INFORMATION AND PROCESS INTEGRATION IN ENTERPRISES:
Rethinking Documents

THE KLUWER INTERNATIONAL SERIES IN ENGINEERING AND COMPUTER SCIENCE

INFORMATION AND PROCESS INTEGRATION IN ENTERPRISES:
Rethinking Documents

edited by

Toshiro Wakayama
International University of Japan
Niigata, Japan

Srikanth Kannapan
Xerox Corp.
Palo Alto, CA USA

Chan Meng Khoong
National Computer Board
Singapore

Shamkant Navathe
Georgia Institute of Technology
Atlanta, GA USA

JoAnne Yates
Massachusetts Institute of Technology
Cambridge, MA USA

SPRINGER SCIENCE+BUSINESS MEDIA, LLC

ISBN 978-1-4613-7512-8 ISBN 978-1-4615-5499-8 (eBook)
DOI 10.1007/978-1-4615-5499-8

Library of Congress Cataloging-in-Publication Data

A C.I.P. Catalogue record for this book is available
from the Library of Congress.

Printed on acid-free paper.

CONTENTS

FOREWORD

As we approach the 21st century, new ways of organizing work are playing an increasingly important role in the global economy. The explosive popularity of the Internet, for instance, illustrates how whole new industries are being built on innovative information processes, and even manufacturers of traditional physical products are realizing that to compete globally, they must develop new information-intensive business processes. For the past decade, MIT's Center for Coordination Science has studied new ways people can work together, including interdisciplinary studies of process modeling, coordination technologies, and technology uses. Thus we were pleased to co-sponsor (along with Xerox Corporation, Fuji Xerox Company Limited, and the Information Technology Institute of the Singapore National Computer Board) IPIC'96, the first International Working Conference on Information and Process Integration in Enterprises.

This conference brought together several strands of work that are critical to the information-intensive enterprises of tomorrow. It sought to integrate approaches ranging from process modeling rooted in computer science to studies of the adoption of new technologies rooted in social science. I believe that integrating these diverse perspectives will be crucial for successful businesses in the 21st century, and this volume presents the valuable intellectual fruits of one such integration effort.

The theme of this first conference, "Rethinking Documents," was a particularly timely focus, as the conference coincided with the surging popularity of a new, document-based software technology--the World Wide Web. Throughout the conference, documents proved to be a crucial focusing device, providing a shared basis for discussing everything from Petri-nets to situated processes to redesigning paper-based processes in new media.

We all have the opportunity to shape, as well as to react to, the enterprises of the future. But we cannot make use of this opportunity if we remain trapped within narrow disciplinary boundaries. The current volume is an important effort at breaking down those boundaries. I believe that managers as well as academics from various disciplines would do well to read these papers and think about the interdisciplinary intersections they represent.

Thomas W. Malone
Patrick J. McGovern Professor of Information Systems
Director, MIT Center for Coordination Science
MIT Sloan School of Management

PREFACE

Issues of information integration, process integration, and the synergy between information integration and process integration are at the heart of effective use of information technology in business enterprises. However, the systemic resolution of such integration issues remains a major challenge. Furthermore, enterprise information and processes have become increasingly distributed. The pace of research must be accelerated to bridge the gap between integration problems and solutions.

This book is a bold attempt to address information and process integration issues as a single body of research and practice. We have also identified the concept of *documents* as a common thread linking the integration issues. Documents, after all, are representations of information, along with representations of the *usage* of the information contained therein. Rethinking the role of documents is therefore central to (re)engineering enterprises in the context of information and process integration.

The chapters of this book are based on papers presented at the *International Working Conference on Information and Process Integration in Enterprises* (IPIC'96), held at MIT on November 14 and 15, 1996. The topics of the chapters cover a range of issues: from the future role of documents in enterprise integration, to emerging models of business processes and information use, to practical experiences in implementing new processes and technologies in real work environments.

Considering the gaps between problems and solutions, we deliberately designed an IPIC agenda with a heavy emphasis on practice. This required us to exercise the necessary evil of declining some theoretical papers of exceptional quality. The topics in the book are also purposefully designed to encourage substantive synergy among the work presented in the chapters. It is through such synergy that collective wisdom may emerge for the benefit of enterprises at large.

The papers in Section I of the book (Chapters 1-5) are attempts to provide conceptual frameworks for thinking about information and process integration. They address the theme of the conference and of this volume, crafting new ways of looking documents as the crucial nexus between information and business processes. The papers in Section II (Chapters 6-9) examine current practice around the use of documents as integrating objects, looking at a variety of settings ranging from vehicle maintenance sites where mobile technicians work to financial services settings.

Section III (Chapters 10-14) contains technical modeling papers.. These new models for integrating information and business processes draw on such tools as petri-nets, partial order data models, and task-oriented modeling. Moving from formal models to field settings, Sections IV and V look at emerging contexts of practice in various realms. Section IV (Chapters 15-18) focuses on industry contexts, with papers looking at electronic document applications as diverse as a repository of legal documents and technology supporting copier field service engineers. Section V (Chapters 19-22) discusses information and process integration in government and educational contexts, including publishing services and classrooms in university settings, and knowledge workers in a military setting.

Section VI (Chapter 23-24) contains two papers – the first consists of case studies of the failed introduction of document image management systems into two companies. In the conference itself, one of the two case studies, that of Dover Service Company, provided the basis for an innovative exercise in information and process integration. As the final event of the conference, teams were assigned either along or across functional lines and the group grappled directly with the implications and problems of changing media from paper to electronic in a particular setting. This exercise highlighted many of the social issues and dynamics that must be taken into account along with more abstract models in order to achieve successful integration of documents into business processes. The second paper (Chapter 24) archives the materials used for the exercise and the presentation materials produced by the groups.

This book would not have seen the light of day, if not for the authors who contributed the chapters, the IPIC advisory board members, and program committee members. Special thanks go to Rick Peebles (Xerox), Francis Yeoh (ITI), Yokichi Itoh (Fuji Xerox), and Thomas Malone (MIT) for their support in funding IPIC activities. George Roth (MIT), Christine Foglia (MIT), Roanne Neuwirth (MIT), Mahmud Hussain (IUJ), and Gwendolyn Baker (Georgia Tech) provided expert assistance to the IPIC steering committee in technical and logistical aspects of the IPIC program. Most importantly, we thank our families for forgiving us for sacrificing precious moments with them as we struggled to complete the book.

The publication of this book marks one major milestone in an arduous journey. In fact, this journey has proved to be a rich experience in information and process integration even for the five of us, as we melded ideas drawn from diverse research disciplines to collaborate across vast geographical distances. We hope that this book has planted the seeds for a community of practice in this body of research. The rethinking process has *begun*.

Srikanth Kannapan
Chan Meng Khoong
Shamkant Navathe
Toshiro Wakayama
JoAnne Yates

ADVISORY BOARD

PROGRAM COMMITTEE

Mark Ackerman, Department of Information and Computer Science, University of California at Irvine

Hojjat Adeli, College of Engineering, The Ohio State University

Paul Cole, Lotus Consulting Group, Lotus Development Corporation

Mark Cutkosky, Center for Design Research, Stanford University

Thomas Davenport, Graduate School of Business, University of Texas at Austin

Daniel Dolk, Naval Postgraduate School

Soumitra Dutta, European Institute of Business Administration (INSEAD), France

P. S. Giridharan, Department of Information Systems and Computer Science, National University of Singapore

Tom Gruber, Knowledge Systems Laboratory, Stanford University

Igor Hawryskewicz, University of Technology, Sydney

Harshavardhan Karandikar, Science Applications International Corporation, McLean, Virginia

Kamal Karlapalem, Hong Kong University of Science and Technology

Wolfgang Klas, Institute for Integrated Publishing and Information Systems, German National Research Center for Information Technology (GMD-IPSI)

Jintae Lee, Department of Decision Science, University of Hawaii

Frank Leyman, German Software Development Laboratory, IBM

Allan MacLean, Rank Xerox Research Center, Xerox Corporation

Matthew Morgenstern, Design Research Institute, Xerox/Cornell University

Hari Narayanan, Department of Computer Science, Auburn University

Helen Samuels, Massachusetts Institute of Technology

Sunil Sarin, Xerox Advanced Information Technology, Xerox Corporation

Avi Seidmann, Simon Graduate School of Business Administration, University of Rochester

Lucy Suchman, Xerox Palo Alto Research Center, Xerox Corporation

LIST OF CONTRIBUTORS

Jun Adachi, R&D Department, National Center for Science Information Systems, University of Tokyo, Japan.
adachi@rd.nacsis.ac.jp

Malcolm Bauer, Human-Computer Interaction Institute, Carnegie Mellon University, USA.
malcolm@cs.cmu.edu

David G. Bell, Palo Alto Research Center, Xerox Corporation, USA.
dbell@parc.xerox.com

Gary A. Benson, BP Exploration (Alaska) Inc., Anchorage, Alaska, USA.
bensonga@akm044.anc.xwh.bp.com

Abraham Bernstein, Sloan School of Management, MIT, USA.
avi@mit.edu

Rao Bhamidipati, Professional Document Services, Xerox Corporation, USA.
rbhamidi@ce.xerox.com

Daniel G. Bobrow, Palo Alto Research Center, Xerox Corporation, USA.
bobrow@parc.xerox.com

Kristin Braa, Department of Informatics, University of Oslo, Norway.
Kristin.Braa@ifi.uio.no

Daniel Davis, Caterpillar Incorporated, USA.

Jasbir S. Dhaliwal, National University of Singapore.

Barrie Gleason, Public Relations Services, MIT, USA.
bgleason@mit.edu

Stephan Greene, Institute for Advanced Computer Studies, University of Maryland, USA.
greene@cs.umd.edu

Keng Joo Heng, Information Technology Institute, Singapore.

Turid Horgen, School of Architecture and Planning, MIT, USA.
turid@mit.edu

Anat Hovav, Claremont Graduate School, Claremont, USA.
hovava@cgs.edu

John Hughes, CSCW Research Center, Lancaster University, UK.

Patrick C.K. Hung, University of Science and Technology, Hong Kong.
cshck@cs.ust.hk

Srikanth Kannapan, Palo Alto Research Center, Xerox Corporation, USA.
kannapan@parc.xerox.com

Kamalakar Karlapalem, University of Science and Technology, Hong Kong.
kamal@cs.ust.hk

Chan Meng Khoong, National Computer Board, Singapore,
chanmeng@ncb.gov.sg

Val King, CSCW Research Center, Lancaster University, UK.

Charles Kukla, Digital Equipment Corporation, USA.
kukla@tnpubs.enet.dec.com

Allan MacLean, Rank Xerox Research Center, UK.
maclean@cambridge.rxrc.xerox.com

Munir Mandviwalla, Temple University, USA.
mandviwa@vm.temple.edu

John A. Mariani, CSCW Research Center, Lancaster University, UK.
J.Mariani@lancaster.ac.uk

Pernille Marqvardsen, Rank Xerox Research Center, UK.

Sham Navathe, College of Computing, Georgia Institute of Technology, USA.
sham@cc.gatech.edu

David Newcom, John Deere Corporation, USA.

Charles S. Osborn, Babson College, USA.
osborn@babson.edu

William Porter, School of Architecture and Planning, MIT, USA.
wlporter@mit.edu

Navi Radjou, National Science and Technology Development Agency, Thailand.

Olivier Raiman, Palo Alto Research Center, Xerox Corporation, USA.

Rostant Ramlochan, Center for Management of Technology, National University of Singapore.

Darrell Raymond, The Gateway Group, Canada.
draymond@gatewaygrp.com

Tom Rodden, CSCW Research Center, Lancaster University, UK.
T.Rodden@lancaster.ac.uk

Anne Rose, Institute for Advanced Computer Studies, University of Maryland, USA.

George Roth, Center for Organizational Learning, MIT, USA.
groth@mit.edu

Noriko Sakai, Graduate School of Engineering, University of Tokyo, Japan.
sakai@rd.nacsis.ac.jp

Craig A. A. Samuel, TRION Technologies, Mayfield Village, Ohio, USA.
samuel@imaging.trion.com

Tone Irene Sandahl, Center for Information Technology Services, Oslo, Norway.
Tone.Sandahl@ifi.uio.no

Thomas L. Sarro, Sarro Associates, Inc., 6311 Holbrook, Chicago, IL 60646.
tsarro@interaccess.com

Wayne Schmidt, Business Processes Division, Construction Engineering Research Laboratories (CERL), US Army, USA.
W-schmidt@cecer.army.mil

Christian Schucan, ETH Zürich (Eidgenössische Technische Hochschule), Switzerland.
schucan@inf.ethz.ch

Mark H. Shirley, Palo Alto Research Center, Xerox Corporation, USA.
shirley@parc.xerox.com

Jane Siegel, Human-Computer Interaction Institute, Carnegie Mellon University, USA.
jals@cs.cmu.edu

Pal Sorgaard, University of Oslo, Norway, and Goteborg University, Sweden.
paalso@ifi.uio.no

Atsuhiro Takasu, R&D Department, National Center for Science Information Systems, University of Tokyo, Japan.
takasu@rd.nacsis.ac.jp

Ankarath Unni, KPMG Peat Marwick, USA.
aunni@kpmg.com

W.M.P. van der Aalst, Department of Mathematics and Computing Science, Eindhoven University of Technology, The Netherlands.
wsinwa@win.tue.nl

Toshiro Wakayama, Graduate School of International Management, International University of Japan.
wakayama@iuj.ac.jp

JoAnne Yates, Sloan School of Management, MIT, USA.
jyates@mit.edu

Gregory Zack, Design Research Institute, Cornell University, Xerox Corporation, USA.
zack@dri.cornell.edu

1 DOCUMENTS, PROCESSES, AND METAPROCESSES

Toshiro Wakayama
Srikanth Kannapan
Chan Meng Khoong
Shamkant Navathe
JoAnne Yates

Introduction

It may seem rather obvious that a well-integrated network information system with abundance of free-flowing digital, online information will inevitably realize truly integrated business operations across time, space, and functional boundaries. Industry experiences, however, show, sometimes painfully, that there is considerable distance between a well-integrated information system and a well-integrated business system that effectively supports people in their work.

The current state of understanding of the gap does not seem to offer a coherent and comprehensive framework in which this diverse set of issues and relationships among them can be meaningfully addressed. Our intent in organizing the working conference on "Information and Process Integration" was to begin an exploration of such a framework that captures interactions of the two systems in both theory and practice. This chapter represents such an exploration by the five of us during the course of conceiving, designing, and organizing the IPIC conference in the fall of 1996 at MIT. Given the complexity of issues involved, and our diverse backgrounds (that we see as a strength), it was a challenge for the five of us to agree with all aspects of the view presented here. Nonetheless, it represents one way of summarizing our exploration and collaborations in the past three years.

The framework discussed here has three components: *documents, processes,* and *metaprocesses*. *Documents*, or information contained in documents (often referred to as *document information*) can, when properly designed, function as a bridge between an information system (container) and a business system (use). In the next section, we will discuss two essential mechanisms that documents are equipped with to support this bridging function.

Information System	↔	Documents	↔	Business System
(Container)		(Contents)		(Use)

Figure 1: Documents as a bridge between Information and Business systems.

The notion of *process*, on the other hand, is actually a collection of related concepts (such as activity, input, output, customer, performance measure, resource, constraint) for generically representing business systems. This generality of the process vocabulary is quite important to us as we are addressing business integration issues across functional boundaries.

Another component critical to general understanding of business systems is the aspect of people and organizations that actively attempt to change and improve existing processes, instead of being merely players in the existing systems. The notion of *metaprocess*, i.e., a process for improving processes, is intended to capture this third component. The process of continuous improvement, or "kaizen", is a good example of a well-practiced metaprocess. As we will see in a later section, the framework of process-metaprocess interactions is a way of capturing organizational and social issues surrounding processes and process changes.

The following sections discuss these three components in further detail and explore relationships among them.

Documents: from data sharing to sharing of "use intent"

Conventional information systems offer relatively mature means of sharing data. Most notably, the decades of advances in database technology have been immensely successful in hiding technical details of the internal organization of information systems under a well-defined interface: e.g., relational database (relational interface language), transaction management (concurrency transparency), and distributed database (location transparency). The end user can then focus on sharing and use of data in the context of organizational needs.

What an organization needs to share, however, is more than just raw data. It needs to share interpretations and meanings of data in the context of its use, in a way that reflects daily work activities driven by larger goals and strategic directions of the organization. This sharing of interpretations takes place in organizations in many subtle as well as explicit ways and often manifests itself in documents; usually as unstructured documents both on paper and in digital form.

This is where *document information,* i.e., the content of documents, comes in. Documents, although still largely in paper form, are equipped with two mechanisms to convey "use intent" of the data they carry, namely metadata and data aggregation. Metadata, or data about data, is actually a very common form of data in the workplace. To see this, observe that business forms are collections of various fields with *descriptions* of the data to be filled in. Thus they represent metadata. Once they are filled out, the resulting documents represent an amalgamation of metadata and data, the latter being structured through the former. According to an estimate, 70 to 90% of documents used in an organization are forms and their filled-out instances. Combined with another estimate that well over 70% of the entire information that an organization uses is in document form, we can say that a typical business deals with a massive amount of metadata. Through meta-level descriptions of data to be used, the business expresses and shares a framework of gathering and interpreting data for coherent organizational use.

Closely related to the metadata mechanism is the aspect of documents that assembles and aggregates data iteratively into hierarchically arranged larger constructs. Such an aggregate structure itself is an expression of the use intent for the assembled information. Thus, for instance, a certain aggregation of inventory data (representing "what is available now") and data on manufacturing schedule (representing "what will be available in future") may represent a use in the customer order department that is acting upon the company's intent to increase the market share through means other than price cut (e.g., retaining customer orders in terms of future availability as well as current availability). While the very arrangement of placing certain inventory data and manufacturing schedule data side by side is an expression of how the aggregate is intended to be used, documents use a variety of metadata to represent such aggregate structures more explicitly (e.g., descriptions of fields in a form, labels for bulleted items, names for section titles, etc.). Consequently, documents are structure-intensive, with an intricate web of conceptual links among data items and metadata items. We define document information in an organizational setting as *information structured to represent its use intent.*

Unfortunately, however, this very richness of structure in document information makes its electronic representation rather difficult. Currently, the state-of-the-art information systems are not sufficiently developed for managing document information at the level of sophistication and reliability available for database information. For sharing and managing database information, we have a mature theory and science of database design, well-developed data design methodologies, and a well-trained pool of database designers and administrators. None of these exists for document information.

There are two recent developments in this regard, however. One is an emerging set of capabilities on top of network infrastructure, known as *middleware,* for creating, storing, sharing, and managing digital documents. This emerging, new *container* for document information is radically different from the paper-based container. Its emergence necessitates a serious rethinking of document information and its use. The following are some of the new ideas from the industry practice in document management in the context of deploying middleware capabilities.

- *Document reusability* as opposed to document reuse: Document reuse implies accepting existing document components whereas document reusability demands that existing components be (re)designed at their creation for optimal reuse opportunity in other (possibly remote) processes. A critical point is that document reusability introduces a process perspective into document design.

- *Intentional documents* (e.g., the *most recent* project report) as opposed to extensional documents (e.g., the project report as of July 15, 1997): In terms of information systems implementation, intentional documents imply separation of intentional specifications (such as document forms) and contents, where extensional contents are computationally derived on demand from intentional specifications.

While this middleware development is about the container, the second development is about the contents, namely the series of document representation and interchange languages such as SGML, HTML, and most recently XML (eXtensible Markup Language, a language vigorously being promoted by the Web consortium as the "SGML for the Internet"). These languages are well positioned to take advantages of the new middleware capabilities. As we have illustrated above, the new container is inviting new notions of the contents, beyond digital simulation of paper documents. Unlike other lower-level document representation languages (e.g., page description languages), the very significance of these languages comes from their rich information- and concept-structuring capabilities.

Our position is, however, that XML documents and other *structured documents* represent only a beginning of an enterprise to enhance the value of information through explicit representation of structures. XML-type of structuring gives building blocks for constructing larger structures to capture higher-level use concepts. For example, shared information spaces constructed collaboratively by a work group are useful in organizing information into different aspects of the work product or process such that the differing perspectives and information needs within the work group can be met efficiently. We expect to see a new structuring discipline that can directly address issues in the domain of business systems.

An important caveat to a structuring discipline is to carefully judge its appropriateness: in the sense that structuring should actually help people in their work and be worth the effort it takes. It is evident from many studies of organizations that a significant proportion of document information is largely unstructured and furthermore not in digital form. More importantly, even independent of the cost-benefit of structuring this class of document information, it is possibly counterproductive to the effectiveness of people to apply a structuring discipline to such documents. For example, notes taken by individuals at a meeting may contain important interpretive and contextual information that derive their power from unstructured-ness and also may carry significant social implications (e.g., privacy) that might argue against a structuring discipline. Based on this insight, it is all the more important to explore the potential impact of structuring information and its limits of applicability and appropriate use. One way to start such an exploration is to focus on process structures and to investigate how they might be related to structures of information that get generated and consumed in processes, which is the subject of the next section.

Processes: mapping process structures into document structures

The concept of a process appears in many different contexts: processes in natural phenomena, processes in computer systems, processes in manufacturing assembly lines, and processes for reaching a political consensus. Processes we are concerned with are about human activities in organizational settings. Even within this context, there are a variety of definitions for process. At a higher level of conceptualization, however, a few general observations can be made. First, "process" is not a single concept, but an aggregate of several concepts, as we will illustrate shortly. Second, it is meant to operate at a level abstracted from functional and other domain-specific contents of business systems. "Process" also serves as a unit for performance measure and enhancement, which is typically driven by customer satisfaction.

Thus, for instance, the process concept can be described as shown in Fig. 2.

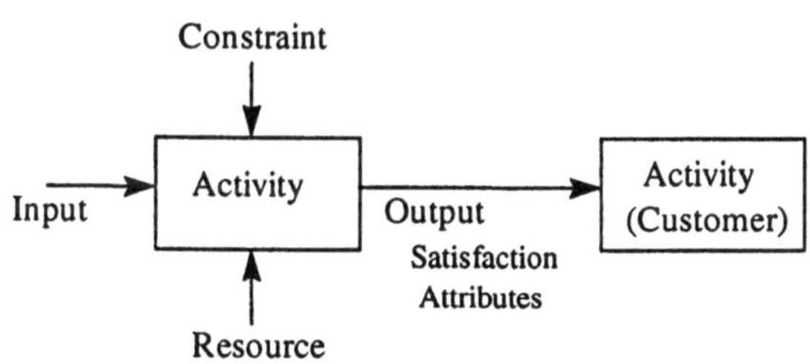

Figure 2: A Simple Process Description

Note that given an actual discourse of business operations, its process representation would be a collection of domain-specific concepts instantiated from the general concepts above and structured by their relationships. For instance, a customer order process might appear as shown in Fig. 3.

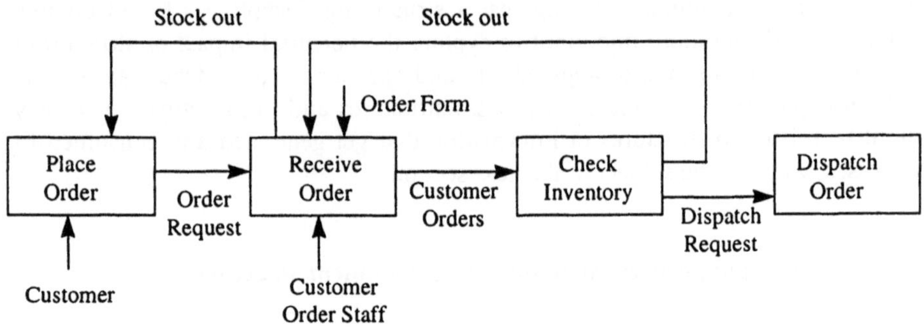

Figure 3: A Customer Order Process Representation

A critical aspect of this order process diagram is that it represents a language, i.e., a set of concepts (such as "Order Form", "Stock Out", "Check Inventory", and "Dispatch Order"), which is customized for collective understanding of the process. "Process", as an aggregate of more general concepts (such as "Activity", "Output", and "Resource"), then serves as a metalanguage for defining the customer-order-process language and possibly other languages. Thus, this language-metalanguage distinction gives a language-theoretic framework for addressing ontological issues of process:

- Can we expect to have a single metalanguage for all forms of work processes?
- If not, are there advantages in having a single (meta-meta)language for defining a family of metalanguages?
- What are the requirements for such metalanguages? Do we have a complete list of requirements?
- How should such metalanguages be related to data modeling metalanguages?

Directly or indirectly, these questions frequently appear, for instance, in the industry efforts to standardize process definition languages, in the design of a software package for process modeling, and in the (often frustrating) practice of process design and implementation using software tools. We think that the issue of process ontology is far from being closed, and that there are still untouched concepts of fundamental importance. Thus, while it is important to pursue a global standard for process definition interface, it is essential to maintain parallel efforts in ontological inquiries of processes.

A case in point is the dependency and trade-off relationship between process structures and structures of information in the process. We will illustrate this relationship through an extension of the customer order process example introduced earlier. Consider the diagram in Fig. 4.

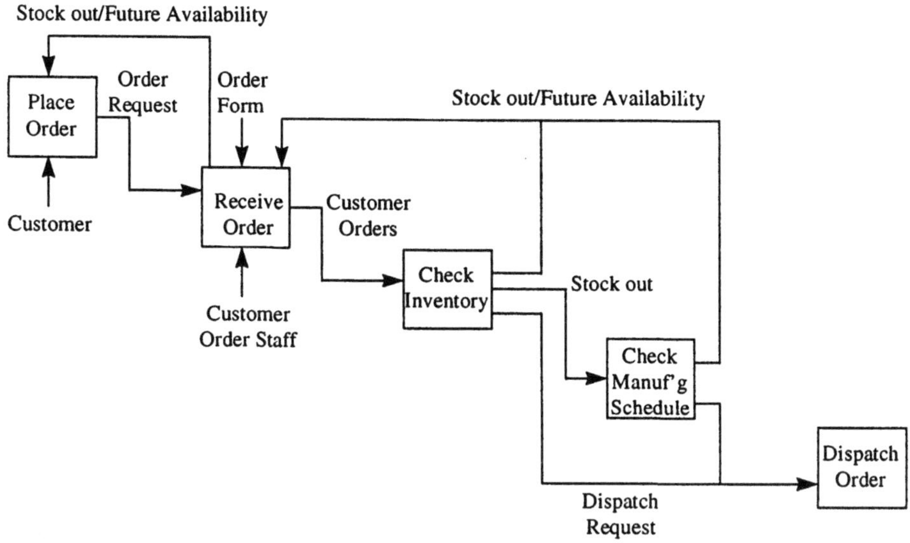

Figure 4: Dependencies between Information and Process Structures.

Also assume that "Customer Orders" is in paper form, "Inventory" in a conventional database, and "Manufacturing Schedule" in an electronic form. Note that these three chunks of information are conceptually related: "Customer Orders" (what is wanted), "Inventory"(what is currently available), "Manufacturing Schedule"(what will be available in future). But, they are rather isolated in use. Thus, a typical scenario of customer order process goes as follows:

- In order to complete a customer order, the inventory needs to be checked.
- But, to do this, the order information in paper needs to be re-entered into the online system. Only then the order gets checked against the inventory.
- If the inventory does not meet the order, that information is routed to the manufacturing division.
- For each stock-out item in the order, its future availability is obtained and routed to the customer order staff and then to the customer.

In this example the conceptual dependency among the three chunks of information is manually traced in the process over time. This is precisely the origin of a substantial portion of the process structure in the diagram. With the emerging capability of middleware to physically establish such conceptual dependencies, however, one can expect to benefit from an integrated document interface with a structure that literally absorbs that extra portion of the process structure. See the diagram in Fig. 5 for an illustration.

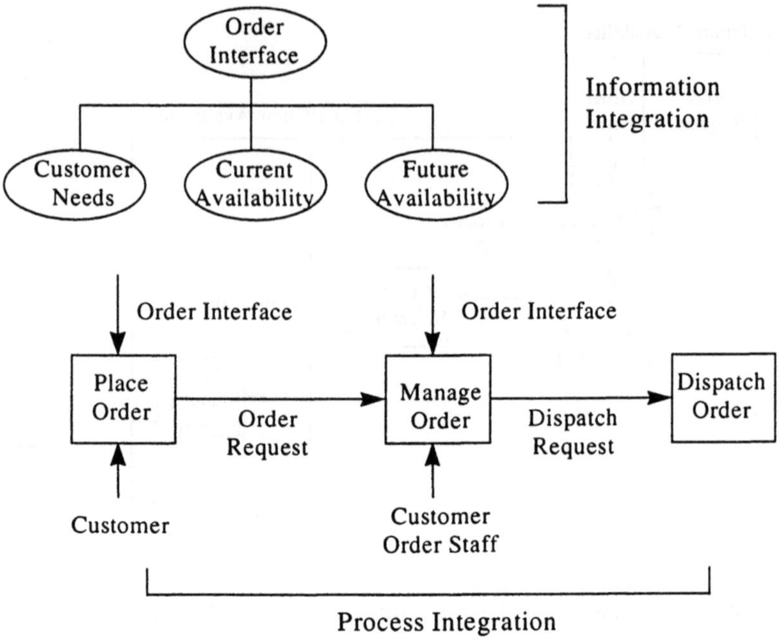

Figure 5: Document Interfaces for Information and Process Integration.

Two mechanisms exist behind this mapping from process structure to information structure, namely *information integration* and *process integration.* Information integration is more than just putting together existing chunks of information (such as "Customer Order" and "Inventory"). It involves reinterpretation of assembled data. For instance, the contents under "Current Availability" will come from the inventory database. But, "Availability" from the perspective of handling customer orders means availability with respect to "Customer Needs". Selecting information from the inventory database and the manufacturing schedule table relevant to a particular order request, structuring that information into a coherent form under labels such as "Current Availability" and "Future Availability", and making it instantaneously available to the customer and the customer order staffs (computationally via middleware capabilities) is an expression of the use intent for the information that was previously too fragmented to carry such an intent.

Process integration is, in many ways, similar to information integration. As in information integration, process integration is not simply "syntactic" pasting together of existing chunks of activities. It addresses "semantic" or functional integrity of processes. Thus, as in information integration, process integration makes sense for a collection of processes with conceptual dependencies among their functions which are not fully exploited. In a strong case of process integration, some functions separately performed by different processes may have such intricate dependencies that it is more natural to merge them together under a single function. For instance, as in the illustration above, receiving a customer order and checking it against the inventory and manufacturing schedule are in reality not a unidirectional chain of activities. Customers are often willing to adjust the contents of their original requests in order to avoid stock-out or slow deliveries due to manufacturing constraints. In such situations, it is more effective if one could merge those functions.

Going back to process ontology, our point is that process structure is ontologically related to information structure. Now observe that process metalanguage represents a language-theoretic approach to process ontology, which has something to do with information structure. Does this mean that there should be a unified metalanguage for processes and information? Does this mean standardization efforts for document metalanguages such as XML and process metalanguages such as the one being pursued by the Workflow Management Coalition should be merged?

Practices and Metaprocesses: Regaining control over processes

Many people share a fundamental mistrust or discomfort with the process-driven paradigm of designing and organizing work-place activities. There are many justifiable reasons for this. One is that the paradigm has not been successful in capturing, within the paradigm itself, the aspects of individuals' highly context sensitive and stylized practices, and the aspect of questioning and challenging existing processes, perhaps in the light of changing markets, emerging technology, or new organizational insights. Consequently, the paradigm tends to subordinate these aspects of individuals to the uniform practice implied by a specific process design.

Theoretically at least, such a chain of activities taking place outside a process and challenging to change the process can be captured as yet another process, even using the same metalanguage. This idea of linking or even amalgamating an object-level construct with a meta-level construct is not unusual in systems sciences. In fact, when practiced carefully, it is known to produce robust systems capable of adapting to changing environments: e.g., amalgamation of a language and a metalanguage (as in natural languages), and the combined practice of learning and meta-learning.

The idea of metaprocess, however, is not just an armchair idea. It is in fact well practiced in many enterprises. From a business perspective, enterprises have sought to develop means to be self-aware of their actual processes and practices. Also, from a social science point of view, there are several research communities who are actively engaged in studying people in organizational settings to develop insights into the way people actually get their work done exploiting aspects of their work setting (e.g., social networks) quite independent of 'official' organization structures and process guidelines. Understanding of enterprise processes and practices driven either from a business or social perspective has the potential to be used both for improvement of organizational effectiveness and individual fulfillment at work (although the two goals are often perceived as difficult to integrate).

A example of a highly stylized metaprocess in an organizational setting is what is known as "kaizen"[1], or continuous improvement. A typical kaizen metaprocess starts with solicitation of improvement ideas from the people involved in the process (see the diagram below). A proposed idea goes through a well-defined (meta)process of various activities such as evaluation/ranking, feedback, selection for implementation, award.

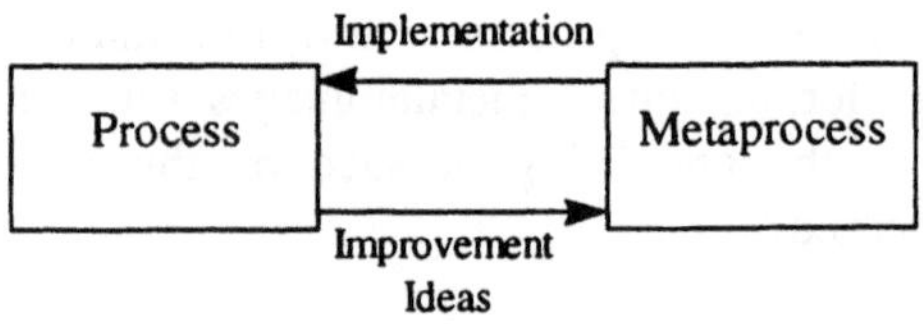

Figure 6: A Typical 'Kaizen' System

A successful kaizen practice does not get built overnight. A manager in charge of building a kaizen practice often spends a few years crafting various aspects of the kaizen system. A challenging part is to solicit good proposals in good quantity from the employees. A key enabler here is proposal forms (called "teian" in the kaizen context) and associated practice to encourage and educate employees for good proposal writing. Kaizen managers put considerable efforts in the design and redesign of proposal forms.

Kaizen is associated with small, incremental changes, as opposed to discontinuous changes involving major innovations. Kaizen changes typically involve physical resources in the process such as tools, equipment, and facilities. But, they occasionally address more structural aspects of the process even across departmental boundaries. In any case, kaizen and innovation are often taken as opposing concepts, where incrementality is the defining characteristic of kaizen. What is more fundamental here, however, is a system of organizational dynamics based on process-metaprocess interactions. A spectrum of differences along the dimension of incrementality vs. discontinuity are of more coincidental nature, stemming from such factors as who is proposing the change, who is in charge of implementing the change, implementation budget, and tools available for designing and implementing changes.

Although many advocates of process innovation prescribe innovation (meta) processes, the kaizen camp is far more explicit about metaprocess implementation. In fact, a more accurate characterization of kaizen seems to be in its practice of organizational dynamics based on process-metaprocess interactions. For instance, kaizen managers are quite keen on full participation of all employees in the

---

[1] Kaizen Teian 1: Developing Systems for Continuous Improvement Through Employee Suggestions, The Japan Human Relations Association, Productivity Press, 1992.

metaprocess, as opposed to exclusively focusing on changes in the target process, which can be proposed by a small number of dedicated employees, or even outside consultants. This drive towards full metaprocess participation is reflected in their design of award systems. Sometimes, kaizen participation even extends to part-time workers. For many employees, it is not an easy task to identify and analyze problems and propose constructive suggestions. Typically, kaizen managers are willing to spend many hours with their employees coaching them on proposal writing. They are also willing to wait a few years till good proposals come out in good quantity. A large portion of the work-force going through years of training and practice for proposal writing and implementation is likely to transform the work-force and attain a new level of organizational capabilities for initiating and managing changes.

As illustrated in the kaizen system, the framework based on process-metaprocess interactions is able to address, beyond documents and processes, a set of issues of organizational and social nature such as change initiation and implementation, work-force education and training, and evaluation and recognition of individual contributions.

Towards Language-based Practice for Systems Thinking

We have discussed documents, processes, and metaprocesses, including their interactions. Collectively, these three seem to cover a scope of issues sufficiently comprehensive to capture interactions of information systems and business systems. We now turn our attention to *language theory*, which seems to be a unifying theme for documents, processes, and metaprocesses, with the hope that we can build a general practice for designing and implementing organizational systems that can take optimal advantages of emerging network information infrastructure.

What is a language?

By language, we mean something specific, namely, a set of concepts having the following:

- a set of named primitive concepts,
- means of composing concepts to construct larger concepts,
- means of abstraction, i.e., means of naming composed concepts.

Thus, for instance, the process metalanguage depicted in Figure 2, as a language according to this definition, has “Activity”, “Input”, “Output”, “Constraint”, and “Resource” as its named primitive concepts. Its means of composition is shown in the depiction. The means of abstraction, not shown in the depiction, can be given by the arrangement that a set of (pair-wise) connected Activities is again an Activity.

Similarly, the Customer Order language in Figure 3 is also a language in the sense of this definition. In this case, the Customer Order language is derived from the process metalanguage by instantiating metalanguage concepts: e.g., "Check Inventory" is an "Activity", "Order Form" is a "Constraint", etc. The Customer Order language inherits its means of composition and means of abstraction from its metalanguage.

From "Fire Fighting" to Systems Thinking

In reality, however, people are more interested in just solving the problem than building a language or organizational knowledge. Are there compelling reasons that they should be building a language before they touch upon individual problems? We will illustrate our answer through an example.

Consider a university library, which is expected to review its journal subscription list every year. The output of this review process is a new list obtained from the old one by discontinuing some journals and adding some new ones. The library solicits inputs from selected students and faculty members. On the basis of these inputs and library policy and vision on journal subscriptions, the library constructs and publishes a new list for general acceptance. But it also stays open for reconsideration of discontinued journals and additional new journals. At this point, the library can be potentially swamped by a mountain of inquiries, complaints, and requests about *specific* journals. However, the very nature of subscription decision is global, i.e., the decision on each journal cannot be made merely on the basis of qualities and characteristics of that journal, but it involves considerations of other journals and other global selection criteria. Each inquiry, on the other hand, is typically about a single specific journal and often unwilling to consider issues beyond that specific journal. "Fire fighting" is one way to describe the resulting situation in which the library staffs are overwhelmed by a large number of inquiries each of which can be quite involving due to the conflict between the specificity of the inquiry and the larger-scale balancing the library needs to maintain.

Now consider another approach to the same task. But, first, we need to introduce a pair of concepts, namely *process schema* and *process instance*. A process schema is a description of properties of process entities and their structural relationships invariant over time. A process instance, on the other hand, is an actual discourse of activities that take place over time. The Customer Order process in Figure 3 is an example of process schema, while its instance is an actual sequence of activities that might start with a specific customer calling a specific staff member at the Customer Order Department. The distinction between *schema* and *instance* is critical, and it parallels the usage of the terms in data modeling.

Now we are ready to describe another approach to the same task of reviewing the journal subscription list. This time, the library designs and publishes the review process (*schema*), including a set of selection criteria for journals and a general policy on its collections. The library gains acceptance for the general review process schema, and then it launches this year's specific review process (instance) which will be guided and protected by the accepted schema. At some point in its discourse, the process (instance) will generate a new subscription list. Due to the general understanding and agreement on the review process (schema), the expectation is that there will be much less fire fighting this time.

We use the term "Systems Thinking" to refer to the conceptual paradigm of problem solving at the level of schema and distinguish it from "Fire Fighting", which takes place at the level of instance as behavior merely reacting to variations of instances without benefits of a general process articulation.

In order to implement and sustain a good practice of systems thinking, however, we need a solid training program. Our claim is that language design, or equivalently schema design, based on a carefully chosen metalanguage, can be an effective component of the program. Particularly if such a metalanguage, or metalanguages, are capable of representing documents, processes, and metaprocesses, including their interactions, and additionally, implemented as an interface language(s) on top the middleware, we would be in a good position to develop a program for implementing language-based systems thinking at workplace.

Conclusions: Co-evolving Technology, Methodology, and Practice

In this chapter, we have attempted to articulate our collaborative experiences in conceiving and organizing a working conference (Information and Process Integration in Enterprises, 1996) in terms of a framework for a field of activity in "general systems science and practice". Our intention was to bridge the perspectives of information systems and business systems while accounting for the socio-cultural contexts of enterprises. We believe that such a bridging of perspectives can be quite powerful in creating new models for enterprises that are both more effective, and more fulfilling to its members. We see documents, and in particular document information, as a basis for exploring the issues bridging these perspectives. We have explored the interesting nature of interactions between enterprise business processes and documents, and shown their relationship to metaprocesses that seek to study or improve actual practices and to bring business process in productive alignment to them.

Achieving the goals of more effective enterprises requires a complex interplay between the distinct perspectives both by systematic modeling efforts and empirical implementation experience while addressing the components of documents, processes and metaprocesses. This interplay can be characterized as a co-evolution of the *technologies* that can support integration of information and process, the *methodologies* for integration that can be designed or emerge from experience, and the *practices* of work that can benefit from new skills and understanding building on emerging technologies and organizational insights.

We hope that the framework presented here is a starting point for such a co-evolution with increasing participation from a community that is representative of the different perspectives that are required.

2 DOCUMENTS AND BUSINESS PROCESSES: UNDERSTANDING THE LINKS

Ankarath Unni and Rao Bhamidipati

Introduction

Much attention has been focused in recent years on the relationship of business processes to business results. Process reengineering and competitive positioning are corporate imperatives in any major corporation in the world today. Whereas the role of effective process design and execution are being more understood in recent years, the role of documents in business processes is much less widely understood. For many people, this idea evokes an image of bureaucrats sitting behind desks piled high with stacks of papers and forms -- pages that shuffle back and forth in an endless loop of red tape, perpetuating "busywork," errors, confusion and redundancy. This picture, although exaggerated, unfortunately bears some resemblance to reality in many organizations. One reason is that, for the most part, most companies never designed their existing business processes, much less the document processes underlying them. Emphasis was placed on functional organizational structures and maximizing efficiency within structures, rather than between and among them. Consequently, in a typical business process one can expect to find a great deal of redundancy and great many documents that do not add value. Document services technologies such as storage, search and retrieval are relatively advanced, and document management discipline has leveraged such technology. However, the document management field is lacking in terms of knowledge, techniques and tools for effectively linking data, documents and technology to business processes.

The document must become a proactive part of the "bottom-line equation" as processes, people and technology. For this we have the challenge of clearly understanding how document can be a proactive enabler as the other three. Once we understand this the industry must come up with concepts, principles, methods, techniques, and tools that become an integral part of the discipline that enables the development and implementation of an integrated holistic business solution to produce optimum business results. As part of this introduction here are a couple of key definitions and concepts:

Business Process: A Business Process is a logical set of activities to produce a defined output of value. It has discrete beginning and ending and has specific inputs and outputs

Process Integration: "Identification, documentation and management of relationships among processes to ensure that all related processes and enablers work as a holistic business system to optimize process, document and organizational performance."

Document: A "Document" is information structured for human comprehension

Basic Concepts

- Business Processes are the primary means of achieving business vision, strategies, and objectives.
- Every business process transforms an input into value-added output.
- Business processes cannot be executed without key enablers such as documents, people and technology.

Understanding the Links

As depicted in the "Business Process Linkage Model" (figure 1), there are four links in the chain connecting processes and documents.

Business objectives are accomplished through business processes

A company would have Enterprise level vision and strategies, as well as individual process level objectives. While lower level objectives can be achieved by a single process or a group of processes, the higher level vision, strategies and targets can be achieved only by integrating and synchronizing all core processes of the Enterprise. Examples of higher level objectives include improvement in customer satisfaction, increase in market share, and higher return on investment. Examples of lower level or individual process objectives would include reduced cost, faster cycle time, and reduced errors. Activities, however small can only be said to be productive when they lead to more effective achievement of the desired business objectives at all levels. Only if a business process is aligned with the corporation's strategic objectives is it adding value to the enterprise. In the current

Business Process to Documents Linkage Model

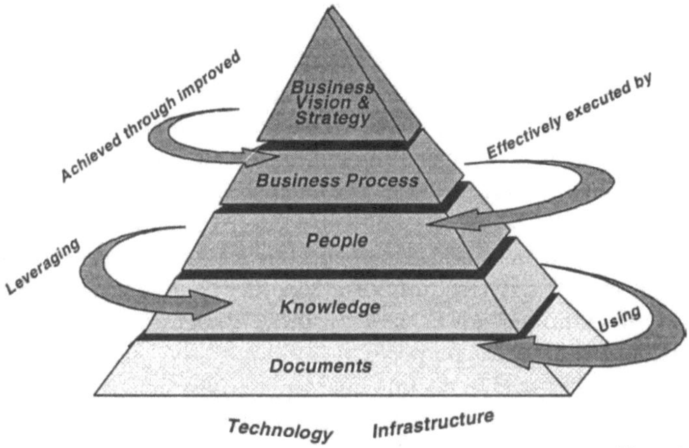

Figure 1

information age, productivity is knowledge-based and value-driven -- adds knowledge as one of the basic inputs -- and measures output, not only by volume but more importantly in terms of quality, elimination of waste, utility, accuracy, timeliness, relevance and so on. Accomplishment of any business objective involves one or many business processes and associated decisions, insight, knowledge, and information. The critical first question that must be asked in attempting to improve a business process is, - Are we doing the right things? Once you have identified the right things to do, design "the right way" to do them.

Most business processes are executed by people

Business processes typically involve people from various parts of the organization, working both as individuals and in work groups. Even those processes that are completely automated involve people who make decisions about them and monitor their operation.

People use knowledge and information to execute business processes

Knowledge implies study, integration and application of ideas. Value is created by applying knowledge to work. Knowledge is necessary both to organize processes and to execute them. Tremendous improvements in business results and productivity can be achieved by consistent dissemination of knowledge.

Documents and document services play a vital role in how people apply and leverage their knowledge and how they interact with business processes

Whenever you have people involved in business processes you have documents. People communicate and create knowledge through documents. Documents are the primary carriers of information, knowledge and interpretations. For many processes, they are the primary output. Documents integrate business processes, people and knowledge. Documents play various roles in a process. They perform different functions --- Transaction documents such as invoices and checks; Reference documents such as manuals; Collaborative documents such as engineering drawings; Learning documents such as competitive intelligence; and Informing documents such as progress reports. Each document has a unique combination of communications and business dimensions to give it value in specific situations for specific purposes.

Document services enable documents to play their integrative role. Document services provide the infrastructure and environment for effective accomplishment of business objectives by enabling interactions among people, processes, knowledge and documents. In concert with a company's technological and organizational infrastructures, document services provide the means for eliminating documents that do not add value, maximizing those that do and ensuring that all documents support a more productive accomplishment of business objectives.

Understanding the links between documents, processes and business results is only the first step. The next step is to apply this understanding to improve value creation.

Exploiting the Links

Documents enable improvements in an organization's effectiveness in four major areas:

- Improving business processes,
- Enabling people to be more effective,
- Leveraging knowledge and organizational learning and
- Leveraging infrastructure and technology.

Improving Business Processes

Nearly every business process includes underlying, sometimes (invisible) document processes that represent its knowledge base. Nearly all documents in a corporation -- invoices, orders, bills of material, reports, specifications, memos,... -- are involved in the execution of business processes.

Documents provide the links in a process value chain, record the actions and results of the process and account for the majority of the inputs and outputs that connect the steps of that process. Documents are the currency that connects business processes. Xerox Business Architecture, an enterprise level framework used in Xerox to manage business processes, indicates that more than 90% of the interfaces among business processes are through documents. Ideally processes must be designed from top-down starting from what are the processes, --"what" are the right things to do --and ending in workflows which details "how" the individual steps in a process will be actually executed. Workflow is the event driven sequence of steps and actions that describes how a process is performed and how the documents flow between steps. Workflow management is the management (mostly automation) of this document flow via a platform of document services technology. Workflows use document services such as document creation, access, use, production, distribution, and so on. Top-down process maps also help in enforcing standards around information and documents. This helps particularly in sharing of common information across an enterprise and in improving consistency in managing by facts.

By improving process productivity, an organization can reduce waste and costs and increase value, quality, customer satisfaction, speed and flexibility. Five "document dimensions" provide a focal point for analyzing processes and a set of techniques for improving their effectiveness.

Document Alignment - Are we using the right documents?

Document alignment involves identifying the documents that add value and those that do not within the context of the desired outcomes of a particular business process. It involves eliminating redundancies and determining whether any new documents are needed. It includes making sure that the right documents are available with the right content, at the right time and right place. Documents in business processes typically function in sets and should be considered in terms of their inter-relationships and may involve integrating information from a variety of documents into one in order to get the right content to the person that needs it in a way that s/he can use it.

Document Design - Are the documents designed for optimum effectiveness?

The design of a document is probably its most tangible factor. It is the element that can have the greatest impact on the effectiveness of documents sent to customers, documents used for presentations and documents that are intended to persuade or motivate people to make decisions or take actions. Beginning with the document's purpose and audience, design encompasses both content and structure and addresses elements of format, such as font style and size, headings, margins, highlights and color.

Examples of the results of redesigning documents abound:

- A new water company bill highlighting information that had been buried results in increased voluntary rationing.
- Direct mail pieces using color typically draw better response than their black-and-white counterparts.
- Clearer presentation of the amount due in bills reduces confusion and

increases payments made correctly.

Use of graphical icons in the table of contents makes an insurance policy more readable by showing at a glance the number of pages in the policy and what each contains.

In addition to adding value to the output, document design can also lead to significant cost savings and can drive process improvement or reengineering efforts. For example, in one insurance company, a design team determined that it would be better to send customers with several types of coverage in a single policy document. Integrating the information required several departments to merge information processes into a single system. The results were reduced processing and mailing costs and increased customer satisfaction.

Document Attribute Alignment - Are we focused on the right document performance attributes?

Once the document alignment process determines that a particular document is valuable, document attribute alignment is applied to ensure alignment between business process requirements and document performance attributes such as speed of creation, method of distribution, frequency, format and medium. Such an analysis might determine, for example, that sending a simple information sheet each month is preferable to sending a glossy quarterly brochure, or that an editable electronic document may be more useful than a paper document. The same document can be used in many ways, for example printed on paper, displayed on-line, or use with hypermedia navigation.

Document Flow Optimization - Are the documents flowing efficiently in the process?

Many workflow techniques were designed at a time when technology could provide a document to only one person at a time. New document processing technologies that enable hundreds of people to look at a document at the same time are leading to the redesign and automation of many workflows.

Document flows, like workflows, often cut across operations. Document flow optimization technique uses the document as a thread to track the steps of a process. The documents and process steps are then analyzed to identify opportunities for streamlining - by making once-sequential steps parallel, by shortening the steps to gain speed and flexibility and by modifying the sequence of steps to reduce waste.

For example, an important and labor intensive process in the pharmaceutical industry is the 'document review' process in which all documents involved in a new drug submission must be approved. In the past, hard copies of the documents were circulated to reviewers sequentially. Now, the reviewers can look at the documents, see the comments of other reviewers and make their own comments, all at the same time. This parallel processing capability has shortened process time in some companies from months to days.

Another way that technology can impact document flow efficiency is by enabling alternatives to the traditional sequence of 'print and distribute'. Many processes can be improved by shifting to 'distribute then print' which greatly reduces distribution costs and time - or to 'print on demand' that eliminates the costs of storage and obsolescence.

Document Life Cycle Management - Are we leveraging the inherent interdependencies among the life cycle stages and is the document process efficient at every stage?

This approach involves taking a "cradle to grave" view of a document, considering all the stages it will go through during its existence. We define these stages as: Construction (via conception, design and creation), Capture (via scanning, storing, organizing, indexing, linking), Production and Distribution (via printing, reproducing, displaying), Usage (via retrieving, querying, searching), Archival, and Disposal.

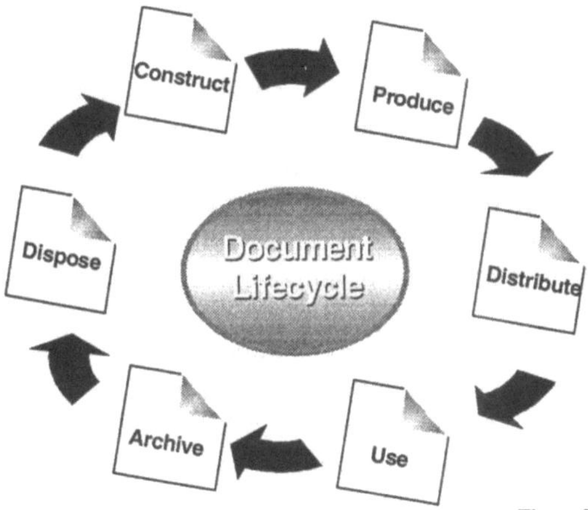

Figure 2

Each stage of a document's life cycle intersects with one or more business processes. At each intersection point, the document is either adding or taking away value from the process. These life cycle leverage points vary from process to process. Examining how a document is used during its entire life cycle can help highlight inherent dependencies among the various stages. For example, the medium, format or platform used to create a document may restrict how, to whom and how fast it can be distributed. The manner in which a document is stored impacts people's ability to retrieve it.

The stages of a document's life cycle are not necessarily sequential or linear, e.g., the distribution stage can take place before and/or after the document is printed, and storage, retrieval and usage can take place repeatedly throughout a document's life.

Document life cycle requirements vary from industry to industry. For example, in the pharmaceutical industry, storage is an especially complicated problem because of FDA requirements that mandate that documents be stored for at least 30 years. In this and some other industries, issues of archival storage must be considered separately from those involved in the storage of active documents.

The life cycle stages of many documents, such as orders, proposals and invoices, travel across process boundaries within an organization and between separate companies. The workgroups that are responsible for a particular stage may not be aware of upstream or downstream requirements. The life cycle perspective provides a tool for transcending organizational boundaries in assessing the enterprise requirements for document processing.

Enabling People to be more Productive

Documents directly impact the productivity of people when they execute processes using documents. People think, convey, feel and decide through documents. They analyze, present, persuade and act using documents.. This productivity impacts at different levels.

Individual Productivity: During the last two decades, productivity tools, many of them document-focused, were primarily aimed at improving individual performance. A new generation of document-focused tools - including Internet - driven by the explosion of information in recent years, promise to bring even greater improvements in individual productivity by focusing on the fundamental ability of individuals to synthesize, organize and retrieve information, to learn and to communicate.

Workgroup Productivity: As more companies recognize the power inherent in groups, structures such as self-managed work teams, multi-functional teams and task teams - increasingly formed on an ad hoc basis - are becoming more prevalent. There is enormous potential for maximizing people's effectiveness through tools that support group activities. A variety of such tools have emerged in recent years and will become more prevalent in the future.

Better sharing of documents simultaneously by team members at multiple locations - e.g. using Lotus Notes to support people in sharing knowledge through distributed documents.

Leveraging Knowledge and Organizational Learning

In our progressively more service-oriented, information-based economy, a company's success will increasingly depend on its ability to maximize its "intellectual capital" - the knowledge and skills of its employees. A document management system can go beyond helping improve enterprise-wide productivity to help businesses maximize their most valuable resource -the knowledge of their employees. Such systems can foster learning by helping people create, acquire, transfer, access, reuse and act on knowledge.

A corporate knowledge base can be built around documents, which can become the key enablers for fostering systematic problem solving, experimentation with new approaches, learning from past experiences, learning from the experiences and best practices of others and transferring knowledge quickly, creatively and efficiently throughout the organization.

A learning infrastructure could prevent the waste involved in reinventing document-based information - such as marketing research studies that, in one large manufacturing organization, were repeated over and over at enormous expense because there was no effective way to easily share the information already collected.

Leveraging Infrastructure and Technology

Processes, people and knowledge, far from being discrete and independent elements, function in a synergistic, integrated way. The document is what enables this integration. The corporation's information infrastructure - including its hardware, software, network, document and information systems and the organizations that manage these - is the vehicle through which the document performs this integrative function.

A company's infrastructure functions either as an enabler or inhibitor of productivity, depending on how well it supports the document processing requirements of the enterprise. Traditionally, this infrastructure evolved over time, driven by technological advances and geared toward data processing rather than document processing. In many cases, a pressing business need, such as ISO 9000 certification of worldwide practices, brings to the surface both the importance and the inadequacy of the organization's document processing practices and supporting infrastructure.

Small incremental investments in document services can result in large productivity gains by leveraging previous investments in computing and communications hardware, software and networks. To realize the productivity opportunities discussed thus far, organizations need to assess and manage their infrastructure from a document perspective. This viewpoint can enhance infrastructure effectiveness in two key areas:

Aligning Infrastructure with Business Objectives: Enterprise document management is an area that is often overlooked by senior managers. In most corporations, no one group is responsible for managing documents on an enterprise level. Managers are often unaware of the document processing environment in their enterprises - the needs of the various customers and the existence (or lack) of management processes, internal and external capabilities and organizational structures to meet those needs. They are also often unaware of the magnitude of infrastructure investments, their returns or the opportunities for improvements.

Managing infrastructure elements collectively as facilitators of document flow through the organization (rather than as disparate elements) can help to ensure that these elements are aligned with productive accomplishment of business objectives.

Optimizing Cost Effectiveness of the Infrastructure: The costs involved in enterprise-wide document processing activities, both internal and external, are enormous. According to the Gartner Group, publishing and document management costs are the second largest expense item in U.S. corporations, accounting for 25 to 40 percent of total labor costs and 5 to 15 percent of gross revenues. An audit conducted by Xerox at one major manufacturing company estimated that managing the firm's document processing activities from an enterprise-wide perspective would yield potential annual cost savings of several million dollars.

Techniques such as Document Resource Assessment can be applied to comprehensively evaluate document resources and how they are managed across the enterprise. Among the issues and opportunities that are addressed in this process are documentation standards, architectures for document management and the connectivity and inter-operability of underlying technologies. Such an assessment would also consider such approaches as outsourcing/insourcing of document processing activities and/or rationalizing the various organizations responsible for document processing within the enterprise. Many services offered by Xerox - including facilities management, outsourcing of document processing, enterprise output strategies and network management services - are aimed at improving the effectiveness of an organization's document processing infrastructure.

Information technology must be used as the key enabler for integration - not only process-to-process integration but also integration of enablers such as people and information technology into a holistic system.

Xerox Examples and Best practices

Xerox Business Architecture (XBA)

Xerox has done an excellent job in identifying the key value chains in the business and modeling them in terms of business processes, and the documents required to perform those processes in this comprehensive document called Xerox Business Architecture (XBA). It is an anchor document used to identify and integrate 'Enterprise Information and Business Processes' -- the main theme of this conference. XBA is a map of the continually evolving process design of Xerox Corporation, including the links and interactions among distinct processes. While many management consultants have defined generic business architectures, XBA is unique to Xerox business processes and the relationships among them. The XBA icon clearly identifies the relationship between management, operational and enabling processes. The core operational processes provide the value chain to the customer. Management processes authorize senior management to direct and measure, and enabling processes provide support. In other words - the operational processes deliver customer value; the management processes focus on effectiveness; and enabling processes are leveraged for operational efficiency.

XBA defines and bounds processes and the dependencies and relationships among them. It basically addresses "what should we be doing" in order to deliver value, which are relatively stable. It then helps you decide the less stable things such as 'how we do it' and 'how we should organize to do it.'

Dependencies and linkages among processes are of primary importance for effective integration of the business enterprise-wide. Since value creation is achieved, in most cases, through documents it follows the concept that documents are the life blood of communications between processes. XBA connects every process with other processes through inputs and outputs which are documents in almost all cases. What XBA provides is the most critical linkage of all -- the linkage of business processes and documents. Additionally it identifies the suppliers of each input and customers for each output. Furthermore, XBA is used to describe the processes and input/output flows with relevant attributes to describe them.

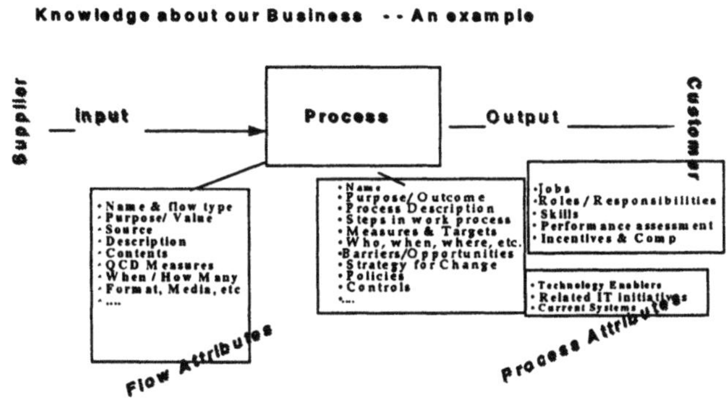

... Process, I/O Flows & Attributes Figure 3

XBA starts with the highest level of processes and progressively decomposes into lower levels that can go all the way down to the workflow level, where the true interactions take place. The Knowledge in the XBA is captured and maintained using a Xerox proprietary tool called Xerox Business Process Analyzer (XBPA). XBPA is a methodology and a software suite for designing, refining, and learning about business processes. Running under Windows™ it facilitates highly productive and collaborative process design over the global network. Underlying the model is a database that captures the process logic and dependencies, and key attributes to describe all aspects of a business process.

Process Ownership

In Xerox every Value Chain (we call them Core Processes) has been assigned an owner. The Core process owner has end-to-end ownership of the core process. The owner creates and manages a 'Process Owner Network' that includes all the stakeholders. The core process owners have responsibility for managing all aspects of the process they own including documentation, design and deployment of solutions. The figure below provides a summary of process owners' roles and responsibilities.

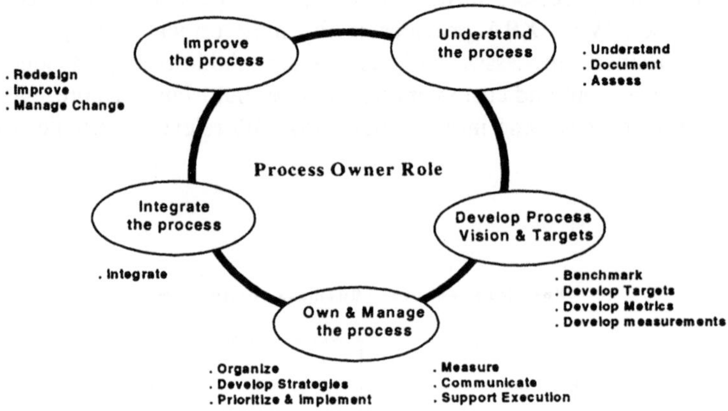

Figure 4

Some of these are the core process owner's exclusive responsibility and some are shared responsibility of the process owner network.

Process Integration Process

The "Integration Process" in Xerox primarily emphasizes the integration of processes through enterprise information structured into 'documents.' The key concepts of the integration process are:

- Each process owner has responsibility of documenting processes in the Xerox Business Architecture
- The documentation includes all the required input documents and their supplier processes or entities. It also includes all the output documents from each process and the customer processes or entities they go to.
- Each of these 'customer-supplier' pairs is called "Touch Points."
- Each touch point is described with 'customer requirements' and 'supplier specifications.'
- After necessary negotiations an agreement is reached and they are recorded as 'agreement documents.'
- These agreements form the basis for all integration activities.

Challenges

Methods

A key challenge is the integration of document improvement and alignment principles and techniques into process analysis and design methodology, and more importantly into the 'information systems' management and development methodologies. This includes

- Understanding the broader definition of "document"
- Separation of data from documents
- Understanding of 'document processing' as opposed to 'data processing'
- Understanding the flow of data between processes as documents
- Integrating document improvement as part of process improvement

Document Architecture

Understanding of what a "Document Architecture" is, and creating and maintaining a Document Architecture. We are getting rather comfortable with Data Architecture, Technology Architecture, and may be Process Architecture. Most of us are still very uncomfortable with Document Architecture. A Document Architecture should include all the key mission critical documents of the enterprise and all the key document attributes such as contents, volume, navigation requirements -- role/relationship to processes and to other documents, media, etc. Document Architecture is quite different from 'Document Services Architecture.'

Another aspect of a Document Architecture is to keep information in document form and people executing processes can retrieve the documents to do the work. Most of the imaging applications, we believe can retrieve static documents, and data processing applications generally create the documents on demand. Users are demanding on-line access to documents with high quality precision and recall capabilities. How will the 'Internet' and 'Intranet' will help meet this challenge remains to be seen.

Document to Data relationship

How can the data (mostly structured in databases) be related to documents defined in the 'Document Architecture?' Currently it is done in ad-hoc fashion largely by individual applications. Of course a pre-requisite to this is a good Document Architecture.

We believe the emerging tools for document to data translation and vice versa hold promise for eventual convergence of data and documents. Imaging alone will not be sufficient. Structuring of digital data for human interaction is vital.

Integrated Repository

Development and use of a truly integrated repository to enable development of holistic business systems integrating all components such as processes, documents, data, people, organizations, applications, and so on.

Bibliography

- What is Knowledge Productivity?, SRI International Business Intelligence Program, Scan No. 2107
- A Business Process Redesign Perspective: Restructuring for the '90s, George Urban, Xerox Corporation
- Using Technology to Support Teamworking, CSC Index Foundation Report, March 1993
- The Action Workflow approach to Workflow Management Technology, CSCW 92 proceedings, Association for Computing Machinery, Nov. 1992
- Automatic Document Generation Systems, New Science Report on Intelligent Document Management, Feb. 1993
- Document Services: Definitions & Relationships, R. Campbell & J. Shono, Xerox Internal Report, President's Summit, April 22, 1992
- Xerox' First Document Symposium Materials, April 1992
- Xerox' Second Document Symposium Materials, April 1993
- Connecticut Mutual Life Insurance Co., BIS Strategic Decisions Third Annual Imaging Excellence Award, BIS Strategic Decisions, 1992
- What's so new about the new economy?, Alan Webber, Harward Business Review, Jan/Feb 1993
- Document Identification: Beyond characters to contextual understanding, New Science Report on Intelligent Document Management, January 1993
- Reflections on workplace learning: Charlotte Linde et al, Institute for Research on Learning, April 1993
- Process Reengineering and Document Management: Xerox internal report, Xerox Ernst & Young Special Report
- Document Services trends: Implications to Xerox, Pete England, Xerox Internal Report, January 1992
- Fuji Xerox, The Document Company BIG M Report, Xerox Internal Report, November 1991
- Reengineering Ends and Begins with the Document, Ken Morris, Siegel & Gate, 1992
- Toward High Performance Organizations: A strategic role for Groupware, Douglas Englebart, Bootstrap Institute, Groupware 92, August 1992
- Knowledge Business Initiative: Tapping the wealth of knowledge within our organizations to increase business agility and robustness, Charles Savage, Digital Equipment Corporation, October 1992
- BYTE June 1992, special issue on Document Management - Color in

Document Design, William Winn, IEEE transactions on Professional Communication, Vol 34, No.3, September 1991

- Using Documents to Integrate Business Information, Datapro Reports on Managing Information Technology, March 1993
- Gartner Group DPS Executive Briefing in Xerox, April 1993
- Conference material on Office Information Systems, Gartner Group, May 1993

3 DOCUMENTS AND DEPENDENCIES: ENABLING STRATEGIC IMPROVEMENT THROUGH COORDINATION REDESIGN

Charles S. Osborn

Strategy implementation and strategic guidance

Evidence from reengineering and process design implies that organizations need to connect high-level strategies more intimately with operation-level work (Davenport 1993; Hammer 1990; Hammer & Champy 1993). In particular, the top-down approaches to strategy implementation perfected by multidivisional command-and-control organizations (Chandler 1962, 1977) appear self-limiting in industries undergoing rapid market change (Eisenhardt 1989, 1990).

As businesses encounter accelerating rates of change, their need for competitive agility increases (Quinn et al 1988). Managers, researchers, and consultants have suggested multiple means for increasing agility; various perspectives have focused on organizational structure (Snow et al 1992), downsizing, information-gathering and surveillance (Aguilar 1967; Rockart and DeLong 1988), control processes (Simons 1995), and process design (Davenport and Short 1990). A consistent thread in this research captures the notion of strategic guidance: the guiding of low-level tasks more effectively towards the execution of intended or emergent strategies[1] (Mintzberg 1978, Simons 1991).

---

[1] Porter defines strategies as "...a combination of the *ends* (goals) for which the firm is striving and the *means* (policies) by which it is seeking to get there" (1980:xvi). Other researchers have emphasized strategies as a pattern of decisions (Andrews 1987:13) that supports a firm's adaptation to external competitive conditions (Lorange 1980:2). This pattern links activities at different levels of the

A separate and growing body of research implies that the ways in which organizations actually carry out work seldom bear much resemblance to the processes that were designed to implement strategic plans (Seely Brown and Duguid 1991; Suchman 1987). The discrepancies often appear so broad that it is tempting to reject ordered visions of strategy (Andrews 1987) and control (Anthony 1965, 1988) in favor of more anarchic models of organizational action (Cohen et al 1972).

Such a choice ignores important trends that are emerging as information technology disperses within organizations. These trends are notable in three areas: (1) the increasing granularity and velocity of business data; (2) the conversion of documents within corporate workflows from paper to machine-readable forms; and (3) the emergence of scalable, systematic process design techniques.

In combination these trends offer a new perspective and new tools for integrating strategic intent with business practice: for providing strategic guidance to improve competitive agility. This perspective suggests an approach to process design and management control that exploits new uses for documents as tools for prospectively coordinating key strategic activities.

Documents and process knowledge

Documents record work. At the level of business transactions, they represent a natural trace of specific organizational activities. An invoice, for example, promises to capture all that we need to know about a specific order. Three successive invoices indicate what occupied the order clerk during part of one day.

Yet documents also aggregate performance. Ten thousand invoices show seasonal sales trends. Ten million, gathered across an industry, describe market share and competitive position. Managers are vitally interested in the trends indicated within such aggregates.

It would be more precise, of course, to emphasize that documents record data rather than work, but this distinction misses two important points. First, at the operational level of many organizations, documenting a task is an integral part of performing the task. Indeed, in many knowledge-intensive businesses, the documents *are* the work. Second, many organizations still employ techniques for document handling and information management that date from decades when

---

firm according to their strategic importance such that operations at a business unit can be seen as "strategic" if they contribute directly to the strategic intent of the organization (Quinn:1980:9). This paper uses the term "coordination strategy" to suggest how organizations choose to coordinate the activities of a business. Such coordination can be "strategically" important when it affects performance constraints that directly influence intended business goals. In these instances coordination strategy aligns very closely with the actual practice of a business strategy. In this paper the term coordination "strategy" is intended to emphasize that alignment.

physical documents represented the only alternative for managing collective knowledge. This paper will argue that in organizational environments whose participants have spent their working lives supporting business processes with documents, workflow documents represent an important unit of analysis in addition to the data that they contain.

In many organizations, documents may represent the only source of process knowledge that is readily available -- or readily used. In a practical sense, documents not only capture data: they also capture what an organization remembers about a process. They are a prop for individual recollection and a source of collective organizational memory.

This perspective suggests that it is reasonable to ask how managers can more effectively leverage the business and process knowledge that existing document stores represent. One alternative is to build more explicit links between business information, process coordination, and workflow documents. This result derives (1) from the increasing velocity and granularity of business performance data; (2) from information systems explicitly designed to leverage proactive linkages between workflow documents and process redesign; and (3) from a unifying theory for applying the intersection of process design, knowledge management, and management decision-making. In combination, these three elements identify documents as a source of leverage for enabling strategic improvement through coordination redesign.

Data velocity and granularity

As information technology affects more companies and industries, the velocity and granularity of data tend to increase. As business performance results become captured in machine-readable form, the incremental cost of distributing information within an organization tends to decrease. Evidence from research into data warehousing and executive information systems suggests that at least two changes can be expected when a company begins to collect external market data or internal performance data systematically and electronically (Rockart & Delong 1988). First, the velocity with which data cycle through an organization increases, sometimes dramatically. Data velocity can be crudely assessed by observing how frequently business performance data are updated across an organization. Second, the granularity of data used in management reporting and management decision-making increases as data behind reported aggregates becomes more readily available, and can be used more systematically. Granularity can be approximated by counting the number of data dimensions that a company tracks to assess market performance.

An example from a longitudinal field study at Frito-Lay, Inc., illustrates how these changes occur, and suggests the role that information systems can play in facilitating them (Linder & Mead 1986; Wishart & Applegate 1987; Applegate & Wishart 1989; Wishart & Applegate 1990). Frito-Lay, Inc. is a Fortune 500 consumer packaged goods manufacturer that dominates the U.S. salty snack foods market. The study focused on information flow and decision-making within four management teams at the top three levels of the company between 1989 and 1991 (Osborn 1992).

In the late 1980s, Frito-Lay, Inc., introduced hand-held computers on its in-store delivery routes. Field sales staff used the computers to generate orders that replenished inventory on retail shelves. This system updated sales records by modem every evening. The data were combined into a multi-gigabyte data warehouse that became the source of a new management reporting system at company headquarters and all regional sales offices. Every Monday morning company managers were informed of cumulative sales performance to the prior Sunday. At approximately the same time, the company began to purchase industry data generated by grocery and retail store checkout scanners. These data were housed in the same database, and became accessible to managers across the company.

Table 1 shows some of the changes in data velocity and granularity that occurred following the introduction of systematically machine-readable internal and external data at the company. First, the speed with which managers knew of market performance (their own and their competitors') accelerated by at least a factor of two, from semi-monthly reporting to weekly reporting. Second, data became available at increased levels of granularity. Where managers traditionally had analyzed company sales at the level of 32 marketing areas, they now could, if they wished, assess trends for each of the company's 400,000 customers. Where market share trends had previously been monitored on the basis of 40 representative markets, external data became available that matched the company's 106 sales districts. Managers tracking internal performance had traditionally emphasized tracking sales growth for each of the company's five major brands. New information systems made it possible to track at least 10 combinations of brand, size, flavor, and region for each product. Traditional external data sources had offered information about 400 competing product variations; scanner data tracked 20,000.

The shift in velocity and granularity at Frito-Lay is perhaps most interesting in

Table 1: Data Velocity and Granularity at Frito-Lay

Criteria	*Internal Data* 1989	*Internal Data* 1991	*External (Market) Data* 1989	*External (Market) Data* 1991
Update cycle	Bi-weekly	Weekly	Bi-monthly	Weekly
No. of performance measures	1	10+	25	110
No. of geographic areas described	32	400,000	40	102
Product SKUs measured	<10	>25	400	20,000
Key performance measurement	Revenues	Profitability	Revenues	Profitability

its effects on the decision-making undertaken by regional management teams. Figure 1 suggests the change in information patterns at the company before and after its networked information systems were installed. One outcome of this change was that the company shifted performance emphasis from sales growth to profitability; this had profound effects on strategic behavior. For the ten years prior to 1989, Frito-Lay had supported its growth strategy by introducing new nationally branded products. In the five years following 1991, the company used its newly available data to understand product profitability rather than growth alone. The realization that profitability varied significantly and unexpectedly across both products and markets led to a renewed emphasis on local market conditions, competitive pricing, and internal cost structures. For a company that had spent decades pursuing sales growth, realignment according to focused profitability represented a major strategic change.

Figure 1: Information patterns and strategy emphasis at Frito-Lay

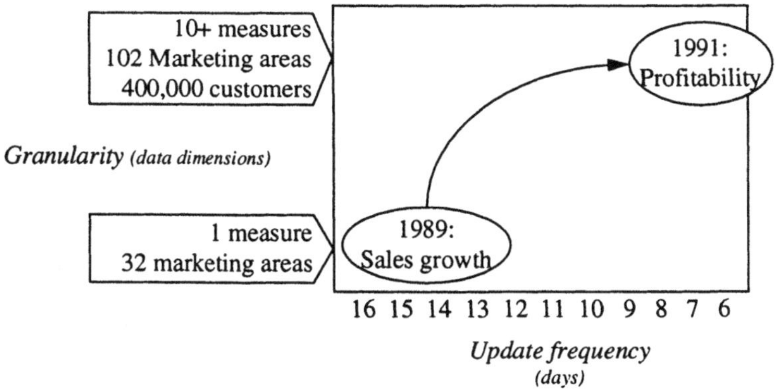

Frito-Lay is an interesting example not only because it suggests how changes in data velocity and granularity can contribute to changes in strategy but because it suggests specific mechanisms for how those changes occur. These mechanisms can be expressed as first-, second-, and third-order changes. First-order change resulted from immediate changes in data update frequency and granularity: more data were available more quickly. Second-order change resulted when the documents that management teams used to support performance monitoring and business decision-making evolved to reflect new analyses based on the new data. The content and conclusions of these analyses at times proved unexpected by company managers. Third-order change resulted after managers thought about, discussed, and reacted to the unexpected results. One third-order effect included the redesign of business monitoring processes, including unanticipated changes in the contents and form of documents used to support operational decision-making. A second third-order result was changes in strategies and tactics across the top three levels of the organization.

Documents, decisions, and strategies

It is perhaps not surprising that the rate and level of change observed within management teams at Frito-Lay was mediated by the documents that managers used in routine business review meetings. In these meetings regional management teams assembled each week and month to assess performance in their market areas. In 1989 business review meetings generally included internal performance reporting using formal slide presentations and accompanying documentation.

Documents used in business reviews reflected the first point at which managers were affected by higher velocities of granular data: as more systematic market knowledge became available, analysts who prepared reports for review meetings began to change content and format in new ways. At first, documents became dense with raw data: some included as many as 1,300 data items per page. As they struggled with this data overload, managers and analysts began to build business models that described determinants of observed data rather than merely results themselves – for example, market-driven causes for variations in profitability. These models began to appear in documents associated with management reporting.

What is interesting about this change is that managers expressed their challenge as one in which the task of redesigning documents was tightly linked with the task of changing strategic behavior. They seemed to suggest that workflow documents became a primary contributor to changes in market knowledge that were shared across levels of the organization: in effect, the documents managers saw led to changes in what they learned and altered how they behaved. In this sense, document redesign contributed heavily to implementing process redesign. As one general manager put it,

> Our challenge is to seek the key causals, the key drivers of our business, and pull whatever data are specifically relevant to those causals from whatever databases that hold that information. We need to provide functional management with a limited set of levers designed around a small set of causals. We need the right information as well as the right analysis because in a command and control organization you too often get what you inspect, not what you expect...Obviously, we've decided that profit and loss reporting is a key component in focusing organizational attention in a productive way. I see the P&L reporting as useful operationally, but also as an educational tool. We need easier tools, more comprehensive and interactive reports. We need a credible information and performance model at the local level. The goal should be to localize knowledge and analysis of the business.

Over the course of eight months, information analysts associated with regional management teams began to develop spreadsheets based on current and historical data provided by the data warehouse. These evolved into machine-readable documents that embedded business performance models. One of the earliest, for example, assessed promotion strategy by examining probable sales cannibalization across product sizes caused by the promotional pricing for a given size. For a given product and region, based on historical relationships sourced from the data warehouse, the analysis asked how much one could expect promotional pricing on XL bags of a product to detract from sales of XXL and Large size bags. This was a sensitive and difficult decision at the company: incremental sales from promotions often increased sales levels by a factor of three for short periods of time, but cannibalization could render the incremental sales nearly profitless.

In effect, as data used in management decisions became increasingly machine readable, the documents used to support management workflows became increasingly embedded with small decision support systems targeted at answering specific questions. Where before 1989 it would have been necessary to pay for a target study of promotion pricing and profitability, it became possible by 1992 to discuss a given promotion's profitability prospectively based on the sales and profits of every promotion decision taken during the past 12 months.

These shifts led to a different kind of document: one that included live analysis (in this example, spreadsheets) and that focused on prospective action (e.g., expected promotion performance) rather than on retrospective reporting (e.g., sales improvements from the promotion just finished). As regional managers worked to redesign business reporting and management processes around profit-driven strategies, they began to build workflows based on machine-readable data and increasingly interactive analyses. As Table 2 suggests, one third-order change that accompanied this evolution was a shift in management perspective from retrospective reporting to prospective analysis.

Table 2: Traditional vs. redesigned workflow documents

Document characteristic	*Traditional workflow*	*Redesigned workflow*
Format	Paper	Machine-readable
Analyses	Presented	Embedded
Frequency	Sponsored study	Systematic
Use in discussion	Reporting	Market knowledge
Focus	Retrospective	Prospective

The picture that emerges from the Frito-Lay example suggests some characteristics of the linkages between data cycles, workflow documents, and process redesign. Over a period of twelve to eighteen months following the introduction of high-velocity market data to management teams, the company redesigned core management processes to reflect strategies focused on profitability rather than sales growth alone. Those processes included workflows built upon documents with the distinguishing characteristics shown in Table 2. Traditional reports had depended on manually-collected data presented on paper. Their conclusions were normally presented verbally during managerial discussions and often based on single-issue studies using data from small test samples. Studies and test samples were largely oriented toward result reporting and providing data that demonstrated the value of past managerial decisions. As a result, their focus was largely retrospective.

Documents associated with the redesigned workflow, however, exhibited different characteristics. They were derived from frequently-updated, machine-readable data and normally included the results of at least one embedded analytical model employed to make sense out of the raw results. The data used were typically collected systematically from all of a region's market areas and/or customers, or could be quickly expanded to equivalent depth. Over time the combination of analyses and systematic data appeared to contribute to changes in the level of market knowledge observed by practicing managers among their functional counterparts and their direct reports.

Using these documents and the redesigned workflow, members of management teams began to focus on what they anticipated to be the results of upcoming decisions rather than reporting and reacting to recent market events. Managerial discussions tended to shift towards prospective rather than retrospective topics, and the company's redesigned processes came to emphasize action rather than reaction. This change in perspective, supported by new documents and tools within the redesigned business review process, spread relatively rapidly within the top five layers of the Frito-Lay management hierarchy, distributing top-down knowledge to the field and bottom-up insights to headquarters using document-based analytical tools that managers at all levels shared and understood.

Process redesign for strategic coordination

The Frito-Lay example suggests the role that electronically-enabled documents can play in process designs devoted to supporting new strategies. It does not, however, provide any assistance in understanding how to improve processes to take consistent advantage of such opportunities.

This paper proposes that a theory describing systematic process redesign in a manner that translates quickly to the level of workflow support can be a key ingredient in generating effective document-enabled strategic guidance as encountered at Frito-Lay. One such alternative is coordination theory as described by Malone and Crowston (Crowston 1991; Malone & Crowston 1993, 1994).

Coordination theory implies a process analysis with three key features. Each contributes to building tighter linkages between strategic intent and actual business practice in ways that enable electronic documents within a workflow to guide as well as record tasks and activities. The features relate to process activities, process variety, and process dependencies.

First, coordination theory suggests that all processes are inherently multi-level: any process is itself made up of subprocesses and any subprocess represents a collection of activities. In this sense it is certainly not unique, but this approach makes it possible to describe any process as a hierarchy of activities ranging from high-level intentions to low-level operations (see Figure 2). Such a hierarchy enables process decomposition in a manner similar to object-oriented design, using inheritance to organize process activities attributes.

Figure 2: Generic process decomposition model

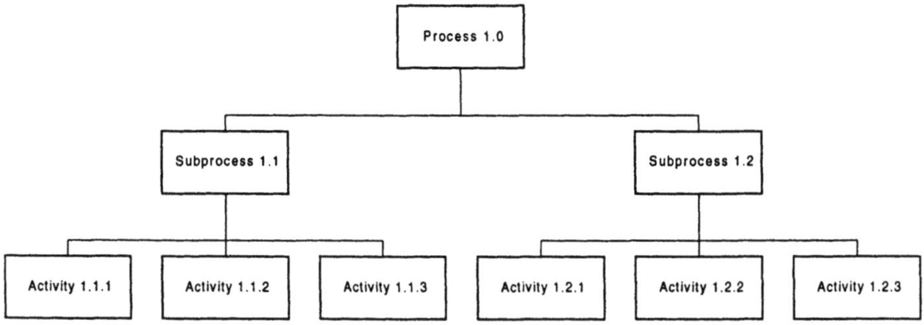

For the purposes of this paper it is important to note where the branches of a particular process decomposition terminate. For practical purposes, for example, the lowest levels in a process decomposition hierarchy represent points at which actual work is accomplished. In many businesses, particularly knowledge-related businesses, this point represents where data are captured in a document. In other words, document creation is intimately connected with accomplishing real work. This is equally the case whether the document created is a transaction record or an analytical artifact, whether it represents entries on paper or in a database, or whether it is a formal or informal presentation of data.

Multi-level process representations: strategies and execution

One of the advantages of process models that explicitly acknowledge the multi-level nature of processes is that they facilitate linking high-level abstractions of process objectives with specific operational-level tasks. A high level description of a process can correlate quite closely with the strategic intent that the process is expected to fulfill. At the same time, a process decomposition can suggest how high-level goals are executed by operational activities. In other words, it can map strategic intent to the practice of real work.

Figure 3 suggests how this approach works for Frito-Lay promotion planning. At the highest level, the process description captures the company's strategic intent in the 1990s: to maximize profitable growth. This process of maximizing growth translates into selling, producing, and delivering product. Characteristics of the salty snack market indicate that sales promotion is an important tool due to the dramatic swings in incremental revenues generated by promotions. Promotion planning thereby becomes a mechanism for expanding profitable sales. At the operational level, this perspective influences the balance between discounts and potential same-brand cannibalization chosen for a given promotion. In practice,

Figure 3: Process decomposition: promotion planning

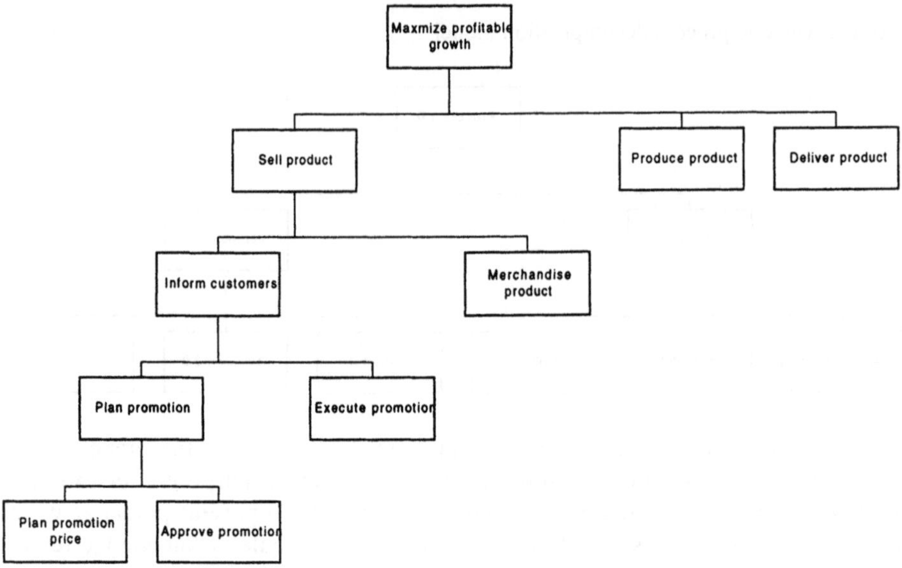

process decomposition of the type suggested by coordination theory can contribute to a shared model of process structure and strategic intent that could be readily understood by managers at several levels within the organization.

It is worth noting that integrating strategic intent across process levels becomes a practical objective using tools that support process decomposition. For example, a workflow system that organized organizational knowledge about strategies and promotions (by generating and collecting electronically-enabled documents to describe promotion data based on current sales) could rapidly illustrate how promotion efforts were contributing to the organization's overall goal. Furthermore, it could do so in a manner readily comprehended by both high-level and field-level management.

Process variety: specialization and strategic guidance

The concepts of specialization used in coordination theory offer an opportunity to describe process variety systematically enough to manage the many dimensions across which instances of a process differ. In this sense, process specialization offers a relatively simple yet flexible way to contrast process characteristics that have given rise to variations in work practice. Models of process specialization offer a technique for making the operational practices that exist in an organization explicit enough so that they can be considered as part of planned process design rather than as informal work-arounds for implicit problems.

Figure 4, for example, suggests how the promotion planning process might differ for salty snacks vs. baked goods. In this example, the factors affecting promotional pricing differ according to the product being promoted. Aggressive promotion prices on potato chips, for example, might cannibalize sales from other versions of Frito-Lay potato chip products on nearby shelves. For a specific baked products, however, the company does not offer many alternatives, so aggressive pricing will affect competitors directly and sales cannibalization is not an issue.

The process decomposition view shown in Figure 4 (b) illustrates how activity descriptions can begin to describe the differences between process specializations (note the differences between activities that make up the Analyze Pricing process). Figure 4 (a) shows how a specialization hierarchy could suggest the same comparison more succinctly. Both illustrations suggest how process modeling that comprehends decomposition and specialization could deliver electronic documents that contained different analytical tools based on the product that was being considered for promotion. For example, the documents analyzing pricing for a potato chip promotion might include an analysis of cannibalization potential, while the pricing analysis for baked goods would include a model for assessing impact on market share. While this is a relatively simple example, it begins to show how awareness of process specializations could contribute to generating workflow support that functions in a process-aware fashion.

Figure 4: Specialization describes process variety

(a) Plan promotion process illustrated as specialization hierarchy

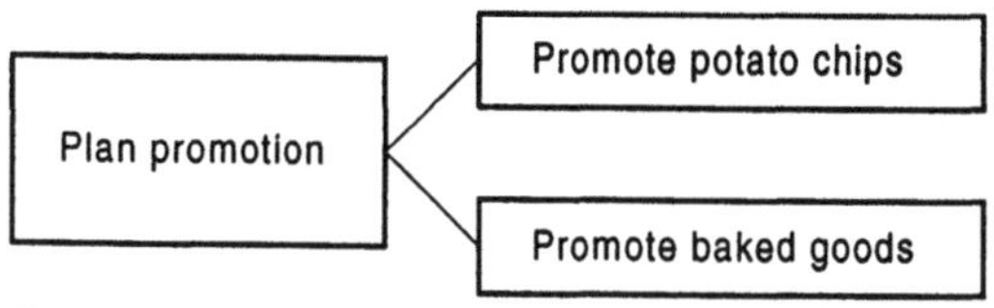

(b) Plan promotion process illustrated as contrasting activity decompositions

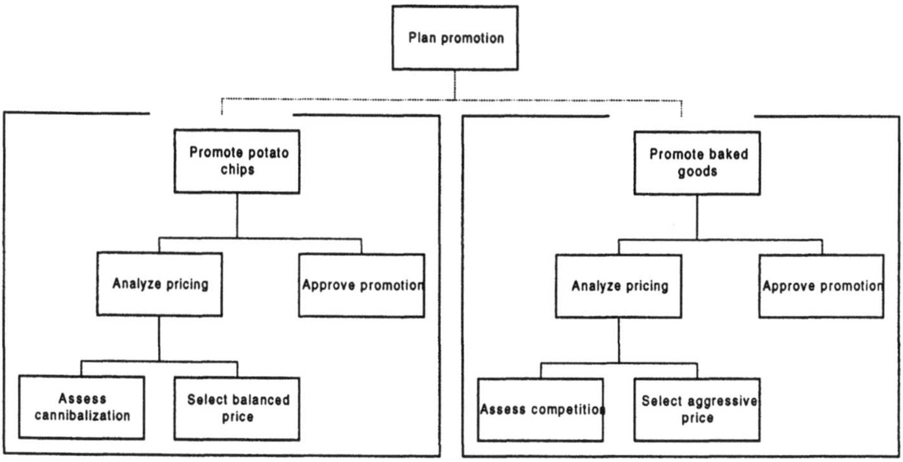

A system based on these structures, for example, would be able to deliver a blank monthly report document to a field manager that included spreadsheets relating to the promotion pricing analysis that was most appropriate for the product under consideration. As more dimensions of specialization are identified and considered, the system would be able to develop workflow support that became increasingly tailored to the task at hand. In effect, the system would be contributing the level of strategic guidance to field-level management that executives would provide if they were able to participate directly in promotion planning at the time (e.g., "We worry about these factors for core product promotions, but we worry most about competitor's pricing for baked goods"). Such considerations to some degree capture big-picture strategic issues in ways that encourage consistency in decisions that are distributed throughout the organization. Such a use of process-based, document-driven tools is of course no replacement for intelligent management discussion, but it may contribute to building shared understanding and common perspectives among widely disbursed organizational participants.

Coordinating dependencies: strategic priorities

A major claim of coordination theory is that dependencies between activities offer significant and systematic leverage for process redesign. Dependencies are articulated as relating to resources that form the outputs of one or more activities and the inputs of a subsequent activity or activities. If two activities share a resource (as output from one and input to the other, or as shared outputs or inputs to a third activity), a dependency is expected to exist between them. Using these ideas, coordination theory describes three common types of dependencies: *flow* dependencies (a resource that is an output from one activity becomes an input to another), *sharing* dependencies (two activities share the same inputs), and *fit* dependencies (two activities produce outputs that must be used by the same consumer). Like processes, dependencies are seen as having decompositions. Managing flow dependencies, for example, includes managing usability constraints (e.g., whether the output is usable to the receiving activity), prerequisite constraints (e.g., whether all the necessary activities been completed before the resource is passed to the receiving activity), and transfer constraints (e.g., whether the resource is provided in the place where the receiving activity needs it).

A second claim of coordination theory is that a generic set of coordination strategies exist for managing a given dependency; furthermore, that generic strategies can prove generalizable across multiple organizational contexts. For example, order entry systems that facilitate taking product requests over the telephone – a technique for managing flow dependencies that uses a first-come, first-served strategy – are expected to be useful to multiple mail-order firms, even if elements of individual order processes differ (e.g., their order processes represent specializations of some more general Order Product process). Figure 5 suggests a technique for representing coordination strategies graphically. Panel (a) shows a flow dependency existing between two processes.

Figure 5: Dependencies and coordination activities

(a) A flow dependency | *(b) A coordination strategy*

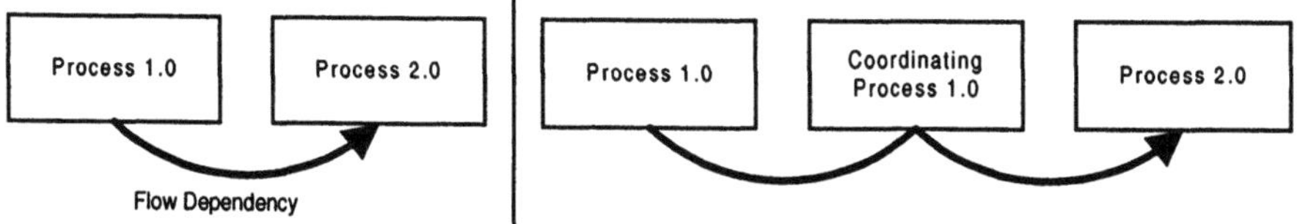

Process 1.0 produces an output resource that is an input to Process 2.0.

Coordinating Process 1.0 represents a process that manages the dependency existing between Process 1.0 and Process 2.0.

Panel (b) suggests that a coordinating process exists which manages that flow dependency according to some coordinating strategy.

Using this perspective, it is possible to describe the implementation of strategic choices with some precision: strategies represent decisions made to select specific coordination mechanisms for managing key process dependencies. For example, consider an industry, such as apparel, where product design plays an important role in ensuring that a producer's output is usable by a consumer (e.g., people don't want to wear pants that don't fit). Traditional coordination techniques within this industry call for designs produced by a manufacturer in many sizes, implying large inventories, long production leadtimes, expensive retail distribution, and heavy advertising budgets. The strategy of manufacturer-driven design is suggested by the specialization represented in the left panel of Figure 6 (b).

Against this coordination approach compare the strategy used by the custom jeans business recently initiated by Levi Strauss, Inc. As suggested by the right panel of Figure 6 (b), this strategy anticipates that the customer designs the product – e.g., by using a scanner to determine the cutting instructions necessary to custom fit a pair of jeans to him or her. Dimensions are transmitted across a network to cutting machines; cut cloth is forwarded to sewing subcontractors. The finished jeans are delivered to the customer by mail within two weeks. This change alters how the dependency between producing the jeans and using the jeans is coordinated. Levi's has discovered that inventory costs are dramatically lower (in terms of store stocking and returns), that leadtimes are shorter (no need to premanufacture for inventory), and that the business is more profitable that traditional distribution (customers are willing to pay a premium for custom fit). The result is a new strategy and a new business segment: custom-fit jeans in batch sizes of one.

While it is clear from this example that changing high-level coordination strategies can have subtle implications for operating levels of a business, consider the leverage which the coordination perspective provides. The approach analyzes key process attributes (e.g., coordination strategies) using electively complex detail (e.g., dependency analysis and process decomposition) while retaining the means for managing process variety (using specialization).

Figure 6: Process redesign as alternative coordination strategies

(a) A systematic approach to process redesign selects alternative coordination strategies:

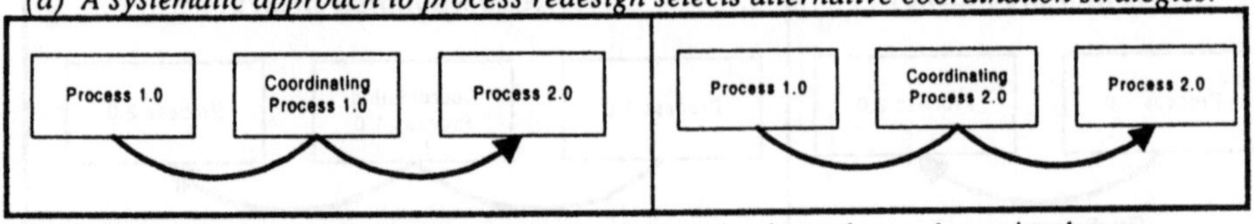

In this example, Coordinating Process 2.0 manages the dependency that exists between Process 1.0 and Process 2.0 using different coordination strategies than Coordinating Process 1.0.

(b) Different coordination strategies are available to customers and vendors who rely on a product:

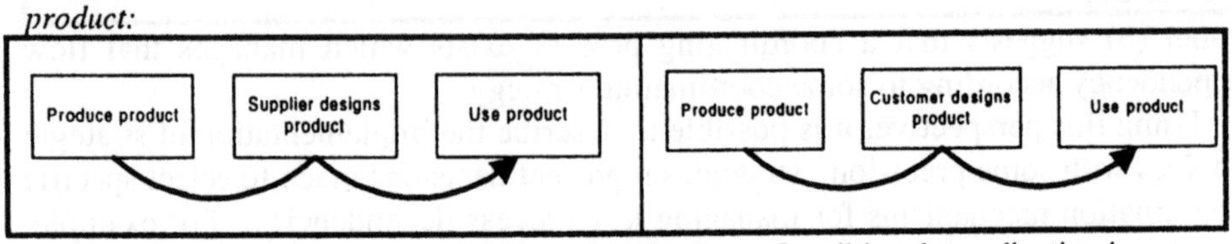

In this case, the process, cost, and delivery implications of traditional coordination in which the supplier designs the product (e.g., market tests, design departments) are different from those of different strategies now being explored in software-supported custom apparel, where the customer designs the fit and chooses the fabric for the product.

Towards document-enabled strategic guidance: an example

Process innovation based on coordination theory focuses systematically on key leverage means for managing process variety (using specialization)., expressed as dependencies between activities. This paper argues that the combination of such a systematic process perspective with systems designed to exploit electronically-enabled documents can encourage workflows whose performance defaults towards delivering strategic intent rather than favoring past practice or local expedience. If such document-enabled strategic guidance systems are practical, it is worthwhile to ask how a combination of process design, coordination analysis, and information technology could deliver these features in an integrated manner.

Coordination theory begins to suggest some characteristics of a systematic methodology for exploiting document-enabled process redesign. It provides a structure that encourages the design of electronic document flows to support top-down knowledge of a process (e.g., strategies), cross-functional coordination (e.g., operational tactics), a focus on dependencies (e.g., key priorities), and rapid response (e.g., efficiency). It further suggests a process guidance role for documents that reverses the traditional relationship between action and documentation by suggesting where documents can provide tools that deliver knowledge to guide actions consistent with higher-level strategies.

To examine these ideas, we will use evidence derived from a process field study of a mailing services company (Osborn, 1995). This study was completed over eighteen months and involved interviews and participant observation covering the activities of 40% of the company's 70 employees, including all of its managers. The company was chosen because its core processes remained simple enough to be readily comprehensible yet its business problems proved sufficiently complex to be interesting.

Overview: the business problem

The company's strategic problem derived from its business mix. The organization specialized in mailing fulfillment services. These services represented contracts though which clients provided an inventory of marketing materials and the company fulfilled requests – e.g., sent individual packages of information in response to requests received by mail or telephone. Normally such contracts covered work over the period of a year. In traditional fulfillment work, instructions rarely changed (e.g., the fulfillment process was well-defined, stable, and repetitive), and jobs could be handled effectively on a batch basis. In order to improve its fulfillment efficiency, the mailing company developed a sophisticated in-house database that processed fulfillment jobs.

By 1992 company management decided to apply the database to the customized fulfillment market. Customized fulfillment represented a different type of business, although at the time company management considered it within the core competence of the company. Customized jobs tended to be generated by trade shows or specific marketing campaigns. They tended to be lower-volume, more diverse, less well defined, and more accelerated than traditional work. Because they often developed from specific events, clients often wanted more customized output than for traditional jobs. Indeed, it was the power of the in-house database for completing such work that encouraged company management to enter the customized market.

By 1994, customized fulfillment contracts represented the fastest-growing part of the company's business but internal operations were nearly overwhelmed and it was not clear to management whether customized jobs were making or losing money. In an attempt to correct these problems the company engaged on a process redesign project to understand how better to manage its growth.

Process analysis: the business problem

To explore how analysis based on process coordination could contribute to integrating electronic documents that encourage strategic guidance for this process, consider the above problem in the language of coordination theory. First, the business problem can be described as a comparison of specializations: company management presumed that the customized database developed for traditional fulfillment would provide leverage in custom markets, but in practice the traditional fulfillment process proved less appropriate for custom work than initially anticipated.

Figure 7 suggests how the specializations of traditional and customized business might differ. Although both businesses retain the same general process structure (e.g., selling to and then servicing clients), the characteristics of the customized business contrasted in important ways.

Figure 7: Traditional vs. customized fulfillment services

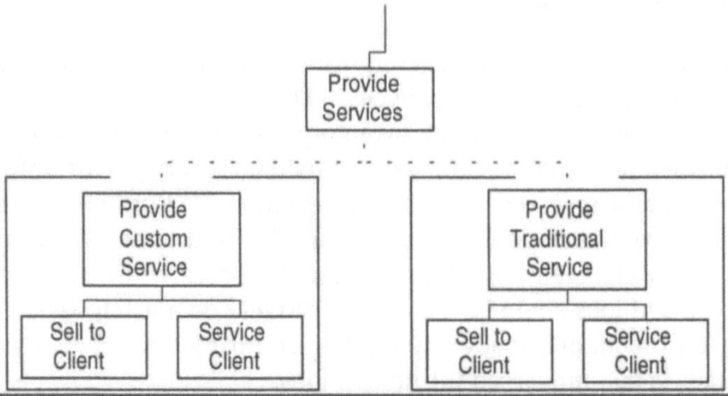

Job	Volume	Duration	Processing	Task order	Deadlines	Contact
Custom	Potential	3-4 mo.	Custom	May vary	Tight	Daily
Trad'l	Certain	Year(s)	Standard	Standard	Set by co.	Quarterly

Figure 7 suggests some of these parameters, not all of which had been obvious to company management when the customized business was initiated. Custom jobs were of shorter duration than traditional work, and included a higher proportion of customized processing tasks. Task order for fulfillment processing could vary for custom work but seldom did for traditional work. For traditional jobs, the mailing company set its own deadlines and reported results quarterly. For custom jobs, customers set deadlines and required daily contact. Finally, traditional contracts all but guaranteed high volumes of business, while volumes associated with custom contracts were contingent upon the client's success at a trade show or with a specific marketing project and was often impossible to predict.

In 1994 the company applied a process to both traditional and custom work that exhibited the structure illustrated in Figure 8 (in the interests of clarity, not all branches of the decomposition hierarchy have been labeled). Within the organization, account executives (AEs) played a key role in selling existing clients on new work, defining custom jobs, and coordinating production. Specifically, AEs were responsible for managing each of the activities described at the lowest level of activities in Figure 8: preparing quotes, setting up jobs, producing the mailing service, and providing status reports.

Figure 8: The fulfillment process

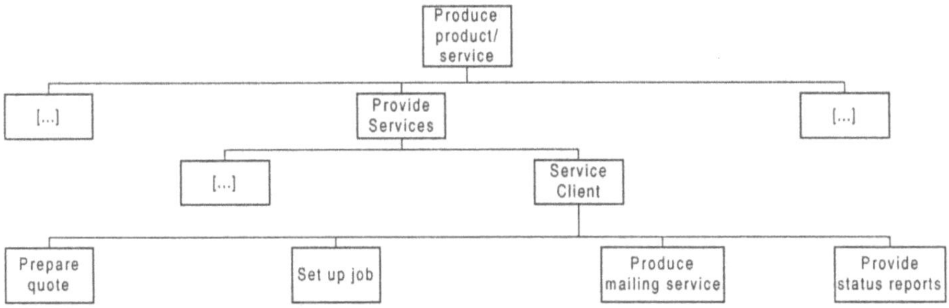

Goals, strategies, and dependencies

To understand how the combination of coordination analysis and process-aware documents can integrate the strategic goals associated with the mailing company's custom-fulfillment business, we can use dependency analysis to focus on how high-level goals were implemented through operational work. To begin with, it is helpful to start at the highest level of the process description shown in Figure 8.

To do so, consider the goal structure of the Provide product/service process. Understood as coordination, this activity managed the conversion of a marketing need experienced by a client into a process where that need was satisfied. In effect, the mailing company inserted itself as a coordination mechanism between two activities in the client's process. If this is a plausible representation, it is possible to describe the company's goal structure as the management of a flow dependency that facilitates the conversion of client marketing needs into satisfactory, qualified sales leads.

Figure 9: Strategic goals as a coordination process

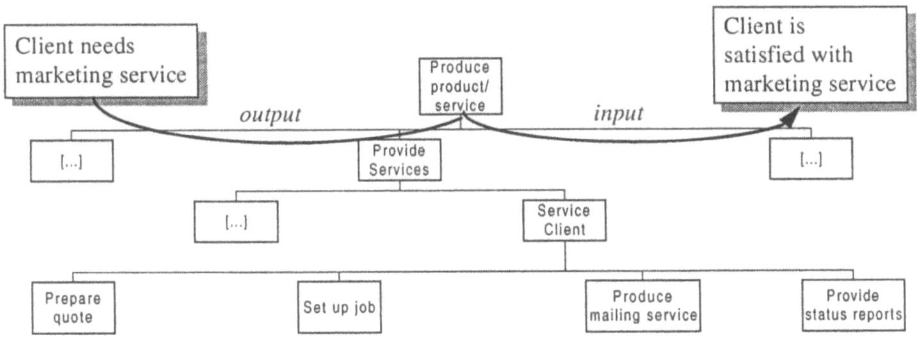

Figure 9 expresses the mailing company's goals as a coordination process in which the company converts outputs from a process that generates a client's need for marketing contacts into inputs that provide useful marketing data with accuracy and response times that fit the client's internal requirements. Coordination theory suggests that any flow dependency can decompose into at least three constraints that must be coordinated: constraints related to usability; constraints related to prerequisites and sequencing, and constraints related to the transfer of products or information. ting a prerequisite dependency.

Figure 10 suggests activities within the Service Client process that coordinate each of these constraints.

By dropping down within the decomposition of Provide Service, it is possible to ask how the process design managed strategies implied by the top-level process. For example, the mailing company used each AE to coordinate the definition of each traditional or custom job by developing a job quote with the customer. The dependency analysis identifies this work as a coordination activity that ensures the usability of the job for both the client (e.g., the client will get an appropriate number and quality of sales leads) and for the company (e.g, the job will prove manageable and profitable).

As part of setting up a job, the AE wrote instructions for each functional department within the company, including the data entry staff who built data records from incoming mail; the system production staff who processed batches of leads using the company's in-house database; the operations staff who picked, packed and sorted personalized letters and mailing materials in the company warehouse; and the technical staff who wrote computer code for completing extreme customized work. Using these instructions, each AE coordinated the work of the operational departments of the company. In this sense, the instructions ensured that each step in a job occurred in proper sequence and with appropriate preparation. From this perspective the Set up Job process can be identified as coordinating a prerequisite dependency.

Figure 10: Managing coordination constraints to implement strategy

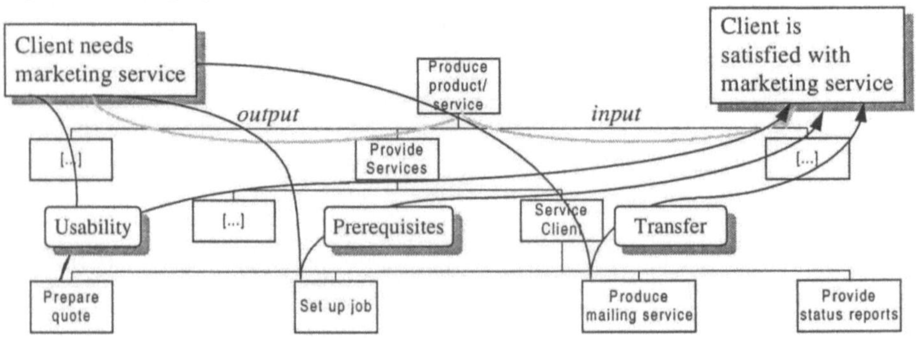

Once a quote had been approved and instructions had been distributed, the production work associated with the job began. This work ensured that the fulfillment requests were completed accurately and rapidly, and that data on qualified sales leads were distributed to the client within the timeframes specified in the quote. This part of the process represented coordinating a transfer dependency. Finally, the AE reported back to the client on the status of the project, a process that also contributed to the usability of the project (the arrow is not shown on Figure 10 for the sake of clarity). In custom work, this reporting could take place as frequently as every day; in traditional work it tended to occur once a quarter.

By focusing on the specific activities that manage key dependencies, this coordination analysis identified three sets of documents – the job quote, the job instructions, and the status reports – that played an important role in supporting the delivery of both traditional and custom work. In 1994, all were prepared and distributed by hand. This method of support was satisfactory for traditional work, but resulted in intense pressure on AEs for custom jobs because of tighter time cycles, shifting requirements, and variable volume. The result of the increased velocity and greater demands embedded in AE workflow was repeated mistakes, each of which had to be resolved by an AE before a job could move forward. Because each job was customized and each quote required intimate knowledge of the company's procedures and cost structures, it proved very difficult to train new AEs and increase new business.

Coordination strategies and strategic guidance

Coordination theory suggests that when a coordination mechanism has been identified as inappropriate for a given process specialization, one alternative is to replace that coordination process with one based on a different coordination strategy. For example, preparing and pricing quotes by hand consumed a large amount of AE time on customized jobs. The coordination analysis demonstrated why and how this activity represented an important strategic priority. It also suggested that the coordination strategy in use for traditional jobs (e.g., negotiating new jobs on an ad hoc basis and manual support for quoting) would not continue to be satisfactory for custom work.

At this point the coordination analysis encourages investigating coordination processes within the Prepare Quote process. This transition, using the same analytical approach applied to the Produce Product or Service process as a whole, begins to ask questions about workflow and documents that would be useful in supporting an improved quoting process. This provides an opportunity to engage in workflow analysis, but with the additional focus provided by prior identification of quote management as a high-priority support issue for custom contracts. While coordination analysis is not necessary to identifying AE quoting as a potential bottleneck, the structure added by the multi-level dependency analysis can be helpful in (a) pinpointing specific process areas where coordination improvements may be most needed, and (b) preserving a higher-level strategic focus when encountering the details of workflow design (e.g., emphasizing during the design of a quoting system that the quoting process ensures the usability of any custom job to both the client and to the mailing company).

Figure 11 suggests how the integration of process coordination and workflow design could contribute to the resolution of quoting and job setup issues at the mailing company. Each dependency is traced to a coordination mechanism that manages a key constraint at the workflow level. The strategy behind each coordination mechanism is then compared with the goal structure of the high-level strategy implied by the flow dependency of which the workflow coordination task is a smaller part. Where the strategy identified at the level of workflow

Figure 11: Coordination processes and coordination strategies

Dependency	*Usability*	*Prerequisite*
Process	Prepare quote	Set up job Prepare instructions / Distribute instructions / Provide sample output to client
Current coordination strategy	Negotiated ad hoc	One-way notification
Potential innovation(s) from redesign	Link with process	Two-way notification
Possible solution	Electronic quote document develops quote and instructions.	Email discussion available around each instruction topic so that questions can be asked and answered. Build in real time alert for important questions and budget review time for AE, functional personnel.

coordination is presumed to be incongruent with the requirements of higher-level goals, the analysis suggests ways in which coordination might be improved. In many cases, it is likely that electronically-augmented documents can play an important role in such improvement.

The Prepare Quote process offers an example of the interaction between high-level goals, process coordination, and document-oriented solutions. As Figure 11 suggests, manual support for ad hoc quoting broke down on custom jobs as AEs struggled to price work that was in nonstandard sequence, to anticipate operational problems with one-time customer requests for specialized features, and to convert the quote to instructions that made sense to operations staff. Analyzing the current coordination strategy suggests that quoting operated as a stand-alone process for traditional work but that it needed to be tightly integrated into the production process for customized jobs.

Possible solutions to the coordination problem arise in part from the ways in which the coordination analysis allows the problem to be stated (Smith, 1988, 1989). A reconceptualization of documents as process guidance tools embedded with some degree of process knowledge suggests the use of workflow support software to provide a quote form that includes knowledge about the tasks and costs associated with specific production processes. An AE could use such a document for three purposes: (a) to explain to a potential client the cost and timing implications of the job that was represented by any specific work request; (b) to price a quote while on the phone with a customer; and (c) to convert the quote into instruction documents more rapidly than allowed by manual procedures. For any AE encountering a job configuration that he or she had not worked with before, the quote form could provide a crude process model that scripted an approach to assessing the value of the incremental business and balancing it against expected costs. Once the quote was accepted, the data associated with it could contribute to generating appropriate instructions for functional staff members. Figure 11 also suggests the analytical steps that suggest the use of emailed documents for improving coordination around job set up and execution. Similar steps can be developed for the Produce Mailing Service and Provide Status Reports processes.

Summary and conclusion

This example suggests how the structure provided by coordination-based process analysis and new tools enabled by electronically-supported documents can contribute to integrating high-level strategic intent with workflow-level task support to suggest a route to integrated process redesign. As the number of companies with access to systematic machine-readable data increase and new document-oriented tools such as hypertext transfer protocols become more widespread, such opportunities for leveraging knowledge of process structure are likely to become more prevalent and more important.

Combining the strategic emphasis of top-down process analysis with the bottom-up insights into work practice afforded by workflow support tools raises the prospect of a more unified and systematic approach to process design. It may be that coordination-aware process analysis can contribute to our understanding of process dynamics in useful ways that increase the levels of strategic guidance available in daily work.

Tools that make greater use of electronically-augmented documents offer the potential for designing workflows that deliver a real-time framework for process guidance. In this paper, the Frito-Lay example offered a view of such a framework emerging unexpectedly; the mailing company example explored how process analysis could increase the likelihood that strategically consistent workflow support can be systematically planned. Such planning goes beyond many workflow and system design techniques currently in use. Coordination theory provides an understanding of process structure and process dynamics to describe the strategic priorities underlying workflow and document design. It offers a means for integrating workflow solutions across multiple levels and branches of a business process.

The guiding premise of this paper has been that recent technological changes are influencing the velocity and volume of data available to managers in large and small business organizations. As the costs of assembling and distributing data fall, the relative costs associated with manual techniques for managing document-based knowledge rise. As machine-readable data become increasingly available, new types of electronically-augmented documents are emerging that can be applied in ways similar to their paper antecedents, but with electronically embedded analyses and process-aware data that did not exist before. What is missing, so far, is a consistent method for understanding processes across levels of abstraction and with control of meaningful process variety so that the design of workflow systems can align more closely with high-level strategic intent. The mailing company analysis described above suggested some avenues toward solving this problem.

Successful efforts to integrate process design and work practice in this direction are likely to result in low-level tasks that remain flexible yet diverge less dramatically from overall strategic goals than under current command-and-control techniques. They are likely to support coordinating documents that leverage existing organizational knowledge and support the accumulation of informed insight at all levels of an organization. By providing real-time frameworks for process guidance, they offer the possibility of a new kind of document that can focus joint organizational attention prospectively and assist in bringing appropriate knowledge to bear on high-priority coordination problems. The combination of process-driven coordination insight and document-driven process guidance is potentially powerful: it can be used to improve organizational performance, change organizational relationships, and extensively alter organizational structures.

References

Aguilar, F. (1967). Scanning the Business Environment. New York, Macmillan.

Andrews, K. R. (1987). The Concept of Corporate Strategy. Homewood, IL, Irwin.

Anthony, R. N. (1965). Planning and Control Systems: A Framework for Analysis. Boston, Harvard University Graduate School of Business Administration.

Anthony, R. N. (1988). The Management Control Function. Boston, Harvard Business School Press.

Applegate, L. M. and N. A. Wishart (1989). Frito-Lay, Inc.: A Strategic Transition (C). Boston, MA, Harvard Business School Publishing Division (Case #190-071, rev. 5/24/90).

Chandler, A. D., Jr. (1962). Strategy and Structure: Chapters in the history of the american

industrial enterprise. Cambridge, MA, MIT Press.
Chandler, A. D., Jr. (1977). The Visible Hand: The managerial revolution in American business. Cambridge, MA, Harvard University Press/Belknap Press.
Cohen, M. D., J. G. March, et al. (1972). "A Garbage Can Model of Organizational Choice." Administrative Science Quarterly **17**(1): 1-25.
Crowston, K. (1991). Towards a coordination cookbook: Recipes for multi-agent action. PhD. Dissertation, MIT Sloan School of Management.
Davenport, T. H. (1993). Process Innovation: Reengineering work through information technology. Boston, MA, Harvard Business School Press.
Davenport, T. H. and J. E. Short (1990). "The new industrial engineering: Information technology and business process redesign." Sloan Management Review **31**(4): 11-27.
Eisenhardt, K. M. (1989). "Making fast strategic decisions in high-velocity environments." Academy of Management Journal **32**(3): 543-576.
Eisenhardt, K. M. (1990). "Speed and Strategic Choice: How managers accelerate decision making." California Management Review **32**(3): 39-54.
Hammer, M. (1990). "Reengineering Work: Don't Automate, Obliterate." Harvard Business Review: 104-112.
Hammer, M. and J. Champy (1993). Reengineering the Corporation: a manifesto for business revolution. New York, HarperCollins.
Linder, J. and M. Mead (1986). Frito-Lay, Inc.: A Strategic Transition (A). Boston, MA, Harvard Business School Publishing Division (Case #187-065).
Lorange, P. (1980). Corporate Planning: An Executive Viewpoint. Englewood Cliffs, NJ: Prentice-Hall.
Malone, T. W. and K. Crowston (1994). "The Interdisciplinary Study of Coordination." ACM Computing Surveys **26**(1): 87-119.
Malone, T. W., K. Crowston, et al. (1993). Tools for Inventing Organizations: Towards a Handbook of Organizational Processes. 2nd IEEE Workshop on Enabling Technologies Infrastructure for Collaborative Enterprises, Morgantown, WV.
Mintzberg, H. (1978). "Patterns in strategy formation." Management Science **24**(9): 934-948.
Osborn, C. (1992). Management support systems, interactive management controls, and strategic adaptation. Unpublished doctoral dissertation, Harvard Business School.
Osborn, C. (1995). MAG Services Company: Process Redesign. Babson Park, MA: Babson College.
Porter, M. E. (1980). Competitive Strategy: Techniques for analyzing industries and competitors. New York: The Free Press.
Quinn, J. B. (1980). Strategies for Change: Logical incrementalism. Homewood, IL: Richard D. Irwin, Inc.
Quinn, J. B., H. Mintzberg, et al. (1988). The Strategy Process: Concepts, contexts, and cases. Englewood Cliffs, NJ, Prentice-Hall.
Rockart, J. F. and D. W. DeLong (1988). Executive Support Systems: The emergence of top management computer use. Homewood, Illinois, Dow Jones-Irwin.
Seely Brown, J. and P. Duguid (1991). "Organizational Learning and Communities-of-Practice: Toward a Unified View of Working, Learning, and Innovation." Organizational Science **2**(1 (February)): 40-57.
Simons, R. (1991). "Strategic Orientation and Top Management Attention to Control Systems." Strategic Management Journal **12**(1): 49-62.
Simons, R. (1995). Levers of Control. Boston, MA, Harvard Business School Press.

Smith, G. F. (1988). "Towards a Heuristic Theory of Problem Structuring." Management Science **34**(12): 1489-1506.

Smith, G. F. (1989). "Defining managerial problems: A framework for prescriptive theorizing." Management Science **35**(8): 963-981.

Snow, C. C., R. E. Miles, et al. (1992). "Managing 21st Century Network Organizations." Organizational Dynamics **Winter**: 5-19.

Suchman, L. A. (1987). Plans and situated actions: The problem of human machine communication. New York, Cambridge University Press.

Wishart, N. and L. M. Applegate (1987). Frito-Lay, Inc.: A Strategic Transition (B). Boston, MA, Harvard Business School Publishing Division (Case #187-123, Rev. 5/24/90).

Wishart, N. and L. M. Applegate (1990). Frito-Lay, Inc.: HHC Project Follow-up. Boston, MA, Harvard Business School Publishing Division (Case #190-191, rev. 4/7/90).

4 ENTERPRISE MODELING WITHIN THE FRAMEWORK OF BUSINESS PROCESS REENGINEERING

K.J. Heng, C.M. Khoong, N.Radjou, J.S. Dhaliwal and R. Ramlochan

ABSTRACT
The enterprise seeking to improve through Business Process Reengineering, needs to first understand its own structures and processes and how they affect each other. It seeks to eliminate non-value adding processes and streamline or change core processes. As a tool for understanding structure and processes, and their effects on each others, we employ Enterprise Modeling technology to model the enterprise and conduct analysis on the model to obtain answers on what-if scenarios. Instead of discarding the model after the analysis, we advocate that it be converted into an operation model (also called an enactment model) to act as a tool for executing the new system. Furthermore, this operation model can collect new operational data for future analysis and evaluation of the new system. We discuss our motivations and the research objectives in detail, share some of the results obtained so far, and explain our intended direction of future research.

Introduction

In this section we introduce the basic concepts necessary to bring the reader to a common understanding for the rest of the paper.

Business Process Reengineering (BPR)

BPR is the fundamental rethinking and radical redesign of business processes to achieve dramatic improvements in critical, contemporary measures of performance, such as cost, quality, service, and speed [Hammer93]. Although highly successful stories of BPR have been published and quoted often, many organizations have failed in their attempts at BPR. One source estimated that two-thirds of American reengineering projects in 1994 failed [Cadwell94]. Some of the reasons for failure are expounded in [Khoong96, Khoong96a]. Clearly, there are pitfalls to BPR, but these can be minimized through formal methodologies during the analysis, evaluation and implementation phases. We propose using enterprise modeling (EM) to create such a systematic methodology within the framework of BPR.

What are Processes?

BPR starts with an understanding of what a business process is and what are the mission-critical business processes within the organization. A business process is a collection of related, structured activities -- a chain of events -- that produces a specific service or product for a particular customer or customers. It has a start, an end, and a purpose. A business process has clearly identified inputs and outputs. The process adds value to the inputs of the process, which are used or transformed to produce the outputs of the process. Sub-processes of activities and tasks within each process create smaller value chains and the output from one sub-process becomes the input for the next part of the chain. Together, all of the processes in an organization form a total delivery system for products and services. Some processes called the core business processes, are the most vital for mission-critical performance and organizational survival and are concerned with satisfying external customers. They directly add value in a way perceived by the customer. They respond to a customer request and generate customer satisfaction. The other main classifications of processes are support processes and management processes. Support process concentrate on satisfying internal customers. They might add value to the customer indirectly by supporting a core process or, they might add value to the enterprise directly by providing a suitable working environment. Management processes are concerned with managing core processes and support processes, or with planning and making decisions at the business level [Ould95].

BPR and Information Technology (IT)

IT plays a crucial role in BPR, but one that is easily miscast. Modern, state-of-the-art IT is part of any reengineering effort; it is an essential enabler. But merely throwing computers at an existing business problem does not cause it to be reengineered. Automating a process is not reengineering, and may be detrimental to the enterprise as it entrenches an existing process that may be sub-optimal. Rather, the effective use of IT in the analysis and decision making processes of a reengineering project can help to speed up the BPR process and assists in critical decision making. Some examples of effective use of IT for the purpose of BPR include modeling, simulation, decision support, knowledge discovery, and groupware & workflow technology. Usually, after introducing changes to a process, new IT systems are needed to aid workers in performing their tasks within this new process. Though important in enacting any changes brought about by the EM process, this secondary use of IT systems is not the main objective of our research into the uses of IT in EM and BPR.

Enterprise Modeling

Enterprise is a term coming into use for what, in the past, might have been referred to as simply a business or an organization. Enterprise is a broader term that can be applied to the conduct of almost any organized purposeful activity or, more specifically, to almost any unit of organized economic activity [Eirich92]. In the broadest sense, an enterprise can be: a consortium, a corporation, an institution, a department, a manufacturing process, a product or service, a business line, an item of complex technology, a body of knowledge, a scout troop, a basketball team, or an information system. However for the purpose of this paper, the term enterprise is considered to imply the functioning of the whole or part of a business, government, military, or educational organization.

An enterprise model is a multi-level logical representation of the enterprise that can be viewed visually on the computer screen or printed onto charts. It offers a holistic representation of the whole enterprise [Khoong95]. EM has the ability for its users to understand the processes and then to simulate changes to observe the outcomes.

An enterprise model can be distributed electronically throughout an organization, and may serve as a standard point of reference for communication within the enterprise. The key to a good model is flexibility. Among other features the enterprise model should have the following [NCR96]:

- It can be built at any level of the enterprise, e.g. a strategic level, a business level, or an activity and workflow level.
- Any aspect of the enterprise can be modeled, e.g. organization, work, processes, products, and goals.
- Any number of different views, e.g. process, people, information, geography, relationships, and schedules, can be taken of any aspect of the enterprise.
- Live valumetric models incorporate or link to simulation tools, allowing multiple dimensions of the dynamic behavior of an enterprise to be viewed.

An enterprise model shows an enterprise's structures, processes, components and the relationships between them that is all-important for a holistic view. A well-modeled enterprise model will enable management to see how the enterprise actually operates, so they need not work from assumptions and traditional views. Using simulation techniques, the model can also reveal dynamic behavior across the enterprise, showing what a change in one place means somewhere else in the enterprise.

Research Background

In this section we briefly describe some published research in similar areas by other research institutions and describe some existing modeling standards and methodologies.

Enterprise Modeling Research - what other researchers are doing in EM

Computer-Integrated Manufacturing - Open Systems Architecture (CIM-OSA)

CIM-OSA provides an architecture to describe the real world of the manufacturing enterprise by providing a unique set of advanced features to model functionality and behavior of Computer Integrated Manufacturing (CIM) systems at three levels: requirements definition; design specification; and implementation description. These descriptions are used to control the enterprise's operation and to plan, design and optimize updates of the real operation environment [Tham96]. The objective of CIM is the appropriate integration of enterprise operations by means of efficient information exchange within the enterprise. This is accomplished with the help of IT. The Open-System Architecture (OSA) defines an integrated methodology to support all phases of a CIM system life cycle from requirement specifications, through system design, implementation, operation and maintenance, and even system migration towards a CIM-OSA solution [Jorysz90].

Purdue Enterprise Reference Architecture (PERA)

Started in December 1990, PERA was particularly developed as an endeavor in EM for a CIM factory by the Purdue Laboratory for Applied Industrial Control at Purdue University. As early as mid-1986, the CIM Reference Model Committee of Purdue for Industrial Computer Systems had recognized the need to establish a basis for the treatment of human-implemented functions in a CIM enterprise. This need formed the focal point in initiating the PERA endeavor [Tham96a].

Toronto Virtual Enterprise (TOVE)

In order to support enterprise integration, it is necessary that shareable representation of knowledge be available that minimizes ambiguity and maximizes understanding and precision in communication. Also, the creation of such a representation should eliminate much of the programming required to answer "simple" common sense questions about the enterprise. The goal of the TOVE project is to create a generic, reusable data model and represents a significant ontological engineering of industrial concepts [TOVE96].

The Enterprise Project

The Enterprise Project is a collaborative project led by the Artificial Intelligence Applications Institute of the University of Edinburgh and includes IBM UK, Lloyd's Register, Logica and Unilever. The main aim is to provide a method and computer toolset that will help capture aspects of a business and analyze these to identify and compare options for meeting the business requirements. This in turn requires the creation of a framework for integrating methods and tools which are appropriate to EM and management of change [Fraser94].

Tools for Inventing Organizations
This is a project carried out at the Center for Coordination Science, MIT. Its intention is to provide a firmer theoretical and empirical foundation for such tasks as EM, enterprise integration, and process reengineering. The project includes collecting examples of how different organizations perform similar processes, and representing these in examples in an on-line process handbook that includes the relative advantages of alternatives. This handbook is intended to help redesign existing organizational processes, invent new organizational processes that take advantages of information technology, and perhaps automatically generate software to support organizational processes [Malone93].

Modeling standards

There are several modeling formats and languages, some quite well established in the modeling community. Some are specific in a form of model, e.g. IDEF0 for process modeling, and Data Flow Diagram for data modeling. Below are some of the standards we have been exploring.

Active Knowledge Models (AKM)
AKM is a reflection of common knowledge and understanding of processes and supporting aspects of organization, product, workflow, and system structures. The model built by one person or team is used by others to create, describe, represent, exchange, interpret, use and manage information, and to assimilate information as knowledge, knowledge as competence and competence as expertise [Lillehagen94]. AKM is used in the modeling tool Metis developed by NCR Norge AS.

Integration Definition (IDEF)
IDEF is a standard, public-domain modeling language that has been successfully used for over twenty years. IDEF0 diagrams use simple rules to govern graphical layouts of a system or process, giving the technique an intuitive appeal and making it easy to learn and use. IDEF0 uses functional decomposition to provide both a big picture and a detailed view of the processes being analyzed. The method's notation encourages simple models that generalizes as much as possible at the higher levels while providing as many levels of low-level details as necessary. For these reasons, IDEF serves not only as a useful modeling tool but also as a tool for communication. IDEF0 is suited for business process improvement projects because it provides a structured description of systems complicated by the interactions of people, computers, and machinery. IDEF includes: IDEF0 for process modeling, IDEF1X for data modeling and IDEF2 for

dynamic and behavioral modeling. The IDEF notations have been designated government standards (USA), Federal Information Processing Standard (FIPS) 183 and 184 [DFIPS93, FIPS93].

ARIS

Professor Scheer developed the Architecture of Integrated Information Systems (ARIS) model. The architecture strives to holistically describe an information system for supporting business processes [Scheer94]. The model tries to simplify the complexity of a system by dividing it into four individual views, namely the Organization, Data, Control, and Function views. Within each view there is defined 3 levels based on their proximity to information technology. The 3 levels are Requirements Definition, Design Specification and Implementation Description. ARIS has many similarities with CIM-OSA. The ARIS methodology is implemented in the ARIS toolset shipped by IDS Prof. Scheer, Inc.

EM Research

By modeling organizations and systems within selected industries, the research intends to identify common EM components that can be integrated into industry-specific reference models so that the process of EM could be formalized and simplified.

The research is aimed at the portion of the BPR process where the system identified for reengineering is being studied. It aims to provide a systematic process for extracting the essentials of the system and putting it in a model. The enterprise model is used first as a static model to understand the current state of the system. As sufficient comprehension is gained, operation parameters and data are introduced into the model to support dynamic analysis through simulation. When the model is sufficiently validated, the user can run analysis of the system using what-if scenarios, perform sensitivity analysis by adjusting some parameters and also perform simulations on variations of the models to gather insights into proposed changes. In this way, the reengineering team can understand the impact of the proposed changes on the organization.

Finally, the model for the system selected would help in implementation, and continue to be a tool for the end users during operation. The idea is that the enterprise model is not to be discarded after the BPR study. It will evolve into an electronic representation of the enterprise and be used by the enterprise itself. The advantages of this approach include:

1. Helps to assess the result of the reengineering exercise and fine-tune the process,
2. Helps to capture future operational data which support future analysis and decision-making,
3. Can plant alarms in the model (possibly through the use of intelligent agents)

to warn users and decision makers of gross deviations from norm, and
4. Guides users on proper procedures of everyday work. This integrates with and supports process quality approaches such as TQM and ISO9000.

From the functional point of view, we are aiming at integrating the 3 enterprise models suggested by [Fraser94]. These are:

- Enterprise Models for Insight: Organizations are influenced by two separate sets of influences that motivate them to try and bring about change. Firstly, there are internal influences and goals that the organization wishes to achieve which necessitates changes. Examples are improving customer satisfaction, increasing profits, decreasing cycle time and costs, making better decisions under uncertainty, etc. Secondly, there are external influences that may force an enterprise to change something. Examples are competitive activity, political legislation, economic trends, technological advances, etc. Several of these factors may act simultaneously and vary in influence with time. Once an enterprise decides to improve its business performance it has to consider what areas are under its control that can be changed to achieve this goal. Areas that can be changed are an enterprise's processes, organization structure, communications and resources. In order to change these areas the enterprise has to understand how it is currently functioning, and to understand how they can be changed to meet new business objectives and environment. Enterprise models can help with this understanding and in intelligently selecting amongst alternative change strategies.

- Enterprise Models for Communication: Access to a common model helps ensure the needs, functions, responsibilities, activities and authorities of people can be communicated to those who need to know them. Such models can indicate the constraints and assumptions behind strategic decisions to all those concerned.

- Enterprise Models for Enactment: Enactment refers to any system, whether automated or followed by humans, which carries out an enterprise's processes. It makes sense to reuse the models created for insight or communication when developing the enactment model. Reuse also helps ensure consistency between the model of what is supposed to happen and what really does happen in the enactment system. If this consistency can be achieved, then changes to the live process can be initiated through changes to the enterprise model. This also leads to the question of being able to automatically generate the enactment model from the enterprise model.

In addition we propose the need for integration of a fourth view:

- Enterprise Model for Decision Support. By Decision Support, we refer to components in the model that link to decision support tools in areas such as simulation, optimization, expert systems, etc. Such tools can provide simulation, optimization, analysis, and control and monitoring capabilities to the enterprise model. For example, users could analyze the benefits of several change options through extensive simulations and reports generated by a decision support tool. Other tools could integrate with the enactment model to optimize, monitor and control the live process. Situations that require immediate or long-term attention may be identified and notified to the users, along with a generated analysis of the problem and possible recommendations, from which the users can base their decisions on. Long-term problems identified through such a mechanism may be candidates for changes that the enterprise should consider. This would lead the enterprise full circle with the enterprise model aiding in deciding areas for future reengineering.

Motivation

The motivation for this research is centered around the fact that many big IT systems in the region, especially in the government services are approaching obsolescence. It is now time to look again at the deployment strategy with respect to the current situation of new business process and social needs, new definition of services, and the enabling potential offered by new IT innovations. Today's operating environment requires a holistic perspective in organizational innovation that integrates together issues pertaining to business processes, technology change, and human resources establishment. In view of the above requirement, the evolution of an EM framework would assist organizations to reengineer swiftly and successfully to face the challenges of the 21st century.

Research Objectives

The objectives of this research are:

1. To develop or fine-tune an existing methodology and toolset for EM that has the following features:
    - reference mechanisms for users to retrieve information about the state of the enterprise from various perspectives,
    - advisory components in software, that can guide users in playing their roles in the enterprise, guided by the EM,
    - enterprise analysis and simulation mechanisms, that organization management can use to understand, measure, improve, and reengineer the organization, and
    - data collection and aggregation from live operations to enable constant monitoring of processes.
2. To deploy the tool in a number of operational environments.
3. To aggregate the components from the tool, i.e. reference mechanisms, advisory components, analysis and simulation mechanism, and data collection

and aggregation mechanism, together with frameworks for different models, e.g., organization, process, data, and system models into a EM framework library. This library will serve as a reference source and workbench for future applications in EM and BPR.

Process, Data and Enterprise Modeling

Investigations of existing standards and methodologies for modeling process and data, and how these could be integrated into an enterprise model will be continually performed to understand the strengths and weaknesses of current methodologies in the light of a holistic enterprise model. The research will also attempt to improve on these methodologies and merge them to form a framework for EM.

Selection and Customization of BPR/EM Tools

There are multiple tools existing in the market for EM and BPR. However most of them concentrate on one aspect of modeling: i.e., either process modeling, data modeling, or simulation. Although some tools attempt to integrate these different aspects, they typically do not have smooth integration from one model type to another. Some tools further integrate with ABC (Activity Based Costing) and process enactment tools.

There are several possible approaches to integrating tools, such as:

1. Using software interfaces, e.g., OLE, DDE, to pass models and data between different tools.
2. Discuss with software vendors to build bridges to standard tools. Examples of existing software bridges include:
    - Interfacing Technologies' FirstSTEP imports data from Computron Software's Workflow (one way only) through the use of the Workflow Process Definition Language protocol WPDL, to simulate workflow designs.
    - MetaSoft's Design/IDEF has a software bridge to its WorkFlow Analyzer, which has a bridge to ProModel's ServiceModel allowing the simulation of workflow models. WorkFlow Analyzer also has bridges to workflow engines (two special versions of this tool creates process models specifically for the workflow engines: FileNet's Visual WorkFlow; and DST's Automated Work Distributor, allowing WorkFlow Analyzer to be used as a full workflow design tool for these engines). It also has a link to an ABC tool (ABC Technologies' Easy ABC Plus).
3. Building our own interfaces between tools through the use of object code or developer's details supplied by the developer.
4. Adopting a tool that integrates these different features together in a seamless

environment that is supported by a flexible methodology. Examples of such tools include the METIS and ARIS tools.

The following features are viewed as the tool requirements:

- Supports a set of important modeling methodologies,
- Networked to support group modeling,
- Dynamic links to other applications,
- Dynamic model supporting simulation and sensitivity analysis,
- Links to workflow process enacting tools,
- Importable and exportable models,
- Process documentation support,
- Provides a set of existing reference models (industry specific models) and supports the creation of new reference models,
- Provides bridges to convert process models and information into specifications for IT systems that support the execution of these processes.

From our findings obtained through actual BPR projects, it was determined that the most feasible approach was to select one (or more) highly integrated tool sets and apply them in different industry settings. The current focus is on applying the ARIS toolset to specific problems from which will lead to the development of ARIS-based industry-specific reference models. ARIS was selected due to its large user base and its high level of integration of different modeling views. ARIS supports 4 modeling views (Organizational, Data, Control and Functional). Within each view are 3 layers that form a link between the models and computer systems that automate and support these models. This greatly simplifies future system design and development. ARIS contains process and data modeling, ABC, workflow, simulation and specific reference models for software design, ISO certification along with many existing industry-specific reference models. Its support of many different modeling methodologies provides flexibility towards the aim of examining and fine-tuning a methodology and modeling views to provide an integrated view of the enterprise. The links to IT systems, such as SAP, BAAN, Oracle, etc., are significant as large enterprise's undertaking an EM effort usually require BPR analysis followed by the development of IT systems. This integrated link to IT systems is lacking in many other tools.

We are continuing to explore the use of Design/IDEF, which through its links to external workflow, simulation and ABC tools provides an alternative approach to obtaining an integrative EM toolset.

Both of these approaches satisfy most of the previously listed requirements. Developing an ideal integrated EM tool would be prohibitively expensive and time consuming as it is a very complex undertaking. The main focus of this project is to improve the state-of-the-art of integrated EM tools and methodologies in actual industry specific settings. As such, it is more suitable to select one or more tools that may become industry standards and examine ways of better using these tools. As alternatives to ARIS (and Design/IDEF) become available they will be evaluated to determine their appropriateness for future study and use.

Evolution of EM Framework

The main goal of the research program is to work through experience, in building enterprise models and abstracting generic and reusable components, towards the evolution of a framework that can be used by enterprises within specific industries. Several industries have been targeted for modeling and the aggregated development result will assist in the identification of generic components for the framework. We are focusing most of our efforts within the transportation and health care sector as these are of significance importance within the Singapore context.

EM Framework and Industry Reference Models

The EM framework consists of EM methodologies and toolsets chosen for their applicability in real business settings. We see that the methodology will evolve into separate reference models for different industries. For each industry, modeling an enterprise will then consist of taking its reference model and customizing it for the enterprise's specific needs. What evolve over time will be specific reference models for each industry. See Figure 1. Although the usage of EM Framework is top-down, the evolution of it is bottom-up, i.e., we derive industry reference models from a set of specific modeling applications.

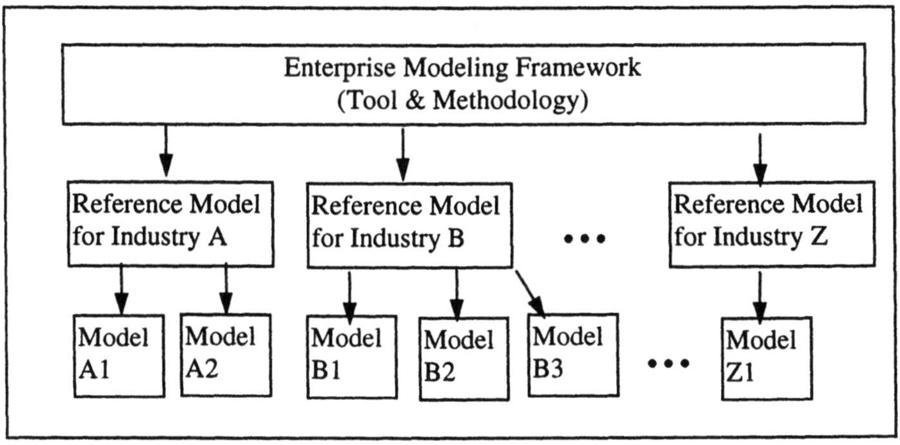

Figure 1: Relationship between EM Framework and Industry-Specific Reference Models

Research into the Modeling of Strategy

In trying to model the enterprise effectively, all functional aspects of the organization need to be modeled and integrated. For processes and data, much work has been done, and research lies more in integrating process and data models. However there has been little work done on less data-centric aspects of business, e.g., strategy modeling and how strategies can be modeled and understood by users of the models. It is suspected that modeling strategies would involve a lot of knowledge engineering, with the models being hybrids of rules, data patterns and structures, case bases, and perhaps some other forms of strategy representations.

Modeling Approach

Within the activity of application modeling, Figure 2 shows the flow of an application model from conceptualization to an operation model. This architecture is independent of any tools or modeling standard. After the requirement study, a static model is first built to validate the system. Then the model enters 2 parallel development activities. The first is to add features to it, such as links to other applications, networking it for multiple users, and then introducing workflow components to support the operation model. The second track turns the static model into a dynamic model by adding parametric information and relevant historical data. The dynamic model is then used for system analysis and modification of the system. When the model is sufficiently verified and validated, it is put online. The result of the 2 tracks is an operation model that end users can use in daily routine. From this operation model IT technologies like intelligent agents, knowledge discovery and

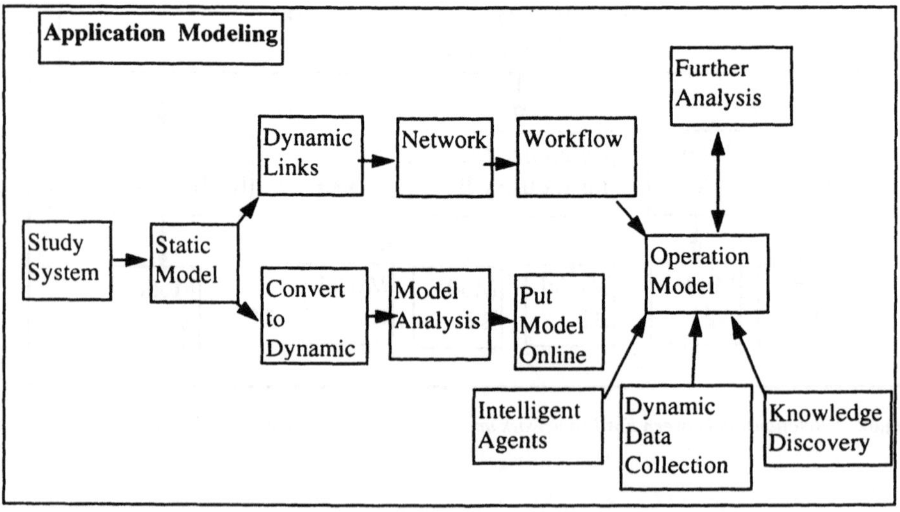

Figure 2: Modeling Approach

data collection can add value to the users and decision-makers. This operation model also provides data for further analysis that leads back to continuous adjustment and fine-tuning of the model.

Figure 3 shows the road map to achieving EM Framework. The activities shown in the boxes denote the duration that we forecast for each of them.

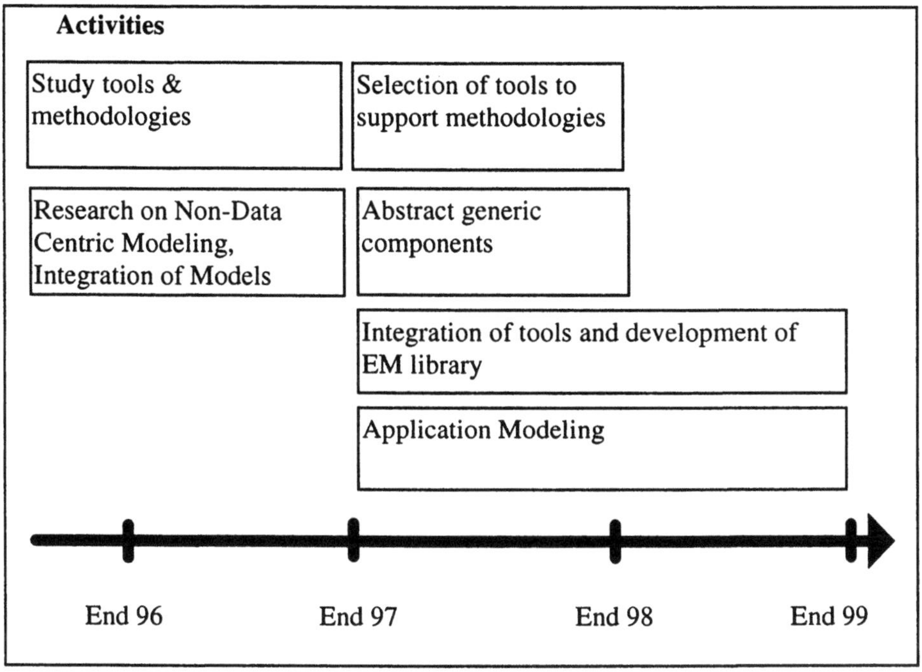

Figure 3. The Road Map to the EM Framework

Research Results to Date

This section elaborates on our on-going research through the application and evaluation of different methodologies and tools within the scope of actual BPR projects. The next phases will see the creation of ARIS-based models within specific BPR projects leading to the development of industry-specific reference models.

Software Application Development Process

ITI's Application Development process was selected as the initial modeling exercise. An enterprise model was built and served as a learning process in modeling techniques and characteristics of specific toolsets. Attempts at converting static models to dynamic models and incorporating workflow tools were attempted. This early project lead to our belief that integrated toolsets commercially available and tested provide the best approach to advancing EM and BPR within business usage.

Student Health Services Process

The School Health Service (SHS) is part of the Ministry of Health and provides free health services to all students in primary and secondary schools as well as selected special schools in Singapore. They provide health screening and immunization programs consisting of a mobile service that visits each school once a year, and follow-up services at specialized health clinics. All of this medical information is collected, stored and used for detailed analysis. SHS has experienced problems with its data entry process. Outdated technology and an acute labour shortage, particularly among the data entry clerks further exasperated this. The objective of the EM and BPR project was to investigate the health care process and recommend solutions that could improve overall performance as well as continue to allow for the capture and analysis of all required data without a resultant increase in staffing levels. Manpower reduction through automation is a primary objective.

By observing and tracking the school visits and the data entry centres, and interviewing the staff involved, enterprise models were developed using Design/IDEF and later redone using FirstSTEP. From these models, as well as our observations and discussions with the staff of the SHS, the major bottlenecks within the data entry process were identified. Three different solutions were proposed. The first two involved the use of optical mark recognition and optical character recognition (OMR/OCR) software to scan and process specially designed forms on which the medical information would be entered. One of the managerial options involved the total outsourcing of the data entry tasks (scanning and processing of the forms), while the other option had these tasks being performed in-house in case of conflicts arising from the confidentiality of this medical information. A third solution was proposed involving the development of a client-server data entry system using a relational database management system. This option is most similar to the current system, and served as an example to explain why this approach was no longer feasible due to its higher development and maintenance costs as well as greater staffing requirements.

IT Master Plan for a Logistics company.

This project's objectives were to develop an IT Master Plan that would guide this company as it redeveloped all of its existing IT Infrastructure (software, hardware and network). The plan outlined all of the necessary IT systems that needed to be developed and provided a schedule that covered the next several years. This company is a leader in its area but saw the need to improve its operations before highly leveraged competitors entered their business. A process-oriented approach was utilized to understand and document their existing processes. As the company is ISO certified it was straightforward to perform these tasks. From the models and discussions with management and users, it was determined that a reengineering of the company to operate in a more integrated fashion was necessary to utilize its resources optimally. The process models were the key to determining the system requirements of the proposed IT Infrastructure and significantly improved the alignment between operational processes and planned IT systems. Significantly, a Lotus Notes-based Intranet was proposed to integrate the different processes, information and systems together. Intranets are fast becoming a key enactment tool supporting BPR initiatives. This project showed the major benefits IT planning, requirements gathering and design can gain from a process-oriented focus. In this project simple process diagrams where utilized. A promising future area of study would be the comprehensive use of EM technology throughout all phases of IT systems planning, design and development to compare it with existing IT methodologies. We envision significant benefits to organizations that use EM as a basis for performing and integrating IT and QA functions.

Process Analysis and IT Planning at a Container Port

Further to our research into the use of EM technology with respect to BPR and IT systems planning and design, we are undertaking a study at a container port to model their core processes and the use and interaction of their existing legacy systems within these process. The goal is to better understand the operations and how the IT systems support them. From an analysis, changes may be made to operational procedures to improve overall performance and to IT systems to better support and integrate operations. The use of an ABC tool integrated with the models will give more meaningful information to operations planning staff in order to determine the costs and profits associated with each set of steps within a process. This will allow staff to make better decisions as to select the most cost-effective changes to existing processes and the most appropriate way of deploying staff and other resources within a process.

Conclusion

An integrative research program for an enterprise modeling framework was presented. We described the existing issues in BPR and EM, and discussed some other research programs in this area. We also discussed some existing modeling standards and methodologies. We outlined the motivations and the objectives of the research. We also shared the result of some of our projects in this research. The initial result is very encouraging but there is still much more research to be conducted before we can realize the vision of creating holistic enterprise models. Finally we presented a road map and outlined an agenda for our continuing research.

Acknowledgment

We would like to gratefully acknowledge the National Science and Technology Board of Singapore for partially funding this project. We would also like to thank Dr. Jacob Lee, Dr. Seok-Hui Ng and Ms. Yuen-Ping Ho of the Faculty of Business Administration, National University of Singapore, and Mr. Hying-Sang Wong of CSPI-NCB, for their valuable contributions in this research.

References

[Cadwell94] Cadwell, B., "Missteps, Miscues", Information Week, June 20, 1994, pp. 50-60

[DFIPS93] "DFIPS 183", Draft Federal Information Processing Standards Publication 183, Integration Definition for Function Modeling (IDEF0), Dec 1993

[Eirich92] Eirich, P. Editor, "Enterprise Modeling: Issues, Problems & Approaches", SIG report at Int. Conf. On Enterprise Integration Modeling Technology, Hilton Head, SC, June 6-10, 1992

[FIPS93] "FIPS 184", Federal Information Processing Standards Publication 184, Integration Definition for Information Modeling (IDEF1X), Dec 1993

[Frank95] Frank, M., "Using object role model to design relational databases". DBMS Interview, Sept 1995.

[Fraser94] Fraser, J., "Managing Change through Enterprise Models", Proc. Applications and Innovations in Expert Systems II, SGES Publications, 1994. Also found at URL: http://www.aiai.ed.ac.uk/~entprise/papers/es_94/paper_contents.html

[Hammer93] Hammer, M., Champy, J., Reengineering the Corporation, Nicholas Brealey Publishing, 1993

[Jorysz90] Jorysz, H.R., Vernadat, F.B., "CIM-OSA, Part I: total enterprise modeling and function view", Int. Jour. Of Computer Integrated Manufacturing, Vol. 3, Nos. 3 and 4, 1990, pp. 144-156

[Khoong95] Khoong, C.M. "Enterprise Support Systems for Business and Daily Life", Proc. Singapore Computer Society Conf. 1995, Singapore, Nov. 22-23, 1995, pp. 122-125

[Khoong96] Khoong, C.M. "'Second Wave' Reengineering: Structure and Methodology", Asia-Pacific DSI Conf. June 21-22, 1996, Hong Kong

[Khoong96a] Khoong, C.M. "Culture-Sensitive Strategy-Level Reengineering", INFORS, vol. 34, No. 1, pp. 43-56, 1996

[Lillehagen95] Lillehagen, F. Active Knowledge Models for Enterprises, Metis Norway

[Malone93] Malone, T.W., Crowston,W.K., Lee, J., Pentland,J., "Tools for inventing organizations: Towards a handbook of organizational processes", Proc. of 2nd IEEE Workshop on Enabling Technologies Infrastructure for Collaborative Enterprises, Morganstown, W.V. April 20-22, 1993

[NCR96] NCR Enterprise Modeling, Homepage of NCR Design and Development Group, at URL http://www.metis.no/home/em

[Ould95] Ould, M. A., Business Processes: Modeling and Analysis for Re-Engineering and Improvement, John Wiley & Sons, 1995

[Scheer94] Scheer, A. W., Business Process Engineering : Reference Models for Industrial Enterprises, Springer-Verlag, 1994

[Tham96] Tham, K.D., CIM-OSA: Enterprise Modeling, Review paper found on URL http://www.ie.utoronto.ca/EIL/entmethod/cimosa/cim.htm, 1996

[Tham96a] Tham, K.D., PERA: Enterprise Modeling, Review paper found on URL http://www.ie.utoronto.ca/EIL/entmethod/pera/pera.htm, 1996a

[TOVE96] TOVE Manual, Enterprise Integration Laboratory, University of Toronto, at URL http://www.ei.utoronto.ca/EIL/tove.htm, 1996

5 LESSONS FROM PAPERWORK: DESIGNING A COOPERATIVE SHARED OBJECT SERVICE

John Hughes, Val King,
John A. Mariani and Tom Rodden

ABSTRACT
The sharing of information plays a central role in most work settings and many applications require facilities which promote cooperative access to shared information. It is important that these facilities are informed from an understanding of the nature of document use in work settings. This paper turns to the use of documents as a means of understanding the use of shared information. The pertinent features of documents are outlined before a critical re-examination of a previous field study is presented. Finally some of the facilities provided by a shared object service are outlined. This service has been motivated by many of the observations presented in the field study.
KEYWORDS
Cooperative Systems, Information Sharing, Observational Studies of Work, Systems Development.

Introduction

Shared information plays a central role in most organizations; it is often the primary means used to develop a shared understanding across a number of cooperating workers. The nature of this sharing, the type of information shared and the forms of cooperation it facilitates vary greatly and the different classes of systems to support this sharing reflect this variety. A wide range of projects and groupware applications have designed and implemented sharing facilities that they believe best meets their particular needs. This pragmatic approach, while producing effective prototypes, has resulted in considerable repetition of effort and facilities. In addition, by adopting this strategy these systems have failed to capitalise on any of the features provided by information management systems and the potential benefits of integration.

Most cooperative applications and groupware systems are in some agreement on the nature of the information they use and have settled on some form of object model[1,2]. As the provision of distributed object systems continues to gain speed in both the commercial and research fields it is important that these systems meet the requirements of user situated with real organisation. The intent of the work reported in this paper is to build upon existing distributed object systems to provide a set of information sharing facilities. We wish to reflect closely on the implications to be drawn for information sharing systems from the nature of documents in organizations. In particular, we wish to consider the intimate relationship between documents and the work they support and how this relationship impacts future information sharing infrastructures.

This paper briefly examines the role of documents in supporting work processes before outlining a shared object service (SOS). The SOS provides an appropriate set of storage mechanisms to allow information to be shared in a manner which encourages rather than prohibits cooperation. In developing the shared object service we particularly focus on outlining infrastructure services based from an understanding of the social nature of information sharing. Our starting point for our endeavour is a critical re-examination of a number of previous ethnographic studies of the use of documents within work.

Understanding the nature of documents

It would be hard to overestimate the importance of documents in human affairs. Much work is explicitly concerned with the production of documents of various kinds: the accountant is concerned to produce a document which records the financial status of an individual or a company; the secretary produces letters, the social worker records, the solicitor contracts. There are also activities in which documents play a key role in such things as denoting status and/or skill, such as a driving license, a certificate of proficiency, a contract, and so on. In addition, and especially with respect to particular types of document, there has grown up an extensive set of procedures for recording, managing and indexing documents, such as the ISBN number for published materials, filing systems, catalogues, version management systems, and so on. The production, maintenance and organisation of documents is an endemic feature of human affairs.

The development of electronic storage and use facilities has typically sought to abstract the informational structure of documents with a view to realising what are, in effect, electronic documents which mimic certain features of paper documents. For example, a database presents the structure of a document as a collection of paragraphs. Similarly, standards such as ODA [5] provides formats for the interchange of documents in an Open environment. This emphasis on structure exhibits a static view of documents even though additional facilities have been developed to exploit the structure dynamically within an electronic medium, most notably with hypertext research [6].

This focus on an abstracted structure has led database system developers to consider the issues surrounding the representation and sharing of information in isolation from its use within a workplace. Effort has been directed toward the construction of abstract representations of information which have no direct relation to actual use of information within work settings. This has been seen by database experts as the responsibility of application developers who exploit the services provided by database systems. However, this state of affairs provides little assurance that the facilities provided are appropriate and effective.

As electronic forms of information play an increasingly prominent role in the workplace so does cooperative information sharing and it will play a significant role in interactive systems. This means that designers need to be informed of the situated character [7] of information sharing and sensitive to the socially organised nature of collaborative work.

General Properties of Documents

What follows is an outlining of some generic properties of documents drawn from a series of field studies of different work contexts in which documents figure as a salient feature of work activities. These include:

- police work [8]
- social work [9]
- invoice processing [10]

First, we outline some of the general properties of documents-as-records which emerge out of the analysis of ethnographic studies of work settings. Secondly, we present a relatively detailed analysis of working with documents taken from an ethnography of a company. Our longer term objective is a find a balance between formulating generic requirements to inform the design outline of a SOS, and the need for further development which will involve more detailed domain specific investigations.

The emphasis is on documents-as-records within socially organised work activities. What we have tried to do is highlight in a general way some of the salient properties of records as socially organised phenomena. In specific organisational settings, such properties will be instantiated in activities in a variety of ways. It also needs to be noted that some of these properties, not surprisingly, make use of the material characteristics of paper within their socially constituted usages.

Documents are part of a socially organised pattern of work

In social life documents do not typically appear 'as documents' but as 'essays', 'contracts', 'draft articles', 'a profit and loss ledger', 'a technical drawing', a 'rail ticket', etc. These descriptions are related to documents' socially organised situations-of-use and evoke and depend upon the contextual practical knowledge which gives them their sense within a set of socially organised activities. Such descriptors are not to be understood as 'merely' alternative ways of describing a more generic and abstract entity (a 'document') but instantiate how and in what ways they are socially constructed as 'objects' within practical activities as these are commonly understood. They are descriptions tied to the nature of the activities within which documents appear.

Documents as representations of organisational objects and actions

Documents-as-records represent the activities of an organisation and can be interrogated for what they say, what they indicate, about an organisation's activities in dealing with its 'objects'. They do not, however, straightforwardly represent the 'actual activities' of an organisation's personnel except in organisationally relevant ways. Records are often couched in conventional formats, using organisational styles, often summaries of what transpired, record decisions taken, and so on. Within organisations some records have an 'official' status in that they are accountably documents of the organisation, and acknowledged as such. These are in contrast to the 'unofficial' documents, such as working notes, 'post it', drafts, etc., often produced by personnel during their work activities. Both kinds are important to understanding the social organisation of work.

Documents as Shared Objects

As organisational objects, records are produced by and for the use of organisational personnel. Records can be said to 'belong' to an organisation both in the sense that they are 'owned' by the organisation and in that they are 'for' organisational personnel. They are produced for specifiable and specified others within the organisation acting in their organisational capacity. This could be said to be the rationale for records. Their point is to be shared by at least some others within the organisation for the purpose of their organisationally relevant activities.

The Procedural Implicativeness of Documents

What records indicate is often the basis for further actions, further activities. A case report in social work, for example, may well form the basis for initiating further organisational action. An 'invoice' not only records 'goods delivered' but specifies 'payment' as the relevant next action. The procedural implicativess of records exhibits their intimate connection with organisational actions, recording and specifying what has been and what needs to be done. This serves to underpin the interdependence of activities within a division of labour. Documents, that is, are to be understood as integral features of the orderliness of activities.

The Accessibility of Documents

Documents can be both normatively and pragmatically regulated in their availability and accessibility. By the former we mean that documents can be surrounded by rights and obligations as to access and use. These rights and obligations can be highly variable in their formality and in their nature. Documents, such as legal and medical records, are typically restricted to authorised users. Others, such as personal letters and diaries, are regulated by informal norms. By pragmatically available we mean that the accessibility is largely a matter of relevance and opportunity. Thus, and typically, public notices are written and displayed 'for anyone who may be interested' or 'for anyone for whom the information is relevant'. The distinction between normative and pragmatic regulation is a rough one only and, in practise, such features are likely to be interwoven. The main point is that documents constitute socially constructed artefacts the sharing of which is socially organised and regulated in terms of access and availability.

The format of documents

Intimately bound up with their public availability and their information carrying property, is that documents are standardised productions; that is, they are formatted artefacts. The format can be understood as a set of procedures for producing and using the document [11] and can be more or less formal, more or less standardised, more or less precise in their specifications. A spreadsheet, for example, is a tight systematic organisation of instructions for ordering and manipulating information whereas a personal letter can be less systematic in its format, though this does not mean that there is no structure to its organisation. Knowledge of formats can, of course, be highly specialised or widely available as in the case of books, letters and newspapers.

The documents as traces

A property deriving from their massively public and standardised qualities is that documents are traces. They can be used to reconstruct activities, agreements, judgements, states of affairs, intentions, and more, since their character is intimately part and parcel of our common-sense knowledge of persons, activities and social structures. Documents have, we might say, properties of representation and documentation. That is, they allow for the construction of records, annals, memorabilia, reminders, and more, which can all be used as the basis for inferences about activities, persons, and events.

The above is an outline of some general properties of records derived from studies of their social organisation of use within a variety of contexts. As such they inform the outline design of the SOS. What follows is a more detailed report of an ethnographic study of record use within a company [10]. While the study itself pursued a number of themes, we extract two sets of procedures, namely, documentary coordination and condensation done by the Senior Accounts Processor as part of her routine work, and processing invoices. These are activities which produce accounts to support organisational monitoring and decision-making.

Paperwork in use: reflecting on a case study

What follows is a report of part of an previous ethnographic study[10] of the top level management of a medium-sized, multi-site 'fast food' company that operates over 50 sites in leisure centres, shopping malls, airports, and so on, and employs, at the time of the study, over 500 persons. Every stock-taking fortnight, each of the unit managers is required to fill in two sheets: a stockcheck sheet and a stock-purchase sheet. Both are broken down into columns which the manager fills out. The stockcheck sheet is a computer print out listing all the items bought centrally for the units. Items not included on the list are added by the manager. The manager fills in all purchases, transfers, present stock and usage; figures which are keyed into the file update at Head Office.

The stock purchase sheet is a similar list of items arrayed by day. The manager lists supplies against the days on which they arrive. The Accounts Processor checks these figures against the delivery notes forwarded by the unit managers. Where there are discrepancies she amends the sheets in accordance with the delivery notes. At the same time she keeps a check on the prices of fresh meat and vegetables. Other prices are standardised and checked by the purchasing section when invoices arrive. This whole procedure takes one week. It is carried out while the figures on the stockcheck sheet are being keyed in.

When the files have been updated, a printout for each unit is extracted. This is the processing sheet which the Accounts Processor works on. The columns are checked row by row against the documents already processed. Where differences occur, then amendments and recalculations may be required. Invoices may be called for and, in some cases, managers required to check further.

The above is the structure into which the work of the Accounts Processor fits. The essence of this work is *modal transformation*. Figures are 'picked up' from one set of sheets and transferred to others. She takes someone else's 'output', that is, the managers' fortnightly sheets, and turns them into another's inputs, namely, the

Management Accounts and summary sheets. One set of materials is turned into another set so that others can work on them.

Her transformations provide a connection between the 'over the counter' activities of the various units and 'managerial decision-making'. Sets of figures, reports, documents, statements, and so on, are turned into a coherent, formatted, systematic and visible 'at a glance' depiction of how things are going in the company. What this involves, first and foremost, is the physical coordination of documentation. She works down the columns looking from one sheet to another, backwards and forwards, checking off the numbers as she goes. The delivery notes are prepared in a day by day sequence so that when she goes through the purchase sheet she will have a bundle that is physically manipulable. The stock sheets are also all filed together unit by unit, as are the stock purchase sheets, the processing notes, and so on. When invoices are required from purchasing, these are pinned to the delivery note to which they apply. The coordination of these physical objects on her desk is achievable only by keeping together the things which go together. Each stands for a particular way of characterising the objects which she has to produce. Her transformation of them involves not a synthesis, not a selection, but an amalgamation.

Representation and Transformation

Although the transformation takes time to produce, it is treated as atemporal. The figures and the accounts refer to how things were at least 2 weeks ago, but are treated as representations of how things are. They exist in what Raffel [12], in talking about clinic records, calls the 'permanent present'. They have a fortnightly sense of now, a sense which is seen but unremarked upon, known but irrelevant for the purposes for which they are constructed. To those engaged in measuring the Company's profitability, there seems no other sensible way of dealing with their operational and organisational contingencies other than freezing activities in fortnightly blocks. This is the level of accuracy that is all that can be practicably asked for.

This brings us to the question of the production requirements for modal transformation. What does the Accounts Processor have to work on? What must she produce? There are some important features which are visible here:

- the formatted character of the Management Accounts. Whatever she produces will be fitted into that format, appear alongside and be used in conjunction with other formatted depictions.
- the transformation is the assembly of an order. She does not need to look beyond the documents she gets to produce the depictions she does. If there is a query it is from the paperwork that it is resolved.
- the tasks are organised as a principle of opportuneness [13]. The whole

> monitoring system is possible because of the centralisation of accounting and purchasing. Much of the coordination of activities she is able to achieve is possible because she is 'going through the paperwork' at the same time as assembling the accounts.

The work of the Accounts Processor is a sheet by sheet, column by column, row by row, modal transformation of one set of documents into another. This is managed by the physical coordination of bundles of documents, documents in files, and documents being worked on. As she works through the lists she leaves a trail of markings so that anyone who knows her routine can come to the files and see where she has got to. The records and documents she produces are a permanent account of the sequential organisation of the tasks comprising account processing in this company. The beginning to end trajectory of the whole sequence is achieved stage by stage, one step at a time, by making sure that everything is to hand that is needed, getting the documents if needed, checking the files when necessary, and so on. It is in her orientation to these things that the orderliness of the Accounts Processor's working life consists as part of a division of labour.

Documents within a Division of Labour

If we turn to the organisation of work around the Purchase Ledger Desk in the company, we can see how the division of labour operates within an environment which is saturated with information. The office consists of a number of positions occupied at any one time by a particular person. The distribution of positions is work specific and is the sedimentation of the local production practices for invoice processing and cheque paying. From the point of view of the accomplishment of such tasks, the work appears as an impersonalised stream of tasks in hand, tasks completed and tasks to be done. Within the bounds of competence, it is of no matter who carries out the work. Rosemary, Eileen, or Amanda could just as easily as Renee fill out the journals and make out the cheques. In this sense, the personnel are locally interchangeable and, often, 'cover for each other' when the need arises. Nonetheless, the task differentiation and specification for the work is seen in terms of 'decisions-that-I-can-make' and 'actions-that-I-can-take' and those which others deal with. The division of labour is organised according to a principle of egological determination [14]. That is, from the point of view of the actor in a division of labour, working through the endless stream, getting things done, means 'doing-what-I-do' and passing on tasks to others so that they can do what it is they do.

The organisation provides an institutionally located and, thus, socially available allocation of activities and tasks. The major line seems to be oriented around the centrality of the individual and bounded by the horizons of their task performance; that is, its egological character.

For the accomplishment of any tasks, some aspects will be problematic. Others will be treated as matters beyond inquiry. For Sue on the Costings Desk to be able to check the prices on the invoices does not require her to worry about the postal service, the grounds on which food and non-food invoices are separated, nor what happens to them when she has passed them on. Once she has finished with them and sent them to Purchase Ledger, they are no longer her concern. Such matters can, of course, be brought under scrutiny. From what 'anybody' knows about the company and how similar enterprises operate, it is possible to discover the reasons why things are done in the way that they are. So, when asked to 'pull an invoice' which she has already passed on, from what she knows about the system and how it works, Sue can find her way through the division of labour at the Purchase Ledger desk and locate the item. Similarly, if required to check an invoice with a supplier, she has little difficulty in working her way through the accounting procedures of another company. She achieves these by treating the division of labour as a distribution of locations for the accomplishment of activities. What she has to find out is where, in the processes for the production of financial accounts, the work she wants to query gets done. It is built upon a presumption that some solution to the problem will have been provided, someone will do the work in more or less known ways, just who and where can be discovered if required.

The egological principle underpinning the working division of labour generates and provides a solution to the coordination of tasks [17]. This is because the division of labour specifies which tasks one has to embed within one's activities and which are, so to speak, institutionally taken care of. This involves anticipating how the institutionalised structures will work. Memo's can be put in pigeon holes in the certainty that they will be eventually read and acted upon. Invoices can be left in baskets for others to pick up. If, later, they have gone from the basket, then they have been collected. Such routine operations of the division of labour provide organisationally specific ways in which those within it can call up, gear into it, and make it work for them, 'Gearing in' is a means of ensuring the smooth performance of the flow of activities by ensuring the fit of one's task performance into that of others and by carrying out 'running repairs'.

Activities are not only organised egologically, but are also zoned according to organisationally relevant dimensions of space and time. The work is clustered around the office in terms of types of audit check. Other distinctions as marked by the Divisional structure of the company are not visible here but are of interest only so far as they bear upon the performance of the tasks in this office. It is an environment of paper processing. To those who know the office and its work, the layout recapitulates the division of labour in that the sequencing of activities can be reconstructed from the mapping of who is where by tracking an invoice through the system and the floor of the office. Thus, when locating where a particular item might be, or some action takes place, a glance around the office suffices as a reconstitution of the organisational plan.

The organisation of activities is not a fixed, given, system-specified phenomenon but an outcome of the routine coordinating work which those working within it perform. When looked at from within a production process, a division of labour, and particularly when looked at in terms of how the features of the objects it produces are recognised and deployed in the taken-for-granted way that they must be, a documentary object passing through it is seen and treated as a stratified record of the work producing it [16, 12, 17]. It displays the locally organised construction of the division of labour for all who know how to see it.

The invoice as a stratified record of work

The company receives invoices in a constant flow but pays them only fortnightly when a series of computerised cheques are run off. As far as food processing is concerned, there are two forms of invoice, Food and Non-food which are treated in different ways. The reasons for this are managerial, financial and organisational. Given the nature of the business, the major proportion of invoices are for food and drink items. One person can deal with these efficiently if they specialise. Given also that food purchases are centralised through main suppliers, the supervisory role can be carried by this person, who can also check that the appropriate prices are charged. A cross-check of food purchases is also obtained through the unit's fortnightly returns on usage. Cross-checks do not occur for non-food items and knowledge of the appropriate prices are distributed among the management. Circulation of the invoices is required for checking purposes alone. Such circulation does, however, allow for the supervision of spending at the respective units; the means by which the Directors keep their fingers on 'what is going on'.

Any invoice has a circulation life within the company, that is, the length of time it takes to process and pay it. The shortest this is likely to be is a week; the longest 6 or 8 weeks. During this life time it passes through a number of hands and across a number of desks. The invoice contains a record of its own passage displayed on a date stamp. Invoices circulate in bundles which start life as 'what is in the post' and accumulate into a 'day's worth' after coding by Purchase Ledger. From there on they accrete into larger sized bundles depending on how quickly they are processed into later stages.

Each stage of the process is dependent on completion of prior stages for its own completion. It is scheduled to 'fit around' the fixed points of the computer input, the weekly wage payments and the fortnightly stocksheet runs. This means that invoice processing is a continuous, fitted-in-where-it-can-be matter for Dawn in the computer room. There is a constant backlog of processed invoices to key in. As a succession of tasks to be done in a series, the processing of an invoice has itself to be fitted into the daily and weekly routines of the those that deal with them. No one deals with just invoices.

As it moves around the paperwork system, the invoice acquires a record of the work done upon it. From the moment it arrives and is date stamped, all production work leaves its mark upon it, either in spaces provided by the date stamp or as appended comments, memos, queries, questions taped to it or stuck on it. In this sense, the orderliness of this record on the invoice is a representation of the orderliness of the work tasks performed. The representation appears as a tick against items that have been checked, question marks against those which are unknown, the initials in the various boxes, and so on. To anyone coming in to an invoice at any moment of its path through the system, the recording on the invoice of what has been and what has not been done, builds up to a stratified representation of the sequence of stages it has passed through and the actions taken in regard to it. Since this sequence and these activities are standardised, a glance at the stratified record is enough to be able to tell what has happened, where things are up to, and what the possible problems might be.

As the boxes are filled in, as the correct codes are written in, the amounts checked and the authorisations given, the normal, unproblematic routine working of the system reproduces itself. Work upon the invoice is, therefore, a distinct sphere of operations for those whose tasks it is to ensure that the paperwork is completed properly. Its horizons, its internal organisation, and its structures are given to them as local and contextual knowledge about how things are done in the company and what, from the invoice, one can say about what has been done and what yet needs to be done. Learning to read an invoice as a record of its production work is learning the paperwork division of labour.

Developing a shared object service

The studies mentioned earlier, and illustrated in more detail through the invoice processing case, were used to inform the outline design of a service to support the cooperative sharing of objects. It is worth noting that many of the key activities discussed in the study highlighted centred on the production and use of documents. As expected, these activities fitted pretty well with the expected behaviour of information storage systems whose concern is the storage, management, manipulation and retrieval of information objects.

The explicit aim of the SOS is to provide a set of services which allow objects to be shared by a community of users. In contrast to existing multi-user storage facilities, it focuses on cooperative sharing across a group of users and the provision of mechanisms which support the management of this sharing. It is intended that the shared object service provides a set of facilities which abstracts from the properties of underlying infrastructure to provide a well defined abstract set of services. This offers the advantages of portability and allows developers to consider the services which need to be provided in terms of an abstract computational model which can then be realised on a number of different distributed object platforms. This arrangement is shown in figure 1.

A full description of the facilities provided by a shared object service are outside the scope of this paper. [See [18] for a more extensive presentation of the shared object service]. The focus here is on those aspects of the service most influenced by our examination of previous studies of the use of documents.

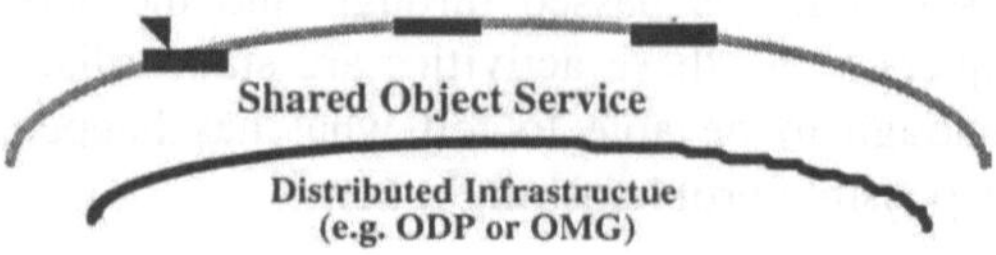

Figure 1 : Role of the shared object service

Access Control

Access has traditionally been handled by a single database administrator. In general each user of the database is considered as a singular client, and each individual client has to have permission granted or revoked to access and/or create data. The general view of access is that it changes infrequently in relation to alterations of information objects. A number of issues surrounding access arise from a social investigation of the nature of work.

The use of roles. Roles are closely tied to work activities. For example, the senior accounts processor cited in the above study, had as one of the tasks of her role to produce the summary sheets for senior managers by transforming material provided by site managers. While it is possible to envisage a storage system which uses this role as a means of determining access to certain objects, it is important to separate this from the determination of action within the role being undertaken by its incumbent.

The point here is not that roles in themselves are inappropriate or serve no purpose within information storage systems. In fact, roles are essential in specifying the relationship between potential users and the information. However, the illusion given is that this relationship determines the behaviour of the role incumbent or that the activities can be specified using a few simple rules. In reality, the working division of labour highlighted in our study, and reinforced by the other studies mentioned, showed users continually re-negotiating their responsibilities. Emerging directly from this consideration of the study is the message that roles are flexible, dynamic and socially organised, and as a consequence the relationship between users and the objects they access needs to be both flexible and dynamic.

The mediation of work. Access rights can be used to mediate and co-ordinate cooperative activities. For example, consider again the use of spreadsheets to generate summary accounts. Summary accounts are calculated by Dawn using a spreadsheet with information provided by site managers. If we consider a system where all of this information is held within a database, access rights mediate the work taking place in a number of ways. These include

The control of interference: By Dawn specifying that only she has access to the information on her spreadsheet she prevents any possibility of distraction from others. A similar management of work was exhibited in our domain of study by the physical location of information. By placing an invoice within an in-tray on her desk Sue controls access to the information and allows herself to work on the invoice with limited possibility of interference.

The sequencing of action: In a similar way to controlling interference access can be used to determine the sequences of action to be carried out on an object. In cases such as the handling of invoices where a sequential ordering of work is observed, users can in turn alter the access to an object to determine an ordering of action. Again this feature was physically managed in our study by moving the invoice from one desk to another within the office. This movement altered the access patterns to the invoice allowing a particular person to work more closely with it.

The publication of work: In actual work settings it is often important to make public to specified others certain features of one's work. For example, consider the way in which site managers in our study make their work public by the submission of monthly reports. This is in effect an alteration of access rights to information to allow a greater community to read it. Similarly, the knowledge of who has particular access rights at a given time facilitates the publication of work. For example, the knowledge that Amanda has a document and can alter it is of direct interest to those who also work with the document.

Cooperative Access and Adapters

Traditional approaches to access have encoded the relationship between roles and information objects within an access matrix. The matrix defines the principal model for the control over a user's access to an object. Problems for cooperative systems using the traditional matrix approach to access which have already been highlighted [19] include -

- It does not provide facilities for the management of roles or groups; individual users tend to be used and dynamic amendment is difficult to do.

- It does not facilitate easy specification of access rights
- It does not offer a mechanism for specification of the access matrix, or for access checking

Building upon our examination of the use of documents, access models within cooperative interactive systems must also allow a number of additional facilities

- They need to be more dynamic with access altering frequently
- They should allow access to be inferred from the state of some activity or a user's role.
- They should provide to allow a group of users to manage changes to access.
- They need to provide a finer granularity of access control than offered by the access matrix.

The current model of a predominantly static access specification has the advantage of simplicity and performance. It also reflects a perspective of protection in that the intent of an access model is to ensure the security of data and protect users from the actions of others. These security needs are in opposition to the trusting and egoless access to information highlighted in the cited study. However, the need for protection and security is a central feature of many existing applications and both forms of access need to coexist. Consequently information sharing and access mechanisms within the shared object service need to be closely associated with shared information objects.

This is achieved by the use of interface adapters which dynamically handle and manage the cooperative aspects of object invocation. The use of object adapters also allows for a separation between the semantic behaviour and structure of the object and the cooperative management of its sharing. The shared object service presents two different means of interaction at different levels of abstraction for the objects within the service. An application or user can interact with an object by:-

- Access to the basic interface provided by the object.
- Access through an interface adapter which abstracts away from the object.

The relationship between these different forms of interaction is one of abstraction (figure 2). An interface represents an object and an interface adapter ID replaces the ID for the interface that it represents. Interface adapters are the principle means used to realise the dynamic access highlighted previously.

The adapter holds a table of presentation conditions for attributes and methods. Each has a different condition entry within the table and the mechanisms to set and retrieve these conditions are provided. In addition, access rights to operations on the object are classified within the adapter into particular access levels. This classification allows users to be granted a particular level of access and to move between levels as necessary in a dynamic manner. The adapter manages the mapping between access levels and the invocation and, with reference to an access manager, verifies access to the underlying object.

Adapters are used throughout the service to manage a wide range of cooperative facilities. Many of these facilities result from an understanding of the use of shared information. A selection of the pertinent use of information and resulting support mechanisms are briefly examined in the following sections.

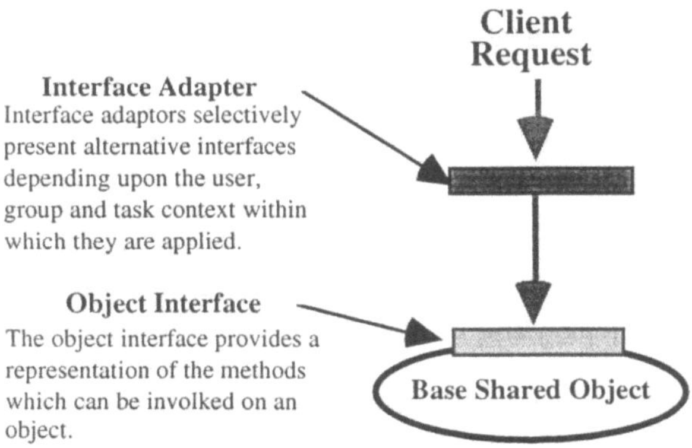

Figure 2: Objects, Interfaces and Adapters

Documents as traces and history

An important feature of our re-examination of previous studies was the observation that a document accumulated traces as it moved through the process which manipulates it. The view of documents as embodying a trace of the actions upon them and the stage they are at within the process highlights the importance of history within cooperative work.

Within the study the application of history was most evident in the use of the invoice as a stratified record of work. The invoice collected on its progress a record of actions associated it. These actions were recorded using stamps, the initialing of the documents, the attachment of notes and memos and the signatures of appropriate people. These marks on the invoice were sufficient to allow a reconstruction of the document history and the actions which have been taken on the document. Similar cues do not exist in electronic document systems and as a result the ability to verify the handling of a document by the reconstruction of its history is missing.

We make a number of assumptions to underpin the representation of history within the shared object service:

- the granularity of a time specification is on a per-attribute basis

- every object requiring history information to be maintained has a history adapter associated with it. A history adapter contains time variables for each attribute. Moreover, multiple values are stored for each attribute. The main object itself always represents the "current" state of the object.
- A Query Specification is capable of including appropriate temporal clauses delimiting the range of a query to a set time period. Using the combination of the main object and the history adapter, it is possible to generate a "temporary" object which represents the state of the object at a given time.

The "Query Engine" of the SOS aims to cope with temporal queries. The generation of an object history requires the identification and recording of significant actions. This can be done within the shared object service by transforming a sequence of actions on the object into history events which are added to the recorded history for the object. Consider an object which represents a file shared between Tom and John. In terms of the object the only interaction either user has is by invocation of methods such as read and write. However, by specifying a sequence of these actions we consider meaningful we can log higher order history events. For example, we could decide that a sequence of the form write(tom), close(tom), open(john), write(john) was a significant transfer of editing to John and record it as Tom passed object to john.

Awareness of action

Tied closely to the notion of history is an awareness of action. Within the processes described in the study much of the constructive nature of the work was predicated on the availability of the actions of others. Most existing database systems support more than one user, in fact multi-user database systems are now the norm. However, while it is true that these systems support a number of users simultaneously interacting with a pool of information, the manner in which this is achieved is problematic when set aside the finding of studies of the use of information. A major design decision within existing multi-user systems is to provide the illusion to each user that they are the only users of the system.

In contrast, we have seen the need to be aware of the activities of other users and to support and encourage the propagation of these activities between users. This ability to make users actions available to others is central to promoting cooperative work. A number of studies have also highlighted the making public of action [3] and importance of information being seen 'at a glance' [4] as a central feature of cooperative work.

In the study, this awareness of action was most evident in the physical arrangement of the offices. The layout of the office allows 'at a glance' the reconstruction of the current status of the work. By seeing where invoices are, the potential workload can be predicted and possible problems and queries flagged. This ability allows users to effectively organise their work so that it closely fits with the work of their colleagues. The availability of others' workload allows an individual's sequencing decisions on their handling of work to be informed by that of others.

In supporting co-operation among a wide set of different users and platforms, a uniform and clean event mechanism is needed. In the shared object service an event handler provides a central facility responsible for the handling and support of requests and subscriptions on events. This portion of the service also maintains a record for the clients of the services and events which are of interest to them. A client, application, or user, can declare interest in a certain event in the system, internal or external, by declaring an interest to the event handler. The event mechanism promotes awareness by informing users of changes to entities.

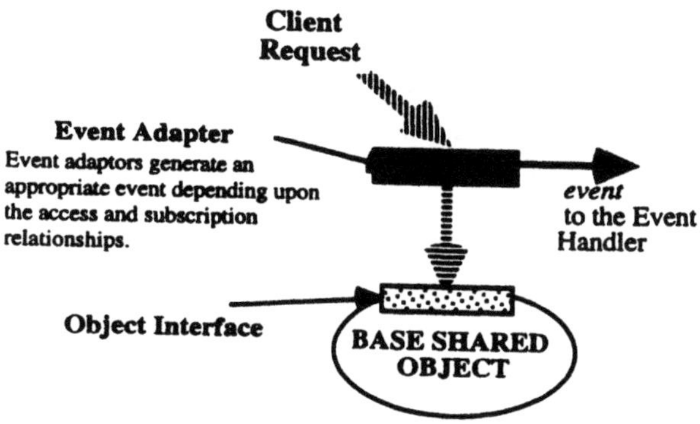

Figure 3: The role of an event adapter

A special form of adapter termed an event adapter is used to inform others of changes in the object (see figure 3). Event adapters are a means of realising event services within the shared object service. An event adapter knows about subscription relationships. If an object declares interest in events to or from another object or agent, then an event adapter 'filters' events to and from the interested object. If an event is of 'public' interest that event is propagated further.

The heterogeneous nature of documents

Finally, we must consider the ease in which a document is grown or extended by stapling other documents to it. Documents have items stuck on, or are date stamped and initialed or have new fields added to them. Thus, documents as they move through a process alter and evolve and assume different significance. Consequently, when we refer to a document within the process, rather than identifying any single entity, we are identifying a heterogeneous collection of entities. Some of these may exist on paper and equally well some may be manifest only within electronic systems. Facilities to manage this heterogeneity is an important part of the shared object service.

As an example of the heterogeneous nature of documents consider again the progress of an invoice within the study. As it moves through the office a set of notes and cover sheets are added which record the actions taken for that invoice. Consequently, an invoice which starts as a single sheet of paper can develop into a collection of associated notes and forms which record the handling of that invoice. In the case where invoices are queried or problematic the effects are more dramatic. An invoice can have a sheet of paper added which transforms it into a query, this in turn can be incorporated into a specialised report outlining problematic invoices. Thus not only can the nature of the type referred to alter as it progresses through the system it may quickly evolve to another type of document with the addition of a single sheet of paper.

The ability of adapters to abstract away from the underlying objects allows us to directly support this evolution. Adapters can present an augmented set of facilities by abstracting across a number of objects. This relationship is shown in figure 4:

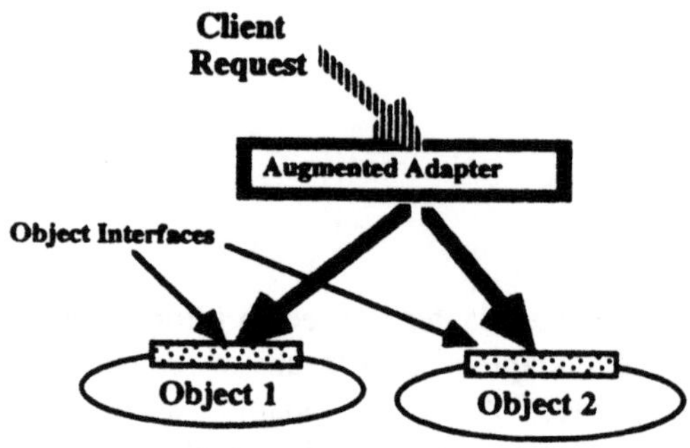

Figure 4: An augmented adapter

From even a cursory examination of the studies described previously, the heterogeneous nature of documents is apparent. There is no reason to conjecture that this heterogeneity will diminish in the case of electronically based objects. In contrast it is likely to increase with a continued need to access paper objects outside the shared object service. It is also important to realise that objects stored within the service may make reference to "real physical" objects every bit as much as they may make references to other objects stored within the service. For example, an electronic catalogue of review forms for a journal may make reference to both electronic and paper instances of the forms sent to the journal editor. Such "physical" objects can be considered as external objects existing outside the service.

In some senses, an object which contains a reference to an external object can be considered as 'incomplete'. Unlike a fully internal object, we do not possess all the information 'at hand' to display, manipulate, indeed generally consider the object. Broadly speaking a number of classes of external object exist.

- Electronic objects which are currently not required and have been removed from the SOS and archived.
- Electronic objects which are detached from the SOS and are not readily accessible. These objects are characterised as being currently relevant but difficult to access. For example, the object may have been placed on a portable or mobile computer.
- Non-electronic objects which are related to the SOS and have some form of electronic manifestation within the service, However, the object itself is not part of the service.

We exploit orthogonality across the service as a means of aiding our representation of external objects. We have chosen to adopt a specialised form of adapter as the means to represent external objects. External adapters act as the electronic manifestation of the externally held artefact. The role of external adapters is to provide a bridge between objects within the SOS and those within the 'real world' which are relevant to the SOS.

On invocation, rather than directly return a result, the external adapter informs the client that the object is external and offers the possibility of some access information associated with the external object. This access information has number of forms:-

- Details of how to retrieve an archived electronic object.
- Details of how to establish electronic communication with a detached object.
- Descriptions of non-electronic objects as a set of textual labels and a description of how to access the external object. This may in turn involve the description of some particular organisational policy or procedure. The description acts as a user resource for accessing the external information.

As in the case of access rights, external accessibility information is held as an integral part of the external adapter. By using external adapters which can act as pseudo representations of objects within the SOS, queries across the database can be handled in a orthogonal manner. In addition, queries can also access external objects and query textual labels in the adapter.

Conclusions

In this paper we have shown how previous studies of work involving the production and flow of documents informed the facilities a shared object service needs to provide. Progress towards increasingly electronic information is occurring in many organisations. CSCW applications require a set of services which promote the cooperative sharing of information. However there is a danger that this infrastructure may lose certain desirable features that paper currently affords.

We do not want to slavishly replicate every feature of the unautomated environment. Not only is this impossible, it is also undesirable as some features are unnecessary for efficient operation. The key to our ongoing re-examination of previous studies is discriminating between features of documents that offer advantages for cooperative work and those that do not. These insights have been used to inform development of a shared object service.

Many other factors have influenced the development of the shared object service including current systems architectures and technical practice. The critical re-examination of previous studies do not in themselves provide a set of requirements. The resulting information is often in too diffuse a form to be turned directly into requirements and some of the desirable features may be impossible or uneconomic to implement. Similarly many of the facilities provided by a shared object service are novel and do not have a counterpart within the manual studies re-examined.

A focus on sharing holds great promise for the development of future CSCW systems. We believe that the development of a set of infrastructure services is beneficial to future CSCW applications and the providers of future distributed infrastructures. By grounding the facilities provided in a social understanding of the nature of shared information we increase the chances of their effective use within cooperative settings. While not replacing the use of direct and target studies a critical re-examination of previous studies has provided this starting point for the shared object service.

Acknowledgements

This work was funded as part of the COMIC project (ESPRIT project no 6225). Our thanks are due to our partners in the project and colleagues at Lancaster.

References

1. Rodden T., Mariani J., Blair G., 'Supporting Cooperative Applications' International Journal on CSCW, Vol. 1, No. 1, September 1992.

2. Greif I., Sarin S. 'Data Sharing in Group Work', ACM trans. on Office Information Systems, Vol. 5, No 2, April 1987, pp 187- 211.
3. Heath C. & Luff P.: (1991) Collaborative Activity and Technological Design: Task coordination in London Underground Control Rooms, In ECSCW '91. Proceedings of the second European conference on Computer Supported Cooperative Work. Dordrech: Kluwer.
4. Hughes, J.A., D. Randall, and D. Shapiro. "Faltering from Ethnography to Design." Proceedings of ACM CSCW'92 Conference on Computer-Supported Cooperative Work. Ethnographically-Informed Design. pp: 115-122.
5. Appelt, W, 'Document Architecture in Open Systems: The ODA Standard', Springer-Verlag, ISBN 0-387-54539-5, 1991
6. Conklin J. ' Hypertext: An Introduction and Survey', IEEE Computer September 1987, pp 17-41.
7. Suchman, L.A. Plans and Situated Actions: The Problem of Human-Computer Communication. Cambridge University Press. New York.
8. Ackroyd, S., Harper, R., Hughes, J.A., Shapiro, D., and Soothill, K. (1992), New Technology and Practical Police Work, London, Open University Press.
9. Wattam, C. (1992), Making a Case in Child Protection, London, Longmans.
10. Anderson, R.J., Hughes, J.A. and Sharrock, W. (1989),Working for Profit: The Social Organisation of Calculation in an Entrepreneurial Firm, Aldershot, Avebury.
11. Sacks, H. (1963), Sociological Description, Berkeley Journal of Sociology, 8, pp. 1-16.
12. Raffel, S. (1979), Matters of Fact, London, Routledge and Kegan Paul.
13. Sharrock, W.W. and Anderson, R.J. (1987), Work flow in a paediatric clinic, in Button, G and Lee, J. (eds.), Talk and Social Organisation, Clevedon, Multilingual Matters, pp. 244-260.
14. Natanson, M. (1986), Anonymity, Bloomington, Indiana University Press.
15. Gurwirsch, A. (1979), Human Encounters in the Social World, Pittsburgh, Duquesne University Press.
16. Garfinkel, H. (1967), Studies in Ethnomethodology, Englewood Cliffs, Prentice Hall.
17. Lynch, M. (1985), Discipline and the material form of images: an analysis of scientific visibility, Social Studies of Science, 15, pp. 37-66.
18. Mariani J, Rodden T, Trevor J "The use of interface adaptors to support cooperative sharing", proceedings of CSCW'94, ACM Press, pp 219-231.
19. Shen, H., and P. Dewan. "Access Control for Collaborative Environments." Proceedings of ACM CSCW'92 Conference on Computer-Supported Cooperative Work. Building Real-Time Groupware. pp: 51-58.

6 INFORMATION INTEGRATION FOR FIELD WORKERS AND OFFICE-BASED PROFESSIONALS: 3 CASE STUDIES

Malcolm Bauer and Jane Siegel

Introduction

This chapter presents three related case studies where interdisciplinary teams at Carnegie Mellon University (CMU) are developing document-centric information systems for use in vehicle inspection, maintenance, and product redesign tasks. The case studies represent three points along the dimension of amount of information integration in different organizations. What is common in the information systems and work processes in all three cases is that they support mobile field workers and their information providers and users. Studies of field workers and their use of information technologies are few. The work reported here is part of our user-centered evolutionary development effort aimed at understanding and supporting the information needs and work processes for mobile workers.

The information needs of inspection, maintenance, and other field workers, e.g., aircraft mechanics or field engineers are different than those of office workers. Tasks include diagnosing and fixing devices rather than brainstorming and authoring. Their work involves interacting with complex mechanical devices outside of the computational environment or information system - there is a need to find information and communicate while being mobile. In addition there are increasingly complex and rapidly changing vehicular configurations and documentation, e.g., in the commercial aircraft business, documentation changes every 90 days and the physical (paper) manuals for one passenger jet would fill about half the cabin space. The brief scenario below illustrates the process and integrated information support field workers require to function effectively today.

Imagine a technician rushing to repair a train or aircraft at a U.S. locale while passengers await departure. The technician has never seen this problem. He accesses a fault isolation process and using a wearable computer linking him to interactive electronic technical manuals (IETMs) isolates the suspected failed component. The integrated information system determines that the documentation in the manuals is the most current. Also, the system finds that a European site experienced a similar problem within the past six months. The technician sends images of the suspected component via a wearable computer and wireless communications to a peer who is at the European site maintaining the same model of train/aircraft. The two technicians discuss the situation via video teleconference (the video camera is mounted on the wearable and is aimed at the suspected failed component). They are able to jointly view the problem context and can annotate the parts illustration to quickly agree on the likely solution. The annotated images and recommendations are sent to the appropriate manager for rapid confirmation and approval to replace an expensive component. The whole incident is archived and notification of the event is sent to the responsible product engineer. The component is replaced and the passengers are on their way with an elapsed time for the whole incident of less than 30 minutes.

Systems to support this scenario are being prototyped and tested in both laboratory experiments and field trials in multiple organizations as part of the interdisciplinary effort underway between CMU and our industry and government partners*. The systems the CMU team is designing and we are evaluating focus on: (1) improving information flow, (2) integrating information from collected documents based upon the immediate needs of field technicians or product engineers, and (3) support for collaboration among multiple geographically distributed workers. To improve information flow, the systems are designed to enable direct transfer of digitized data (via wireless transmission) for use by others in the organization. This differs from the current process where information is physically recorded and then manually entered into the information system. For document integration, we have created an information space that allows for the integration of many documents in different formats and mediums (paper, electronic) residing in many different places. Support for collaboration involves enabling joint annotation of documents coupled with high quality communication (audio and, at times, video).

Creating a system that allows for the incorporation of existing documents, the access to information contained in these documents presented in a meaningful way, and the authoring of new documents, poses four significant technical and organizational challenges which we describe. Then we provide three brief case studies and a summary about the status of the document-centric information integration work underway at CMU.

---

* Due to the proprietary nature of some of our work, we are unable to list our partners at this time.

Challenges

1. Interfacing with legacy databases

In most organizations significant repositories of documents already exist that are in various formats and maintained and accessed by particular software applications. For example, one of the organizations we are working with maintains a vast database of schematics and is only accessible through a custom application developed in-house. To access these documents along with technical manuals or parts information it is necessary to develop an interface to the custom database program. To integrate different classes of documents to support work processes in organizations is it necessary to develop a system to access many different legacy databases in which these documents reside.

2. Providing access to systems while mobile

In all of our case studies, the systems under development are providing information to field technicians whose job requires them to work in, around, and under large vehicles. They need their hands free to work. They also need access to vast information repositories to guide their troubleshooting, repair and redesign work. Providing hands-free access to this information and allowing them great mobility is a difficult problem. The nature of their work also restricts the ways in which field workers can interact with the system. In one of our case studies, field technicians work on a moving train with passengers present. Using a speech recognition system is one interface that allows hands free input, yet if the train were having a problem, technicians speaking aloud trying to solve it would worry passengers, an option that is not acceptable to the transit company.

3. Providing on-line access to documents that is more efficient than paper

There have been numerous studies evaluating the efficiency and usability of on-line hypertext versions of manuals in comparison to paper manuals (Landauer, Egan, Remde, Lesk, Lochbaum, and Ketchum, 1993). Very few show an advantage for hypertext systems over paper. For example, McKnight, Dillon, and Richardson (1991) describe a study in which they compared a carefully constructed hypertext system to a paper manual generated from text files of the hypertext system and arranged in a somewhat arbitrary order. They found that information retrieval using the electronic hypertext version was significantly inferior to the paper manual, and that participants preferred the paper manual. The study made every effort to give an advantage to the hypertext system. Usually manuals are designed for paper first and then converted to a hypertext version of the paper manual. In this instance the system was first designed for hypertext and converted to paper format. Many other studies (Gordon, Gustavel, Moore, and Hankey, 1988; Marchioni and Shneiderman, 1988) point to the fact that it is a difficult problem to design electronic document delivery systems that are even as good as paper.

The retrieval problem. Typical findings for retrieving desired documents are that searchers find 10-40 percent of the existing relevant material and retrieve 30-60 percent irrelevant material. The findings hold for paper (e.g. libraries) and for a wide range of computer retrieval methods (e.g. Boolean search queries). Recent methods (e.g. LSI, (Deerwester, Dumais, Furnas, Landauer, & Harshman, 1990), Clarit (Evans & Lefferts, 1995)) increase this hit rate significantly to has high as 80%. Employing these methods on-line may be one way to give computer-based systems an advantage over paper.

The navigation problem. There are numerous studies that show that people have difficulty traversing hierarchical lists to reach desired information. Typically people get lost by going down the wrong branch of a tree. This appears largely due to the wide variance in conceptual structures in people, in this case between the authors and users of hyperlinked documents. (Landauer et al, 1993). Merely converting paper documents to electronic format with simple rules for deciding on links is even worse, yet the problem of reauthoring existing paper documents is a daunting task as well. Additional issues arise when incorporating parts illustrations or large schematic drawings (ranging from 11 x 17 inches to 36 x 60 inches in physical copy). How users will scroll or track their location is unresolved. Designing large hyperlinked electronic documents that are easier to use than paper documents remains a difficult problem.

Limited screen real estate. Resolution on computer screens has increased significantly in the past few years, but it is still far lower than what is typically available on paper. Small portable systems that give field workers significant mobility typically have worse resolution than larger desk top computers (VGA (i.e. 640x480) vs. SVGA (i.e. 600x800)). Presenting the wide range of documents needed by the field worker (including schematics, diagrams, procedural information) on smaller screens is especially challenging.

4. Organizational challenges

The kinds of systems the CMU team is building offer unprecedented opportunities to individuals to share information within an organization. Yet information is a valuable commodity even within an organization and sharing it freely may not necessarily be in the immediate best interests of all people in the organization. In addition, in many companies there is a quality assurance issue with respect to information. For example, traditionally manuals, policies, procedures, etc. are often written by a central documentation group who assure that the information is accurate and current. Maintenance workers and engineers expect that the procedures they follow are correct and the central documentation group will be held accountable if it is not. On-line systems potentially give everyone the ability to become authors - to have employees offer ideas and share potential solutions to problems, and to have these created documents immediately available to all other workers. Yet, allowing this ability potentially degrades the quality of information and makes accountability difficult if it circumvents evaluation and approval processes for information that had been in place.

Understanding the role of different types of documents and how they are used by various people uncovers potential information sharing problems but does not solve them. Putting in place systems that support information and document integration allows more information to be shared by more people. These systems have the potential to make work processes and associated problems public that were before known only to a few individuals. They allow people to collaborate much more closely. This sharing may expose differences in beliefs, policies, and practices and potentially create an environment where these differences can be resolved or result in great conflict. In short, information and process integration requires organizational change - both to enable the integration and resulting from the integration.

Change is hard and organizational change which is effective often is slow (Kaufman, 1981) which is why we advocate and employ an evolutionary approach to process and information integration. A central part of the work underway at CMU is baselining the processes and documenting the information flows, roles, responsibilities, dependencies and tasks in sufficient detail to inform the design of the system. In one organization, the process for engineering changes to products was documented and presented to management in March, 1995. Major improvements are being realized as the company re-engineers that process , creating a new position, altering the set of engineers and managers and their decision process. This changed process is supported by the new system described in case 3 which allows easy access to integrated historical information from both the field and headquarters.

Now that we have outlined some of the problems associated with our work we describe our prototype systems. As mentioned, we take an evolutionary approach to design and development. The current systems represent a compromise between deployment speed and functionality. The team picked processes that we believed would yield immediate benefits. As the systems are used we expect the organizations to change in response. We expect to grow the information integration systems over time continually expanding and changing them in response to the changes caused in the organizations. With that said, we describe the current systems. The three systems show a progression in information integration.

Case 1: Marine Vehicle Inspections

The domain of the first effort is inspection of marine amphibious vehicles. Before the development of the CMU system, the marine inspectors used paper checklists consisting of more than 500 items that they carried on a clipboard with them as they moved about the vehicle. The inspectors checked off whether a particular part was faulty and hand wrote a two or three word description of the problem for each faulty part. A clerk typed the fault/no fault and free form information about the nature and severity of the problem into a database for use in scheduling and performing maintenance tasks. Because the handwriting of the descriptions is typically poor, and because the people retyping the document are one-step removed from the problem, the maintenance personnel who actually fix the faulty part do not trust the description and typically do another inspection/diagnosis before performing the maintenance.

The system the CMU team is developing with substantial end-user involvement consists of wearable mobile computer with an on-line checklist that can be completed by use of a dial input device (Bass, Kasabach, Martin, Siewiorek, Smailagic, & Stivoric, 1997) which is almost hands free instead of the paper checklist that the marine maintenance personnel use to perform the inspection. The CMU team is also developing a voice recognition system that will allow users to do data entry by speaking the status and problem descriptions. Trials of prototypes of this system (using a Toshiba laptop worn in a backpack) showed the potential gains to inspectors of having a hands free means to input information. Essentially we have created an electronic version of an existing checklist that the maintenance personnel use as they work in, around, and under the vehicle. The two photographs in Figure 1 present examples of people using the system. The information users enter is downloaded directly to a database from the wearable computer after each inspection. This removes the need for retyping the document from handwritten text and provides another major time savings (previously a two or three day temporal delay occurred while the checklist information is in process and thus is not accessible to the maintenance personnel). The maintenance personnel who actually fix the problem will be reading the problem description and looking at text spoken (and verified) by the person who actually inspected the vehicle reducing or eliminating the need to reinspect.

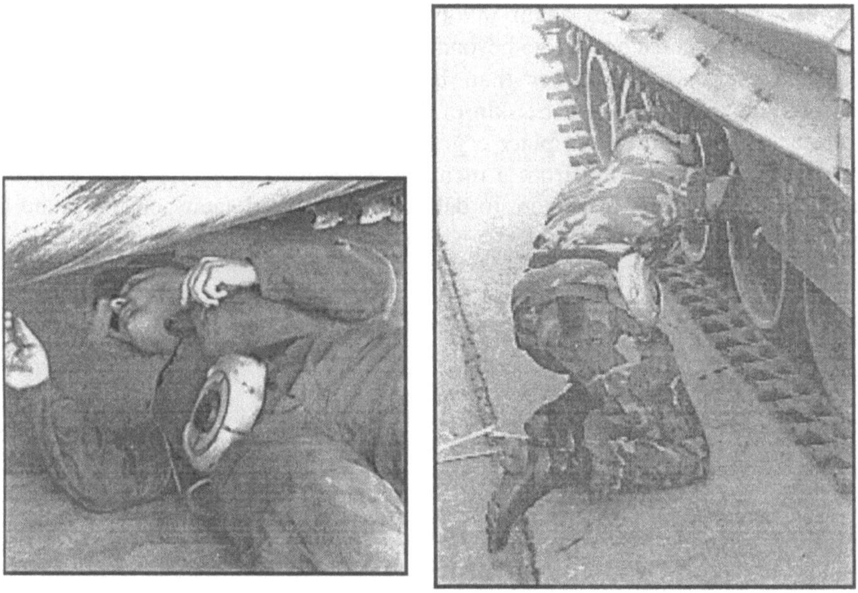

Figure 1: Wearable System in Use During Marine Vehicle Inspection

Case 2: Airplane Inspections

The domain for the second effort is airplane skin inspection. The aircraft involved in this case is the KC-135 (similar to a Boeing 707) used for refueling of jets by the U.S. military services. The planes are about 30 years old and the Department of Defense hopes to keep these planes in service for another 20 years. They are stripped to bare metal periodically to determine whether cracks, corrosion, or other flaws need to be repaired. Like the previous example, in the existing process, the inspectors also use a clipboard and describe each fault that they find in their own words. Also, they record the coordinates of each fault, and place tags or marks with a special pencil on the actual aircraft to show the location of most faults. They then enter these faults into a computer database that gets used by planning personnel to schedule the actual maintenance tasks. The scheduled tasks are printed out on cards that the maintenance personnel use.

The new CMU system again involves a wearable mobile computer system. However, the process changes go beyond the mere electronic automation of the first effort in several ways. Rather than being a checklist, the inspectors use an electronic, navigable map of the skin of the plane. When they find a problem area on the actual plane they can place a graphical marker on the electronic map and label the fault by choosing from a menu of predefined categories (see Figure 2). The system allows the inspectors to delineate a group of faults on the plane and

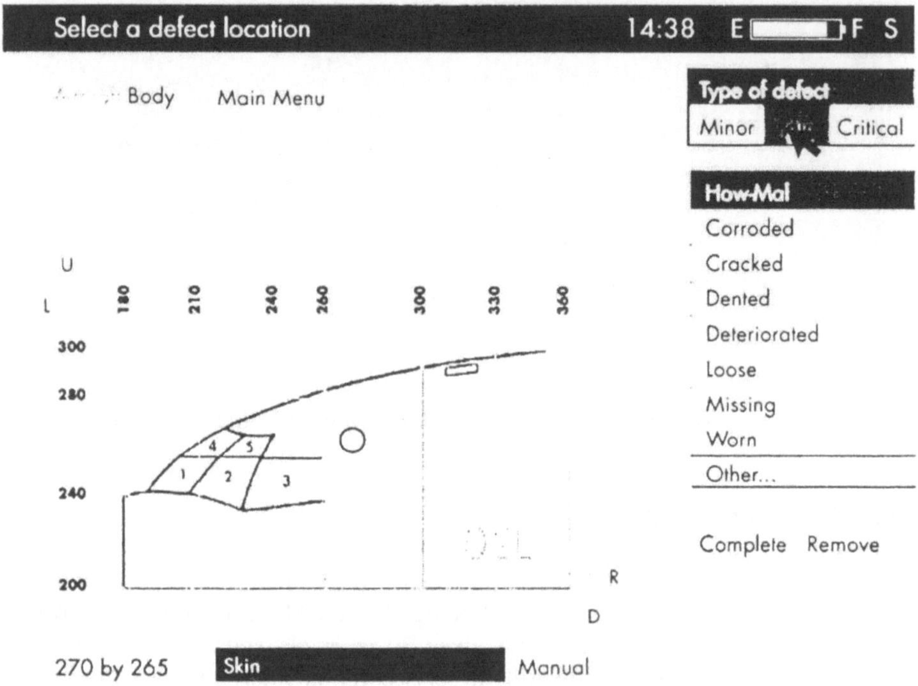

Figure 2: Airplane Skin Inspection Interface

categorize them all at once. Also, it enables them to indicate the severity of the problem. This goes beyond automation of the existing process in that the information they are saving now consists of precisely defined faults and their coordinates in relation to other features on the skin of the plane. The expected benefit of replacing the physical marks or tags on the aircraft with the print-out of the fault locations is a major time savings and a reduction in the the risk of injury/physical strain for inspectors who currently must reach from hydraulic lifts to place marks/tags on the planes. Like the marine system, the inspectors can download the information directly into a database, eliminating the data re-entry task. Unlike the original process, the information is represented in a way that many people can quickly and easily interpret. Thus it can be used by planners, managers, and maintenance personnel.

Case 3: Vehicle Maintenance and Redesign

The domains for the third effort are technician training, and maintenance and redesign of large vehicles. In the existing processes maintenance and redesign are largely independent with little information flowing between them. The maintenance teams at various field sites communicate with each other and with the engineering design team through an array of formal paper documents and via phone in cases of emergency. Creating a system to support these work processes is considerably more ambitious than the previous two applications which involved field inspectors working in isolation. This system must support both field and desk workers collaborating across space and time. In addition, the workers are collaborating over a wide range of documents including technical manuals, schematics, problem reports, change requests and notifications, and diagnostic data from vehicles. Our current system supports the following work processes:

Preventive Maintenance. These are regularly scheduled maintenance procedures that technicians perform on the trains. Technicians need to refer to manuals and procedures while having their hands free to work on the vehicles especially for infrequently performed and complex tasks.

Corrective maintenance. When a train breaks down there is an urgent need to correct the problem quickly. Technicians and engineers often need to collaborate to solve problems. Often a technician or field engineer in another site, in another country, has solved a similar problem, but currently there is no effective way to know that or to access the knowledge.

Training. Field site technicians and engineers need refresher training, and training on new procedures. To advance in their careers they need to become proficient in new procedures. Also new employees need significant training to perform even basic procedures.

Authoring. As new trains are built and as designs and maintenance procedures change, up to date information must be made readily available to the field technicians and engineers. Authoring these documents and issuing updates to the field is a difficult and costly task. While there are often many common subsystems across products that would allow reuse of document subsections, tracking these in the design process has proved difficult.

Engineering Feedback. Technicians and engineers involved in train maintenance have learned much about the systems designed by engineers at headquarters. But this information resides only in the minds of field personnel or in documents to which product engineers do not have ready access. There is a need to make the collective experience of field personnel available to product engineers at the right time in the design cycle to improve the next product release.

We describe the basic functionality of the system and then discuss issues relating to information and process integration. The unifying concept of our system is that many work processes within a company create information that other processes can use. The CMU team, collaborating with the end-users in the organization, technicians and other professionals, is developing a system that allows people throughout the company to bring to bear the collective knowledge of the company to help solve their immediate problems.

In the new system, maintenance technicians, engineering personnel, management personnel, and even equipment systems can exchange information through a document-centric information space. The information space provides access through a simple browser to: Interactive Electronic Technical Manuals, the parts catalog, schematic drawings, an expert system for troubleshooting problems, the inventory and parts ordering system, data from vehicles for use in preventive maintenance modeling, policies and procedures, phone/mail/address directory, discussion databases, and email. The system captures trend and fault data from the vehicles and uses it for predictive maintenance and diagnostic functions. Field problems are communicated to engineering for assistance in repairs and for information needed to develop new products or improve current ones. The system will enable technicians at maintenance facilities and engineering personnel to access technical manuals and schematics, view filtered data from the diagnostic subsystem, provide process descriptions and current process status information, and store various documents developed and used in various aspects of training. Technicians will access those on-line, hypermedia documents for refresher training as their schedule permits. The system also supports people-to-people collaboration, e.g., joint annotation of schematic drawings among field maintenance sites and engineering, and allows individuals to store the results of these sessions and refer to them at a later time. The system integrates information and processes in several ways.

1. Vehicle maintenance and document authoring

The documentation and training group at headquarters produces large sets of paper manuals which are delivered to the field sites when train systems start up. Over time field employees create their own notebooks containing relevant sections of the manuals with their own additions to procedures and specializations for their particular sites. The notebooks also contain schematics with important circuits highlighted and diagrams of mechanical systems with their own annotations added. The technicians refer to the notebooks regularly and share their notebooks with others at this site. They leave them in established public places so anyone at the site can have access to them. The notebooks represent a reorganization of much of the relevant information found in the manuals with important information added by the technicians. Currently, this information rarely finds its way back into the "official" manuals yet represents an important source of company "know-how."

The new system provides a way for technicians to copy and annotate pages from the manuals and schematics and construct notebooks on-line. The annotations are stored separately from the manuals and schematics and different sets of annotations can be viewed by different people allowing technicians to share insights and build on each others knowledge. The system includes a hierarchy of read and write protection allowing users different levels of privacy, e.g. viewable only by themselves, by the local site, by a set of sites, and by headquarters. This annotation ability allows for a new level of information integration. The technicians are constructing new documents by assembling relevant pieces of other documents and adding new knowledge by annotation. The on-line system allows these documents to be more easily constructed and to be shared across sites. We expect this will allow technicians as a whole to crystallize both important lessons learned and innovative changes to procedures. It allows technicians to become part authors of the documents they use. Their notebooks become living, growing, repositories of the current maintenance practices in the company.

This raises the issue of quality of information and accountability as discussed above. How can we be assured that the information being added by technicians is correct? Allowing technicians to add annotations freely to documents and allowing others to use these annotations circumvents the standard evaluation and approval processes for adding to official documents. If a technician at one site uses a modification to a procedure recommended by a technician at another site and a problem occurs who is responsible? For the value of this sort of information integration to be successful, changes in process integration between the field sites and the documentation and training group are essential and are being addressed now. One option is for the documentation and training group to collect annotations from the field site notebooks on a regular basis, evaluate them, noticing common changes and innovations, and integrate these useful additions to the official manuals. In this way, the document information flow that was formerly one-way, from the documentation and training group out to the field sites, becomes a cyclical process with the technicians taking an active role. This model of document creation and integration allows for bottom up generation of useful information (technician, trains, day-to-day communications) with useful parts becoming more accessible and stable as they are incorporated into standard documents by the more centralized documentation and training groups.

2. Vehicle Redesign

Our system enables a somewhat different process and information integration between the vehicle design and maintenance processes. Field sites produce several different kinds of documents containing information about train status and problems. These include weekly status reports, incident reports, notices suggesting design changes, etc. Over time these documents develop into a kind of detailed history of the vehicle with lessons learned about the vehicle included from the experiences of the field site technicians and engineers. This information will be useful to the product engineers as they develop new products and improve existing designs. Currently the information exists as a distributed collection of paper documents. As a result the product engineers cannot access it in any meaningful way. The new system provides flexible access to these documents through the use of an integrated information space with a robust search engine, Clarit. (Evans & Lefferts, 1995). When redesigning a train component, engineers can ask the integrated information space for relevant status reports, problems, etc. written by field technicians. Sets of company documents that were purely archival before can now be analyzed by design engineers to track recurrent problems across field sites and inform the design of new products.

3. Training

New employees, employees needing refresher training , or employees preparing for competency testing to advance their careers using the new system can access the integrated information space from multi-media equipped desktop computers at their worksite. They can select a module or modules related to the hydraulic system or whatever system/subsystem they want to learn more about for a given session. The system provides a personal history of training modules the individual employee has completed as of that date. Once the employee selects a module, he/she has the option to link to related information such as technical manuals, schematic drawings, parts information, or video clips of experts performing the tasks of interest. The employee also may link to an expert system for use in fault isolation and may interact with that system for training in troubleshooting processes. The new system supplements the formal classroom and on-the-job training available to employees. It is expected to be particularly useful in providing more flexible, yet formal delivery of interactive training for globally distributed employees where turnover in staff may occur every few months.

Summary

In all three cases, we expect that conversion of documented information to support multiple users and the processes they are executing will have substantial impact on organizational performance. Initial results from the marine case study and the skin inspection case study support this expectation. The three cases represent three points along the dimension of amount of information integration.

In the amphibious marine vehicle system, there is little integration of information from different sources. The performance gains come from reducing the information reentry process. Instead of clerks interpreting and retyping the documents created by the inspectors, the system allows the inspectors to download the information in a format so that the mechanics can get the information directly. Also, the information in the documents has greater precision and reliability. In a sense this is process integration because we have removed the middleman and brought the inspector and the mechanic closer together through the use of information technology.

The airplane skin inspection system goes one step beyond this. By integrating the map of the airplane skin and the faults, it incorporates knowledge that was previously only implicit (the map) with explicit knowledge contained in documents (the list of faults). This allows many more people to easily understand information that was previously not accessible.

The train maintenance and redesign system involves the greatest amount of information integration. Using the document-centric information space, many different people with different roles and responsibilities can dynamically integrate information from a wide array of documents containing different kinds of information (text, schematics, video clips of procedures, and diagnostic data).

Because these systems and the work processes are undergoing formative evaluation and are still evolving, we are unable to report data from formal evaluations of their impact at this time. Measures of success being considered/used in this work include both subjective and objective measures. We are looking at benefits for three parties in these efforts:

- end-users view success in terms of: ease of use, ease of learning, faster error recovery, less frustration, less fatigue, improved work quality,

- user's organization success measures may include: improved productivity and effective work time of personnel, or decreased training and support costs

- developers and the development organizations consider: decreased development time and costs, increased product quality, increased customer satisfaction and sales volume.

We and the end-users already see substantial potential impact e.g., in preliminary trials in case 1, the marine vehicle inspection task, there was a time savings of approximately 40 percent by using the wearable computer (Smailagic & Siewiorek, 1996). Similarly, for case 2, the aircraft skin application, we found a reduction from 56 minutes to 3 minutes for passing inspection data from the inspector to the maintenance scheduler.

References

Evans, D. A., and Lefferts, R. G. (1995). CLARIT-TREC experiments. *Information Processing and Management*, **31**, 3 pp. 385-395.

Deerwester, S., Dumais, S.T., Furnas, G.W., Landauer, T.K., and Harshman, R.A. (1990). Indexing by latent semantic analysis. *Journal of the American Society for Information Science,* **41**, 391-407.

Gordon, S. , Gustavel, J., Moore, J. , and Hankey, J. (1988) The effects of hypertext on reader knowledge representation. In Proceedings of the Human Factors Society 32nd Annual Meeting (pp. 296-300). Santa Monica, CA: Human Factors Society.

Kaufman, H. (1981) *The Limits of Organizational Change.* The University of Alabama Press, 124 pps.

Landauer, T., Egan, D, Remde, J., Lesk, M., Lochbaum, C. , and Ketchum, D., (1993) Enhancing the Usability of Text Through Computer Delivery and Formative Evaluation: the Super Book Project. In *Hypertext: a psychological_perspective* (Eds.) McKnight, Cliff, Dillon, Andrew, and Richardson, John. E. Horwood, New York, 202 pps.

Marchioni, G. and Shneiderman, B. (1988) Finding facts vs. browsing knowledge in hypertext systems, *IEEE Computer*, 21, 70-80.

McKnight, C., Dillon, A., and Richardson, J. (1991). A comparison of linear and hypertext formats in information retrieval. In R. Macalese and C. Green (Eds.) *HYPERTEXT: state of the art.* Oxford: Intellect.

Smailagic, A., and Siewiorek, D. P. (1996). Modalities of interaction with CMU wearable computers. *IEEE Personal Communications.*

Acknowledgments: We would like to thank the primary system designers and developers including: Dick Martin, Dan Siewiorek, Len Bass, Chris Kasabach, John Stivoric, Asim Smailagic, and Bernd Breugge. This work was supported by the Advanced Research Project Agency and the Daimler-Benz AG. We especially want to thank Len Bass for his feedback about this work.

7 CROSSING THE BORDER: DOCUMENT COORDINATION AND THE INTEGRATION OF PROCESSES IN A DISTRIBUTED ORGANISATION

Allan MacLean and Pernille Marqvardsen

ABSTRACT
This chapter explores issues in the coordination of distributed processes across different departments in a nationwide financial institution, and also how these relate to, are impacted by, and integrated with external customers and organisations which are part of the process. The specific example we examine is the processing of applications for a mortgage. In the organisation with which we have been working, this process involves gathering and integrating information from different sources to produce a file of documents. This file is used as a basis for assessing risk, making a decision about whether or not to lend on the case and providing a record which makes the decision accountable.

Introduction

This paper describes work that aims to help develop technologies to better support the integration of distributed organisational processes. It is concerned with how different parts of an organisation coordinate their activities to provide a service at the national level, how the "same" process is enacted in different locations within the organisation and how the organisation relates to relevant third party customers and suppliers. Our current focus is in the financial sector, in particular the approval and provision of mortgages for house purchase (or sometimes home improvement). We draw on an example from our recent work which has investigated how documents required to support the granting of a mortgage are collected and interpreted by a UK Building Society (henceforth "the Society"). We discuss the relationships to the formal organisational processes and to the distribution of work across the organisation.

Our starting point for considering technologies in this kind of distributed domain builds on the common observation that current systems for supporting the enactment of distributed work, such as workflow systems, often lead to failure and frustration rather than improvement in business efficiency. For example in a recent study of the print industry, Bowers et al. (1995) reported how the introduction of a system for supporting the organisation and management of shop floor printing required significant work-arounds to get the work done effectively. It also led to overtime being required to handle work which could previously be carried out in the normal working day. Their observations point to fundamental mismatches between the model of work embodied within the system and the working practices which it was intended to support.

There are a number of reasons for this kind of problem. Two of the most important are that the process model used may not provide an adequate reflection of what is required to get the work done and, more subtly, control over *how* the work gets done may be moved implicitly from the worker to the computer system, with disastrous consequences. The approach we are taking relies on developing requirements for process support which take better account of work practices, and on developing ways to use process representations as a resource to support getting work done. We build on previous work done both within our own laboratory and elsewhere to develop techniques for analysing and modelling processes and for implementing technologies based on these models. The aim is to do this in such a way that the models used enable users to retain appropriate control over their work, rather than hand over control to the technology.

To ground this work, we are carrying out two specific kinds of research. The first is oriented around field studies to help us better understand some of the requirements for supporting distributed work. The second is developing potential technology solutions to help us explore how some of the more subtle and complex requirements may be realised.

This paper focuses on the field studies side of our work. We will outline some of the characteristics of distributed work from one of these studies, and point to some implications for what needs to be taken into account to improve support for it. We should stress, however, that our emphasis in this paper is to articulate an understanding of how work is coordinated rather than jump into specific technological solutions. More detail of the kinds of technical solutions we are exploring can be found in Dourish et al. (1996).

The Organisation

The Society is a major UK Building Society (roughly equivalent to a US Savings and Loan). It has over three thousand employees nationwide, a central headquarters, about three hundred and fifty branch offices across the UK, and a number of regional and community offices. The Society offers a range of financial services including savings, loans and insurance.

The results and insights reported here are based on information from a number of sources. The first is a "top-down" view of the organisation, which was gained from taking part in a one week intensive workshop at the Society's head office. This involved a number of senior members of the Society and a number of representatives from sales, marketing, technical and research arms of Rank Xerox. The Society is a large customer of Rank Xerox and the primary motivation for the workshop was to develop further the customer-supplier relationship by providing each organisation an opportunity to understand the other better. Rank Xerox Research Centre was involved for two additional reasons. First, to help provide insights into the kinds of technologies and services currently in the research laboratories, which the Society might expect from Rank Xerox in the medium to long term. Second, to look for opportunities to learn more about longer term requirements for organisations like the Society. Much of what was learned from this exercise concerned the organisational structure and values, and the formal processes around which the Society was organised.

The second source of information is a "bottom-up" view of the organisation. This was derived from starting at the "end-nodes" of the Society, such as high street branches where business is generated. To provide a focus we concentrated on the Mortgage Application Process and "followed" it through the organisation, from the points where an initial application is received to where the cheque is issued if the loan is approved. We visited six branch offices, four Initial Approval Units (IAU) and two Final Approval Units (FAU) over a period of about nine months. Data was gathered from a combination of observation of work in progress, and from interviews with members of each department.

The Mortgage Application Process is an excellent example of a highly distributed, knowledge intensive, and document intensive process. At the moment, the Society relies heavily on paper documents for carrying out the process. However, it is beginning to introduce new technologies to improve support for the process, which makes this a particularly appropriate time to be working with them.

We will continue by giving an outline of what the Mortgage Application Process entails and then look at how this is reflected in the organisation's formal processes and the ways in which it is actually enacted in different parts of the Society. We will pay particular attention to the ways in which information is passed and communicated across the various boundaries between departments in the organisation, and with the various third parties with whom these departments have to liaise.

The Mortgage Application Process

The Mortgage Application Process is primarily about risk assessment. It entails building a file on each application. The file is developed by checking and summarising information provided and gathering additional information. This is used to support assessment of the risk: if the Society lends this person the requested amount of money on this property, is it likely that the repayments will be made reliably and if they are not, is the property worth enough to safely cover the loan. Once a decision has been taken, the file becomes an accounting device to justify the decision.

Figure 1 characterises the flow of the application through the Society, and shows some of the interactions with third parties which elicit further information and/or carry out additional checks.

The process starts when a customer applies for a loan to buy a house. The customer walks into a high street branch, discusses requirements with an adviser and fills in an application form. This form, along with supporting documentation, is sent along to the Initial Approval Unit (IAU) (labelled "mortgage desk" in figure 1) which takes input from a number of branches in the local community.

The IAU takes the information provided by the customer at face value. They check the information provided and carry out a credit check and check for any signs of fraud. If there is no problem, they issue a preliminary offer to the customer and pass the application on to the Final Approval Unit (labelled "mortgage processing unit" in figure 1). This unit carries out further more detailed checks (e.g. getting input from third parties such as the employer and a valuer), and enters the information into the Society's central computer system. If all is well, they issue the formal offer and liaise with the customer's solicitor and their own head office to issue the loan to the customer at the appropriate time.

There may be deviations from this process depending on the precise case. For example, a large number of mortgage applications actually come from third party "introducers" rather than "direct" customers who walk into the branch. These introducers are other financial institutions or financial advisers who mediate in negotiations for a loan on behalf of their own clients in return for a fee. A manager in charge of introduced business is typically associated with each IAU.

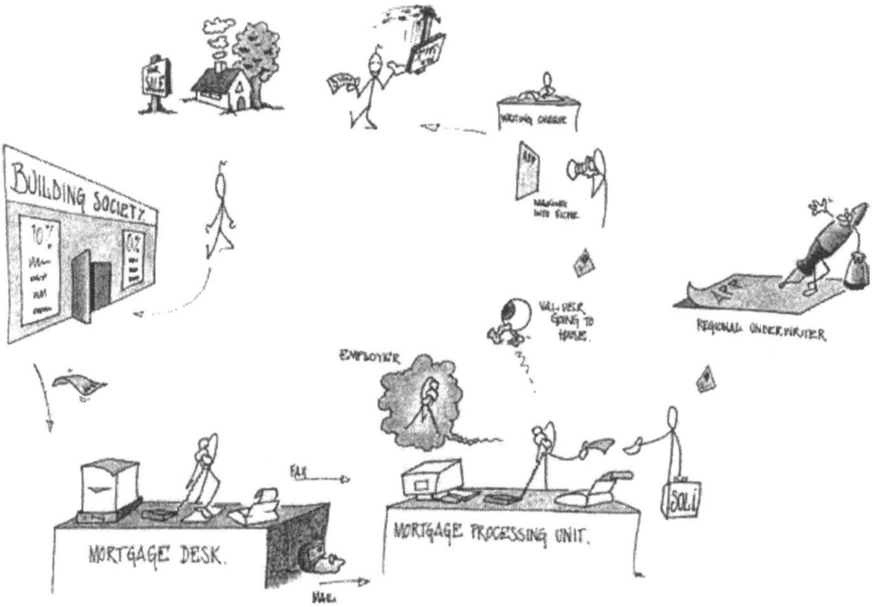

Figure 1. The flow of the Mortgage Application through the Society.

Once the processing gets underway there is little difference between introduced business and direct business in terms of formal processes although, as we shall see later, there may well be some differences in the details of how it has to be dealt with. Another example is a request for a loan that is greater than 75% of the value of the property. This has to go through additional checks (known as "SG referral") to obtain a "Security Guarantee" which involves more stringent credit checks on the customer and additional insurance to cover the risk of the property value being insufficient to reimburse the Society should the borrower default on payments. In this case, the application has to go through the office of the Regional Underwriter.

Since our aim in this paper is to focus on coordination across intra- and inter-organisational boundaries, we have only given a brief account above of the activities performed by each participant in the process. However, this should be sufficient for present purposes to give a reasonable feel for the kinds of activities that are involved.

Normative and routine processes

We shall now move on to consider more formal representations of the Mortgage Application Process. Figure 2 shows a high level process description from the Society's Mortgage Application Process Manual.

The manual goes into considerably more detail about what is involved in carrying out the various risk assessments - what has to be checked, etc.. However, it pays little attention to how these are distributed across the organisation, or how any distribution is coordinated.

The Distribution of Normative Processes

In an attempt to produce a representation in which the distribution of the process across the organisation was clearly presented, we have developed a notation we refer to as Role Interaction Diagram (RID). It is derived from the Role Activity Diagram notation (see Ould, 1995), but is simplified to emphasise interactions across roles and play down detailed activities within roles. Figure 3 shows the same normative process as figure 2 restructured within this notation. The "roles" around which it is organised correspond to the key units within the Society responsible for processing the mortgage application, and the key external people and organisations with whom they liaise. Note that the people carrying out these different roles are therefore typically separated geographically.

Even at the level of detail presented, figure 3 is simplified in two ways. First, it does not distinguish between a direct application from a customer, which would be submitted via a high street branch and an application that comes via a third party introducer. Thus the role of customer here may be filled by the customers themselves, or by their representatives in a branch or external organisation. Second, this diagram does not include additional people within the Society, such as the regional underwriter, who may have to be involved in special cases, for example involving higher risk or lending outside the normal policy guidelines.

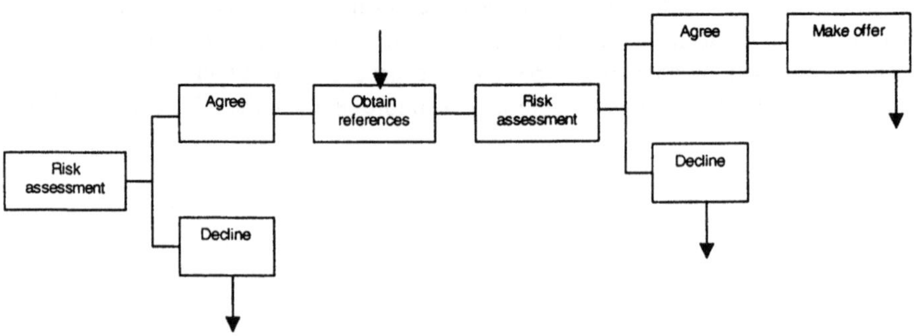

Figure 2. The Mortgage Application Process (based on the Society's process manual).

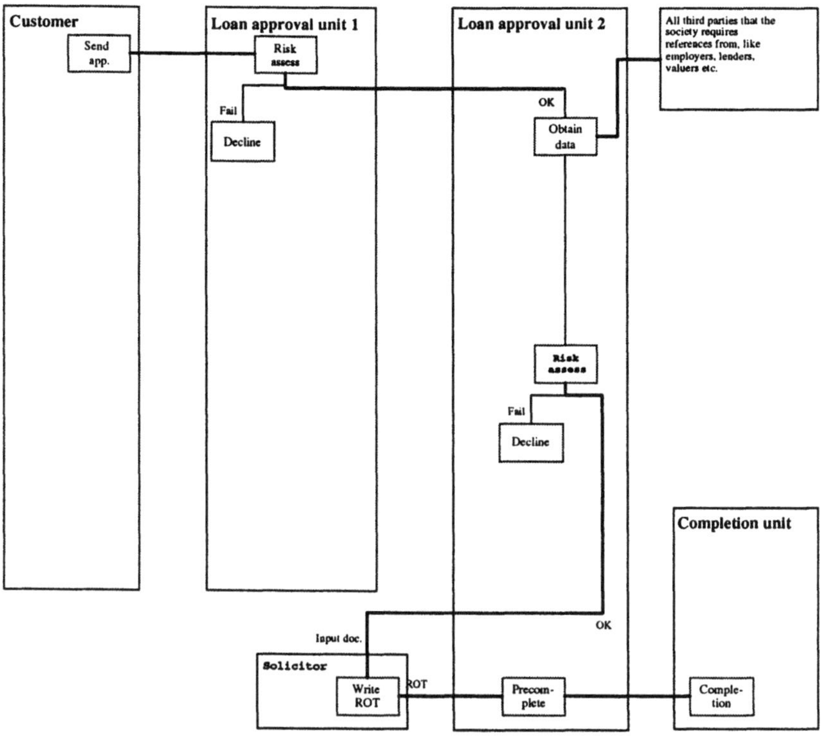

Figure 3. The "Normative" Mortgage Application Process RID (Role Interaction Diagram), showing how the process is distributed across the organisation and the relationships to the customer and key third parties. [Loan Approval Unit 1 corresponds to the IAU, Loan Approval Unit 2 to the FAU and the Completion unit is centrally located at the Society's headquarters.]

Nevertheless, we shall see shortly that the distinctions drawn out here are sufficiently rich to provide insights into how coordination takes place across the various people, departments and organisations which are involved.

Routine Processes

Although the formal process as defined centrally is fairly straightforward, and implies a one way flow of information through the Society, in practice a much richer set of considerations need to be taken into account. The "perfect" application which has all the correct supporting material required, and where it is clear that the Society's loan is secure, is actually fairly rare. To quote an employee working in one of the IAU's:

> "invariably you need more information, it's very rarely that you get an application fully packaged with all the information that you could possibly want"

and in a similar vein from another employee:

> "So I get the case, I get the file and I get the forms and in 99 out of 100 cases, something is missing"

The effects of this are very apparent in the activities we see in the processing of the mortgage applications. There are many more interactions across roles (which, remember, typically involve coordinating across geographical locations). Figure 4 shows the interactions we observed in our field studies and adds these to the normative processes shown in figure 3. We should emphasise, however, that these interactions are not *exceptions* to the normative process, they are very much *part of the day to day routine* of how the work gets done. We therefore refer to the set of activities used to describe the process in figure 4 as the routine process (cf. Suchman, 1983).

Although it looks much more complicated, there are really only two underlying phenomena which account for the 'extra work' implied by the increased interactions shown in figure 4. One involves chasing up required information. Most applications require phone calls to be made to chase up missing information. This includes information that has not been provided, which is wrong or incomplete, has been lost within the Society, or is out of date. The other involves answering queries from customers about the status of their application. Since the process can be distributed across up to four or five different parts of the Society [not all shown in figure 4], some queries require further information gathering before they can be answered. Although we do not have detailed measures, we estimate that, in some offices, as much as 75% of the day can be spent in pursuing these "extra" activities rather than directly carrying out the tasks specified in the normative process.

The Society has a strong ethic of putting itself out to satisfy customers. This results in a flexibility that is manifested in a number of ways. For example, they are generally prepared to make further enquiries about cases that pass the credit check with an "amber" rating - i.e. they do not strictly fall inside the guidelines for low risk credit, but the Society believes they may nevertheless be an acceptable risk. The people who handle applications also answer telephone queries from customers. This ensures a satisfactory response to customers, even though it slows down application processing. Finally, much of the Society's business comes from third party "introducers". The quality of application these people produce varies widely, and indeed the Society may be prepared to negotiate different commission rates that reflect the amount of work they need to get an application "into shape".

Variations across the organisation

The previous section has presented the normative and routine processes as a characterisation of work across the Society. Although obviously based on the information gained from the various locations we visited, we have no reason to believe that these characterisations do not reflect the activities carried out in the many similar units across the country. However, even within the sample we have examined, if we look in more detail at precisely how these activities are reflected in different places, there can be considerable variation between different units which have the same role in the process.

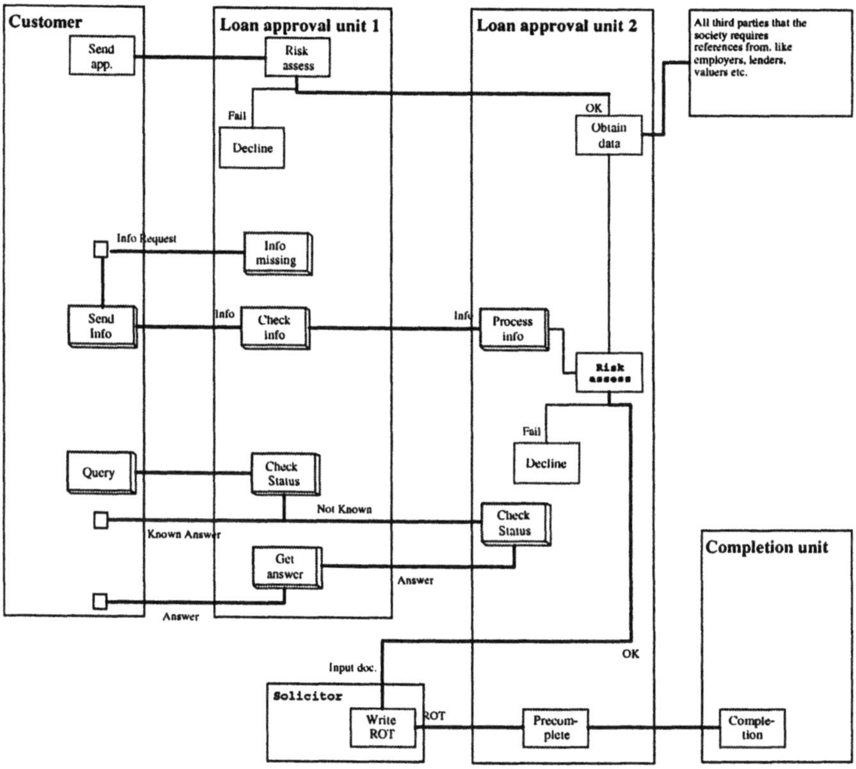

Figure 4. The "Normative" Mortgage Application Process RID (from figure 3), augmented by the "Routine" activities which characterise coordination within the process.

Before giving some examples of this variation, it is important to understand a little bit more about how the Society implements its processes. Although significant effort goes into designing and supporting the core business processes centrally, it is also recognised that they can never capture all the details required to carry them out. Consequently, there is also a strong emphasis on team based working, where the implementation of processes is achieved by a series of teams with partially overlapping membership. This gives an excellent forum for locally developing ways of working and making sure that problems which emerge can be dealt with. It is clearly effective in terms of the sense of belonging to the Society, and in the empowerment that it engenders. This was obvious from our interviews both with people who had only been employed by the Society for a short time and had gone through the initial induction course, and with people who had been around for much longer. However, it also provides a framework that allows different ways of working to emerge in different places which have the same role in terms of responsibilities for business processes. We will go on to give some examples, continuing to focus in particular on how coordination activities are structured, and on how coordination requirements are directly affected by the ways in which other parts of the work are carried out.

Requesting References

In the normal course of events, initiating requests for inputs from third parties, such as employers' references, are initiated from the FAU. Traditionally this was because the system into which FAU employees enter the data about the case also generates the form letters to ask for this information. However, it might take two days before a file sent from the IAU reaches the FAU. Moreover, once it has been sent off, the IAU has no direct control over how quickly it is processed, so the IAU will sometimes send off requests for references etc. before passing the case to the FAU:

> "We're instructing the references simply because again we know it's a fairly urgent case this one"

This may happen when they know it is urgent, perhaps because completion is due soon, or because the case has been slow to be dealt with by the IAU and they want to try to get it through within the benchmark time. In another case, we were told this had been done to speed up processing of a case to reassure a new introducer about the efficiency of the Society in dealing with applications.

One IAU told us:

> "The FAU said no, just send us the application form and we'll get the references. But it wasn't working, it just took longer and we had no control over it and we were in the firing line"

This IAU was in fact one of the few with access to a new computer system that gave them access to the relevant form letters. They therefore decided to routinely initiate reference requests themselves for all cases:

> "We package everything ourselves, all references, instruct valuer, get fees and then send it off to [FAU B]"

These variations in how the work is organised provide a good example of ways in which process improvement takes place. There are good reasons why it is appropriate to send the reference requests from the FAU in terms of minimising effort in producing the letters, but it is recognised that a downside is the process being carried out more slowly. In the examples given, this tradeoff is managed by either putting in more effort to maximise the speed of dealing with urgent cases, or where the up-front effort can be reduced significantly (with the new computer system), re-organising how the process is carried out. There are of course further side effects of this in that the information required to ensure smooth coordination between the IAU and FAU is made more complex. We shall see shortly how some aspects of this are dealt with.

Dealing with interruptions

One of the "routine" activities which we identified as sometimes causing enormous overheads was dealing with interruptions, especially those caused by fielding telephone enquiries about the status of applications. This was clearly recognised as a problem. As one IAU employee put it:

> "The phone calls from the customers and the introducers isn't the worst, The worst is that you might have to make more calls to deal with their problem"

and in another case where we were asking what a phone call had been about:

> "They phoned [another employee in the same office] earlier and asked him if they could get the valuation report and now they can't understand it... I'm interrupted"

A number of different strategies were tried to deal with this kind of problem. For example, one manager responsible for introduced business would sometimes start his day by calling all introducers he thought may have queries to update them on current status. He reasoned that doing it this way kept him more in control of his time and reduced the likelihood of random interruptions later in the day.

Another strategy that had been tried, but failed, was to get phone calls answered by someone who was not directly responsible for processing applications, such as a secretary or temp. However, they quickly found that so many queries required a detailed knowledge of current cases that this was not effective.

One IAU was able to adopt a more radical strategy:

"We rarely have customer contact, the branches are asked not to give our phone number away. They can either talk to their introducer or their branch"

This seemed to be fairly effective, essentially getting calls fielded by someone with a reasonable knowledge of the case. A side effect would seem to be slower feedback to the customer in cases where the branch or introducer had to make further enquiries. However, it appeared that IAU had less overall pressure from interruptions from phone calls.

Another office dealt with the problem by assigning some workers to a corner without a phone:

"We shield some of the others from phone calls, the two over there aren't to be disturbed"

They took this "no interruptions" strategy so seriously that we were also asked not to interrupt the people who were assigned to that corner during our visits.

The Society places great value in developing and maintaining personal relationships with customers. Although the problems this can produce are well-recognised, it is acknowledged that the people who are responsible for processing the application are also the ones who are best able to give an accurate and knowledgeable reply to queries, despite the impact interruptions may have on other aspects of their work.

Managing the Coordination of Information

The Society provides a large number of standard forms which are used to support the Mortgage Application Process. One critical one used by the IAU to track the status of all applications is the MAPR (Mortgage Application Processing Record). This contains information about the location of each file and the status of information required (e.g. references, valuation reports etc.). However, when a file is sent from the IAU to FAU it requires additional status information to be attached to each case. Despite initial implications that the IAU is responsible for one part of the processing, and the FAU another part, as we saw earlier, it may not be quite so straightforward. It is not the case that exactly the same processing will have been carried out on each file. Remember that each FAU deals with files from multiple IAUs. Depending where it came from, or even the particular case, some requests for references may already have been made, or some information may be missing. The precise information "crossing the border" between the IAU and FAU is therefore not well defined, but it is generally seen as important that delays do not happen while waiting for further information to arrive before sending a case on. As one FAU employee said:

"It's better that they send it to us as soon as possible with information 'to follow'" and she also pointed out an example where there had been a problem to make the point:

> "Whoops, we should have made an offer today but that's the branch's fault. They sent out for references and didn't send the rest to us...So they waited till they had all the material"

The complexity in keeping track of who has done what has serious implications for the coordination of activities across the different units. Support for these coordination needs does not seem to be provided from central sources. Each FAU has developed its own "submission sheet" which they require IAUs to attach to the front of every case that is forwarded. This sheet summarises exactly what has been done for the case, and the status of information that might be required (e.g. attached, not relevant, to follow). However, even though the processes are the same, because these sheets have been developed independently, they are sufficiently different that problems can occur. As an employee from FAU A said about the submission sheet FAU B use:

> "I saw [FAU B's] submission sheet and it was very confusing"

To bring home the impact this can have, during the period we were visiting the various locations, one of the IAUs moved from dealing with FAU B to FAU A. The manager of FAU B claimed:

> "It doesn't create problems that we (the FAU's) change communities [i.e. deal with different IAU's]"

However, the situation from the point of view of the IAU was quite different:

> "Everything varies from FAU to FAU"

Dealing with different forms is one part of the problem, but not the only source. For example, the importance of personal contact came out very strongly:

> "I think by moving us from [FAU B] to [FAU A] we lost out on the continuity in the relationship. ...We had one person just specifically to deal with our cases at [FAU B] ... I think we have really noticed the difference from having one person dedicated to all the cases"

Finally, as a reminder of the effects physical location has in the coordination of work, it happens that the local IAU for FAU B is located in the same large office. One of the employees of this IAU whom we were observing got some new information on a case and told us:

> "I'll advise the FAU on this because they also have him in their system. I'll just walk over there and give them a copy"

In this case coordination can therefore be managed in a much more lightweight way.

Overall, the coordination requirements for this process are fairly complex. However, one of the most striking aspects is the impact that different ways of doing the same job can have when coordination is required, and in particular when changes are made to configurations which are isomorphic from an organisational point of view.

Conclusions

The aim of this paper has primarily been to focus on an account of document intensive work in distributed settings and to look at how the practicalities of the work relate to the organisational processes which describe it. One important feature of the work described here is that it entails different groups carrying out "the same" process. One effect of this variability is that it produces opportunities for individual groups to develop new ways of working which can then be shared with others. (The Society does in fact have mechanisms to support sharing via its team-based approach, although we did not look at how effective these are in the work reported here.) On the other hand, it is clear from some of the findings in earlier sections that when different ways of working have been developed and not shared, they can have serious consequences for attempts to reconfigure relationships within the organisation. They introduce boundaries with properties which are not fully understood by those who have to communicate across them. This would appear to be one area where there is potential for improved process integration by paying special attention at the organisational level to the development of the interfaces across which different groups have to communicate. The characterisation of the process to include what we referred to as normative and routine activities provides a way to describe the coordination activities which need to take place, and thus may provide a route to giving them organisational legitimacy in the development of core processes.

Implications for Technology Support

One of our goals in doing this work is to give us a richer baseline from which to develop process support technologies that take good account of the practicalities of getting work done. We would not want to claim that the route to technological support lies in simply fitting technology into the processes and practices as they are currently enacted (cf. Davenport, 1993, Hammer and Champy, 1993). Nevertheless, we believe that developing technologies without an understanding of what it is to do the kind of work being supported is doomed to failure (cf. Landauer, 1995, Button, 1993).

As an example of the kinds of implications we can draw, one of the phenomena which was commonly observed was proceeding in the process with incomplete information from "earlier stages". In their discussion of issues for next generation workflow systems, Abbott and Sarin (1994) identify knowledge work, and this kind of characteristic as ones that need to be addressed. In another part of the project reported here, we have been developing novel techniques for supporting this kind of flexibility in the ordering of workflow (Dourish et al., 1996). The basic techniques we use make use of the process representation as a resource to help guide user action rather than something that "takes over" the enactment of work, which tends to be the effect of most current workflow systems in the marketplace.

It is very likely that some of the overheads which are currently present in the Society's processes could be reduced significantly (e.g. with common access to an on-line database to get more up-to-date status information). It is also clear that many of the interactions which are required could not be easily incorporated into current process support technologies. As one example, direct interaction with customers can be very open-ended. As another, it is inevitable that there will be queries over how to interpret some of the information provided, and indeed as new information comes in, it may force a re-interpretation of older information. The last observation would be important, for example, when considering how to move more information online earlier in the process. It suggests that it may not be sufficient simply to confirm that corroborative information such as bank statements or identity have been checked, but to maintain scanned images of the material for later perusal.

It is clear that some of the vagaries in organising and dealing with information cannot easily be removed since they rest on the customer understanding what is required and making it available. As one of the headquarters staff lamented to us (slightly tongue in cheek!) when discussing process design:

"the biggest problem with customers is they don't understand our processes..."

References

Abbott, K. and Sarin, S. (1994) Experiences with Workflow Management: Issues for the Next Generation. In Proc. ACM Conference on Computer Supported Cooperative Work, CSCW'94, Chapel Hill, NC, October 1994.

Bowers, J. Button, G. and Sharrock, W. (1995) Workflow from Within and Without. In Proc. European Conference on Computer Supported Work, ECSCW'95, Stockholm, Sweden, Sept. 1995.

Button, G. (Ed.) (1993) Technology in Working Order: Studies of Work, Interaction and Technology. Routledge, London.

Davenport, T.H. (1993) Process Innovation: Re-engineering Work Through Information Technology. Harvard Business School Press, Boston, Mass.

Dourish, P. Holmes, J., MacLean, A., Marqvardsen, P., and Zbyslaw, A. (1996) Freeflow: Mediating between Representation and Action in Workflow Systems. In Proc. ACM

Conference on Computer Supported Cooperative Work, CSCW'96, Boston, Mass, Nov 1996.

Hammer, M. and Champy, J. (1993) Re-Engineering the Corporation: A Manifesto for Business Revolution. HarperCollins, New York, NY.

Landauer, T. 1995 The Trouble with Computers: Usefulness, Usability and Productivity. Bradford Books, MIT Press, Cambridge, Mass.

Ould, M. (1995) Business Process Modelling and Analysis for Re-Engineering and Improvement. Wiley, Chichester.

Suchman, L. (1983) Office Procedure as Practical Action: Models of Work and System Design. ACM Transaction on Office Information Systems. 1(4), 320-328.

8 APPROACHES TO STANDARDIZATION OF DOCUMENTS

Kristin Braa and
Tone Irene Sandahl[1]

ABSTRACT
This paper identifies and compares different approaches to standardization of documents in order to enable electronic document exchange based on SGML. Case studies applying the different approaches were conducted. The dilemma between standardization and flexibility is emphasized. An analytical framework has been developed as a means to reveal and categorize limitations, problems and new possibilities associated with the different standardization approaches.

Introduction

This paper focuses on the design and implementation of electronic documents in organizations. Although at least 80 % of corporate electronic information in organizations is in the form of documents, as opposed to database records (Reinhardt, 94), current systems have little access to this information. Traditionally, documents have been static, represented as files on disks. Until PCs were networked, these files usually belonged to only one user and passed from one person to another in printed form. Along with the adoption and diffusion of Internet communication technology, there is a growing interest in exchanging and distributing documents through data networks. Document distribution is necessary not only as a means of exchanging information between people but also as a means to integrate systems.

To enable exchange and distribution of documents through networks, some standardization is necessary (Hanseth et al., 96). In the case of the World Wide

[1] The authors are presented in alphabetic order only.

Web (WWW), the text is marked up in HTML (de facto standard). Thus, all WWW browsers[2] can read and present text (documents) on the Internet in a suitable way, whichever hardware platform is used.

This paper evaluates and compares different approaches to standardization of documents in order to enable electronic document exchange based on SGML. These are approaches to building the infrastructure for document exchange within organizations, and approaches to the division of labour for accomplishing the process. Using SGML is not the only way to achieve standardization. RTF, PDF, and ODA are other examples. However, the case studies presented are concerned with document exchange systems based on SGML.

We have identified three main approaches to standardization: One approach, **"soft" standardization**, is to let the producers of a text write freely and then hire people to go through the text and mark it up. Another approach, which we call **guided standardization**, is to guide text producers to use styles in a word-processor and then convert the documents to SGML. With the third approach, **enforced standardization**, the producers of a text produce the SGML-coded text themselves.

The aim is to study standardization processes, based on different approaches. This paper is based on a comparison of examples of the different approaches, studied in three different organizational settings. An analytical framework is developed as a means to reveal and categorize limitations, problems and new possibilities associated with the different standardization approaches.

The paper is organized as follows: First, the research approach and the theoretical framework are outlined, followed by a brief presentation of SGML. The application of the framework in the organization is then considered. There is a section discussing our findings, which are then summarized in the conclusion.

Research Approach

In this section we will state the background for the selection of cases, and show how we came up with the theoretical framework for analyzing the approaches to electronic document exchange systems found in the cases.

Empirical Work

Comparative case studies were conducted in organizations where different approaches to standardization of document exchange were applied, with special emphasis on the organizational setting and application domain. The selection of cases reflects the ongoing discussion within the SGML community about different approaches to converting non-SGML documents to SGML. Van Herwijnen (90) presents five different approaches: i) Tagging documents with a non-SGML editor,

---

[2] Vendors are making their own version of HTML, this may over time change the compability between the browsers.

ii) using editors that give formatting feedback (e.g. LEXX and DECwrite), iii) adding the tags with a program, iv) imposing structure with style sheets, and v) using native SGML input systems. Organizations that apply at least one of the approaches above were selected. We were, however, not able to find organizations in Norway applying approach i) or ii). The selected cases are: Case 1, Organization of Web service; Case 2, Production and exchange of administrative handbooks; and Case 3, Production of a university catalog, representing approaches iii), iv) and v), respectively. However, we reframed and renamed the approaches (see following section). The theoretical framework presented in the following section was applied as an analytical tool in the comparative studies.

The chain of work tasks in the standardization process involves people in several roles from different parts of the organization. Qualitative interviews were conducted including all those involved in the document exchange process - text producers, text providers, editors, converters, managers, and technical staff - representing use perspectives, organizational perspectives and technical perspectives. In addition, electronic documents that were written by text producers were analyzed with respect to the use of styles (Van Herwijnen´s approach iv). Technical reports documenting the process of standardization were studied, and emails sent to internal distribution lists, reflecting text producers' experiences with the standardization process, were analyzed.

Approaches to standardization of documents

There are several ways to standardize documents for electronic distribution and exchange (e.g. Van Herwijnen, 90). These approaches are, however, viewed from a technical perspective that does not include the use situation or the organizational context. We found that a use perspective on standardization approaches was more applicable and richer, since Van Herwijnen's technical approaches imply preconditions on use practices that are not dealt with. We have, more generally, characterized approaches to standardized document exchange systems as:

1. **"Soft" standardization**: the producer may produce text as before, but the text will be standardized/structured by others or partly converted by programs (related to iii).

2. **Guided standardization**; quasi-standardization where the producer has to follow predefined style sheets and where other people or programs are used to convert the text to suitable code. In terms of SGML, the producer deals with styles to “mark” text elements instead of using tags (related to iv).

3. **Enforced standardization**; the producer of text must work according to the standard. In terms of SGML the producer must mark up the text with use of tags (related to v).

Within the **"soft" standardization** approach the producers of a text use traditional word processing products, like Microsoft Word, AmiPro or WordPerfect. There are no rules or standards that must be applied in the text processing process. Authors usually format the document by choosing the font, font size, margins, and so on, from a toolbar. They are not required to define the different text elements (title, heading, paragraph), nor to define the document structure (title before heading, and heading before paragraph). With respect to understanding the content and the structure in a document, this approach satisfies human user needs, but for the computer it is more or less incomprehensible. Programs may do some conversion, but manual structuring is necessary to standardize such documents in SGML. In this case, the text producers (with their word processor) do not create documents that are "ready" for the SGML-based document system, and manual editing has to be added.

In the **guided standardization** approach, the producers of a text use style sheets in word processors like Microsoft Word, AmiPro and WordPerfect. In terms of SGML, the producer deals with styles to "mark" text elements instead of using tags. There are possibilities for representing structure with the use of style sheets, but the possibilities are restricted (Johnson & Beach, 88; Woods, 91). With the correct use of style sheets, a conversion to SGML can be done automatically using conversion programs (Van Herwijnen, 90).

With **enforced standardization** the producers of a text use an SGML editor, and encode the text in SGML directly. An SGML editor "reads" and "understands" the definition of the document type (DTD). The editor knows the content and the structure, and therefore helps the authors follow the "standardized structure" in the text processing process. The author marks up the text using tags. In SGML the marked title may look like this: <title>This is a title</title>. When one uses an SGML editor, the text is marked up directly. If the coding is done correctly, no further conversion is necessary.

The "soft" standardization approach focuses mainly on the use perspective, while the enforced standardization approach mainly views the standardization process from a technical perspective. The three different approaches to producing SGML-encoded documents are viewed as ideal types, meaning that in reality one may find that different approaches are applied at different stages of the process.

Quality perspectives

To be able to evaluate and compare different approaches to standardization in an organizational context, we apply perspectives in Braa's (95) IS quality framework. The IS quality framework is an analytical tool for understanding and evaluating information systems in an organizational context. The perspectives are the use quality perspective, organizational quality perspective, and technical quality perspective. These perspectives provide a useful contribution to evaluating document exchange systems as well, since in the end designing quality systems is what designing computer-based document exchange systems is all about.

Use quality is seen from a subjective perspective: the end users' actual experience of using the system. Different users and user groups will have different experiences and ideas about what good quality is. In applying a use perspective, the consequences of using SGML for different kind of users (authors, editors, readers etc.) are emphasized.

Information systems are operative in an organizational context and social practice, so that organizational perspectives on quality are also relevant for judging quality.

Quality seen from a technical perspective refers to the software system's structure and performance. The technical quality of a software system is the basis of its functionality (the computer must perform according to expected operations), thus often regarded as the most important.

Braa (95) concludes that neither of the perspectives is sufficient when the aim is to evaluate and understand the quality of information systems in an organizational context. The relationships between the perspectives are closely intertwined, e.g. a robust technical artifact is needed if the system is to function effectively and the artifact is used in an organizational setting, for an organizational purpose. If an IS is not used, it does not have any qualities. How to evaluate the use quality will depend on the perspective of the user or group from which it is regarded.

The approaches to electronic exchange systems, "soft" standardization, guided standardization and enforced standardization, combined with the IS quality perspectives from Braa (95), constitute the collective framework for analyzing and comparing the different cases.

Scope of the research

The study focuses on different approaches to standardization of documents based on SGML. The aim is to study the standardization process, not to do an evaluation of SGML itself, nor to discuss different ways of processing the SGML documents into further applications.

The choice of SGML is based on the fact that it is an international standard (ISO 8879) for describing documents independently of specific processing systems, operating systems, and document models, designed for data longevity and portability, and the fact that there is a fast growing interest in SGML within the private as well as the public sector in Norway.

Standard Generalized Markup Language

There are at least two different ways to achieve document interchangeability between systems: standardization of applications, so that the applications can work on each other's documents, or standardization of the document itself, so that it can be processed by any application. SGML supports the latter solution.

SGML is used to describe the structure and the content of a document (descriptive markup), not its appearance (procedural markup). A descriptive markup system uses markup codes, which provide names to categorize parts of a document. Markup codes such as <descrip> identify a portion of a document and assert of it that "the following item is a description". All the text is coded as plain text. SGML thus enables the interchange of text across platforms, because there is no need for "translation" to any machine-dependencies. The same document can readily be processed by many different pieces of software, each of which can apply different processing instructions to those parts of it that are considered relevant. In addition, different sorts of processing instructions can be associated with the same parts of the file. Since only the structure and/or content of a document is marked, a given viewer of that document can decide what the "look" will be. The markup of the document never changes; only the way that it is interpreted does.

SGML supports the notion of a document type, and hence a document type definition (DTD). An SGML document always has an associated DTD that specifies the rules of the model of the document; for example, a DTD might specify that the document must have a description, and cannot have any warnings that are not immediately followed by one or more specifications. Its parts (description, warning, specification, etc.) and their structure in the DTD formally define the type of a document.

A basic design goal of SGML is to ensure that documents encoded according to its provisions should be portable from one hardware and software environment to another without loss of information.

Application of the framework in the cases

In this section we describe the approaches applied in three different organizational settings. We found that each case mainly applies to one approach. Hence, the approaches are described by our findings from the cases. The description is viewed from the three perspectives: use, organizational, and technical perspective.

"Soft" standardization

Case 1: **Organization of Web service.** The organization is a major public bureaucracy, consisting of several large and independent departments. A common externally oriented Web service was launched in 1995, where governmental information, press releases and publications are published. The aim is to inform the public, thus the service is considered politically important.

A newly established unit herein referred to as the technical editorial board operates the Web service. The technical editors receive documents for publishing via email, on floppy disks, and sometimes on paper. The documents come from a variety of sources. Most employees in the organization use PCs, using AmiPro, Microsoft Word or WordPerfect for word processing. Within the departments individuals decide which documents will be published on the Web service. Documents are normally received directly from the authors, but large publications such as governmental committee reports are often obtained from print shops. These latter documents are already coded in SGML when the technical editors receive them.

The organizational strategy seems to minimize changes in work in the text producers' use situation. The "soft" approach can be explained by the role of the technical editorial board of the Web service. The technical editors have no authority to instruct authors, and make documents available on an "as is" basis, taking whatever steps may be needed (in some cases retyping the text). The staff of the technical editorial board has to manually go through the documents, identifying and understanding the structure. Further, they must either add styles for subsequent conversion to HTML[3] or code the document directly in HTML in order to get the document into a standardized format. Often hybrid documents are received, where some of the styles are simulated in WYSIWYG editors. New tools for conversion are brought into use as they become available. Thus experimenting with tools has been undertaken in order to build competence.

Guided standardization

Case 2: **Production and exchange of administrative handbooks.** In the spring of 1994, it was decided to collect information about existing and related procedures of formal work routines applied in administrative work in a large educational institution. The information was collected into two books: the regulations handbook and the administration handbook. The first step was to make printed documents, standardized by means of styles in Microsoft Word. The next step was to convert the books into SGML and HTML for presentation of the electronic books in the Web viewer. The styles were designed based on negotiation in a working group.

Working with style sheets was perceived as time-consuming by the text producers. They were unfamiliar with the use of styles, and spent much more time than expected in applying styles. The analysis of the styled documents showed that they did not use the style sheets completely. About 25% of the styles in the style sheets were not applied. Instead they used, for example, the style "normal" even if it was logically a heading or a quote. Consequently, manual structural proofreading was necessary before automatic conversion could be accomplished. Thus, the technical situation became more like that in the "soft" standardization approach, with a need for recognition of the structure and adding styles by the technical staff.

A training manual was written, in which the styles were presented and explained. All the text producers received this manual, but very few used it. No training was provided. The result was that the text produced was inconsistent and difficult to use as standardized documents, and was no more standardized than in the situation of "soft" standardization; further use is dependent on manual reconstruction. The results from our study of the use of style sheets show that text producers, as well as technical editors, spent more effort on creating a handbook

---

[3]According to SGML terminology, HTML is a DTD.

than before. The assumptions about automatic conversion failed, because the text producers did not use styles consistently. It was necessary to establish support personnel for completing the styles in documents before conversion, to make up for the lack of consistent use.

Enforced standardization

Case 3: **The production of a university catalog**[4]. Case 3 is a pilot project developing a solution for the production, exchange and distribution of a university's course catalog by means of SGML. The catalog was previously only published on paper. There are about 40 text producers, distributed among about 20 units, involved in maintaining the catalog. The text producers use an SGML editor. The SGML editor incorporates a validating parser that makes it possible to avoid markup errors and invalid structure during editing.

Responsibility for the production of different parts of the catalog is divided between different units at the university. The text producers in the central administration maintain information about all parts except the information from the faculties. They coordinate contributions from other units at the university that will be presented in the catalog. At a lower level, each unit (department) is responsible for its part of the catalog, collecting information and distributing updated information to the students and staff.

The technical staff developed the DTD, which represents the model of the structure and the content of the catalog, with some participation from text producers. The intention was to make the DTD rich enough to be able to retrieve information from databases, to link to other information and to have functions for presenting different views of (some of) the information in the catalog. Programs have been developed for conversion both to HTML, so that the catalog can be presented on the Web, and to PostScript through TeX/LaTeX, for presentation of the catalog on paper. When the information is ready in SGML, the technical staff merges the files to produce the catalog. The catalog as a whole is parsed, and conversion to Web and paper can be done whenever needed.

Users found work with the document exchange system hard and frustrating, especially in the beginning. Use of SGML requires discipline as to the way text is written. Structuring the information according to a DTD creates limitations on work styles. Usually, people can present information their own way using their preferred tools. Dealing with SGML, they felt that flexibility was limited. Others pointed out that work with the catalog had changed. The catalog is still the product; however, using SGML has changed the process. They spent more time writing and editing the catalog than before, because of the new tool and the structuring. Because of the time-consuming process, some got fewer work tasks, and ended up as "experts" on the catalog. In other words, introduction of SGML created specialized work tasks, more like typing pools.

---

[4] A more detailed presentation of this case can be seen in (Jenssen & Sandahl, 96)

From a more organization-oriented perspective, the introduction of SGML required much effort in training and support. Even with planned training, the text producers needed to have access to some form of constantly available user support. They needed help to solve technical problems, to figure out what to do with the different parts of the information, and how to code and where to put the markup. User support created a heavy workload for the technical staff.

As a benefit of introducing SGML, the organization wanted to offer some new services to customers, such as publication on the Web, integration between the catalog and relevant databases, and providing facilities for a matrix on room allocation. From a technical perspective, this is easy to implement because the capabilities are embedded in the structure of the information itself. However, one year after implementation the database integration and the room allocation service were still not implemented.

There has been a change in administrative routines and distribution of responsibility since the SGML implementation. Before the introduction of SGML, the central administration unit was responsible for the production process - deadlines, proofreading after the deadline, new kinds of information in the catalog, etc. Some time after the first production of a computer-based catalog, the technical department assumed responsibility for the production process, without any clear agreement.

From a technical perspective, the document exchange system imports and processes the SGML-encoded document automatically using predefined programs. However, the technical staff detects numerous syntax inconsistencies during the conversion process. Errors in the documents are possible because when users experience too many failure messages on syntax, they switch the validation checker off. The technical staff then has to manually check and mark up the document.

Discussion

The three different cases described above mainly represent three different approaches to standardization of electronic documents. The approaches to standardization are presented in relation to three perspectives: use, organizational, and technical perspectives. This constitutes the framework applied in the discussion below. An outline of the results is presented in Table 1.

Use perspectives

From a use perspective, the "soft" standardization approach differs significantly from the other two approaches. In the "soft" approach the text producers have little, if any, change in their work. They use their word processors the same way as before the introduction of standardization. They format their text manually using a toolbar within the word processor, and the paper copy of the text is seen as the final product. The work organization of the text producers is as before. They do not deal with the standardization directly. There are, however, some restrictions on the layout in some of the documents they produce. The organization wants to have a common profile on some of its information. In this respect, the text producers "fake" the profile using manual formatting. The appearance of the text on paper complies with the profile, but the electronic versions of the text are quite different, because of the use of spaces, tabs, fonts and font sizes. The text producers do find themselves in a flexible work situation when it comes to production of text, and they do not experience any limitation on the process.

Table 1: Summary of the results, applying the framework to the cases.

	"Soft" Standardization	*Guided standardization*	*Enforced standardization*
Use perspectives	• Little change in work content • Little change in work organization • Little change in roles	• Some structure in work • Requires common understanding of styles • "Workaround"	• High structure in work • Change in work content • Change in work organization • New roles emerge • "Workaround"
Organizational perspectives	• Allocation of parallel organizational unit • Allocation of resources to technical staff	• Common agreement on styles • New roles emerge	• Allocation of - training support - user support • common agreement on DTD
Technical perspectives	• Manual conversion • Reconstructing the structure of document • Low compatibility • "Workaround" • Need for creative conversion tools	• Medium automatic conversion • Medium compatibility • Need for tools (text processors) facilitating styles	• Automatic conversion • High compatibility • Need for development of advanced editors

Within the guided approach, the text producers have to use predefined styles. Observations in the second case study show that text producers have problems using styles correctly and consistently. They are not familiar with the use of styles and think of them as "difficult to use". Some text producers stated that the style mechanisms have an unsatisfactory design, and do not necessarily support the idea of structuring. When they did not know how to use a style, or which style to use, they just dropped it and used "normal" instead and then simulated the layout. Further, they might use the style "quote" on an ordinary paragraph, because they knew that the "quote style" was formatted as italic text. Gasser (86) defines "workaround" as the development of new ways of using computer systems, which were not intended by the original design. Working around the predefined style sheets by "faking" the styles is easily done, and many text producers did. Thus, the situation of text processing was not experienced as very standardized. It seems that motivation for using styles as a part of the standardization process was lacking. An emphasis in user training on understanding how use of styles is part of the standardization process, and why consistent use is crucial for achieving that, might help.

In the enforced standardization approach, both the work routines and tasks were changed because of SGML and the SGML tools. The text producers' work situation was structured by the predefined DTD, and was experienced as restricted with respect to the order of work tasks, as well as the work itself. However, when they experienced the structure as too annoying they switched the validation checker off. This "workaround" occurs and creates a breakdown in the automatic conversion routines.

From the use perspective, the "soft" approach is the most flexible, and few changes are observed in work situations. The standardization process will not affect the text producers. In the guided, and even more in the enforced approach, the users feel that the work is strongly affected by the standard.

Organizational perspectives

From an organizational point of view, the three approaches have different effects. Within the "soft" approach there was a need for establishing an additional unit within the existing organization - just for converting the documents into formats that are more appropriate in relation to standardization. Since the text producers are left out of the standardization itself, others had to do the job. In case 1, the staff developed competence by experimenting with the conversion tools. This resulted in delays in publications on the Web.

In the cases of "soft" standardization and guided standardization the technical staff is part of the work chain of standardization, and will easily be seen as a bottleneck between the text producers and the final product. The text has to go through a standardization process in another part of the organization before it is ready for further application.

Within the guided standardization approach the organizational effort is on at least three different levels. First of all, it is necessary to negotiate common style sheets (templates) for different document types. These style sheets are standardized for the organization. Second, the text producers have to learn to use the style sheets, and how to style documents. As observed in case 2, production of administrative university manuals, and also reported in Sørgaard and Sandahl (97), this is not necessarily a trivial task. The assumptions about automatic conversions failed, because the text producers did not use styles consistently. Third, a parallel organizational unit was established and given resources to make up for the lack of standardized documents received from the users. Our experience is that an understanding of the rationale for using styles consistently is necessary; the role of styles in the standardization process should be emphasized.

Within the enforced standardization approach, the workload is placed on the shoulders of the text producers. They have to work within a structured environment enforcing standardized work tasks, and to learn the principles of SGML as well as a new tool. There has to be an agreement on a DTD, which is an organizational challenge (Jenssen & Sandahl, 96). Modeling the DTD in a way that supports the work processes. not only modeling the document as a product, needs to be an organizational effort. Much user training and user support is needed, and the organization has to allocate resources to do this. In addition, SGML expertise is necessary, which takes time to achieve. Technical competence is important in this approach.

Table 2: "Workaround" creates breakdowns and leads to a technical situation as in "soft" standardization.

	"Soft" Standardization	*Guided Standardization*	*Enforced Standardization*
Use Perspective		Workaround (faking the style use)	Workaround (switching off the checker)
Organizational Perspective			
Technical Perspective	-Manual standardization -Reconstructing the structure of document -Low compability -Need for creative convertion tools		

In the case of the catalog production we observed a change in responsibility for the production process, which was transferred from the department (or faculty) level before SGML implementation to the technical department coordinating the whole production process. As far as we know this was not due to a conscious decision.

From a technical perspective we see that the potential for document exchange systems can be achieved at the organizational level, but this has so far not been implemented. Managers have little involvement in the implementation of document exchange systems. This is often regarded mainly as a technical task. Organizational perspectives need to be addressed explicitly; this implies challenges for further research.

Technical perspectives

From a technical viewpoint, the "soft" approach necessitates a great deal of manual conversion. Software tools that identify layout as structure can do some conversion;

otherwise people have to standardize the text manually by using styles or directly into SGML. Since the text has a restricted structure, and no defined content, the text has to be treated before further use is possible.

The guided approach could provide for automatic conversion, if the styles were used in a correct and consistent manner. Since the use of styles in a way defines the structure and to some extent the content of the document, conversion to other formats is easier to provide (Sørgaard & Sandahl, 97).

In the enforced approach, the technical condition for further processing is directly present. This, however, requires correct and consistent code.

"Workarounds" in the text production create breakdowns of the standardization process in both guided and enforced standardization, and must be compensated for by manual conversion efforts like those in "soft" standardization (Table 2). Observations in the cases reported on in this paper show that breakdowns occur easily, lead to bottlenecks in the standardization process and cause delayed or unpublished documents. To avoid breakdowns and gain the benefits of standardization, adequate support is needed, with regard to both better tools and training.

Standardization and Flexibility

The application of the three perspectives shows that there are differences in who gets the benefits and who performs the work, as discussed in Grudin (94), depending on which approach is applied. Working according to standards will doubtless limit the flexibility of work styles but may create new flexibility in terms of new services or products. The relationship between standardization on the one hand and flexibility on the other is illustrated in Table 3.

The relationship between standardization and flexibility appears different depending on which perspective and which approach is applied. In the "soft" standardization approach the use perspective is considered dominant and flexibility in the use situation is very much present. The conversion routines in the same approach provide a low degree of standardization, thus implying manual reconstructing of documents and manual conversion.

In the enforced standardization approach, the technical perspective is dominant and flexibility with respect to developing new technical solutions will be supported, while the work processes are conceived of as highly standardized. The DTDs enforce a high level of detail for encoding the information. To support the design of new functionality and provision of new services based on information in the document, the DTD has to be well defined. On the other hand, if the DTD is very structured, more user problems will occur. Technically, it is easier to go from a highly structured DTD towards a less structured one, than to add structure. Consequently, the future functionality and services must be envisioned from the very beginning of the DTD modeling. This represents a challenge in DTD modeling.

The DTD modeling is seen as a model of the document, thus a technical matter, not as a model of the work with documents in an organizational context. A DTD that seems appropriate as a technical solution may not be appropriate for the text producers. IT departments are the driving force in DTD-modeling, and their understanding of the work in organizations is limited. In the end, the standardization effort done in the organization might not give the expected flexibility, because the DTD is not satisfactorily designed and can be difficult to change.

Table 3: Standardization and Flexibility

	"Soft" Standardization	*Guided standardization*	*Enforced standardization*
Use perspectives	• high degree of flexibility in use • low degree of standardization of work routines	• some flexibility in use • some standardization in work routines	• low degree of flexibility in use • high degree of standardization in work routines
Organizational perspectives	• low degree of flexibility regarding new applications • low degree of control of product / work	• some flexibility regarding new applications • some control over products	• high degree of flexibility regarding new possibilities of applications • high control over products and work routines
Technical perspectives	• little degree of flexibility regarding (developing) new technical solutions • low degree of standardization of conversion routines	• some flexibility regarding (developing) new technical solutions • some standardization of conversion routines	• high degree of flexibility regarding (developing) new technical solutions • high degree of standardization of conversion routines

The guided standardization approach is a hybrid attempting to provide some flexibility in use situations and some standardization in conversion routines. However, our observations in the cases discussed in the present paper show that consistent use is critical in order to avoid breakdowns in conversion routines, which create a technical situation similar to the "soft" approach (Table 2).

In the organizational perspective, the tension between standardization and flexibility appears as the trade-off between the costs of dealing with standardization (e.g. user support, training) and the benefits of flexibility with respect to new services and products. To create flexibility from an organizational point of view, such as providing new services and products, standardization is required.

The relationship between the approaches

The boundary between two of the categories, "soft" standardization and guided standardization, is blurred in the case of the organization of a Web service. As an initial step, the "soft" standardization approach was chosen. The costs were that a heavy workload was imposed on the technical editorial board (reducing the number of documents being published). After a new conversion tool became available, in which the technical staff saw the potential of using styles, they subsequently begun to emphasize the use of templates (style sheets). Products and tools change fast in the early stage of Web technology, and, as observed, they affect work practices. However, use and availability of document templates or style sheets vary widely between the units. We saw several examples of difficulties in applying styles consistently; consequently, manual conversion work was still needed.

The organization's longer-term aim turns out to be to proceed with an enforced standardization approach. The plan is to install SGML editors at the front desks in the departments, and have the coding done by the receptionists in addition to their customary work tasks. At this stage this has not been implemented. Time will show whether this is a realistic strategy or not. However, it seems that different approaches were applied step by step due to increasing maturity in use, motivation, technology and competence. The strategy seems to be to start small with "soft" standardization in order to gain motivation, knowledge and experience, and then to proceed with the next approach.

Going from the "soft" and guided standardization approaches to the enforced standardization approach involves changing the text producer's tools. In the "soft" and the guided standardization approach, well-known WYSIWYG editors are usually applied. SGML editors are not necessarily WYSIWYG and are more loosely connected to the end product. Traditionally, with the use of WYSIWYG editors, the text producers control the whole process: from editing through manipulation, formatting and presenting the documents. When an SGML editor is applied, this is not necessarily the case. In addition, the DTD sets restrictions on how to edit, because of the predefined structure, and to some extent, content. Thus, the transformation process from word processors to SGML editors can be hard for the text producers.

Conclusion and further research

The aim of this paper has been to discuss different approaches to the standardization of documents, and to categorize limitations, problems and possibilities within the different approaches according to use perspectives, organizational perspectives and technical perspectives. The framework has been applied in three organizations to analyze the experience and to present the results. Although the borders between the identified approaches, "soft" standardization, guided standardization and enforced standardization are blurred in some situations, the characteristics of the approaches proved to be useful. We found that the framework supports a more holistic evaluation of the standardization process and of the possibilities of achieving success, by explicitly regarding each perspective. By applying this framework, different, problematic, and possible defective aspects of the approaches may be revealed. An overview of the resources needed to improve the process may then be achieved.

Which approach to choose will depend on a variety of factors, i.e. staff competence, organizational effort, technical support and technical infrastructure - or it could be dealt with as an organizational choice: where to implement changes in the organization.

For each approach, we have found contrasts in who will get the workload and who will get the benefit. Due to the chain of work tasks involved in document exchange, it is not obvious that those doing the work will be those experiencing the benefit. This situation creates a motivation problem and is a major obstacle to the accomplishment of successful document exchange.

In the "soft" standardization approach the technical staff got the extra workload, due to the effort to convert the text into SGML, and the producers of the text got the benefit in the sense that no changes in work situations were added. In the enforced standardization approach the producers of the text had to apply a new authoring tool, and, to some degree, make use of SGML. Consequently, the text producers definitely experienced an extra workload, especially in the beginning. The technical staff benefited because there was little or no correction in the SGML files. However, they were busy providing user support and solving user problems. The user problems of working with the standard have to be solved in order to more easily achieve the text producers' acceptance of the document standardization. In the guided standardization approach, success depends on whether, or how, the styles are applied. If the style mechanisms are consistently used, it is proportionately easy to convert automatically to SGML. We have found that "workaround" in use situations in both guided and enforced standardization approaches imply a technical situation like that of "soft" standardization.

The issue of standardization and flexibility will be different depending on the perspective and the approach being applied. Flexibility in use is experienced within the "soft" standardization approach, while the technological solutions within the same approach are not flexible at all. While the work processes are conceived as highly standardized and difficult to apply, flexibility in technological solutions is supported within an “enforced standardization” approach, although not automatically adopted. Organizational effort and acceptance are necessary. Seen from the organizational perspective the tension between standardization and flexibility results in the costs of dealing with standardization (e.g., user support, training) while the benefits of flexibility appear as new services, products, etc.

Independent of the strategy applied, we have observed that the organizational potential of SGML has not been realized so far. The situation is rather that the documents are implemented as an electronic version of paper documents, and new functionality is seldom added. This can partly be explained by the fact that the work related to text production, user support, corrections and conversions is so time-consuming that the further development of new functionality has little priority. Another important factor is that organizational and managerial involvement and commitment are lacking. We have indicated the necessity of considering organizational needs as early as the DTD modeling stage. So far it seems that the organizations are only paying the costs of the standardization, and not yet obtaining the advantages. Since the potential is not realized, there may also be reason to ask questions about the usefulness of SGML itself. Challenges on how to take advantage of the potential of the new medium, as well as firm evaluation of SGML itself, need to be addressed in further research.

Time and product development are significant variables in this area of early adoption of electronic document technology, making it necessary to carry out longitudinal studies. A challenge for further research will be to develop tools and techniques to reduce the bottlenecks; tools for supporting the use of styles; tools for "embedding" the standardization into the document processing; as well as techniques for including users in the standardization process - in addition to putting organizational needs on the agenda from the very beginning of the design of the document exchange systems.

There are, however, some problems in comparing the cases for various reasons: The products are different. They exist in different domains, and the document exchange systems have been introduced for different reasons. However, this study "paints a picture" of typical application domains and of a chaotic situation of immature technology as well as lack of competence and experience.

Acknowledgments

Sincere thanks to Joan Greenbaum, Ole Hanseth, Andrew Clement, Pål Sørgaard, Håvard Fosseng and Jonathan Grudin for constructive comments on drafts of this paper. This work was supported by the Research Council of Norway through its grant to the BEST program and the Swedish Transport & Communications Research Board (Kommunikationsforskningsberedningen) through its grant to the "Internet project."

References

Alschuler, L. (1995) ABCD ... SGML A users guide to structured information, International Thompson Computer Press, London

Braa, K. (1995) Beyond Formal Quality of Information Systems Design, Ph.D Thesis, Department of Informatics, University of Oslo.

Checkland, P. & Scholes, J. (1990) Soft Systems Methodology in Action, John Wiley & Sons, New York.

Derose, S. J., Durand D. G. (1994) Making Hypermedia Work. A User's Guide to HyTime. Kluwer Academic Publishers.

Gasser, L. (1986) The Integration of Computing and Routine Work, in ACM Transactions on Office Information Systems, Vol 4, No. 3, p 205–225.

Grudin, J. (1994) Eight challenges for developers, Communications of the ACM, Volume 37, Number 1, p. 93–105.

Goldfarb, C., F (1990). The SGML Handbook, Claredon Press, Oxford.

Gruber, T., R., Vemuri, Sunil, Rice, J. (1995) Virtual documents that explain How Things Work: Dynamically generated question-answering documents, at http://www-ksl.standford.edu/people/gruber/virtual

Hanseth, O., Monteiro, E. and Hatling, M. (1996) Developing information infrastructure standards: the tension between standardization and flexibility, Science Technology and Human Values, 1996 (To be published??).

Kim, K. K. (1989) User Satisfaction: A Synthesis of Three Different Perspectives, in Journal of Information Systems.

Kitchenham (1989) Software quality assurance, in Microprocessors and Microcomputers, Vol. 13 (6), pp 373-381.

Jenssen, A. E, Sandahl, T. I. (1996) Conflicts between the possibilities and the reality in the field of structured electronic documents. Experiences from a large-scale SGML-project. In Proceedings of the 19th Information Systems Research Seminar in Scandinavia, 1996

Johnson, J., and Beach, R. J. (1988). Styles in document editing systems. Computer, 21(1), January 1988.

Reinhardt, A. (1994) Managing the New Document, in Byte, Vol 19, No. 8, August 1994.

Smith, J., M. (1992). SGML and related standards. Document description and processing language. Ellis Horwood Limited.

Sørgaard, P, and Sandahl, T.I (1997) Problems with styles in word processing: a weak foundation for electronic publishing with SGML. In 30th Hawaii International Conference on System Sciences (HICSS), Wailea, Hawaii, Jan 7-10, 1997

Travis, B. E. and Waldt, D. C. (1996) The SGML implementation Guide, Springer, 1996

van Herwijen, E. (1990) Practical SGML. Kluwer Academic Publishers, Dordrecht, Boston, London.

Woods, M., J. (1991) Techniques for textual mark-up using Microsoft Word. University Computing, 1991, 13, 171-179.

9 INFORMATION AND PROCESS INTEGRATION FROM USER REQUIREMENTS ELICITATION: A CASE STUDY OF DOCUMENTS IN A SOCIAL SERVICES AGENCY

Stephan Greene and Anne Rose

Introduction

The Maryland Department of Juvenile Justice (DJJ) is designing a new information system to replace its legacy system for youth case management. DJJ is responsible for juveniles who have violated the law or who are a danger to themselves or others. The major goal of the new information system is to improve the process of juvenile case management, and thus deliver more effective services to youths, by better facilitating the tracking of case information and the production and handling of case-related documents.

The primary challenge in designing the new system is to optimize the integration of existing processes, information, and documents. The Human-Computer Interaction Laboratory (HCIL) at the University of Maryland, in conjunction with Cognetics Corporation, is working with DJJ to develop detailed designs for the new system, to be specified in a request for proposals (RFP) distributed to contractors bidding to implement the final system. The design effort has included a great deal of close interaction with DJJ personnel at all levels.

This case study discusses the value of, and some practical methods for, a detailed analysis of enterprise documents, including direct elicitation from users of their document-centered information requirements. We discuss the benefits to process integration resulting from the document-centered work. As this work has been done in the context of the design and specification of a new information technology application, from a user-centered design perspective we discuss in particular the benefits of coupling the results of the document analysis effort with innovative user interface techniques, including visualization techniques for personal histories and Personal Role Management (Shneiderman and Plaisant 1994). Role management is an approach to user interfaces that organizes information in terms of the separate roles users play in an enterprise, rather than requiring users to manually graft these information links onto the usual file-oriented, hierarchical mechanisms of desktop management. Data collected during the document analysis directly supports the application of these user interface techniques for organization and visualization in the system design. The result is better support for user role management, particularly of documents, which will increase the system's potential for fostering enterprise-wide information and process integration.

Context

A role for information technology in business process re-engineering (BPR) is well recognized, though not without more than a bit of controversy, disagreement, and lack of predictive empirical research (Barothy, Peterhans & Bauknecht 1995; Davenport 1993; Hammer and Champy 1993; Kaltoff 1994). Ongoing efforts on many fronts are working toward developing methodologies for designing appropriate information technology to support organizational process improvement. For the purposes of this paper, we will consider aspects of information technology design in support of *process integration*, defined as the general "reorganization of structural relationships among process entities for enhanced performance" (IPIC 1996). This definition captures the central emphasis on structural changes to process rather than the replacement of specific process entities, leaving the existing process structure intact.

Process integration is highly interrelated with *information integration*, defined as "the creation of new, value-added information out of existing information, often from multiple, unrelated sources" (IPIC 1996). Information integration can be seen as a way to support new business interpretations and decisions from the existing collection of possibly unrelated information available within an enterprise. Information integration is thus "a means of bridging information and processes by generating an actionable interpretation of information in the context of a specific process" (IPIC 1996).

Documents are increasingly recognized as a class of information-conveying vehicles that are highly critical, indispensable business process components. At the same time, document content is least amenable to information integration given the structural complexity and demanding life cycle management requirements of documents (Bearman 1994; Cox 1995; IPIC 1996; Penn 1983).

Background

Most documents at DJJ are produced manually, often involving the compilation of aggregate information, repeated copying of previously collected information, or the referencing of disjoint records distributed across many offices. In addition, DJJ feels that its legacy system is not able to provide the database reports needed to conduct useful analyses of DJJ operations. Data entry into the old system is considered a black hole from which little of use is extractable. Many reports are only possible through special requests submitted to central system administration and require several days' turnaround time. Addressing these functional shortfalls in database reporting and document production and handling should bring significant benefit in terms of time and cost savings, and should be attainable with a cost-effective level of effort (Saunderson 1995).

Many DJJ documents are not only critical and actionable interpretations of information, but are also legally required and admissible instruments. Given the significance to DJJ of document-based information, the design of the new system must not only accurately capture on-screen data and functionality for end users, it must have a fully integrated document production component. Completely eschewing the myth of the paperless office, DJJ recognizes the permanence of the document. In all its forms, the document is a key business process artifact that is valuable for its unique graphic abilities to support human comprehension, produced and maintained for its evidentiary or reference purposes (Johnson 1983a). DJJ's new information system must represent a migration to a truly comprehensive workflow management system that includes support for the production and routing of documents. The analysis of documents has emerged as a focal point for defining system functional requirements, as documents emphasize information content, information flow, and recordkeeping requirements. Documents are a reflection of the character of an organization.

A number of organizational constraints complicate current document use and will affect the effort to improve the handling of documents. To begin with, DJJ in not monolithic. At a high level, DJJ is an independent agency of the executive branch of state government that answers directly to the state governor. Both the governor's office and the legislature determine DJJ's operating context, and place specific information demands on DJJ in formulating relevant legislation, budgets, and regulations.

At a lower level, DJJ must interact closely with many external, independent entities which control information input to DJJ and control information output by DJJ. For example, the State's Attorney's Office (SAO) must review cases recommended by DJJ for formal court action. The SAO may approve, reject, or modify the recommendations of DJJ, which must then pursue the case as directed by the SAO. Each jurisdiction in the state has its own police department with its own standards for police reports and for the formulation of specific criminal allegations related to the relevant incidents and perpetrators. In addition, the judicial system varies among jurisdictions with respect to many procedures, and even varies at the level of the individual judge. These differences have direct impact on the case management processes of DJJ and on the documents it must produce in the course of carrying them out. These regional and jurisdictional variances must be accommodated within the new information system; they challenge the degree of standardization and information integration attainable. The key to this work will be to identify and exploit opportunities for information and process integration where possible, while maintaining the ability to deal with varied external constraints. Work on the design of the new system, in particular document-related functional requirements assessment, has highlighted these issues within DJJ and is driving new policy initiatives which, while just beginning, may eventually begin to support integration with external processes at a higher level, perhaps through interfaces to external systems, affording some greater potential for document standardization as well.

These issues suggest that process integration in a public social services agency like DJJ is not straightforward. It will be difficult to quantify success, given that at DJJ success means to improve the lives of troubled youth and their families and to protect public safety. The potential of the new system is to allow case managers to spend more time with youths and less time seeking information and composing or referencing documents. In addition, the new system should afford better data analysis on aggregate youth information, and more sophisticated reporting and documentation of that analysis, to better measure performance.

The constraints outlined above highlight the fact that a not-for-profit, social services organization such as DJJ presents some significant and unique complications in achieving process integration. At the same time, the potential benefits to the organization and to the society it serves make the effort worth pursuing. Many other types of organizations undoubtedly operate under similar circumstances, and could perhaps benefit from our results.

Approach

We have used iterative, interlocking methods for determining how best to accommodate documents in the design of the new system. They included data gathering from stakeholders at DJJ, analysis of the data gathered and of the documents themselves, and evolving system prototypes subjected to iterative usability testing. Our approach to gathering and analyzing information about documents is grounded in the literature of information and records management, and archival theory, where the unwavering significance of the document as an information source has long been recognized (Johnson 1983a, 1983b). An information and records management program is an organizational attempt to more effectively and systematically manage information resources, which is a major goal of the new DJJ system. To ensure a successful program, a comprehensive and detailed survey of existing records is considered the crucial first step (Kane 1978; Kubicki 1985; Saffady 1992). Records may be in any form or media, including paper, electronic, and others. Within DJJ, virtually all records are in the form of paper documents, with a small portion produced on paper from electronic sources. Thus for DJJ, the records survey was essentially a survey of paper documents. We began the survey by compiling an inventory of existing DJJ documents.

To complete the records survey, the document inventory was annotated with information about each document's content and the context of its use. This information is required for effective information management in general (Wolchak 1986), and is recognized as critical to the design of information technology to address the management of documents (Barry 1994; Hendley 1995a; Kay 1994). In deciding how to properly characterize a document, we were guided by a particularly thorough set of functional requirements designed for electronic records management, including the management of documents, that is being developed at the University of Pittsburgh by Richard J. Cox and his associates (Cox 1995). To mention them briefly, these requirements hold that electronic records must be:

- Compliant with regulations
- Responsibly managed
- Implemented and employed at all times
- Consistently used to insure credibility
- Comprehensive, to cover all organizational transactions
- Identifiable as to their discrete purpose
- Complete, reflecting the content, structure and context of the events they document, and thus:
    - Accurate
    - Understandable
    - Meaningful
- Authorized by appropriate records creators
- Preserved, maintaining content over time, and thus:
    - Inviolate
    - Coherent
    - Auditable
- Removable, with authorization, leaving an audit trail
- Exportable to other systems
- Accessible, meaning:
    - Available
    - Renderable
    - Evidential
- Redactable, in that contents can be masked for security reasons.

These functional requirements speak to the need for the adequacy of records, or as in this case study, of documents. Adequate records are those that allow reconstruction of the activities or decisions that created them. An organization such as DJJ deals with sensitive family and personal issues, and must comply with the appropriate legal standards in doing so. The issue of adequate records, or adequate documentary information, is thus intimately tied to many of DJJ's organizational processes. In the design of new information technology for DJJ, we have attempted to begin to meet the requirements of adequacy by gathering the right information and conducting or facilitating appropriate analyses of existing DJJ documents. We have identified the persons involved in the creation and use of each document in order to meet requirements such as compliance, responsibility, authority, and accessibility. We have analyzed and redesigned documents in order to meet requirements such as consistency, identifiability, and completeness. And we have prioritized documents in order to gauge the relative importance of each of these requirements for individual documents.

Data Gathering

Working from the compiled inventory of documents, we began with a cursory survey of the documents, creating a record for each in a relational database to be used to manage data in the analysis. Documents were identified as either forms, short reports, aggregate statistical reports, or correspondence. They were then clustered according to their relevance to functions within DJJ, such as intake procedures, medical care, education, and interaction with the courts. Multiple variations of the same document, in use at different offices, were identified and grouped. Excluded from entry into the database and thus from further consideration were all documents not related to youth case management, such as personnel documents. The new system is not intended to support any functionality in those areas. The assigned document categorizations were later revised and refined in consultation with DJJ, as no general system of document classification was in use internally at DJJ. Taking all document types together, the resulting inventory contained roughly 300 distinct documents, 57 of which had two or more variants, with some having as many as eight or nine variants.

We used a set of user segment names to begin to identify individuals involved with each document. The user segments were previously defined from information gathered during site visits and interviews with DJJ personnel, and from analysis of a set of process maps produced internally. The user segment definitions had been circulated to and approved by stakeholders at DJJ, and have been serving as a common reference list of explicitly defined target end users that guides the system design. In attempting to identify the user segments relevant to each document, however, we discovered that the process maps, formal descriptions of all internal DJJ processes, did not systematically encode information about documents. It became clear that eliciting information about documents directly from DJJ personnel would be necessary. Thus we held a series of document workshops with approximately 20 representatives from DJJ with the knowledge and authority to describe and revise documents. For context, we started the first workshop by giving participants a general introduction to the issue of adequacy and of the role of documents in organizational function in order to stimulate broad, critical thinking. This was followed with a discussion of specific questions about documents.

Time limitations forced us to focus on a few key points during the workshops. Specific questions were grouped into two main tasks. The first task was to annotate each document with meta-information about its users and its priority. The second task was to identify, analyze, and, if needed, revise and standardize the information content and structure of each document. Participants were asked to systematically examine each document in the inventory and supply requested information, organized as follows:

- Document Meta-information:
  - Identify source users and divisions
  - Identify destination users and divisions
  - Identify users with access
  - Identify users with authorization
  - Prioritize according to:
    - Frequency
    - Effort
    - Criticality

- Document Content:
  - Identify field contents
  - Review field structure

The document content coding scheme in terms of field contents and field structure is broadly defined. Many DJJ document are forms, or have parts that are forms, but others contain significant narrative portions. Generally, there is some structure to the narrative sections, and these areas were considered "fields" for the purposes of the workshops.

There is an inherent danger in attempting to characterize a document in any fixed sense. Workshop participants were instructed to provide a snapshot of their current thoughts about documents, with the knowledge that changes would certainly occur and that the system would be flexible enough to accommodate them. In addition, factors such as changes in criticality will be accommodated within the system by allowing user-specified alerts to be attached to documents, with appropriate routing and email notification taking place. Documents subject to greater variability were not systematically encoded as such, but as these concerns were revealed, informal notes were made and links to specific functional requirements have been articulated in the RFP.

Document Meta-Information

The identification of **source users** and **divisions** is an attempt to capture the context of the document's creation. The source user segments are the original producers of the document. Source divisions are defined as either the organizational divisions internal to DJJ or the external agency in which the document is typically produced.

The identification of destination users and divisions is an attempt to characterize how documents are put to use. Destination users are the varied consumers of information in documents, including, in this case, both DJJ user segments and individuals at external agencies. Participants were encouraged to augment the list of internal user segments to adequately capture the flow of documents. Users at external agencies, such as judges, prosecutors, and federal auditors, as well as individuals such as parents of trouble youths or victims of juvenile crimes, were not part of the internal user segment list, but were identified on an as-needed basis. In addition, a case file or other form of permanent storage was suggested as an important kind of pseudo destination user. Destination divisions include the DJJ division of internal users, and external entities, such as the educational, medical, law enforcement, or judicial agencies with which DJJ regularly exchanges documents in the course of youth case management.

Access and authorization are important concerns for DJJ, where confidentiality and clear lines of responsibility must be maintained. Using the augmented user segments, participants were asked to identify the users with clearance to access the information in a document, as well as those who must give signed authorization to the document.

Prioritization of documents is very important given limited resources for system development and the likelihood of its incremental rollout. In addition, eliciting information about the priority of documents helps to identify those for which certain functional requirements, such as compliance with regulations, are most important. Three separate scales were used to characterize priority. The scales were the frequency of a document's production, the amount of effort required to produce a document, and a document's criticality with respect to decision making and organizational activity. Priority will be given to those documents most frequent, critical, and difficult to produce. Frequencies were expressed in terms of the percentage of the appropriate "situations" in which a document is produced. For example, an Intake Decision Report document was characterized as being produced for "100% of admissions." Other documents were characterized on a periodic basis. For example, a case manager's monthly case load report was characterized as being produced monthly for each case manager. Coupled with statistics on the number of intake cases and case managers on staff in each office, reasonably accurate measures of the volume of each document can be estimated.

Document Content

The **content** and **structure** of each document was evaluated for its completeness, identifiability, and consistency. Participants were asked to standardize variants of equivalent documents, to analyze each document's structure and content, and to produce example revised versions of each document. Emphasis was placed on analyzing a document's information fields. Participants were asked to consider the appropriateness and adequacy of both the discrete and narrative information fields found in documents, and to identify the typical content of each field. Field contents may be a limited set of possible field values, or a discrete value such as a case or petition number. Other fields may be structured narratives, in which something like a psychological evaluation is documented in narrative fashion with prompts for specific areas of content. By analyzing and potentially revising each document's structure and content, and identifying its typical use within the organization, the documents are not only improved but made more understandable to those outside the organization, with system designers and implementers being the primary beneficiaries. There was no conflict between the document characterizations provided by their users and creators, and the desire of designers and implementers to create a standard coding scheme. The workshops collected information at a level well above implementation details.

Results

Although the workshops were an aggressive attempt to carefully analyze over 300 documents, they were extremely productive in gathering useful information. Despite some initial resistance by participants to addressing lengthy and sometimes tedious issues, overall response to the workshops was extremely positive. Participants recognized the benefits of the effort for the design of the new information system, as well as for immediate application to their current jobs. Responses to the requested information were agreed upon, and revised and standardized versions of documents were successfully negotiated. The document meta-information was entered into a relational database holding the inventory of documents to support further analysis and to provide reports on documents for the system specification. Revised and annotated versions of all documents were entered into word processing files and will serve to further specify the system design. In addition, the information gathered on document content was linked to a data dictionary based on the data elements in the current system and on data elements mandated by regulation. Given the variety of documents used and produced by DJJ, we will also be certain to meet the information content needs of daily case management as well as research and reporting on the effectiveness of DJJ programs and services. The meta-information in the database describes each document in terms of the user segments that handle each document, and in what way. In addition, it characterizes the routing of the document for authorization. Functional requirements for workflow support of different users segments can thus be linked directly to the documents that must be handled by that user.

Current document status results from the document workshops are as follows:

Supported by the system as electronic documents:	**61**
Supported by the system as images:	**10**
Not supported by the system:	**135**
Merged into other documents:	**29**
Eliminated, no longer in use:	**7**
Local Documents:	**16**
Status Pending:	**19**
Subsumed by the system's user interface:	**21**

The documents to be supported as electronic documents have been revised and annotated, entered into electronic word processing files, and checked against the data dictionary to ensure database support for their production. The revised versions of these 61 documents reflect the content of the 29 documents that were merged into them. Some documents, mostly external documents and medical documents, will be supported only as images. The 135 documents not to be included in the system were designated as such for various reasons, such as them being rarely used, or used only by certain offices, and/or simply not being significant enough to consider for inclusion. Local documents are those in use only at specific offices, and which will be considered for inclusion in later iterations of the system. A few documents were found to be no longer be in use, and the status remains unclear for 19 documents, pending policy and program reviews and discussions with others in the department not participating in the workshops. The 21 documents marked as "subsumed" are those for which the desktop interface of the system will provide identical information, along with options for printing. They will not be considered further as documents, although their content was checked against the data dictionary as well. Typical of these documents was a caseload list for an individual case manager. Such as list is now central to the system view designed for case managers.

In addition, roughly equivalent contents were found for about a third of the contents of more than two dozen functionally distinct documents, primarily consisting of youth identification information such as name, address, date of birth, and case numbers. The standardization efforts worked to make these contents identical, thus streamlining information and simplifying the specification of system requirements. These results should facilitate process integration by allowing the collection of information about youths at any point in their interaction with DJJ to be usable at other points of contact within the department. With agreement on document content, information can be collected once and used repeatedly by workers throughout the department with responsibilities in vastly different areas, such as counseling, medical care, or education. Little or no information capture was lost from the standardization work. Participants from different jurisdictions generally found that information being collected by others would be of use to them as well. As an example, in the case of fields containing enumerated types, standardization produced a superset of existing type enumerations, (along with some terminological standardization). While not all users may make use of all options in an enumeration, no useful differences were eliminated, as discussions focused successfully on what information really mattered to the work at hand. In the end, greater but more precisely articulated options were provided.

The examination of some specific documents provided a unique forum for the discussion of long entrenched and recalcitrant problems within the organization. Lively debate was sparked, new information was shared among representatives from different jurisdictions, and some significant policy initiatives were undertaken. In analyzing document contents, occasionally opposing responses emerged, and points of contention were often settled by reference to internal policy documents, when available, or by turning to the Annotated Code of Maryland as the final authority. The design of revised documents benefited from these policy revisitations by ensuring their compliance to regulation, identifiability as to their purpose, and the consistency of their use and thus the credibility of their contents. A planned second review of documents by executive staff will further ensure the regulatory compliance of all documents. The document analysis tasks of the workshops were thus extremely valuable starting points for discussing important issues of process and policy.

Discussions of documents and policy have in some cases led to the identification of specific opportunities for process integration at DJJ. These results illustrate the interrelationships between distinct organizational components. Policies (and standards) constrain processes, which are in turn implemented by procedures that are supported by tools, such as information technology. Our results underscore the fact that documents are supporting tools in the implementation of processes that are closely allied with information technology tools. Both must support procedures in the implementation of processes while conforming to policies and standards. More importantly, desired changes to the documents that ultimately implement policy can suggest opportunities to affect process improvements and, in turn, policy modifications.

An example comes from a policy initiative motivated by the examination of a document involved in the tracking of youth income information. This document is used to determine eligibility for federal reimbursement of nutrition expenses for youths in DJJ residential facilities. Currently, this document is prepared at facility admission solely to indicate an income class code for a youth. Federal auditors visit the facilities and manually review this document in each physical case file to determine overall reimbursement figures for a given time period. Workshop participants suggested this income class code could be included on the standard admission form, eliminating this extra document and simplifying the admission process. DJJ initiated correspondence with the appropriate authorities to determine if this change, specifically if implemented in an electronic environment, was acceptable under the terms of the reimbursement program. Initial approval has been granted, provided the eligibility code determinations are easily linked to individual admissions. This concern is met given that the admission sheet is generated at every admission. Moreover, with eligibility codes entered electronically at every admission, determining overall reimbursement information can be done with a simple database report generated at a personal computer. This approach integrates information from numerous documents at each facility across the state into a single document at one site. Not only is the admission process simplified, but the administration of this entire program will require less time and fewer personnel for both DJJ and the external auditors. This initiative, leading to information and process integration, has involved policy makers as stakeholders and has specified additional functional requirements for the new system. It was a direct outcome of the analysis of documents, as the potential for the new system to support the program in this way had not been previously articulated.

Another interesting example was the Service Plan document, which is intended to detail the provisions of the treatment plan devised for an individual youth. Discussion of this document was rather controversial. Some workshop participants not only found its structure inadequate, but voiced the opinion that it should be eliminated entirely. Its value in contributing to effective case management was seriously questioned, as was its secondary role as a method of evaluating case managers. Others felt the document was a useful tool. A heated debate ensued, and avenues for revising the policy requiring this document were identified. In the end, evaluation of this document led to the most significant potential workflow change, pending executive approval and implementation, to the entire process of assessing a youth, recommending a plan of action, and following the progress. This process involved several documents, the Risk and Needs Assessments, the Service Plan and the Progress Assessment. The Risk and Needs Assessments are used to quantify the youth's risks and needs. The Risk score is used to recommend a level of supervision, ranging from minimal to institutional, and the Needs score is used as a baseline to measure the youth's progress. Based on the identified needs, a Service Plan is created that outlines the plan of action and the Progress Assessment is used to measure how well it is working.

The major problem with the current process is that the existing Service Plan is not directly tied to the needs identified in the Needs Assessment. The form allows case managers to record a series of objectives and services. It does not match an objective to a need, but the Progress score is based on the youth's needs. As a result, the case managers claim that the Service Plan is not used as it was intended since it is not integrated into the planning and evaluation very well.

Because the purpose of the Service Plan was to propose a plan of action based on the youth's needs, the Needs Assessment and Service Plan were combined into one document. Space was provided after each need to specify any objectives and services. The Progress Assessment was also modified to allow space for the objectives and services. This allows the case managers to modify the objectives and services as they monitor the progress.

These are the most salient examples of the effect that the elicitation of user requirements through document analysis has had on issues of process and policy at DJJ. We expect to identify further examples of information and process integration as the system is deployed and DJJ begins to fully exploit the use of information technology. While this work was motivated by the needs of information system design, many benefits can be realized even if the system were never to be built, as DJJ has now revised and specified its documents with precise statements of their contents and purpose.

We believe the approach used here will be of most benefit to organizations with similar circumstances: those with little or no existing information technology support, multiple jurisdictions with little standardization and coordination, and minimal funding or infrastructure to specifically support document coordination. It may also be of use in the case of mergers, where the coordination of documents between the merged entities might benefit from detailed comparisons and the exchange of work methods and information.

Coordination with the User Interface

For the critical areas of youth case management and individual workflow support, the emerging user interface design for the new system tightly couples documents to novel graphical presentations and tailored user functionalities. The information elicited from users at the document workshops helps define the important events in youth case management, what documents and information are relevant to these events, and which users must be given access to the information and documents. The framework of the interface design and the content provided by the document analysis combine to take the system beyond workflow or document management systems by integrating the management of both within comprehensive, graphic representations and customized but flexible user views.

The system's user interface has been partially mocked-up using desktop rapid prototyping tools. These prototypes will be included in the RFP as supporting specification of the user interface. As detailed in Rose, et. al. (1996), user interface designs for the new system are being based on the concept of creating a customized "view" of the central system database for different user segments. The functionality defined for each view features links to the documents that must be produced or handled as part of the procedures supported within that view, in direct support of user workflow. Links to documents will either display electronic documents or provide a pointer to non-electronic documents. A number of documents in the inventory, however, are entirely subsumed by the design of the user views as noted above. These consist primarily of spreadsheet or list documents showing, for example, all youths assigned to a case manager that have court hearings scheduled on a particular day. The user views (see Figure 1) include list display areas and simple query mechanisms for creating and printing lists of records, providing both pre-defined and ad-hoc query and reporting functionality. This approach makes a far greater variety of such documents available to users.

Various DJJ forms and reports are related to individual youths, such as psychological assessments or court orders. These documents are bundled in the youth record by events. The youth record (see Figure 2) is a display that provides an overview of an individual's history with DJJ. It also provides access to all the relevant documentation. The LifeLines display of the youth record (Plaisant, et. al. 1996) is a graphic timeline interface that shows the youth's status using color to indicate the depth of penetration into the system. Users can pull down menus from each status indicator to see a list of documents related to the activities associated with the status of the youth at that point in time. Choosing one of the menus items

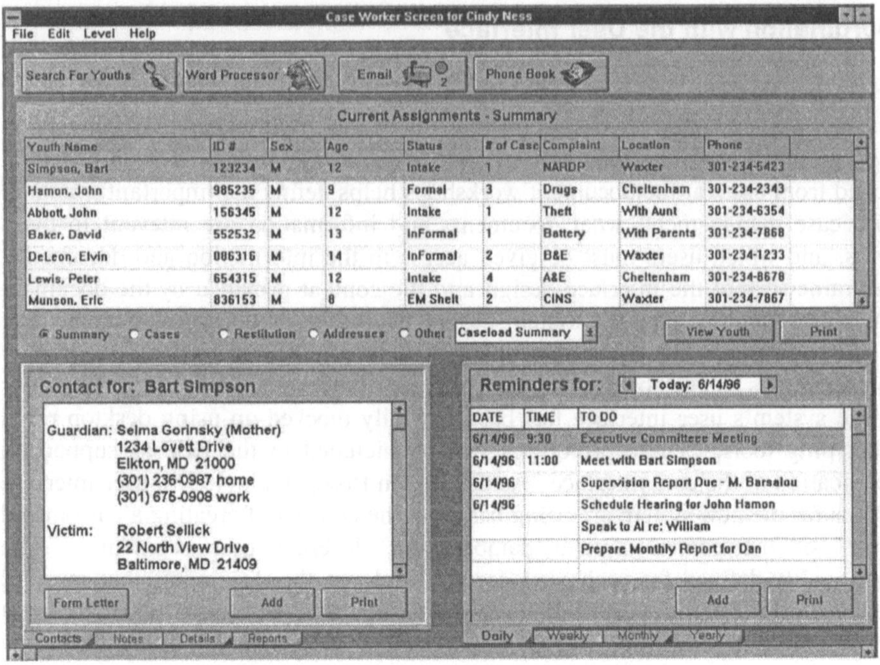

Figure 1 (above). A sample case manager view. Fig. 2 (below). The Youth Record.

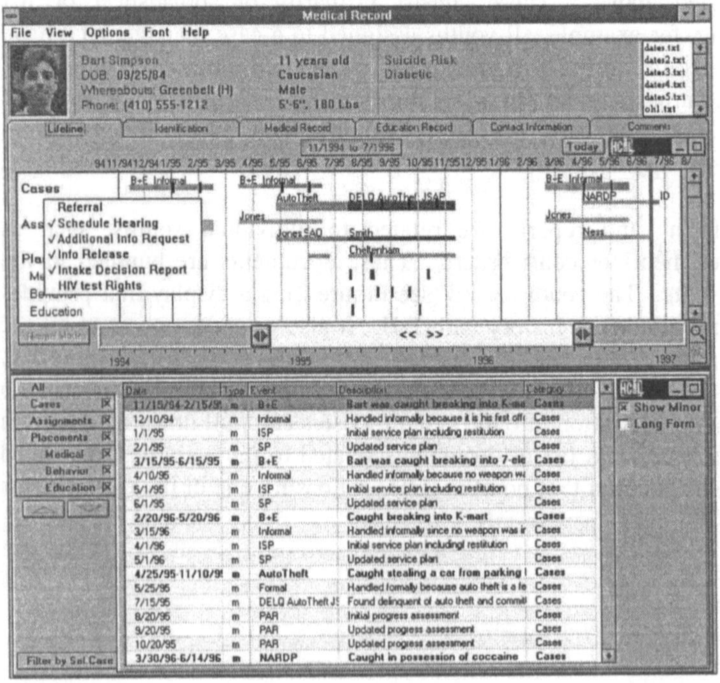

opens a window in which the associated document is shown. In addition, significant discrete events such as medical evaluations, special behavioral incidents, and educational assessments are represented on the LifeLines with tick marks, which provide similar navigation to the supporting documents that detail the event. The LifeLines thus give users a graphic overview of a youth's entire history, with quick access to details, on demand, in available documents. This design achieves information integration by gathering documentary information on a youth, from distributed sources, in a graphical, single-screen life history representation that is of use to diverse workers attending to distinct aspects of youth case management. The design indicates the existence of, and provides access to documents without requiring a search of any kind.

The graphical overview thus provides a quickly discerned summary of a youth. Rather than rifling through a case file, where behavior incident reports may or not be present, a worker can, for example, quickly see the presence of behavior incidents on the LifeLines, and know whether or not the youth is likely to be troublesome. A case manager may have greater need than a nurse to navigate down to the details in behavior incident report documents, but the information is available to both at whatever level of detail is preferred. The youth record also includes a filterable, tabular list of events, tightly-coupled to the LifeLines, which provides slightly more textual detail than is possible on the LifeLines, while stopping well short of the level of detail of the supporting documents. The information represented in the youth record in an integration of information that was previously distributed across a case file of linearly arranged paper documents and dozens of separate screens of the current information system. While ultimately the information content of both approaches may be nearly identical, the youth record creates value-added information with its graphical overview coupled with access to details and documents on demand. The data gathered during the workshops will be used as the system is implemented to place documents and events appropriately within this interface. Both the user views and the youth record displays exhibit one of the principles of the Role Management approach, which is to have all information related to a task or role, at least at some level of abstraction, on the screen at the same time. The relevant documents are represented abstractly in these displays, and their rich information content is easily navigated to with typical graphical user interface mechanisms.

Conclusion

This work has demonstrated the utility of document analysis in the context of information system design to achieve process and information integration. The DJJ document workshops spawned a new kind of self-examination for the organization, which explored entrenched and problematic activities long ignored. The results will positively affect process changes and will lead to a better information system design. Fostering user discussion of existing documents helps define existing processes and information requirements, and highlights areas where process changes can effectively be made and what system features are needed to support them.

In addition, information integration can be achieved with innovative graphic representations that collect information, particularly documents, from diverse sources and of multiple types, into single screen overviews. These developments in user interface design can benefit both the organization and the individual user. For organizations, new system administrative tools with graphical user interfaces are being developed to aid in the collection and analysis of business process information and the design and specification of process models and information technology. For the user, the recent work of Shneiderman and Plaisant (1994) on Personal Role Managers (PRM) (also Plaisant and Shneiderman 1995) begins to suggest ways to structure individual work in harmony with their roles in an organization, effectively becoming personal process support tools. Graphical interfaces to both personal role management and organizational modelling must accommodate process artifacts, or documents. The elicitation of specific information about documents, as demonstrated in this case study, can have great benefit for the documents themselves as well as their optimal accommodation by system design.

These results suggest a valuable synthesis of principles and research from the fields of human-computer interaction, information and records management, archival theory, and process theories and technologies Some future research opportunities now seem apparent. Workflow management systems, document management systems, and process technologies have evolved separately and targeted distinct markets. Only recently have such systems begun to move toward closer integration (Hendley 1995b; Jablonski 1995; Karagiannis 1995; Medina-Mora, et. al 1993; Teufel and Teufel 1995; Watson Jr., et. al 1995). Methods for integrating process definition and modelling, requirements analysis, and document and workflow management should continue to be pursued because these research fronts can all contribute to the goal of enterprise process integration.

Acknowledgments

We thank the DJJ workshop participants, who have worked so hard in analyzing documents. We thank Linda Parker Gates for many valuable discussions of process concepts and thoughtful reviews of this chapter. Catherine Plaisant provided many useful comments on early drafts, and Ben Shneiderman provided valuable guidance at the beginning of this work. Cognetics Corporation and the HCIL design team have created the overall system design to which the work described here contributes. The preparation of this chapter was supported by funding from the Maryland Department of Juvenile Justice.

References

Barothy, Thomas, Markus Peterhans, and Kurt Bauknecht. 1995. Business process re-engineering: emergence of a new research field. *SIGOIS Bulletin* 16(1):3-10.

Barry, Richard E. 1994. Electronic document and records management systems: towards a methodology for requirements definition. *Information Management & Technology* 27(6): 251-256.

Bearman, David. 1994. *Towards a Reference Model for Business Acceptable Communications*. Manuscript. http://www.lis.pitt.edu/~nhprc/.

Cox, Richard J. 1995. *Putting the Puzzle Together: The Recordkeeping Functional Requirements Project at the University of Pittsburgh; A Second Progress Report.* Manuscript. http://www.lis.pitt.edu/~nhprc/.

Davenport, Thomas H. 1993. *Process Innovation: Reengineering Work through Information Technology*. Boston: Harvard Business School Press.

Hammer, Michael and James Champy. 1993. *Reengineering the Corporation: A Manifesto for Business Revolution.* New York: HarperCollins.

Hendley, Tony. 1995a. Planning and implementing an integrated document management system: a checklist of points to consider. *Information Management & Technology* 28(2): 63-66.

Hendley, Tony. 1995b. New developments in workflow, imaging, and document management. *Information and Management Technology* 28(4):152-158.

IPIC. 1996. International Working Conference on Integration of Enterprise Information and Processes. Manuscript. http://www.iti.gov.sg/conference/ipic96.html.

Jablonski, Stefan. 1995. On the complementary of workflow management and business process modelling. *SIGOIS Bulletin* 16(1):33-38.

Johnson, Edward N. 1983a. The document as an information source. *Information Management* 17(May): 21-25.

Johnson, Edward N. 1983b. Document base management: a concept for document control and use. *Information Management* 17(June): 23-25.

Kaltoff, Robert J. 1994. Imaging success and business process reengineering. *Information Management and Technology* 27(5):216-217.

Kane, Gerard J. 1978. Techniques for conducting a records management survey. *ARMA: Records Management Quarterly* 12(July): 8-11.

Karagiannis, Dimitris. 1995. BPMS—Business process management systems. *SIGOIS Bulletin* 16(1):10-12.

Kay, Michael H. 1994. Document content management: towards an object-oriented approach. *Information Management & Technology* 27(1): 27-30.

Kubicki, Mary. 1985. Information resource management requires data analysis. *ARMA : Records Management Quarterly* 19(January): 10-14.

Medina-Mora, Raúl, Terry Winograd, Rodrigo Flores, and Fernando Flores. 1993. The action workflow approach to workflow management technology. *The Information Society* 9():391-404.

Penn, Ira A. 1983. Understanding the life cycle concept of records management. *ARMA : Records Management Quarterly* 17(July): 5-9.

Plaisant, Catherine, Brett Milash, Anne Rose, Scott Widoff and Ben Shneiderman. 1995. LifeLines: Visualizing Personal Histories, in *Proceedings of CHI '96 (Vancouver, BC, April 13-18 1996)*, ACM, NY, 221-227.

Plaisant, Catherine and Ben Shneiderman. 1995. *Organization overviews and role management: inspiration for future desktop environments*. HCIL Technical Report CAR-TR-771. University of Maryland, College Park, MD.

Rose, Anne, Jason Ellis, Catherine Plaisant, and Stephan Greene. 1996. *Life Cycle of User Interface Techniques: The DJJ Information System Design Process*. HCIL Technical Report, University of Maryland, College Park, MD.

Saffady, William. 1992. *Managing Electronic Records*. Prairie Village, KS: ARMA International.

Saunderson, Sandy. 1995. Minimum pain and maximum gain: counting the cost of not installing an electronic document management system. *Information Management and Technology* 28(3):117-118.

Shneiderman, Ben and Catherine Plaisant. 1994. The future of graphic user interfaces: personal role managers. *People and Computers IX, British Computer Society's HCI '94 (Glasgow, Scotland, August 1994)*, 3-8.

Teufel, Stephanie and Bernd Teufel. 1995. Bridging information technology and business—some modelling aspects. *SIGOIS Bulletin* 16(1):13-16.

Watson Jr., James K., Jeetu Patel, Paul Burian, Bob Puccinelli, Ninju Bohra. Doculabs' enterprise workflow benchmark evaluation. *Inform* (October):22-36.

Wolchak, William H. 1986. Conducting a systems analysis. *ARMA: Records Management Quarterly* 20(July): 16-19.

10 THREE GOOD REASONS FOR USING A PETRI-NET-BASED WORKFLOW MANAGEMENT SYSTEM

W.M.P. van der Aalst

Abstract: Currently, the Dutch Customs Department is building a nationwide information system to handle all kinds of declarations related to the import and export of goods. For this purpose the Petri-net-based Workflow Management System (WFMS) named COSA has been selected. During the selection process, it turned out that there are several reasons for insisting on a Petri-net-based WFMS. The three main reasons for selecting a Petri-net-based WFMS are discussed in this paper. In our opinion these reasons are also relevant for many other projects involved in the selection or implementation of a WFMS.

1.1 INTRODUCTION

At the moment more than 250 Workflow Management Systems (WFMSs) are under development. This signifies that the term 'workflow management' is not just another buzzword. The phenomenon workflow management will have a tremendous impact on the next generation of information systems [HL91, Kou95, Sch96, AH97]. To appreciate the relevance of workflow management one should look back in history. In the sixties an information system was composed of a number of stand-alone applications. For each of these applications an application-specific user interface and database system had to be developed, i.e. each application had its own routines for user interaction and data storage and retrieval. In the 70-ties data was pushed out of the applications. For this purpose Database Management Systems (DBMSs) were developed. By using a DBMS, applications were freed from the burden of data management. In the 80-ties a similar thing happened for user interface management. The emergence of User Interface Management Systems (UIMSs) enabled application developers to push the user interaction out of the applications. In our opinion WFMSs are the next step in pushing generic functionality out of the applications. The 90-ties will be marked by the emergence of workflow software, allowing application developers to push the business procedures out of the applications. Figure 1.1 shows the phenomenon workflow management in a historical perspective.

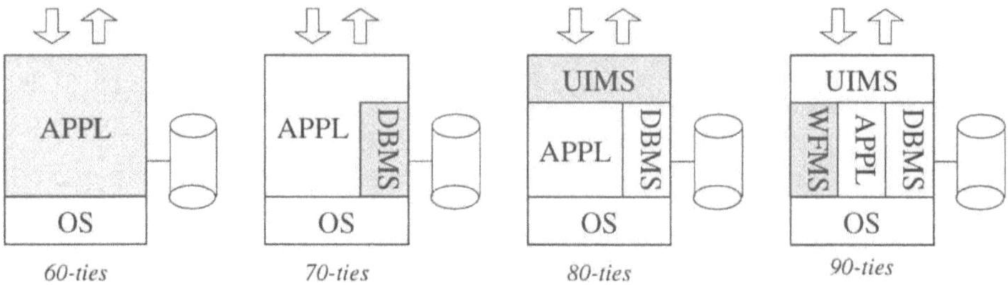

Figure 1.1 WFMSs in a historical perspective.

The Workflow Management Coalition (WFMC), founded in 1993, is an international organization whose mission is to promote workflow and establish standards for WFMSs. In January, 1995 the WFMC released a glossary which provides a common set of terms for workflow vendors, end-users, developers and researchers [WFM96]. In this glossary a WFMS is defined as being a system that completely defines, manages and executes workflow processes through the execution of software whose order of execution is driven by a computer representation of the workflow process logic. Instead of the term 'workflow process logic' we prefer the term 'business logic' to reflect the fact that the configuration of the WFMS is subordinate to the underlying business processes.

The benefits of a WFMS are comparable to the benefits of an UIMS or a DBMS. Flexibility, integration of applications and a reduction in development costs are the incentives for using a WFMS. The importance of workflow management was also recognized by the Dutch Customs Department when they started a project for the development of a nationwide information system for the handling of Customs declarations. The project was named after the name of the information system under development: *Sagitta-2000*. Since the regulations with respect to Customs declarations are very complex and subject to change, the flexibility and the capability to integrate applications of workflow management software were the prime incentives to start the selection of a WFMS for the realization of Sagitta-2000.

WorkManager
Workparty
FloWare
OPEN/workflow
Powerflow
EPIC/Workflow
Inconcert
Echo
Teamflow
Teamroute
COSA
Imageplus
Flowpath
Trimco
Staffware
ProcessIT
Event manager
Smartstream
Keyfile
Visual Workflo

Figure 1.2 Some of the leading WFMSs.

During the selection process some of the leading WFMSs were evaluated using a list of generic selection criteria and a list of functional requirements specific for the Sagitta-2000 project (see Figure 1.2). In the beginning the results were quite disappointing. First of all, the selection process was hampered by the fact that, despite the efforts of the Workflow Management Coalition, standardization is lacking. Secondly, most of the leading WFMSs fail to represent the business processes of the Dutch Customs Department in a natural manner. Many WFMSs have restrictions with respect to the nesting and/or mixing of parallelism and alternative routing. Moreover, most of the WFMSs do not allow for the explicit modeling of states. As result it is not possible to handle triggers and external choices properly (See Section 1.4). Thirdly, only a few WFMS could be used in the technological environment (i.e. hardware platform, operating system, DBMS, etc.) of the Dutch Customs Department. During the selection process it dawned upon the people involved in the Sagitta-2000 project that a Petri-net-based WFMS could meet all of the functional requirements needed. It turned out that there are at least three good reasons for selecting a Petri-net-based WFMS:

- Formal semantics despite the graphical nature.
- State-based instead of event-based.

- Abundance of analysis techniques.

On the basis of these observations the Petri-net-based WFMS COSA [SL96] was selected for the local hardware platform. For the central workflow engine of Sagitta-2000 there were no suitable candidates. Therefore, the Dutch Customs Department decided to start building a proprietary workflow engine based on the Petri net formalism. We would like to emphasize that these decisions were based on objective arguments. The people responsible for the selections were not biased towards Petri nets. In fact, most of them had no prior knowledge of Petri nets.

The reasons for selecting a Petri-net-based WFMS are quite universal and certainly not specific for the Dutch Customs Department. They hold for most situations where the introduction of a WFMS is considered. In the remainder of this paper we introduce the Sagitta-2000 project followed by a discussion on each of the three main reasons to use a Petri-net-based WFMS.

1.2 SAGITTA-2000

The Sagitta-2000 project started in 1994. The goal of this project is to develop a nationwide information system for the processing of all kinds of Customs declarations. The processing of a Customs declaration is a very complex process which is subject to change. Activities that are needed to handle a declaration are typically related to the registration, checking and control of movements of communal goods. For some types of declarations more than 50 activities can be identified.

At the moment the handling of Customs declarations is partly automated. A number of legacy systems support the management of data related to the processing of declarations. The management of the processes is hardly supported at all. Paper documents form the pivot on which the processing of Customs declarations turns. As a result, the processes are hard to manage and service to the customer is poor. Moreover, the legacy systems are poorly integrated and form a patchwork which reflects the history of Dutch Customs regulations. The goal of the Sagitta-2000 project was to build a flexible well-integrated information system which also supports and manages the process itself.

One of starting points of the Sagitta-2000 project is the separation of information logistics and the implementation of Customs tasks. From the start, it was clear that it would be nice to use a WFMS for the information logistics. By using a WFMS as the basis for Sagitta-2000, it should be easy to accommodate the system to the continual changes of the regulations with respect to

Customs declarations. Flexibility, maintainability and the ability to integrate applications were the keywords that served as a stimulus for using a WFMS.

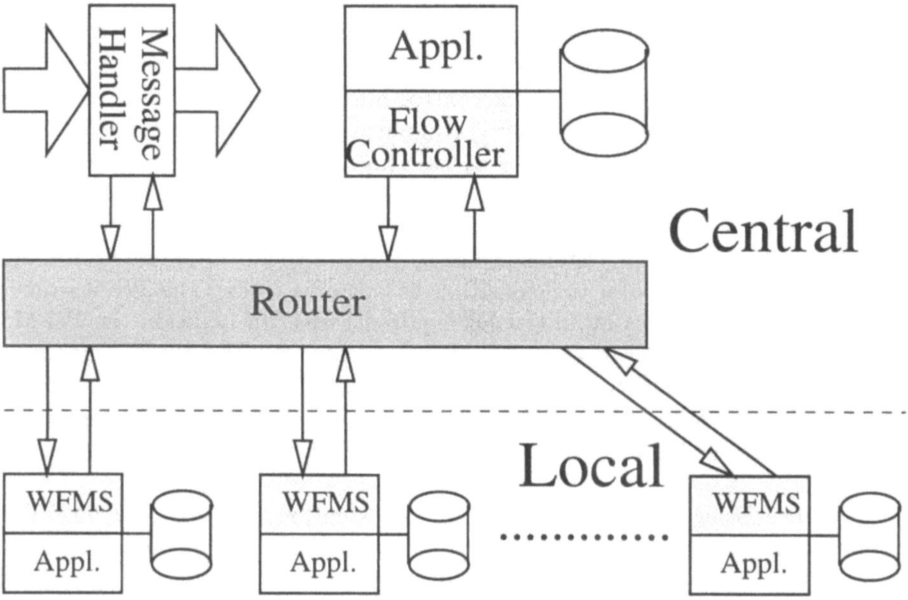

Figure 1.3 The architecture of Sagitta-2000.

Sagitta-2000 will be a distributed information system, composed of a central system in Apeldoorn and dozens of local systems (one for each Customs office). Figure 1.3 shows the architecture of Sagitta-2000. Messages which relate to Customs declarations are received by a *Message Handler*. The Message Handler translates these EDI-messages to an in-house format. At any moment a case, i.e. a Customs declaration, is being handled by one of the local platforms or by the central system located in the city Apeldoorn. The *Router* sends an incoming message which relates to a specific case (Customs declaration) to the proper location. Customs information about declarations is stored in a central database. About 50% of the cases do not require user interaction and are handled completely automatically by the central system. The other 50% require user interaction and need to be handled at a specific Customs office. Cases which require interaction with a Customs officer are partly handled by the central system and partly by one of the local systems, i.e., a case is transferred from the central system to one of the local system the moment user interaction is required. The Router system takes care of these case transfers and the routing of messages. The central system which takes care of the processing of tasks for specific cases is split into two parts: (1) a *Flow Controller* and (2) a set of *applications* for the execution of Customs tasks. The Flow Controller is a system which takes care of the case logistics, i.e., it decides when to execute which task for a specific case using control information about the case. The functionality of the Flow Controller is comparable to the 'engine' in a WFMS. The Flow Controller initiates tasks by starting the proper applications. Note that only the applications can access the Customs information about declarations. The local platform has an architecture which is similar to the central system. Each of the local systems is also split into two parts: (1) a *WFMS* and (2) a set of *applications* for the execution of Customs tasks. The WFMS takes care of the case logistics by initiating required tasks. In addition the WFMS assigns interactive tasks to Customs officers. Note that the applications executed at the local platform which require user interaction cannot be executed by the central system. For performance reasons only, Customs information about declarations handled locally is temporarily stored in a local database.

Performance issues are a constant point of attention for Sagitta-2000. The estimated number of declarations per year is more than 10.000.000. Moreover, there will be days on which more than 70.000 declarations have to be handled! The number of Customs officers using Sagitta-2000 will be more than 5000. These figures show that the Sagitta-2000 project is a very ambitious project. At the moment nearly 100 persons are involved in the development of Sagitta-2000.

The logistics part of the information system is the crux of the Sagitta-2000 project. The workflow procedures used by the local WFMS and the central Flow Controller need to be a good reflection of the business processes at hand. Although there are, from a technical point of view, a lot of differences between the local and the central platform, the business processes are platform-independent. Therefore, the Sagitta-2000 project started with the modeling of the business processes. Each business process describes which tasks need to be executed in order to handle a Customs declaration (case). A business process also specifies which tasks can be executed in parallel, whether there are alternative tasks or iterations. For this purpose the Sagitta-2000 team developed a diagraming technique which is based on Petri nets and inspired by the Glossary of the WFMC [WFM96]. Figure 1.4 shows an example of a business process[1]. Tasks are modeled by rectangles. For each task it is specified how it is triggered and which application is initiated by the triggering of this task. Tasks are connected by triangles named 'work-stores'. Work-stores specify enabling conditions for a task to be triggered. In Petri-net terms work-stores correspond to places and each task corresponds to a small network taking care of synchronization, triggering and the execution of the corresponding application. The diagraming technique has been used to model the business processes relevant to Sagitta-2000 successfully.

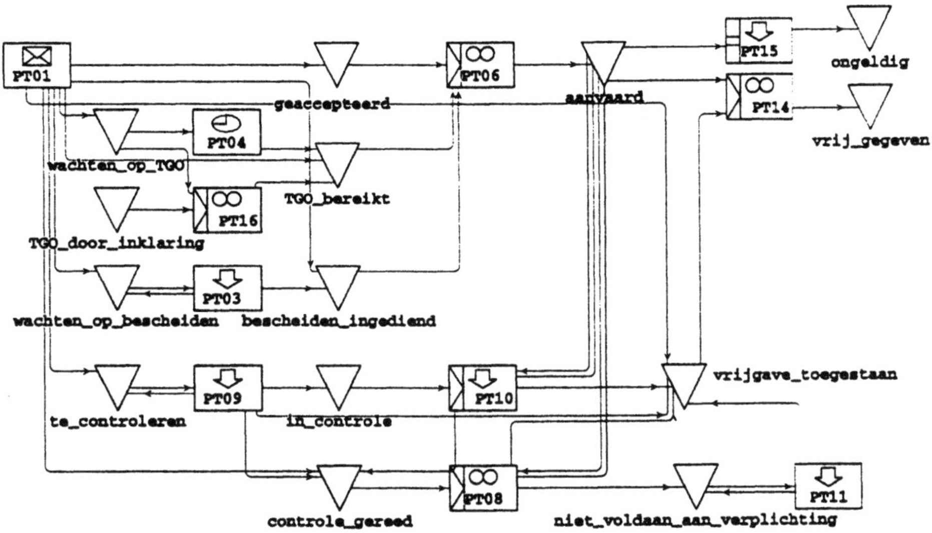

Figure 1.4 The business process 'basis-aangifte' (in Dutch).

Parallel to the definition of the business processes the technical infrastructure (hardware/software) has been selected. For the central system an IBM ES9000 mainframe will be used. The DBMS used for the central system is DB2 and the Message Handler, the Router and the Customs applications are being implemented using Cobol, CICS and DB2. Since suitable workflow products are missing for the mainframe, the Flow Controller is also implemented using Cobol, CICS and DB2.

For the local platform a client/server architecture is used. The server is a HP 9000 connected to dozens of client PCs using a Novell network. The server runs under UNIX and the clients are using Windows. The DBMS used for the local platform is Sybase. For the interactive applications the combination of Powerbuilder, C++ and Sybase is used. The Open Server for CICS is used to exchange Customs data between the central DB2 database and the local Sybase database. The exchange of cases will be handled by the IBD, a service offered by the Dutch PTT. Figure 1.5 shows an overview of the chosen technical infrastructure.

Given the technical infrastructure and the functional requirements, the Sagitta-2000 team had to select a WFMS for the local platform. Based on the technical infrastructure we made a first selection. The WFMS should be able to operate in a client/server environment (UNIX/Windows). Moreover, the WFMS should be able to communicate with Powerbuilder and use Sybase for data management. Using these technical requirements and the vendor profiles we made the following shortlist: OPEN/Workflow (Wang), Workparty (Siemens), COSA (Software Ley) and Visual WorkFlo (FileNet/Olivetti). We used this shortlist and the functional requirements as the basis for a further selection. After visiting some of these vendors and looking at the brochures of many other WFMSs we became very pessimistic. Most of the WFMSs did not meet the functional requirements needed. Business processes which were easy to formulate in the Petri-net-based diagrams were difficult to implement using most of the WFMSs we evaluated. Fortunately, we also selected the Petri-net-based WFMS COSA [SL96]. COSA met all the functional requirements. In fact, it was possible to translate the Petri-net-based diagrams for the business processes semi-automatically into workflow procedures for COSA. At that moment we realized that the use of a Petri-net-based WFMS for the local platform was essential for the success of Sagitta-2000.

At the same time we tried to select a WFMS for the central system. Unfortunately, we discovered that workflow management software is focussed on client/sever technology. The only interesting product was Early Cloud's Message-Driven Processor (MDP), a message-oriented middleware workflow product which runs on mainframes (MVS/CICS). A more thorough investigation showed that MDP was not a suitable candidate for the Flow Controller. Therefore, the Dutch Customs Department decided to develop a tailor-made workflow engine using Cobol, CICS and DB2. At the moment this workflow engine is being built. Based on the success of the Petri-net-based approach for the modeling of the business processes and the local WFMS, the Flow Controller is also based on Petri nets.

For the Dutch Customs Department and in particular the Sagitta-2000 project, the selection of Petri-nets as a vehicle for modeling and implementing the central and local workflow turned out to be very promising. Moreover, we are convinced that the use of a Petri-net-based WFMS has a number of real advan-

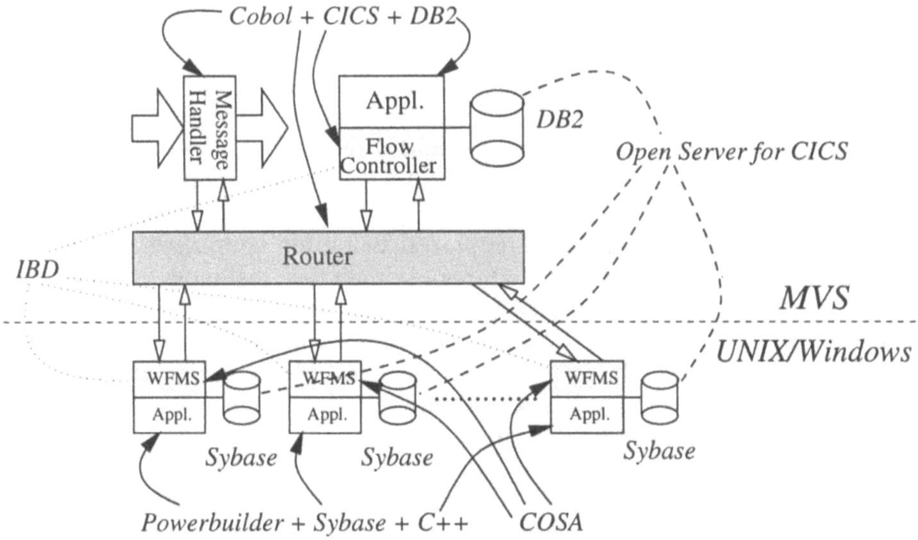

Figure 1.5 The technical infrastructure of Sagitta-2000.

tages which are not specific to the Sagitta-2000 project. Any other information system which supports complex business processes can benefit from the use of a Petri-net-based WFMS. Therefore, we present three universal and solid reasons for using a WFMS based on Petri nets.

1.3 REASON 1: FORMAL SEMANTICS DESPITE THE GRAPHICAL NATURE

The first reason for using a Petri-net-based WFMS, is the fact that business logic can be represented by a formal but also graphical language. The semantics of the classical Petri net and several enhancements (color, time, hierarchy) have been defined formally [Hee94, Jen92, Mur89, Rei85]. In this section we will show that a Petri net can be used to model the primitives identified by the Workflow Management Coalition [WFM96]. These primitives are also present in today's WFMSs. To discuss these workflow primitives we start by introducing some terminology.

The objective of a WFMS is to handle *cases* successfully. Examples of cases are insurance claims, orders, mortgages, tax-returns and loans. A *task* is a piece of work whose execution contributes to the completion of a business process.

Synonyms for task are process activity, logical step and work element. A *task instance* is a task that needs to be executed to handle a specific case. Task instances are executed by *resources*. A resource is a human, an application or a combination of a human and one or more applications. Synonyms for resource are actor or participant. The capabilities of a resource are given by a set of *roles*. Each task requires a specific role. Roles are used to map task instances to resources. A *workflow procedure* defines a partial ordering of tasks to handle cases of a specific type. A *workflow process* definition comprises a workflow procedure, a set of resources and a strategy to map task instances to resources.

One should clearly differentiate between workflow process definition and workflow process execution. Workflow process definition is concerned with the design of tasks, procedures, roles and resources using a design and analysis tool. Workflow process execution is concerned with the enactment of cases and task instances using a workflow engine.

Features of a Petri-net-based WFMS are most prominent in the design and analysis fase. Therefore, we concentrate on the workflow process definition.

Figure 1.6 shows how the six workflow primitives identified by the Workflow Management Coalition [WFM96] can be mapped onto Petri nets. Tasks are mapped onto transitions and causal relations are modeled by places. Transition *t1* models the synchronization of two subflows (AND-join). Transitions *t21* and *t22* model an OR-join: two subflows are merged into one subflow. Transition *t3* models an AND-split: a subflow is split into two parallel subflows. Transitions *t41* and *t42* model an OR-split: a selection is made between two alternative branches. Iteration can be modeled by adding a feedback transition (*t52*). Connecting two transitions (*t61* and *t62*) by means of an intermediate place, results in two sequential tasks.

The state of a case c is given by the distribution of tokens corresponding to c over the places in the Petri net. To distinguish between tokens corresponding to different cases we use a high-level Petri net model [Jen92, Hee94] extended with color. The color or value of a token contains information about the case the token belongs to and some additional information (e.g. routing parameters, due-date, responsible or preferred resource). Note that each transition which models an AND-join requires a precondition to prevent tokens corresponding to different cases from being mixed.

To illustrate the use of Petri nets for the modeling of workflow procedures, we consider the processing of complaints.[2] A complaints desk handles complaints of customers about the products produced by the fictitious Company X. Each complaint is registered before it is classified. Depending on the classification of the complaint, the complaint is ignored, a letter is sent to the customer or

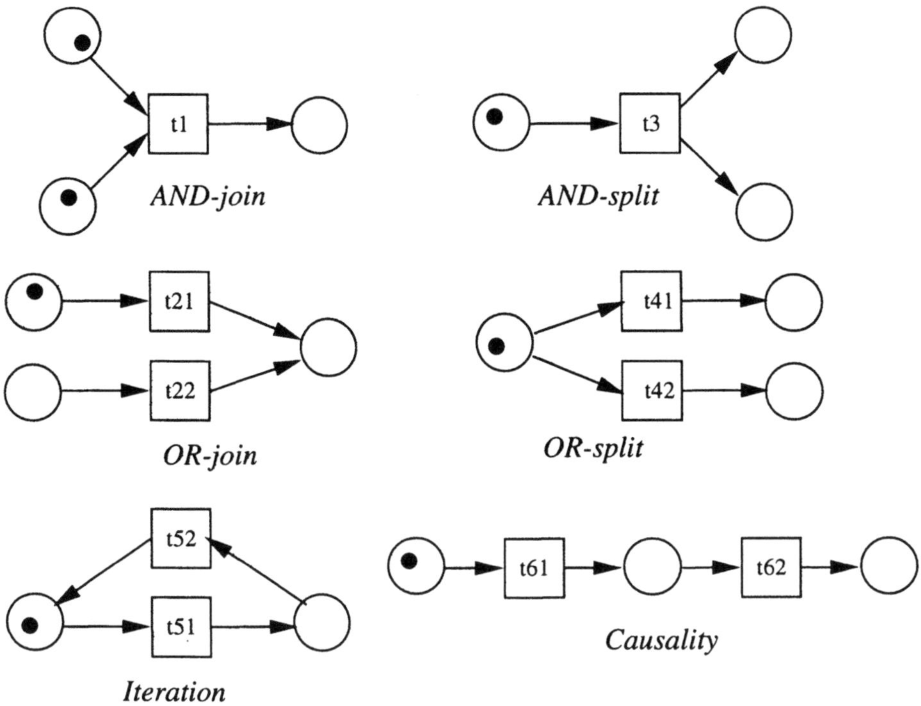

Figure 1.6 Workflow primitives.

an inquiry is started. The inquiry starts with a consultation of the department involved, followed by a discussion with the customer and the management of the department (in parallel). Based on this inquiry the necessary actions are taken. Finally, the dossier is filed. At any time between the registration of a complaint and the moment the complaint is filed, the customer may inform about the status of the corresponding complaint. Figure 1.7 shows a specification of the workflow procedure used to process complaints. Even for this simple example we need all the primitives identified by the WFMC.

The workflow primitives shown in Figure 1.6 are used to define workflow procedures. However, to complete the definition of a workflow process we have to add another dimension: the dimension which takes care of the mapping of tasks to resources. The dimension of workflow procedures and the dimension of resource management are orthogonal and therefore difficult to visualize in one Petri net. Nevertheless, it is possible to model workflow procedures and

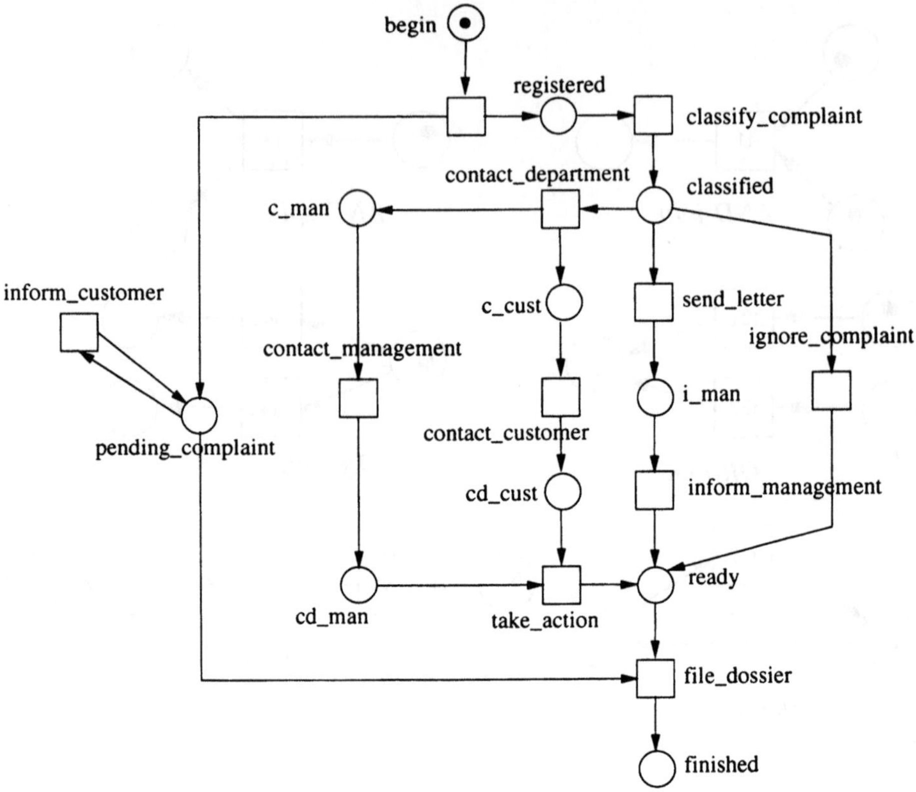

Figure 1.7 A Petri net describing the workflow procedure used to process complaints.

resource management in an integrated way by using an high-level Petri net extended with color and hierarchy. For more information the reader is referred to [AvHH95, AH96, AH96, AH95].

Experiences in the Sagitta 2000 project showed that Petri-nets can be used to model workflows in a natural manner. People that had no prior experience in computer science were able to specify workflow procedures. Although Petri nets are easy to use because of their graphical nature, they are well-founded and formal semantics are available. The fact that workflow procedures are specified using a technique with formal semantics is vital to the success of workflow projects such as Sagitta 2000. The fact that Petri nets have formal semantics has a number of advantages.

- A workflow procedure specified in terms of a Petri net is *unambiguous*, i.e., the meaning of each construction is clear and there is no room for multiple interpretations. This way, it is possible to avoid interminable discussions about the precise meaning a workflow procedure specification.
- A Petri net description of a workflow can serve as a *contract* between subdepartments. The formal semantics can be used to resolve conflicts over the interpretation of common workflow procedures.
- The interpretation of a Petri-net-based workflow procedure is *tool independent*; it does not change when a new version of the WFMS is released.
- The formal semantics allow for *reasoning about properties* of a given workflow procedure. It is possible to prove (the absence of) dynamic properties such as deadlock, livelock, etc.
- The formal semantics form a prerequisite for the application of all kinds of *analysis techniques.*

Many of today's available WFMSs provide ah-hoc constructs to model workflow procedures without any formal semantics. Moreover, there are WFMSs that impose serious restrictions on the workflow primitives shown in Figure 1.6. For example WANG's OPEN/workflow does not support the nesting of parallel flows. Some WFMSs also provide exotic constructs whose semantics is not 100% clear. To avoid these problems one could use a Petri-net-based WFMS having formal semantics. This does not mean that some 'syntactic sugaring' to facilitate the design process should be avoided. Note that the exchange of workflow process definitions between two Petri-net-based WFMSs is easy compared to the exchange of workflow process definitions between two WFMSs based on different concepts.

For more information on workflow modeling with Petri nets, the reader is referred to [EN93, Aal96, Aal97, AH97].

1.4 REASON 2: STATE-BASED INSTEAD OF EVENT-BASED

In contrast with many other process modeling techniques, the state of a case can be modeled explicitly in a Petri net. Process modeling techniques ranging from informal techniques such as dataflow diagrams to formal techniques such as process algebra's are *event-based*, i.e., transitions are modeled explicitly and the states between subsequent transitions are modeled implicitly. Today's WFMSs are typically event-based, i.e., tasks are modeled explicitly and states between subsequent tasks are suppressed. Figure 1.8 shows a typical diagram which defines a workflow procedure. The tasks *A, B, C, D, E, F, G* and *H* are represented explicitly in contrast to the state.

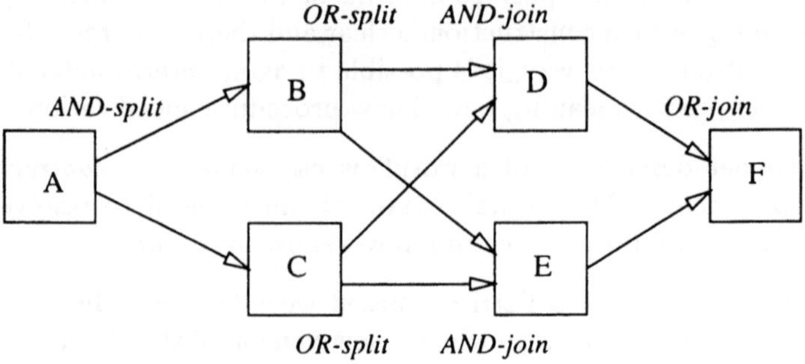

Figure 1.8 An event-based description of a workflow procedure.

If we convert the event-based description shown in Figure 1.8 to a Petri net, we obtain the net shown in Figure 1.9. The tasks are modeled by transitions and intermediate states are modeled by places. Note that in contrast to the description given in Figure 1.8 it is possible to refer to states between the execution of subsequent tasks.

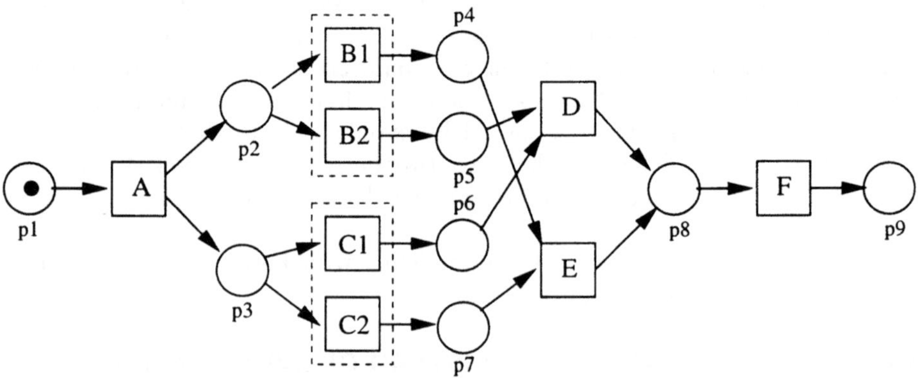

Figure 1.9 A state-based description of a workflow procedure.

The distinction between an event-based and a state-based[3] description seems to be very subtle, but turned out to be of the utmost importance in the Sagitta-2000 project. In general, there are several reasons for using a state-based description. These are discussed in the remainder of this section.

First of all, a state-based description allows for a clear distinction between the enabling of a task and the execution of a task. Since the enabling of a task does not imply that the task will be executed immediately, it is important to have this distinction. To illustrate this, we need to discuss the *triggering* of tasks in more detail. The execution of a task instance for a specific case starts the moment the task instance is triggered. A task instance can only be triggered if the corresponding case is in a state which enables the execution of the task. Consider Figure 1.9. Task D can only be triggered for case c if there is a token in each of the input places of D which corresponds to c. There may be tasks which are not triggered by the WFMS itself. In Sagitta-2000 there are four kinds of triggering:

- Automatic: a task is triggered the moment it is enabled. This kind of triggering is used for tasks which are executed by an application which does not require human interaction.
- User: a task is triggered by a human participant, i.e., a user selects an enabled task instance to be executed. In a WFMS each user has a so-called 'in-basket'. This in-basket contains tasks instances that are enabled and may be executed by the user. By selecting a task instance the corresponding task instance is triggered.
- Message: an external event (i.e. a message) triggers an enabled task instance. Examples of messages are telephone-calls, fax messages, e-mails or EDI messages.
- Time: an enabled task instance is triggered by a clock, i.e., the task is executed at a predefined time. For example, the task 'remove document' is triggered if a case is trapped in a specific state for more than 15 hours.

Only for automatic tasks the enabling and the execution of a task coincide. Therefore, it is important model the intermediate states explicitly.

Another reason for the explicit modeling of states is the possibility of *competitive tasks*. Two tasks are competitive if they are both enabled and only one of them may be executed. Figure 1.11 shows two competitive tasks B and C. We use the symbols shown in Figure 1.10 to denote the way each task is triggered. Task A is triggered by an external message. The execution of task A is followed by the triggering of B or the triggering of C. If the user selects the instance of task B before some predefined time, then B is executed. Otherwise, task C is executed. Note that the execution of task C implies that task-instances have to be removed from the in-baskets of the participants which are allowed to execute task B. To model this situation we cannot use an event-based description. The choice to do task B or C is not made during the execution of task A. The choice

Figure 1.10 Four kinds of triggering.

to do B or C is implicitly made by the environment of the WFMS while the corresponding case marks place $p2$. There are many WFMSs which are unable to model the situation shown in Figure 1.11, simply because the intermediate state $p2$ is suppressed. As a result an enabled task instance is required to be executed: once a task instance appears in an in-basket it remains there until it is executed.

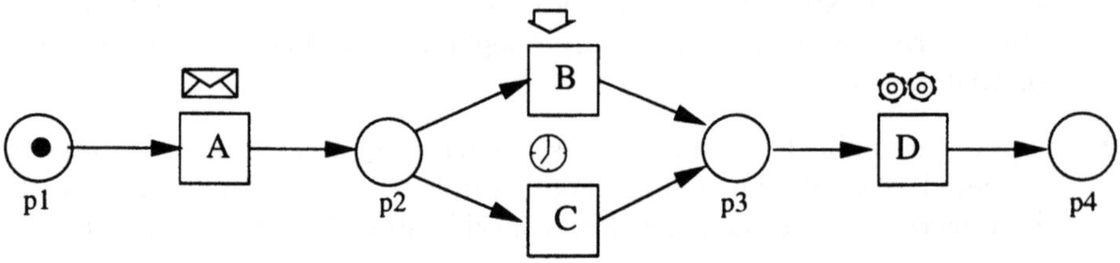

Figure 1.11 Task B and task C are competitive.

Sometimes it is necessary to withdraw a case. For many event-based WFMSs, this is difficult situation. Task instances have to be removed from the in-baskets of the participants. In a Petri-net based WFMS such a withdrawal is quite easy: simply remove all the tokens and triggers that correspond to the canceled case.

Today, a WFMS is often used within a single department. In the future, enterprise-wide workflow systems will become a reality. For example, Sagitta-2000 will be a distributed system composed of many independent autonomous workflow subsystems. Each of these subsystems runs on a local platform having one server and many clients. Although each location is autonomous, cases are exchanged frequently. There are several reasons for moving a case from one location to another. There may be a compelling reason for such a transfer, e.g. a task can not be executed at the current location. However, a case transfer can also be issued to balance the workload. Anyhow, there has to be a way to transfer a case from one WFMS to another WFMS. For state-based WFMSs this is quite easy: remove all tokens which correspond to the case to be transferred and move them to the other WFMS. Note that this is only possible if the workflow procedures in the two WFMSs are compatible. Clearly, exchanging cases between event-based WFMSs is much more difficult.

There are many reasons for using a state-based WFMS instead of an event-based WFMS. Event-based WFMSs can only be used satisfactorily in situations where the workflow engine is leading, i.e., tasks are triggered by the WFMS instead of the environment of the WFMS. In many situations this is not very realistic. The WFMS should follow and guide the environment instead of imposing all kinds of restrictions.

1.5 REASON 3: ABUNDANCE OF ANALYSIS TECHNIQUES

Petri nets are marked by the availability of many analysis techniques. Clearly, this is a great asset in favor of a Petri-net-based WFMS. We have showed that the Petri net formalism allows for a representation of the workflow which is close to business process at hand, i.e., it is possible to model the workflow in a natural manner. This representation can be used as a starting point for various kinds of analysis. In a sense, the Petri net representation serves as an interface between the business process at hand and the method(s) of analysis. In fact, Petri nets provide a 'solver-independent' medium that can be used to make a concise 'blue-print' of the workflow definition we want to analyze. This blue-print may be used at different levels of decision making and can be used as a starting point for various means of analysis. Compared to the usual algorithmic approaches (where the emphasis is on the analysis process rather than the modeling process), this approach is characterized by the fact that during the modeling process the user is not shackled by the techniques which are going to be used to analyze the model.

For an overview of the many analysis techniques developed for Petri nets the reader is referred to [Hee94, Jen92, Mur89, SV90]. In general these techniques can be used to prove properties (safety properties, invariance properties, deadlock, etc.) and to calculate performance measures (response times, waiting times, occupation rates, etc.). In this way it is possible to evaluate alternative workflows.

Let us focus on analysis techniques that can be used to prove properties of a given workflow procedure. By constructing the occurrence graph, we are able to verify whether a desired property holds. For example, we can use the occurrence graph to detect deadlocks and undesirable states. However, it is also possible to use techniques which exploit the structure of the underlying Petri net. For example, we can generate place invariants to verify safety properties. We also developed an analysis technique which verifies in polynomial time whether the workflow procedure satisfies the following requirements [Aal97]:

- There are no 'dangling tasks', i.e., tasks which do not contribute to the processing of cases.
- For any case, the procedure will terminate eventually. (Given some fairness assumption.)
- The moment the procedure terminates for a specific case, all references to this case have been removed.

A procedure which satisfies these requirements is called a *sound* workflow procedure. In [Aal97] this soundness property is defined formally and a technique is presented to verify this property in polynomial time. This technique is based on the rich theory developed for free-choice Petri nets [Bes87, DE95]. If we analyze the procedure shown in Figure 1.9 using this technique, we detect an error. The workflow procedure is not sound: executing task *A* for a specific case followed by *B1* and *C1* results in a deadlock. For the workflow procedure shown in Figure 1.9 this result is trivial. However, for the workflow procedures used by Sagitta-2000 it is far from trivial to verify the soundness property. (A workflow procedure contains typically 50 tasks.) Nevertheless, we succeeded in proving the soundness property for each of the procedures by using this technique.

Before introducing a new or revised workflow procedure it is important to have estimates of the important performance measures such as response times, waiting times and occupation rates of resources. Some of the leading WFMSs provide a simulation facility to evaluate the performance of a given workflow process without actually enacting the workflow procedure. There are many Petri-net based simulation tools. Therefore, it is easy to link a Petri-net-based WFMS to an existing simulation tool. If the duration of a task can be modeled by a negative-exponential distribution, then the corresponding Generalized

Stochastic Petri Net (GSPN) can also be analyzed by Markovian analysis techniques [MBC86]. If the duration of a task can be modeled by a pessimistic and an optimistic estimate (i.e. an interval), then the corresponding Interval Timed Colored Petri Net (ITCPN), can be analyzed using the MTSRT method presented in [Aal93]. In either case, standard tools are available for performance analysis of the workflow process at hand.

Clearly, the abundance of analysis techniques developed for Petri nets, enables the user of a Petri-net-based WFMS to analyze a workflow process in various ways (including simulation). In the Sagitta-2000 project we used the Petri-net-based analysis tools ExSpect [ASP94] and INA [Sta92] for simulation purposes and structural analysis.

1.6 CONCLUSION

Today's situation with respect to workflow management software is comparable to the situation as regards to database management software in the early 70-ties. In the beginning of the 70-ties most of the pioneers in the field of DBMSs were using their own ad-hoc concepts. This situation of disorder and lack of consensus resulted in an incomprehensive set of DBMSs. However, emerging standards such as the Relational Data Model [Cod70] and the Entity-Relationship Model [Che76] led to a common formal basis for many DBMSs. As a result the use of these DBMS boosted. There are many similarities between today's WFMSs and the DBMSs of the early 70-ties. Despite the efforts of the Workflow Management Coalition a real conceptual standard is missing. As a result many organizations are reluctant to use existing workflow management software. In our opinion Petri nets constitute a good basis for standardization. Inspired by practical experiences, we have come to realize that many of the features of the Petri net formalism are useful in the context of workflow management. In this paper we have given three solid reasons for using a Petri-net-based WFMS. For the Sagitta-2000 project these reasons turned out to be crucial:

- Formal semantics despite the graphical nature. For the Sagitta-2000 team it was important to have a concise set of terms and an unambiguous diagraming technique. The diagraming technique is easy to use for the people involved in the Sagitta-2000 project. Moreover, the formal semantics of the diagraming technique enable the use of diagrams as a 'contract' between the (sub)departments cooperating in this project.

- State-based instead of event-based. In the beginning the Sagitta-2000 was hampered by the use of event-based diagrams typically used in many workflow products. It was difficult to handle case transfers, rerouting of cases, case withdrawals and external triggers. By using a state-based approach these problems were solved quite easily. This was one of the prime reasons for adopting Petri nets.

- Abundance of analysis techniques. Simulation was used to validate the business processes and new concepts. In addition advanced Petri-net-based analysis techniques were used to verify the correctness of the complex workflow procedures for Sagitta-2000. These techniques allow for the verification of future changes of the workflow procedures.

Based on these reasons the Dutch Customs Department decided to select COSA for the local platform and to build a Petri-net-based workflow controller for the central platform.

Acknowledgments

The author would like to thank the Sagitta-2000 team, in particular Peter van der Toorn, Silvia de Kloe, Jaap Rigter and Hans-Rob de Reus, for their contributions to the results reported in this paper.

Notes

1. The terms related to the processing of Dutch Customs declarations are too specialized to be translated. This is the reason we focus on the lessons learned rather than expatiating on on specific Customs processes.
2. We use a fictitious example because the workflow procedures in Sagitta 2000 are too complex and require extensive knowledge of the jargon and the processing of Customs declarations.
3. We use the term state-based to denote that states are modeled explicitly. Clearly, a state-based description also incorporates state transitions, i.e., events.

References

[Aal93] W.M.P. van der Aalst. Interval Timed Coloured Petri Nets and their Analysis. In M. Ajmone Marsan, editor, *Application and Theory of Petri Nets 1993*, volume 691 of *Lecture Notes in Computer Science*, pages 453–472. Springer-Verlag, Berlin, 1993.

[Aal96] W.M.P. van der Aalst. Petri-net-based Workflow Management Software. In A. Sheth, editor, *Proceedings of the NFS Workshop on Workflow and Process Automation in Information Systems*, pages 114–118, Athens, Georgia, May 1996.

[Aal97] W.M.P. van der Aalst. Verification of Workflow Nets. In P. Azema and G. Balbo, editors, *Application and Theory of Petri Nets 1997*, Lecture Notes in Computer Science, page (to appear). Springer-Verlag, Berlin, 1997.

[AH95] W.M.P. van der Aalst and K.M. van Hee. Framework for Business Process Redesign. In J.R. Callahan, editor, *Proceedings of the Fourth Workshop on Enabling Technologies: Infrastructure for Collaborative Enterprises (WETICE 95)*, pages 36–45, Berkeley Springs, April 1995. IEEE Computer Society Press.

[AH96] W.M.P. van der Aalst and K.M. van Hee. Business Process Redesign: A Petri-net-based approach. *Computers in Industry*, 29(1-2):15–26, 1996.

[AH97] W.M.P. van der Aalst and K.M. van Hee. *Workflow Management: Modellen, Methoden en Systemen (in Dutch)*. Academic Service, Schoonhoven, 1997.

[ASP94] ASPT. *ExSpect 4.2 User Manual.* Eindhoven University of Technology, Eindhoven, 1994.

[AvHH95] W.M.P. van der Aalst, K.M. van Hee, and G.J. Houben. Modelleren en Analyseren van Workflow: een Aanpak op Basis van Petri-netten. *Informatie*, 37(11):590–599 (in Dutch), 1995.

[Bes87] E. Best. Structure theory of Petri nets: the free choice hiatus. In W. Brauer, W. Reisig, and G. Rozenberg, editors, *Advances in Petri Nets 1986 Part I: Petri Nets, central models and their properties*, volume 254 of *Lecture Notes in Computer Science*, pages 168–206. Springer-Verlag, Berlin, 1987.

[Che76] P.P. Chen. The Entity-Relationship Model: Towards a unified view of Data. *ACM Transactions on Database Systems*, 1:9–36, Jan 1976.

[Cod70] E.F. Codd. A Relational Model for Large Shared Data Banks. *Communications of the ACM*, 13(6):377–387, June 1970.

[DE95] J. Desel and J. Esparza. *Free choice Petri nets*, volume 40 of *Cambridge tracts in theoretical computer science.* Cambridge University Press, Cambridge, 1995.

[EN93] C.A. Ellis and G.J. Nutt. Modelling and Enactment of Workflow Systems. In M. Ajmone Marsan, editor, *Application and Theory of*

Petri Nets 1993, volume 691 of *Lecture Notes in Computer Science*, pages 1–16. Springer-Verlag, Berlin, 1993.

[Hee94] K.M. van Hee. *Information System Engineering: a Formal Approach.* Cambridge University Press, 1994.

[HL91] K. Hayes and K. Lavery. *Workflow management software: the business opportunity.* Ovum, 1991.

[Jen92] K. Jensen. *Coloured Petri Nets. Basic concepts, analysis methods and practical use.* EATCS monographs on Theoretical Computer Science. Springer-Verlag, Berlin, 1992.

[Kou95] T.M. Koulopoulos. *The Workflow Imperative.* Van Nostrand Reinhold, New York, 1995.

[MBC86] M. Ajmone Marsan, G. Balbo, and G. Conte. *Performance Models of Multiprocessor Systems.* The MIT Press, Cambridge, 1986.

[Mur89] T. Murata. Petri Nets: Properties, Analysis and Applications. *Proceedings of the IEEE*, 77(4):541–580, April 1989.

[Rei85] W. Reisig. *Petri nets: an introduction*, volume 4 of *Monographs in theoretical computer science : an EATCS series.* Springer-Verlag, Berlin, 1985.

[Sch96] T. Schäl. *Workflow Management for Process Organisations*, volume 1096 of *Lecture Notes in Computer Science.* Springer-Verlag, Berlin, 1996.

[SL96] Software-Ley. *COSA User Manual.* Software-Ley GmbH, Pullheim, 1996.

[Sta92] P.H. Starke. *INA: Integrierter Netz Analysator, Handbuch*, 1992.

[SV90] M. Silva and R. Valette. Petri Nets and Flexible Manufacturing. In G. Rozenberg, editor, *Advances in Petri Nets 1989*, volume 424 of *Lecture Notes in Computer Science*, pages 274–417. Springer-Verlag, Berlin, 1990.

[WFM96] WFMC. Workflow Management Coalition Terminology and Glossary (WFMC-TC-1011). Technical report, Workflow Management Coalition, Brussels, 1996.

11 LOGICAL STRUCTURE TRANSFORMATION BETWEEN SGML DOCUMENTS

Noriko SAKAI , Atsuhiro TAKASU , and Jun ADACHI

Abstract: Many documents comply with SGML (Standard Generalized Markup Language), since documents with logical structures have advantages in utilization. However, diversified structures lead to problems in full-text database systems of those documents.

This paper proposes a transformation method of logical structure and it enables database systems to provide users with a unique logical structure for retrieval or browsing. The proposed method transforms logical structures as follows: 1.Specify the transformation rules, 2.Extract necessary elements from the original document according to the transformation rules, 3.Arrange extracted elements, and 4.Create and accept elements for a new document.

In this method, elements are expressed with *path* expressions relevant to tree structures and the relations between intermediate nodes in the paths of original and transformed elements are defined in the transformation rules. This relationship judges original elements to be merged in a new document as cases of repetition or combination.

11.1 INTRODUCTION

Explicit description of a logical structure is an essential aspect of writing electronically processed documents, since the formatting of text using defined descriptions increases the versatility of generating, storing, laying out, exchanging, and utilizing the text. SGML (Standard Generalized Markup Language) [1], the international standard (ISO 8879) expressly developed for this purpose, allows those who handle their own documents, such as publishers, academic societies, and database managers, to define logical structures depending on their individual preferences, a capability which markedly improves the flexibility and ease with which highly expressive documents can be produced. However, when such documents are stored in a full-text database, differences in logical structures lead to difficulties in data retrieval and document browsing, e.g., easily identifying retrieved elements with non-uniform formats and quickly comprehending various page layouts. For documents in the same domain, specifically scientific documents, logical structures are similar to a certain extent but may have different logical structures.

Another important aspect which must be considered is the costs associated with data entry. That is, it is much more efficient to store documents as originally generated in an SGML-based logical structure and then dynamically transform them on demand into a uniform logical structure that is unique to the database system used.

In addition to SGML, other methods have also been developed for easily describing logical structures: HTML (Hyper Text Markup Language) and LaTeX are currently the most commonly used formatting tools. HTML is based on SGML, yet its logical structure lacks flexibility with regard to distinctive descriptive capabilities. On the other hand, LaTeX is not based on SGML, and its usefulness is limited due to its loosely defined logical structures and layout-oriented commands.

Therefore, assuming that documents are stored in a full-text database as originally written, we have been developing a data retrieval system expressly designed to handle SGML-formatted scientific documents. In our approach, the database system responds to any input query by dynamically transforming all documents matching the query so that they have a uniform structure when provided to the user. A brief description of the operation of the systems follows (Figure11.1).

1. As a part of the system design process, assignment rules between logical elements of the database system and those of stored original documents are specified.

2. Queries are issued based on the logical structure of the database system.

file=overview.eps,width=8cm

Figure 11.1 An overview of the proposed database system for SGML documents.

3. Matching documents are dynamically transformed into system logical structures and provided in a uniform format.

The method used for dynamic transformation is the key consideration in system operation, and although several such methods have been proposed, they either cannot perform complex transformations or are not user-friendly since programming skills are required. Our method, however, overcomes these drawbacks by defining assignment rules between logical elements of original and transformed documents, called specifications, so that equivalence between them can be maintained.

Section 11.2 describes SGML standards and transformation problems due to differences in logical structures, while Section 11.3 discusses the inherent drawbacks in previously proposed transformation methods. In Section 11.4, an overview of our transformation method is presented, and in Section 11.5 we explain the assignment rules between system and original logical elements. Section 11.6 provides a detailed description of system operation. Finally conclusions and future tasks are described.

11.2 SGML AND LOGICAL STRUCTURE TRANSFORMATION

11.2.1 SGML Standards

Any document described using SGML standards consists of the following parts:

1. SGML Declaration – Declaration of the character set to be used within a document. This declaration is also used for other, more complex functions.

2. Document Type Definition – Definition of the logical structures which are constructed using elements. A document type definition (DTD) is used to define the specific logical structure meeting an individual requirement.

3. SGML Instance – Documents themselves are described explicitly with logical structures and *marked up*, i.e., character strings are recursively set between *tags* which indicate the name of an element. Tags coming before a character string are termed *start tags*, while those following it are termed *close tags*.

```
<Recordlist><Record><Title>Doc1</Title><Author><Surname>Smith</Surname>
<Firstname>Bob</Firstname><Middlename>Thomas</Middlename><Affiliation>
NACSIS</Affiliation></Author><Author><Surname>Jones</Surname><Surname>
Nelson</Surname><Firstname>Mary</Firstname><Affiliation>NACSIS
</Affiliation></Author><Ref>reference1</Ref><Ref>reference2</Ref>
</Record><Record><Title>Doc2</Title><Author><Firstname>Michael
</Firstname><Surname>Brown</Surname><Affiliation>Univ. of Tokyo
</Affiliation></Author></Record></Recordlist>
```

Figure 11.2 Typical SGML marked-up document.

file=rei.eps,width=

Figure 11.3 Possible differences between original and transformed documents

Figure11.2 shows an SGML instance of a document marked up in SGML as an example of a typical original document. This document has a logical structure containing numerous logical elements. For example, **<Title> Doc1 </Title>** is one element, where **Title** is the element name, and **<Title>** and **</Title>** respectively indicate the start and close tags of the contents corresponding to character string **Doc1**. It should be noted that since the start and close tags are recursively described, the defined logical structure is similar to the logical structure defined by a conventional tree expression.

11.2.2 Differences in Logical Structures

To develop a suitable transformation method, the differences between the logical structures must be identified and classified.

Figure11.3 shows the tree expression corresponding to the original document example (Figure11.2), where it and its parts are referred to as "original," e.g., original document, original elements, etc. Also shown is the tree expression representing the original document following transformation, where it and its parts are correspondingly referred to as "transformed." These documents are used to clarify the differences in logical structures, all of which fall into one of the categories described below. The numeric suffixes of the element names indicate ID numbers that are not included in element names.

Identified differences are as follows:

1. Selection of elements – An element defined in the original document has no equivalent element in the transformed document, e.g., **Middlename** (*3*). Conversely, if the transformed document has an element for which the

original document has no equivalent, the transformed document simply assumes that there is no content to that element. Equivalence of two elements means that those hold the same information, such as the author name.

2. Names of elements – Equivalent elements have different names, e.g., **Title** (*0*) and **subject** (*c*).

3. Depth of logical structures – An element in the original document is at a higher or lower depth of logical structure than the equivalent transformed element, e.g., **Affiliation** (*4*) and **affiliation** (*b*), **Ref** (*9*) and **ref** and (*d*), respectively.

4. Original elements with the same name and position are either (i) merged together so that they are equivalent to a single transformed element or (ii) not merged together so that they are equivalent to a new transformed element at the same position, e.g., **Affiliation** (*4* and *8*) to **affiliation** (*b*) and **Ref** (*9* and *10*) to **ref** (*d* and *e*), respectively.

5. Two or more original elements are combined to form an equivalent transformed element, e.g., **Surname** (*1*) and **Firstname** (*2*) make **author** (*a*). This assignment is termed *combination*.

6. Order of elements – The order of two original elements is reversed in the equivalent transformed element, e.g., original element **Title** (*0*) appears before **Surname** (*1*) but **subject** (*c*) comes after **author** (*a*).

The proposed method is designed to transform documents with different logical structures into a uniform structure for use by a particular database system. If the database system incorporates this method, many different structures can be handled so that upon retrieval or while browsing, users are furnished documents with uniform structures.

11.3 RELATED TRANSFORMATION METHODS

Many studies have focused on the processing of structured documents. Their objectives vary, such as editing, laying out, summarizing, and so on. Here we refer to some which deal with the transformation of logical structures.

11.3.1 Transformation of Highly Structured Text

Blake et al.[2] proposed a method to automatically transform a marked-up Oxford English Dictionary (OED) into a more concise edition. In their approach, the highly structured contents of the OED were described by a tree expression and simple operators were defined to manipulate subtree and leaves of the tree, such as "*choose an element which is a child of X.*" This transform method, however, is not flexible enough for our application because SGML documents have a more complex structures.

11.3.2 One-to-One Transformation

Warmer et al.[4] proposed a method to transform SGML documents by defining actions for specific tags. This method can be applied to transform SGML-formatted documents into electronic mail format. For example, if a document contains an element like "**<Mail><Sender>Smith</Sender><Recipient>Jones </Recipient><Body>Hello</Body></Mail>**," then a division word "**From:** " is output when the start tag "**<Sender>**" occurs, and a new line marker is output when the close tag "**</Sender>**" occurs.

Similar transformation methods based on the occurrence of elements and tags were also adopted by Prices et al. [3] and others, although such one-to-one transformations cannot use contextual information regarding the occurrence of elements or combine multiple elements.

11.3.3 DTD-based Transformation

Warmer et al.[5] also tried to implement transformation of SGML documents with writing specification in DTD. Their specifications are functions for the appearance of each element, described in C and embedded in DTD. This method has the advantage that specifications can be described distinctly depending on the logical structure.

On the other hand, this method is not particularly flexible to operate, such as for combination. Furthermore, the editing specification makes it difficult to revise DTD because the original DTD is lost.

11.4 OVERVIEW OF THE METHOD

The following procedure is used by the proposed transformation method.

1. Specify assignment rules between original and transformed elements.
2. Analyze the original document and extract necessary elements for creating a transformed document.
3. Arrange extracted elements regarding repetition or combination.
4. Determine a set of elements describing a transformed document and sequentially arrange them to construct the transformed document.

Steps 1 – 4 are discussed in further detail.

11.5 ELEMENTS AND SPECIFYING ASSIGNMENT RULES

We assume that a defined logical structure consists of logical elements, that an actual document is an ordered list of element instants having values such as character strings or figures, and that the position of an element is expressed as the path from the root of the logical structure to it. The path consists of a list of *components* corresponding to elements of the SGML standard. Components are delimited with slashes "/" and, if necessary, are uniquely identified by a numeric suffix referred to as an *ID*.

For example, an element instance named **E'** with value **Smith** is described by the path "**/Recordlist1/Record1/Author1/Surname1**." Hereafter, complete paths are called *elements*, each of which consists of *components.*

Definitions for a formal expression of our method and an explanation of how to describe assignment rules and how they work are provided below.

11.5.1 Superiority of Components

Assignment rules describe which of one or more original elements compose a transformed element and, as mentioned above, elements are distinguished by their names and IDs. However, the following two cases need more information in order to evaluate the required transformation. For this purpose, *superiority* of components is defined.

Superiority has two roles. The first is relevant to the relation between element instances in the same original document. For old element instances with paths having the same names, it is necessary to distinguish cases where repeated elements are to be merged and those where merging is not required. Consider an assignment rule, original element "**/Document/Chapter/Section/Paragraph**" that is defined to become a transformed element "**/document/section**," and original element instances with different IDs only in **Paragraph** to compose the same transformed element instance. This case is called *repetition.*

According to this rule, "**/Document1/Chapter1/Section1/Paragraph1**" and "**/Document1/Chapter1/Section1/Paragraph2**" are merged and become an element instance. On the other hand, an original element instance with a different ID in **Section**, "**/Document1/Chapter1/Section2/Paragraph3**," composes another transformed element instance.

Superiority indicates the distinction of these two occasions. Since **Section** is decisive, it is defined as superior, and **Paragraph** is not. Superior components are much more common than those not, and non-superior components are marked with "**!**."

The second case arises from the possibility that the length of the paths, that is, the numbers of components in the paths of the equivalent original and transformed elements may be different. For this situation, the relation of file=iroiro.eps,width=

Figure 11.4 The role of superiority and effect of various superiorities.

components in paths must be defined. For example, in the same case as before, the change of **Paragraph** is neglected and treated as a repetition of the previous instance, and original elements having **Section** with different IDs are not.

For transformed element instances, the change of **Section** in the original document is reflected as the change of **section**. That is, when original elements which have different IDs in the components beneath **Section**, are repetition and become the transformed element "**/document1/section1**," and an element which has different ID on **Section** becomes a transformed element "**/document1/section2**," which has a different ID in **section**. To meet this requirement, **Section** and **section** are key and superior with the same sequence of superior components in the paths. Therefore, the number of superior components, e.g., components without symbol "**!**" in the assigned transformed and original elements should be the same.

From the example in this paper, one rule which describes the relation between the original and transformed elements using superiority is shown in Figure11.4 *(0)*.

Figure11.4 also shows how other superiority affects in various cases. In case *(1)*, the change of ID of the original component **Author** is not neglected and affects the change of the transformed component **author**, in addition to *(0)*, which is in the example assignment rule. Then the former two and latter two original elements are merged and become transformed elements with different IDs in **affiliation**.

11.5.2 Expression of Elements

Elements are used in two ways: for specifying assignment rules and for analyzing and constructing documents, defined as element "*A*" and element instance "*D*," respectively. *A* and *D* are described using the following attributes.

1. Elements of Assignment: *A*
   - The path is denoted as *A.path*. It expresses the position in a logical structure. It could be "**/Recordlist/Record/Author/Surname**."
   - A *COMB* or *NOT* flag indicates whether a particular *A* contains a combination, denoted as *A.comb*.
2. Element instances in Document: *D*

- The path of D is denoted as $D.path$. A document is constructed by an ordered list of D and paths represent the position of D. It could be "**/Recordlist1/Record1/Author1/Surname1**."
- The value of D represents actual data and is denoted as $D.val$, i.e., $D.val$ could be "**Smith**."
- $D.ass$ represents an assignment rule by which an element instance is transformed.

Components in a path expression are denoted as C and the attributes of C are defined as follows:

1. The name of a component is denoted as $C.name$.
2. Each C is allocated a numeral ID denoted as $C.id$. $C.id$ is unique in a particular sort of C.
3. A flag to indicate whether C has superiority and is denoted as $C.sup$. Superiority is applied to the whole path expression of transformed elements and original elements if the assignment does not have a combination and to the common part of paths of original elements if a combination exists. Values are SUP, NOT, and $COMB$ for the cases if a component is superior, not superior, and in the other parts of the path of elements to be combined, respectively.

The path or fragment of path, composed of a list of components, is represented as P, and P has three types. They are P, P_{SUNO}, and P_{COMB} for the cases if $C.sup$ is not determined or is irrelevant, SUP or NOT, and $COMB$ respectively.

The components of two paths having the same names and/or IDs means that the components of each path have the same name and/or IDs throughout the paths, from the roots to leaves.

Original elements, original paths, and original components are expressed with primes "$'$," such as E'.

11.5.3 Specification of Element Assignments

At the start of system operation, it is necessary to specify the assignment rules of elements between original and transformed logical structures. This procedure is performed in advance as a part of the design of the database system, in most cases by the authors of the documents or the manager of the database system.

The database designer basically defines how a transformed element is composed of an original element. Here the assignment rules contain:

```
   #1. Cases without Combination
0. /recordlist /record !/subject; /Recordlist /Record !/Title
1. /recordlist/record!/affiliation;/Recordlist/Record!/Author!/Affiliation
2. /recordlist /record !/other /ref; /Recordlist /Record /Ref;

   #2. Cases with Combination
3. /recordlist/record!/author;/Recordlist/Record!/Author/;Surname;Firstname
```

Figure 11.5 Specification sample (Numbers at the beginning of lines are for explanation.)

- How one or more original elements compose one transformed element.
- How superiority between components of original and transformed elements is arranged.
- How the formation of transformed element is specified.
  In this paper, the detailed explanation of processing data format is omitted in order to focus on the description of how logical structure transformation works.

To describe these functions, an actual specification is described as follows. First, as the simplest case, when a transformed element consists of an original element, the assignment rule is a list composed of the transformed element itself and the original element, which is equivalent to the transformed element, in a path expression delimited by ";," such as:

```
/recordlist/record!/affiliation;/Recordlist/Record!/Author!/Affiliation
  (transformed element)              (original element)
```

This means an original element instance "**/Recordlist/Record/Author/Affiliation ... NACSIS**" becomes a transformed element instance "**/recordlist/record/affiliation ... NACSIS.**"

When a transformed element consists of more than one original element, the assignment rule is a list in which the transformed element comes first, followed by the common part of paths of the original elements assigned to that transformed element, and finally as many remaining parts of paths of the original elements come as the number to be combined, delimited by ";" such as:

```
/recordlist/record!/author;/Recordlist/Record!/Author/;Surname;Firstname
(trans. element)    (common part of orig. elements)    (the other parts)
```

This means that the original element instances "**/Recordlist/Record/Author /Surname ... Smith**" and "**/Recordlist/Record/Author/Firstname ... Bob**" make the transformed element instance "**/recordlist/record /author ... Smith, Bob.**"

In our example, the assignment rule is as shown in Figure11.5.

```
D'.ass {C'.name:C'.id:C'.sup }+ D'.val (sup:  1=SUP 0=NOT -1=COMB)

 1. 0:/Recordlist1:1 /Record1:1 /Title1:0 : Doc1
 2. 3:/Recordlist1:1 /Record1:1 /Author1:0 /Surname1:-1 : Smith
 3. 3:/Recordlist1:1 /Record1:1 /Author1:0 /Firstname1:-1 : Bob
 4. 1:/Recordlist1:1 /Record1:1 /Author1:0 /Affiliation1:0: NACSIS
 5. 3:/Recordlist1:1 /Record1:1 /Author2:0 /Surname2:-1 : Jones
 6. 3:/Recordlist1:1 /Record1:1 /Author2:0 /Surname3:-1 : Nelson
 7. 3:/Recordlist1:1 /Record1:1 /Author2:0 /Firstname2:-1 : Mary
 8. 1:/Recordlist1:1 /Record1:1 /Author2:0 /Affiliation2:0 : NACSIS
 9. 2:/Recordlist1:1 /Record1:1 /Ref1:1 : reference1
10. 2:/Recordlist1:1 /Record1:1 /Ref2:1 : reference2
11. 0:/Recordlist1:1 /Record2:1 /Title2:0 : Doc2
12. 3:/Recordlist1:1 /Record2:1 /Author3:0 /Firstname3:-1 : Michael
13. 3:/Recordlist1:1 /Record2:1 /Author3:0 /Surname4:-1 : Brown
14. 1:/Recordlist1:1 /Record2:1 /Author3:0 /Affiliation3:0 : Univ.ofTokyo
```

Figure 11.6 Results of extraction from an original document (list of extracted elements).

11.6 PROCESSING METHOD

The following sections explain how this method works using above specification.

11.6.1 Extracting Elements from Original Documents

Original element instances referred to in the assignment rule are necessary to compose a transformed document and they are extracted by a way of lexical analysis. This is processed by judging whether each path of an original element instance has the same components in its names as that in one of the assignment rules.

For this example, the results of extraction are shown in Figure11.6. This figure contains the list of element instances, and each line has $D'.ass$, a path expression of an element instance, and $D'.val$ in succession. Path expressions have $C'.name : C'.id : C'.sup$ for each component.

11.6.2 Arranging Element Instances from Original Documents

The system then recognizes repetitions and combinations. If repetitions or combinations occur, those element instances are merged and their values are transformed into new formats. This step is divided into three parts.

Repetition of an Element Instance to be Combined
An author name, for example, is usually composed of a surname and a first-name, but an author possibly may want to register two surnames. To process such a case simply in the next step, the system merges those surnames.

In general, the system finds element instances that have components of common parts with the same names and IDs and components of the remaining with the same names, and merges those element instances. For example, according

```
 1. 0:/Recordlist:1:1 /Record:1:1 /Title:1:0 : Doc1
 2. 3:/Recordlist:1:1 /Record:1:1 /Author:1:0 /Surname:1:-1 : Smith
 3. 3:/Recordlist:1:1 /Record:1:1 /Author:1:0 /Firstname:1:-1 : Bob
 4. 1:/Recordlist:1:1 /Record:1:1 /Author:1:0 /Affiliation:1:0 : NACSIS.
 5. 3:/Recordlist:1:1 /Record:1:1 /Author:2:0 /Surname:2:-1 : Jones(Nelson).
 6. 3:/Recordlist:1:1 /Record:1:1 /Author:2:0 /Firstname:2:-1 : Mary
 7. 1:/Recordlist:1:1 /Record:1:1 /Author:2:0 /Affiliation:2:0 : NACSIS
 8. 2:/Recordlist:1:1 /Record:1:1 /Ref:1:1 : reference1
 9. 2:/Recordlist:1:1 /Record:1:1 /Ref:2:1 : reference2
10. 0:/Recordlist:1:1 /Record:2:1 /Title:2:0 : Doc2
11. 3:/Recordlist:1:1 /Record:2:1 /Author:3:0 /Firstname:3:-1 : Michael
12. 3:/Recordlist:1:1 /Record:2:1 /Author:3:0 /Surname:4:-1 : Brown
13. :/Recordlist:1:1 /Record:2:1 /Author:3:0 /Affiliation:3:0 : Univ.ofToky
```

Figure 11.7 Results of processing of repetition in combination.

to an assignment rule *3.*, two original element instances *5.* and *6.* in Figure11.6 are recognized to be merged because the components have the same names and IDs for the common part "**/Recordlist/Record/Author**" and the remaining components have the same names. On the other hand, an original element instance *13.* is not merged.

The results for this example are shown in Figure11.7. The fifth and sixth element instances in Figure11.6 are merged and the fifth element instance in Figure11.7 is generated.

Combination

When judging combination, the common part of paths must have the same names and IDs. For example, depending on the assignment rule, a surname and a first name of the same author are to be combined, but those of other authors are not. In general, according to an assignment rule *3.*, two original element instances *5.* and *6.* in Figure11.7 are recognized as to be combined because components in the common parts have the same names and IDs, and in the remainder, they are the same as the remaining parts in the assignment rule. On the other hand, the original element instance *12.* is not to be combined since a component in the common part **Record** has a different ID.

The results for this example are shown in Figure11.8. The second and third element instances in Figure11.7 are merged and the second element in Figure11.8 appears with only the common part of the path.

Repetition

Contents which appear many times in an original document are restricted so far as possible to appear only once in a transformed document. In our example, the elements of authors' affiliations appear twice for one record in the original document but repetition in the transformed document is prohibited. This restriction is represented in an assignment rule using superiority.

```
1. 0:/Recordlist:1:1 /Record:1:1 /Title:1:0 : Doc1
2. 3:/Recordlist:1:1 /Record:1:1 /Author:1:0 : Smith, Bob
3. 1:/Recordlist:1:1 /Record:1:1 /Author:1:0 /Affiliation:1:0 : NACSIS
4. 3:/Recordlist:1:1 /Record:1:1 /Author:2:0 : Jones(Nelson), Mary
5. 1:/Recordlist:1:1 /Record:1:1 /Author:2:0 /Affiliation:2:0 : NACSIS
6. 2:/Recordlist:1:1 /Record:1:1 /Ref:1:1 : reference1
7. 2:/Recordlist:1:1 /Record:1:1 /Ref:2:1 : reference2
8. 0:/Recordlist:1:1 /Record:2:1 /Title:2:0 : Doc2
9. 3:/Recordlist:1:1 /Record:2:1 /Author:3:0 : Brown, Michael
10. 1:/Recordlist:1:1 /Record:2:1 /Author:3:0 /Affiliation:3:0 : Univ.ofTokyo
```

Figure 11.8 Results of processing combination.

```
1. 0:/Recordlist1:1 /Record1:1 /Title1:0 : Doc1
2. 3:/Recordlist1:1 /Record1:1 /Author1:0 : Smith, Bob / Jones(Nelson), Mary
3. 1:/Recordlist1:1 /Record1:1 /Author1:0 /Affiliation1:0 : NACSIS / NACSIS
4. 2:/Recordlist1:1 /Record1:1 /Ref1:1 : reference1
5. 2:/Recordlist1:1 /Record1:1 /Ref2:1 : reference2
6. 0:/Recordlist1:1 /Record2:1 /Title2:0 : Doc2
7. 3:/Recordlist1:1 /Record2:1 /Author3:0 : Brown, Michael
8. 1:/Recordlist1:1 /Record2:1 /Author3:0 /Affiliation3:0 : Univ.ofTokyo
```

Figure 11.9 Results of processing repetition.

The system finds element instances which have components if they are superior with the same names and IDs and if not superior only with the same names, and merges them. According to an assignment rule*1.* two original element instances *3.* and *5.* in Figure11.8 are recognized as to be merged because components "**Recordlist**" and "**Record**," which are superior, have the same names and IDs, and component "**Title**," which is not superior, has the same names.

As a result of this processing, the original element instances become as shown in Figure11.9. The third and fifth element instances in Figure11.8 are merged, and the third element instance in Figure11.9 is generated.

11.6.3 Setting Element Instances and Composing a Transformed Document

By the process described up to here, one original element instance is equivalent to a transformed element instance. Thus, the system can set up a suite of transformed element instances which comply with the original element instances. In this step, differences of IDs in the original superior components are reflected in the IDs of the transformed superior components in the same order from the root of the paths.

In the example, according to the assignment rule *1.*, a transformed element instance *3.* in Figure11.10 is set for the original element instance *3.* in Figure11.9. For the original element instance in which the second superior

{C.name:C.id}+ D.val

```
1./recordlist0 /record0 /subject0 : Doc1
2./recordlist0 /record0 /author0 : Smith, Bob / Jones(Nelson), Mary
3./recordlist0 /record0 /affiliation0 : NACSIS/ NACSIS
4./recordlist0 /record0 /other0 /ref1 : reference1
5./recordlist0 /record0 /other0 /ref2 : reference1
6./recordlist0 /record1 /subject1 : Doc2
7./recordlist0 /record1 /author1 : Brown, Michael
8./recordlist0 /record1 /affiliation1 : Univ.ofTokyo
```

Figure 11.10 Results of fixing a set of transformed elements.

component has a different ID from the former *8.* in Figure11.9, a transforn element instance in which the second superior component also has a differ ID from the former *8.* in Figure11.10 is created.

Finally, transformed element instances are put in an order that is appropri for a transformed structure and are accepted in a way of syntactical analy and SGML tags are added.

11.7 CONCLUSION

We proposed a transformation method between documents using SGML w various structures, and explained how to designate a specification of the tra formation and how the system processes documents.

In a database system with this transformation capability, only one logi structure, user-interface, processing application is needed since the diversity logical structures is absorbed by dynamic structure conversion. Therefore, s systems can store various documents from many societies or publishers as t are originally prepared and provide users with browsing and retrieval opti using logical structures.

In the next phase, we will extend this method to enable flexible specificat of transformation using relative expressions of paths. We will implement t method as a prototype to evaluate the effectiveness of this approach.

Acknowledgments

This research was partially supported by Japan Society for the Promotion of Scier and by the Grant-in-Aid for Scientific Research of the Ministry of Education, Scier Sports and Culture, Goverment of Japan.

References

[1] van Herwijnen, E: "Practical SGML," Kluer Academic Publishers.

[2] Blake, G.E., Bray, T. and Tompa, F.WM.: "Shortening the OED: Experience with a Grammar-Defined Database," ACM Trans. Info. Syst., Vol.10, No.3 (July 1992), pp. 213–232.

[3] Price, L.A. and Schneider, J.: "Evolution of an SGML Application Generator," ACM Conf. on Document Processing Systems (1988), pp. 51–60.

[4] Warmer, J. and van Egmond, S.: "The Implementation of the Amsterdam SGML Parser," Electronic Publishing Vol.2-No.2 (July 1989), pp. 65–90.

[5] Warmer, J. and van Vliet, H.: "Processing SGML Documents," Electronic Publishing, Vol.4-No.1 (March 1991), pp. 3–26.

12 TASK ORIENTED MODELING OF DOCUMENT SECURITY IN CapBasED-AMS

Patrick C. K. Hung
and Kamalakar Karlapalem

ABSTRACT
The CapBasED-AMS (Capability-based and Event driven Activity Management System) deals with the management and execution of activities. A Problem Solving Agent (PSA) is a human, or a hardware system, or a software system having an ability to execute activities. An activity consists of multiple inter-dependent tasks that need to be coordinated, scheduled and executed by a set of PSAs, where each task is an atomic activity executed by exactly one PSA. A task can potentially involve some processing of documents. Since many of the documents have sensitive information, document security issues have to be modeled, specified, and managed by the activity management system. In this paper, we present security issues for document management in CapBasED-AMS from the point of task execution by using a PSA role based document security model. We present a task coordination model for document security control from the PSA viewpoint, task viewpoint, and activity viewpoint by adapting role-based document security model. A major contribution of this work is to integrate the security requirements, and mechanisms from these viewpoints into a logical framework which can be used to model, manage, and impose security driven activity execution.

Introduction

The CapBasED-AMS (Capability-based and Event-driven Activity Management System) developed in [1,3,4,5,9] deals with the management and execution of activities. There are two approaches developed by researchers [6] for managing access control of documents. Discretionary Access Controls (DAC) is used to model the security of objects on the basis of a subject's access privileges defining what kind of access a subject has to an object, and a set of predicates to represent content-based access rules. In Mandatory Access Control (MAC) the security objects and subjects are assigned to a security level. The access rule is based on pre-defined predicate which compares the security levels of objects and subjects. But these approaches to document security modeling do not consider the task semantics, and the security requirements imposed by the task. The task semantics include aspects derived from the coordination of task in the activity, the PSA to execute the task, the documents needed and the organization factors like constraints involved in the execution of task. We will adopt DAC for addressing PSAs/Tasks access to documents, and we will adopt MAC to allow PSAs manage the security specification of documents. Based on the role based document security model [7,8], we present a task coordination model for document security control from the PSA viewpoint, task viewpoint, and activity viewpoint.

Concepts and Terminology

Activity management consists of decomposition of activities into tasks, coordination and data sharing among multiple PSAs executing the activity, and monitoring, scheduling and controlling the execution of multiple tasks of an activity. A software system that facilitates the specification, maintenance, and execution of activities is known as an Activity Management System (AMS).

Figure 1 shows the CapBasED-AMS architecture which consists of two parts: (1) the capability-based activity specification and decomposition component consisting of an Activity Specification Language (ASL) processor, an Activity Decomposer (AD) and a Match Maker (MM). ASL facilitates the description and specification of the activities. The Document Management System (DMS) facilitates the specification and management of documents. AD decomposes an activity into tasks. MM identifies PSAs to execute the tasks. AD and MM generate a coordination plan using a Task Specification Language (TSL) as addressed in [4,5]. (2) The event-driven activity execution component deals with propagating information, coordinating PSAs, scheduling and monitoring execution of tasks of an activity. And the activity execution is supported by three modules, namely the Document Manager (DM), Activity Generator (AG) and the Activity Coordinator (AC). The DM manages the document flows and enforces the security control on documents during activity execution. The AG acts as a pre-compiler. It takes a specification in TSL (the ActivityID.tsl in Figure) to generate the activity graph, ECA rules and define runtime data schema. The AC acts as an execution manager for activity execution.

As the focus of this paper is on security issues, we refer you to [4,9] for further details on activity specification, decomposition and execution.

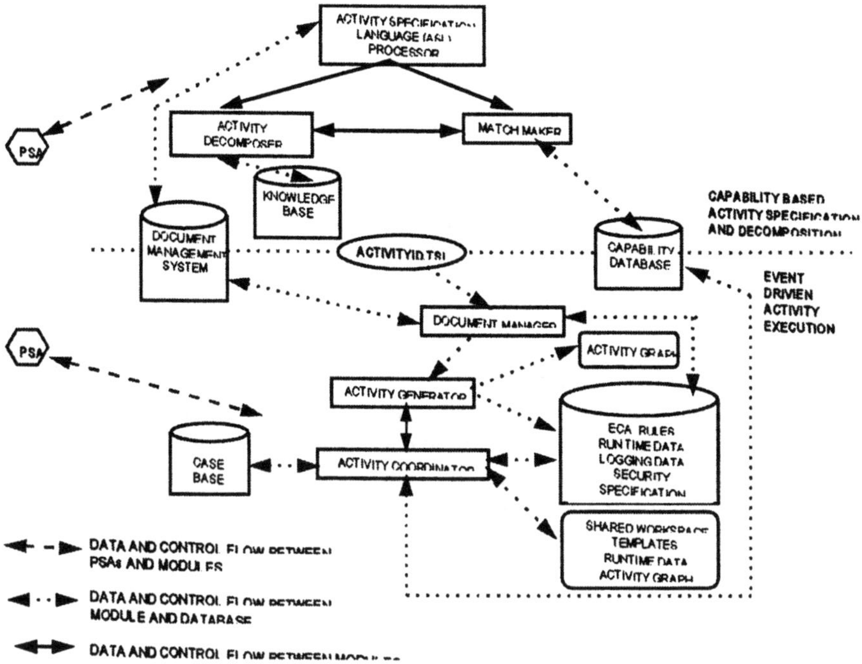

Figure 1 Arichitecture of CapBasED Activity Management System

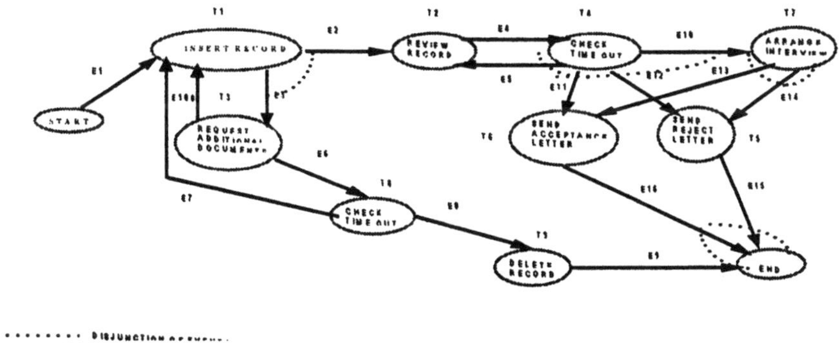

Figure 2 The Coordination Plan for Graduate Admission Activity

Example: The Graduate Admission Office (see Figure 2) processes the applications of the potential graduate students twice a year by using a set of university and departmental guidelines. The graduate admissions committee headed by Graduate Coordinator, supported by the Graduate Secretary and consisting of few faculty members review the applications. Each time a batch of new student application forms come, and then the clerk will check the completeness of the students application. If the students application is incomplete, a message requesting additional documents by a due date is sent to the candidate. If the application is complete, the graduate coordinator initiates a task to review the students application by decision due date, during which time the status of students application is "pending". The result of the review process can be i) accept the student, and a letter of acceptance is sent to the student, ii) reject the student, and a reject letter is sent to the student, and iii) interview the student, an interview call letter is sent to the student. either to accept or reject the student.

Note that the above mentioned activity will process a set of documents like letter, application and evaluation form during its execution. This activity will be used as a running example to illustrate the document security in CapBasED-AMS. The rest of the paper is organized as follows, the next section describes the document classification, the following section describes the security modeling and enforcement in document scope and flow, and the last section presents the conclusions.

Security Modeling of Documents for Task Execution

Document provides semantic information and data for the execution of task, and the document is represented by the occurrence of input or output event. Table 1 presents some output event specifications for the Graduate Admissions activity.

Event Id	Doc Id	Source (s)
E100	Application_folder	DMS
E200	Pending_folder	DMS

Table 1 Event corresponding to Documents

Each of the documents Doc.id defined above must have the Taskorg which is the task where the document is originated from and Taskdest which is the task where the document is destined to. Each document Doc.id is directly retrieved from some source, e.g., Document Management System (DMS). The Source is the field which specifies where the document is from. At the execution time, a PSA can retrieve the document from the specified source or create a new document. Document plays five different roles in CapBasED-AMS: input, new, archive, retrieval and output document. Input document is the document embedded in the input event of the task before execution. New document is the document created during the execution of task. Archive document is the document archived in the DMS during the execution of task. Retrieval document is the document retrieved from the specified source like DMS which is not included in the input document of task. Output document is the document embedded in the output event generated by the task after execution. Task takes one or more kinds of input documents In Doc represented by input events and then the PSA may perform certain operations on these In Doc, or the PSA may create some new documents New Doc, archive or retrieve some documents Archive Doc. or Retrieval Doc. during the execution of task. After the execution of the task a set of output documents Out Doc represented by output events generated by the task govern the flow of documents during the activity execution.

Security Classifications

In order to manage the security control systematically, there are four security classes managed by the CapBasED-AMS, namely, World, Group, Owner and System. World means all the PSAs and users in the environment have the authorization to access the specified document. Group means a set of specified PSA roles or instances have the authorization to access the specified document. Every instance of a PSA role is authorized to access some documents by default. The instance inherits all authorizations from its role by default, and every instance can have some additional authorizations on the document regardless of its role and group. The security administrator is responsible for creating a group and assigning the PSA roles or instances to it by specifying it declaratively.

Let *Instance(PSA_Role)* be the function which returns a set of instances of a PSARole. The set of PSA instances excluded *Inst_Excluded* specifies the set of PSA instances which is a subset of *Instance(PSA_Role)* excluded from this group. On the other hand, the set of PSA instance included *Inst_Included* specifies the set of PSA instances which is not included in the included in this group explicitly. In our example, there may be a group ``Graduate Admission Committee" as shown Table 2. ``Dr. Smith" and ``Dr. Shepard" are the instances of role ``Lecturer" and ``Research Associate" respectively. And then, ``Dr. Smith" is excluded from this group explicitly even though its role ``Lecturer" is in the ``PSA Role" field. On the other hand, ``Dr. Shepard" is included in this group explicitly even though its role ``Research Associate" is not in the ``PSA Role" field.

Group Identifier	Graduate Admission Committee
PSA Role	Graduate Coordinator
	Graduate Secretary
	Lecturer
PSA Instance(s) Excluded	Dr. Smith
PSA Instance(s) Included	Dr. Shepard

Table 2 Group Instance Specification

Every document in the CapBasED-AMS has a owner (the user/PSA who creates the document). In our example, ``Prof. Fred" who is the ``Graduate Coordinator" creates the ``Evaluation Form" for each application form. Therefore, ``Prof. Fred" is the owner of the ``Evaluation Form". System means only the CapBasED-AMS and/or security administrator have the authorization to access the document. In our example, after the graduate admission activity specification and decomposition module will generate an intermediate file (activity.tsl) for the activity execution module [9] to facilitate the execution of the activity. Such a document in the CapBasED-AMS can only be accessed by the system class or security administrator.

Access Privileges

There are a set of access privileges for executing operations on document in CapBasED-AMS such as read, write, modify and security-specification. The set of access privileges are all self-explanatory except the security-specification. Furthermore, some abstract access privileges such as ``verify" and ``evaluate" for an applicant's form can be defined by user as well. The security-specification means the privilege to modify the security control on the documents, and it has two levels of specification, one is the specification of security class to the specified document and the other one is the specification of access privilege to the specified document. Each PSA role will be assigned a security level number which is an numeric value assigned by the security administrator at the specification time by evaluating the security organization factor of the PSA. The security organization factor is the index to represent the accessibility of a document by a PSA in an organization. The instance inherits the security level number from its role by default. The PSA instance can also be assigned a specific security level number other than the default one inherited from its role. At the execution time, the security administrator can explicitly assign a specific security level number to PSA according to new requirements in a dynamic environment. For example, the PSA ``Lecturer" has 7 as security level number in the graduate admission activity. But his security level number may be amended to 9 which is higher for some other activity like ``Teaching Database Course", it is because ``Lecturer" with security level number 9 is the main role participate in this activity. In a more dynamic environment, a PSA can have different security level numbers for different documents in the same activity. The function SecurityLevel(PSAID, DocID) calculates the security level number of PSAID for accessing DocID explicitly. Thus, the security level number of a PSA may be different for different documents.

The main purpose for assigning security level number is when a PSA grants the security-specification privilege to others, the awardee must have the security level number which is greater than the security level number of the granter. If it grants to world or group, only those instances in the world or group which have higher security level number than the granter has this privilege. The reason from having security level numbers is to remove cyclic grants. A PSA does not want one of the descendants who has the ability to change the security control to come back and revoke its access privileges again. There is a system log which is only accessible by the system class, to keep track of the grant history for recovery once the security control is violated. Furthermore, the same access rights may be granted from different sources. Therefore, the log also keeps track of each source of granted access. If a granter's authorizations is revoked, then all the descendents which are granted authorizations by it will also be revoked completely. But if the recipient has the authorizations granted from other unrevoked source, then the recipient keeps its privileges.

Security Classes in Logical Document

In CapBasED-AMS, the document is treated as a logical document which can be divided into a set of logical sub-documents shown in Figure 3 based on the security classes. In our example, an ``Postgraduate Admission Application Form" can be treated as a logical document which includes a set of logical sub-documents like ``Personal Particulars", ``Academic Background", ``Relevant Working History" and ``Confidential Recommendation". Each of these sub-documents is mapped to different security classes, and to a physical sub-document.

Owner inherits the access privileges of sub-documents from the pre-defined template created by the security administrator. Whenever a document is created,

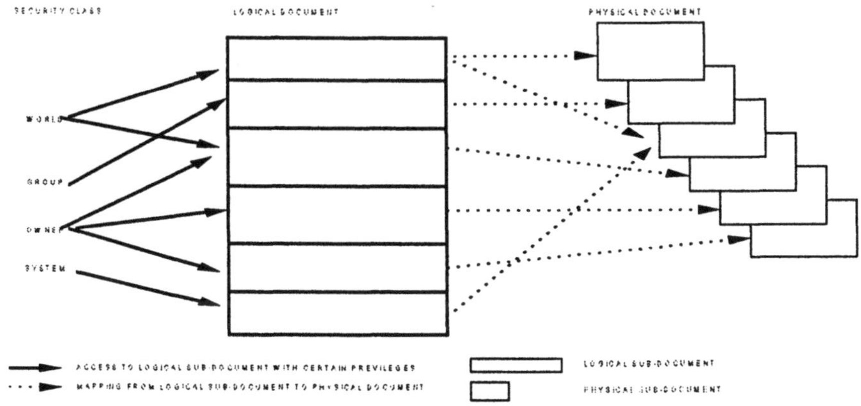

Figure 3 Security Control in Logical Document

Document ID	Graduate Admission Application Form (No: 93856543)
Sub-Document ID	Academic Background History, Relevant Working History, Confidential Recommendation
Authorizations	Read, Security-Specification, Approve
PSA Role(s)/Group ID	Postgraduate Committee, Administrative Officer
PSA Instance(s) Excluded	None
PSA Instance(s) Included	Dr. Shepard

Table 3 Document Access Privileges

the document owner is able to grant the inherited privileges from the sub-documents to others. That is, one can specify which PSAs are allowed to execute the operations on specified sub-documents by specifying it declaratively. The security administrator has the privilege to grant any security authentication to any group of PSAs. In our example, after the ``Executive Officer" in the admission registration office receives the application form from the applicant, it may grant the privileges of accessing this form to the appropriate PSA in the department in order to execute the graduate admission activity as shown in Table 3.

Privileges can also apply to a set of documents as generic privileges. Furthermore, based on the world, group, owner, and system classification, the documents which have the same logical template and attributes can also be classified into different groups for easing the management of security authorization specification. In our example, all the Postgraduate Admission Application Forms can be organized once a semester in the academic year, for example, ``1996 Fall-Semester Applications". Therefore, the ``Graduate Committee" who examine the potential candidates is granted the authorization to access this document group instead of granting authorization to the application forms one by one. A set of documents can be assigned (as a single unit) generic privileges. In order to limit the access to document by the PSAs only when they are executing the task, we develop the concept of a session. A session is the time interval during a task is executed. A PSA can access the document only during a session, but a PSA can also access the document out of a session when the security specification of PSA to the documents it allows to do so. In our example, when there is an acceptance letter returned from the post office, the ``Clerk" is allowed to read and check the correctness of applicant's mailing address from the applicant's form even though the execution of task ``Send Acceptance Letter" is completed.

In Figure 4, the document security model shows the relationships among the PSA Instance, PSA Role, Activity, Task and Document in the CapBasED-AMS. The mapping between the PSA role and instance is many to many and each PSA instance is assigned to a role during a session. The activity is decomposed into a set of tasks where each task is matched with exactly one PSA role, and the PSA is matched to a task may need to access document during the task execution. The constraint factor ``the document can not be updated by two or more PSA concurrently" and session factor ``the PSA can only access this document only when the task is executing." can determine the document access by a PSA. The authentication of a PSA to access a document is determined by the security class and access privilege specified on the document.

Security Modeling of Documents and Enforcement

Every task has input and output event(s) except the ``START" and ``END" task in the coordination plan as defined in [4,5], and there may be documents represented by the events as shown in Figure 5. Let *In Doc.1 ... In Doc.N* be the set of documents represented by the subset of input events. During the execution of the

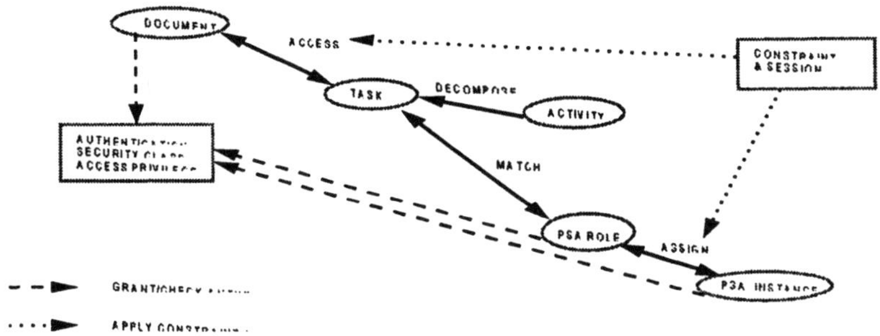

Figure 4 Document Security Model for CapBasED-AMS

task, the PSA may perform certain operations on these input documents, and a set of new documents *New Doc* may be created by the task. In our example, the ``Graduate Coordinator" must be able to create a document such as ``Evaluation Form" for each applicant to record the evaluation status of the application. Each type of the document may have some pre-defined template. The default security control requirements on the document may also be specified by the security administrator. In our example, the ``Evaluation Form" of each applicant may only be accessed by the ``Graduate Admission Committee" group by default.

On the other hand, some documents from *In Doc, New Doc or Retrieval Doc* may be archived in the DMS by the PSA. Thus, the output document Out Doc may include the documents from the input document *In Doc*, new document *New Doc* and additional retrieval document *Retrieval Doc.* from a specified source like DMS. Further, the *Out Doc* does not include the document *archived Archives Doc.*, i.e., *Out Doc.* $\subseteq$ *(In Doc.* $\cup$ *New Doc.* $\cup$ *Retrieval Doc.) - Archives Doc.* and a PSA can archive any document that is retrieved, i.e., *Archival Doc.* $\subseteq$ *(In Doc.* $\cup$ *New Doc.* $\cup$ *Retrieval Doc.).* In the Figure 5, one can see that the output document of ``Task 1" is the input document of next coordinated ``Task 2", i.e., *Out Doc1* $\rightarrow$ *In Doc2.* In our example, the task ``Insert Record" will generate the output event ``Insert(``ApplicationComplete")" which is an application form as input event of the task ``Review Record".

Let the function ``Scope(PSAID, ActivityID)" return the set of TaskID's of ActivityID executed by the PSAID. On the other hand, the function ``Scope(DocID, ActivityID)" returns the set of TaskID's of ActivityID which access the document DocID. The function ``Flow(DocID, ActivityID)" which returns a set of EventID's and the corresponding TaskID's accessing the document DocID. This set of EventID's should be the input/output events of the set of TaskIDs generated by ``Scope(DocID, ActivityID)".

The algorithm ``DocumentSecurityConflictDetection" as shown in Figure 6 detects the conflicts among the PSA, document and task during specification time. It will check all the tasks of an activity, and then it tries to gather all the documents including input, new, archive and output which are needed by the task. Further, it checks the access privilege ``PrivilegeID" for each document that needs to be accessed by the PSA matched to execute the task. If the privilege is not a security-specification, then it will call the function ``DAC" to authenticate it. If it is a security-specification, it will prompt the user to input the PSA ``ToPSAID" (whose security-specification is being changed) and then call the function ``MAC" to authenticate it.

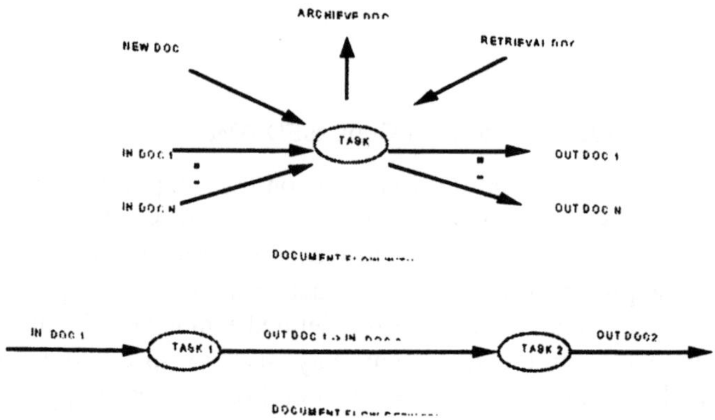

Figure 5 Document Flow with respect to Tasks

The function ``DAC(DocID, PSAID, PrivilegeID)" as shown in Figure 7 applies Discretionary Access Controls (DAC) to validate the access privilege of document by a PSA. It takes a document DocID, a PSAID, and PrivilegeID which are document operations such as, read, write and modify. A list of subdocuments of DocID which will be accessed by the PSA is retrieved, and then the authentication of each subdocument will be checked. The security authorization check is implemented by using Event Condition Rule (ECA) based security specification. If the security privileges are valid, then the PSAID has the authorization to access the document DocID with the PrivilegeID. If one of them is invalid, then the PSAID is denied from performing the PrivilegeID and ExceptionalHandling procedure will takeover to resolve this conflict.

```
Algorithm DocumentSecurityConflictDetection(ActivityID)
FOR  ALL TaskID ∈ Tasks(ActivityID) DO
BEGIN
 DocIn = InDoc(TaskID);
 DocNew = NewDoc(TaskID);
 DocArchive = ArchiveDoc(TaskID);
 DocOut = OutDoc(TaskID);
 PSAID = MatchMaking(Task);
 DocSet = DocIn ∪ DocNew ∪ DocArchive ∪ DocOut;
 FOR ALL DocID ∈ DocSet DO
 BEGIN
  PrivilegeID = Access(DocID, TaskID);
  IF (PrivilegeID ≠ SecuritySpecification) THEN
   IF DAC(DocID, PSAID, PrivilegeID) = INVALID THEN;
    ExceptionHandling(PSAID, DocID, PrivilegeID, NULL);
  ELSE
  BEGIN
   Input(ToPSAID);
   IF MAC(DocID, PSAID, ToPSAID) = INVALID THEN;
    ExceptionHandling(PSAID, DocID, PrivilegeID, ToPSAID);
  END
 END
END
```

Figure 6 Algorithm Document Security Conflict Detection

```
Algorithm DAC(DocID, PSAID, PrivilegeID)
InvalidList = Empty;
SubDocList = AccessSubDoc(DocID);
 FOR ALL SubDocID ∈ SubDocList DO
 BEGIN
  IF CheckAuthentication = DENIED THEN
   InvalidList = InvalidList ∪ SubDocID;
 END
IF InvalidList = Empty THEN
 RETURN (VALID);
ELSE
 RETURN (INVALID);
```

Figure 7 Algorithm Discretionary Access Control

```
Algorithm MAC(DocID, PSAID, ToPSAID)
InvalidList = Empty;
SubDocList = AccessSubDoc(DocID);
 FOR ALL SubDocID ∈ SubDocList DO
 BEGIN
  IF SecurityLevel(PSAID, SubDocID) ≤
    SecurityLevel(ToPSAID, SubDocID) THEN
   InvalidList = InvalidList ∪ SubDocID;
 END
IF InvalidList = Empty THEN
 RETURN (VALID);
ELSE
 RETURN (INVALID);
```

Figure 8 Algorithm Mandatory Access Control

In function ``MAC(DocID, PSAID, ToPSAID)'' as shown in Figure , we applied Mandatory Access Control (MAC) theory to validate the ``Security-Specification'' privilege on the document DocID. Every PSA is assigned a security level number. The access rule is based on pre-defined predicate in the previous section which compares the security level numbers between granter PSAID and awardee ToPSAID. If the security level number of awardee is greater than the granter's, then the PSAID has the authorization to grant the PrivilegeID to the ToPSAID.

If the authorization is not given, then the PSAID is denied from performing the PrivilegeID and ExceptionalHandling procedure will be applied to solve this conflict as well. A task cannot be executed if the PSA does not have the authorization to access/process/transfer the relevant documents to the next task. After a PSA is matched to a task, the PSA should be able to perform certain operations on the documents in order to execute the task. If the authorization is not given by applying functions DAC or MAC, an algorithm of ExceptionalHandling procedure as shown in Figure is used to address resolve this conflict.

This algorithm will handle different exceptional cases. If the requested document does not exist, then it may call the document manager to retrieve it from the DMS since it may have been archived previously. Otherwise, it will call the security administrator to handle it. On the other hand, if the function ``DAC'' or ``MAC'' is invalid, then it will find the another similarly capable PSA as a substitute or ask the security administrator to handle it. Finally, the last step of the caller procedure will be re-executed again in order to test it again. The purpose of performing exceptional handling procedure is to avoid failure of any task due to invalid document access, since a failed task will cause the whole activity to be suspended.

```
Algorithm ExceptionalHandling(PSAID, DocID, PrivilegeID, ToPSAID)
IF Inexistent(DocID) THEN
BEGIN
 IF Archived(DocID) THEN
   Request(Document Manager);
 ELSE
   Request(Security Administrator);
END
ELSEIF Invalid(DAC) OR Invalid(MAC) THEN
BEGIN
 ( NEWPSAID = EquivalentMatch(PSAID);
 PSAID = NEWPSAID) )
 OR
 Request (Security Administrator);
END
REVIVETHESTEPBEFORECALL;
```

Figure 9 Exception Handling Algorithm

Enforcement of Task Oriented Modeling of Document Security

The document security information will be stored using ECA rules, and will be used by the execution module of CapBasED-AMS. The security administrator is responsible for enforcing and monitoring the document security during the execution of tasks of an activity. Security control on the document is enforced by using Event-Condition-Action (ECA) rules. During the execution of task, ECA rules will be triggered when the document is accessed for performing some operations by the PSA. The event ``process(operation, document)" is generated by the PSA which involves an instance of the ``Document Process Subactivity" to be created by the system. Three tasks ``Document Process" which is executed by the PSA, ``Check Authentication" and ``Exceptional Handling" which are executed by security administrator will be decomposed from this subactivity as shown in Figure . And then, in the task ``Check Authentication", the conditions such as whether the PSA can perform the operation on this document or not will be checked. Based on the satisfaction of these conditions an action will be taken to allow the operation on the document. If the PSA has certain privilege on the document, the action will be to allow the PSA to perform the operations on the document in ``Document Process". SNOOP language is used to specify events for accessing the document by the PSA. By using the event detector in the document management system, once the event is detected, the condition evaluator will evaluate and verify whether certain operations can be performed on the document by the PSA. In our example, the ``Graduate Coordinator" needs to read the applicant's form during the execution of the task ``Review Record", then the Event: process(read, applicant's form) will trigger the execution of Condition: Check

Authentication to validate if the ``Graduate Coordinator" has the authentication to read this document or not. If the ``Graduate Coordinator" has the authentication to read it, then the Action: read(applicant's form) is performed. Note that there can be separate events for satisfying the security constraints from the point of view of the activity, task, PSA, and the document, before the document is processed by the PSA. Thus ECA rules enable independent and integrated treatment towards security enforcement from different view points in the CapBasED-AMS. On the other hand, if the PSA is denied to access the document, then the ``Exceptional Handling" task will be triggered. If the ``Exceptional Handling" can solve the conflicts, then it will trigger the event ``retry" to ``Check Authentication" again. Otherwise, it will trigger the event ``failed" and return back to the original task. In order to prevent cyclic process between the two tasks ``Check Authentication" and ``Exceptional Handling", the user can specify some constraints on it, e.g., maximum number of cyclic execution, time out or etc.

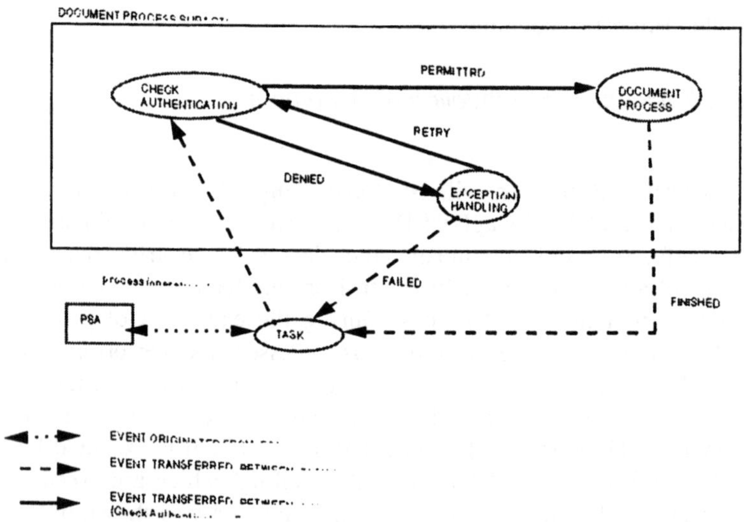

Figure 10 Document Process Subactivity

Events logging for document operation are done during the execution of tasks by security administrator. This logging is done by the active database manager as described in . This events logging is useful for recovery if there is any failure during tasks execution. This allows for active security enforcement, monitoring, and control, which is very essential for activity management systems.

Summary

We presented security issues of the document in CapBasED-AMS from the point of task execution with the PSA role based document security model. PSA role based document security model states that each PSA instance performs a certain role in the organization. Based on its role and organization, every instance is authorized to perform a specific set of operations on a document. The instance inherits all authorizations from its role and organization by default, and every instance can have some additional authorizations on the document regardless of its role and organization. In some cases, an instance can be excluded from inheriting some authorizations based on its role and organization. Furthermore, based on the role and organization, the documents can also be classified into different groups for easing the management of authorizations. Whenever a document is created, the document creator or the security administrator is able to grant the authorizations directly. That is, one can specify which PSAs are allowed to execute which operations on documents. Security control on the document is enforced by using Event-Condition-Action (ECA) rules. ECA rules are triggered when the document is affected by certain events such as initiation of document operations by the PSA, then the conditions such as whether the PSA is to perform the operation on this document or not will be checked. Based on the satisfaction of these conditions an action will be taken to allow the operation on the document. This allows for active security enforcement, monitoring, and control, which is very essential for activity management systems.

References

[1] Sharma Chakravarthy, Kamalakar Karlapalem, Shamkant B. Navathe, and Asterio Tanaka. Database Supported Cooperative Problem Solving. International Journal of Intelligent and Cooperative Information System, September 1993.

[2] Sharma Chakravarthy and Deepak Mishra. Snoop: An Expressive Event Specification Language For Active Database. Data and Knowledge Engineering, November 1994.

[3] P. C. K. Hung, H. P. Yeung, and K. Karlapalem. CapBasED-AMS: A Capability-based and Event-driven Activity Management System (Demonstrations). Proceedings of the ACM SIGMOD Conference on Management of Data, June 1996.

[4] Patrick Hung. A Capability-Based Activity Specification and Decomposition for an Activity Management System. Master's thesis, The Hong Kong University of Science and Technology, 1995.

[5] Kamalakar Karlapalem, Helen P. Yeung, and Patrick C. K. Hung. CapBasED-AMS - A Framework for Capability-Based and Event-Driven Activity Management System. Proceedings of the Third International Conference on Cooperative Information Systems, 1995.

[6] G. Pernul. Canonical Security Modeling For Federated Databases. Proc. of the IFIP TC2/WG2.6 Conf. on Semantics of Interoperable Database Systems, 1992.

[7] Ravi S. Sandhu, Edward J. Coyne, Hal L. Feinstein, and Charles E. Youman. Role-Based Access Control Models. IEEE Computer, 1996.

[8] C. C. Woo and F. H. Lochovsky. Role-Based Security in Database Management Systems. DBSec, pages 209--222, 1987.

[9] Helen Yeung. An Event-driven Activity Execution for An Activity Management System. Master's thesis, The Hong Kong University of Science and Technology, 1995.

13 THE PARTIAL ORDER MODEL OF DATA: ENTERPRISE INTEGRATION VIA A UNIFYING MODEL

Darrell Raymond

Introduction

For some twenty years, researchers in document systems have struggled to define and establish document processing as a research area in its own right. In the process, we often felt the need to portray documents as a unique kind of data, not susceptible to traditional data processing or database approaches. It is ironic that having erected a wall between document systems and other systems, we now need to seek a way to breach that wall, in order to re-integrate documents with the enterprise.

There were good reasons for pursuing a distinct theory of documents, the main one being that existing database systems were clearly unsuitable for managing documents. The dominant logical model for enterprise data—the relational model—seems inappropriate or incomplete for many of the areas of concern to modern enterprises, such as documents, product data management, resource planning, and workflow. Non-relational systems have been constructed in each of these areas, but they are generally lacking in a solid mathematical theory of the objects and operators that they embody.

Integrating enterprise data requires a unifying theory of the objects and operations of the enterprise. This theory need not, and probably should not, discuss products, workflow, resources, or even documents: the relational model, after all, does not found itself on the business processes to which it is normally applied. The strength of the relational model is that it roots itself in set theory, rather than domain issues. Similarly, a unifying model for the enterprise should be rooted in a mathematical abstraction that is applicable to a variety of areas and is flexible to changes in the enterprise.

This paper discusses such a model: the partial order model of data. Like Codd's relational model, the partial order model attempts to be a general-purpose, domain-independent, algebraic model. The key difference between the two models is that where the relational model is based on the theory of unordered sets, the partial order model is based on the theory of ordered sets. Order is a fundamental property of many types of data, particularly documents.

Codd's purpose in restricting the relational model to unordered sets was to eliminate one of the key problems of his day—the embedding of access structures in the logical model of the data. While access structures are almost always ordered, it is not therefore true that order is always due to an access structure. Order is a fundamental property of data (Pratt 86) (Parker 87, 89). In the partial order model, order is the key characteristic that is preserved and managed.

The partial order model

A partial order is most simply thought of as a directed acyclic graph of some collection of objects. Figure1 shows some examples of partial orders.

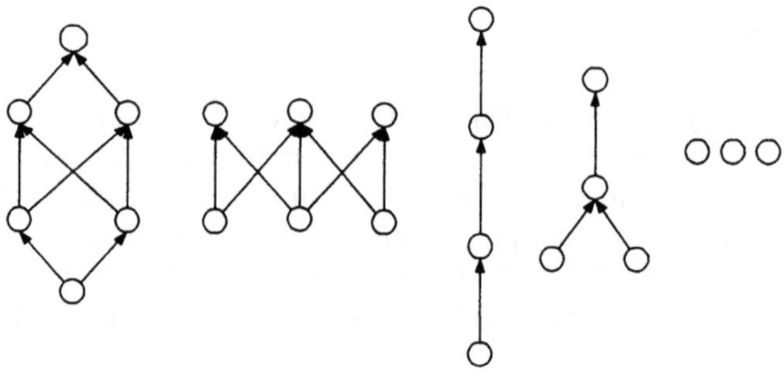

Figure 1. Examples of partial orders.

Two special kinds of partial orders are totally ordered sets (known as chains) and completely unordered sets (known as antichains). The relational model deals only with sets; hence, it can be thought of as an antichain-based model. Current document systems, on the other hand, tend to focus on totally ordered notions of data. SGML, for example, views documents as nested collections of sequential characters. Such models can be thought of as chain-based models. If one approach specializes in chains and the other in antichains, it seems a natural question to consider a model that can express structures that are chains, antichains, or somewhere in between. Such a model could serve a unifying function, as it would span the range between relational and existing document models, and include novel structures that are currently unsupported by either.

We follow Codd's lead in emphasizing an algebraic approach to a data model. The partial order model provides a set of operators that can be used in an algebraic fashion; the operators are applied to partial orders, and produce partial orders as their result. The key operators in the model are the following:

- *max*—select the maximum elements of the partial order
- *up*—select the suborder above a particular element
- *dual*—invert the ordering relationship. In combination with max and up we can construct min and down.

In addition, there are the operators of lexicographical sum Σ and cross product $\times$. Lexicographical sum, roughly speaking, allows us to substitute the elements of a partial order **P** with members of another set of partial orders **Q**; the result is that the member partial orders of **Q** are themselves partially ordered according to the order specified in **P**. The cross product of **P** and **Q**, on the other hand, allows us to produce a partial order that satisfies both **P** and **Q** simultaneously. Cross product is roughly analogous to the relational join. The well-known partial order operators of linear sum and disjoint union are actually special cases of lexicographical sum.

Generally one wants an to have the property of closure; in this case, we want the result of any operation to be a partial order. The main restriction introduced by closure is that we cannot have a difference or complement operator, since in general the result of either operator is not a partial order. More information on the operators, properties, and implementation of partial order databases can be found in Raymond (96).

Next we consider how a partial order view of data can lead to interesting new notions in modelling documents.

Rethinking documents as partial orders

Text gains its expressive power from two fundamental inventions: the alphabet and the use of positional notation (Goodman 76) (Harris 86). The alphabet is a small set of atomic characters that can be composed into a very large number of structures through the use of positional notation. Positional notation is an ordering of characters; from positional notation we get words, sentences, chapters, headings, footnotes, marginalia, parallel translations, tables, page furniture, and most of the other structures in documents. Computerized documents also permit dynamic orders; that is, the ability for the user to change the order of the components (Raymond and Tompa 88) (Raymond 92) (Raymond 93). Whether dynamic or static, any system that relies on positional notation clearly has order as an integral aspect. Thus, it seems clear that order should take a primary role in any model for documents.

There are many different ordering relationships in documents. We shall show how it is possible to build up a model for documents by exploring each of these relationships in turn.

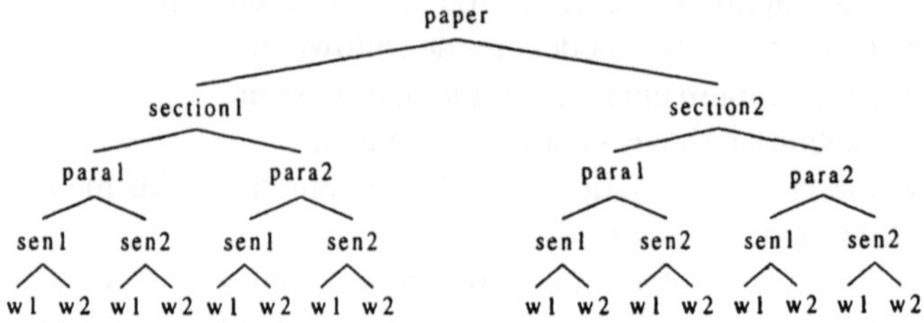

Figure 2. Partial order **L**.

The most recognized class of ordering relationships in documents is *containment*. Containment expresses the fact that some parts of a document are components of other parts. A commonly recognized example of containment is the so-called 'logical' structure of documents; for example, a research article is a collection of sections, each section is a collection of paragraphs, each paragraph is a collection of sentences, and each sentence is a collection of words, as in Figure 2. This structure is often called the 'logical' structure of a document (or even 'the' structure of a document). We will denote this structure by **L**. **L** is hierarchical, and thus partially ordered.

The elements in Figure 2 are numbered because documents generally consist of ordered parts: thus, a sentence is not a set of words, it is a sequence of words. For the moment, we will ignore these sequences, and treat all collections as sets.

The relationships presented in Figure 2 are only one of several forms of containment. Figure 2 is not itself the document; rather, it is one representation of the document, a highly redundant one. In a document of reasonable size, words and phrases are certainly repeated many times, and if the document has 'boilerplate' text, then even sentences or sections may be repeated. Normally we think of these redundant values as equivalent. This equivalence, or alternatively, this redundancy in data, can and should be expressed in the data model, since that is the only way that it can be abstractly managed.

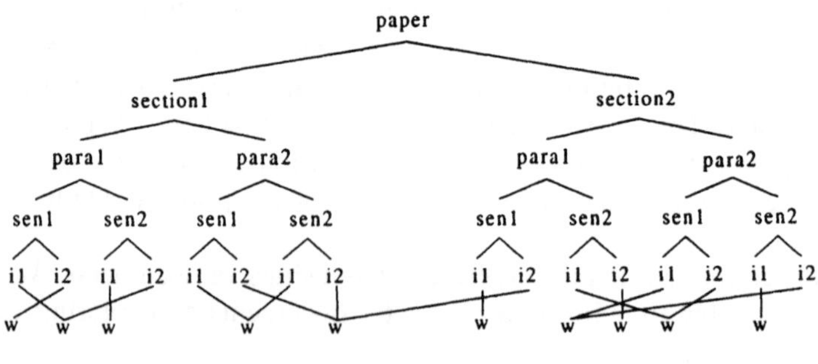

Figure 3. Partial order **C**.

Figure 3 shows **L** along with a new partial order, **R** that captures the equivalence of words. The new structure distinguishes between words and the uses of words: we call the latter *instances*. Words are values, while instances are occurrences of those values in some ordered structure. **L** organizes instances, and **R** organizes words. If $a < b$ in **R,** this implies that a contains b; thus, the word w contains its instances i_j. **L** and **R** can be viewed as two partial orders that meet at their 'fringes'. We refer to the combination of **L** and **R** as **C.** [1]

Because it separates the notion of 'word' from that of 'instance', **R** is capable of describing situations in which words have a variety of non-identical instances. This permits us to capture surface differences such as capitalization ('Army', 'army'), abbreviation ('Dr.', 'M.D.'), spelling variation ('draft', 'draught'), ligatures (hemorrhage, hæmorrhage), hyphenation (boiler room, boiler-room), line breaks (hyster-esis), special symbols ('&' for 'and', '$' for 'dollars') and digits and numbers ('2' and 'two').

Figure 3 shows a structure in which only shared words are represented, but it is also possible to express the sharing of individual characters, of sentences, or of other fragments. The choice of what to model in **R** depends partly on the types of queries we want to support, and partly on the constraints we need to enforce during update.

Structures like **R** have the interesting property that they are abstractions of *indexes.* **R** captures redundancy, but in so doing it also expresses the essential property of an inverted list—the unification of copies of data. Both **R** and inverted lists support querying based on data values. **R** goes beyond the basic inverted list, however, since it organizes the values into a partial order, expressing the transitivity between 'inverted' values. Thus, we might think of the various **R** structure as 'transitive value' structures.

Note that **R** captures the abstract notion of an index, but it does not mandate a specific data structure for that index. **R** supports querying of ordered data values, and states the relationships of sets or sequences of values to one another, but does not specify how these relationships are to be stored or updated. It is possible to develop several data structures that can support **R,** but they belong to the implementation layer of the system, rather than the modelling layer.

Next, let us consider the sequential structure of the data. Typically, each element of **L** is totally ordered within its parent; thus, a sentence is a total ordering of words, a paragraph is a total ordering of sentences, and a section is a total ordering of paragraphs. A totally ordered structure is not mandatory; hypertexts, for example, may have a variety of possible orderings for paragraphs or sections, and sentences may have words that can be reordered or contain incomparable alternatives (such as the ubiquitous 'and/or'). We will capture the partial order of the sequential components by **S.** **S** for our example is shown by the dashed edges in Figure 4. Since **S** represents the sequence structure explicitly, we no longer require subscript numbers.

---

[1] The 'combination' of these two partial orders is not a union, since the orders are not defined on disjoint sets. We have no operator that produces this structure; it is simply a structure consisting of two partial orders that share some elements.

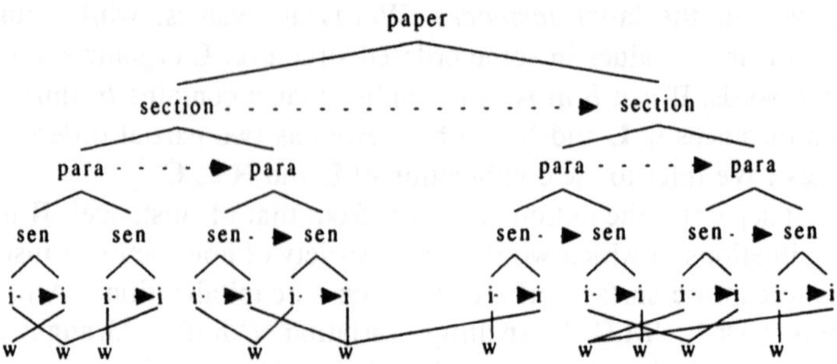

Figure 4. Partial order **T**.

S is a union of disjoint sequences, so **S** is trivially partially ordered. The combination of **S** with **C** is also a partial order. **S** orders only incomparable elements within **C** and therefore does not conflict with either **R** or **L**. We will refer to the combination of **S** and **C** as **T**.

Using these structures, we can solve queries such as the following:

- Find the first paragraph in every section
- Find all sections between section *m* and section *n* that contain the words 'compact' or 'compress', but not 'automata'.
- Find all sentences in which the word 'fast' precedes the word 'compression', possibly with some intervening words.

We can solve these queries algebraically, using only the operators previously described; solutions to the queries can be found in Raymond (96).

The constructs that make up a document consist of ordered structures of characters. Some of these constructs are sets, some are total orders, and some have incomparability (and so, are non-degenerate partial orders). It is the combination of these constructs that makes it difficult to employ purely set-based models to manage documents.

The example we have examined has mostly hierarchical components. However, the partial order model (and the example queries that have been shown) will apply even if documents contain non-hierarchical , such as tables.

Software for making tables has been available since at least 1979 (Lesk 79), but the problem does not appear to be a solved one, as research into tables continues (Beach 85) (Vanoirbeek 92) (Wang and Wood 93a, 93b) (Shin *et al.* 94). The main issue that keeps researchers interested in tables is separating the purely presentational aspects of tables from their logical structure. Partial orders do not address all the issues of table layout, but they do provide interesting insights into the problem of separating presentation from abstraction.

Consider the following simple two-dimensional table:

	x_2	x_4	x_3	x_1
y_2				
y_3				
y_1				

The key idea in the partial order approach to tables is separating the description of the data values from their layout. Our example has two dimensions, X and Y. The dimensions contain individual values x_1, x_2, x_3 and x_4, and y_1, y_2, and y_3. Every data point in any valid table layout is denoted by one value from each of these dimensions; hence, the total data space is the expression $X \times Y$; that is, the binary relation over all data values.[2] If we were not displaying the values in a table, this cross product would be a complete and sufficient description of the data. A table, however, is something more than the data values: it is an ordered presentation of the data values. In the partial order model for tables, we let the data space be defined by the cross product of a collection of data dimensions, and we specify the layout by ordering those dimensions. By ordering the individual x_i and y_j within X and Y, and by using a partial order cross product instead of a set cross product, we derive a layout of the data corresponding to a table. A different table can be constructed simply by changing the order of one or more of the dimensions. Changing the order of a dimension corresponds to interchanging rows or columns of the table.

In the partial order model, then, a *data space* is the cross product of two or more data dimensions:

$$M = A \times B \times C \times \ldots$$

A *table* is a layout of a data space that is specified by ordering the values of the dimensions:

$$\mathbf{M} = \mathbf{A} \times \mathbf{B} \times \mathbf{C} \times \ldots$$

A data space is produced by a set-theoretic cross product operator; a table is produced by a partial-order cross product operator. The partial order model thus clearly separates the data from its layout; the former is unordered and manipulated with set-based operations, while the latter is partially ordered and manipulated with partial order operations.

A simple cross product is the right model if the data dimensions are independent and orthogonal. Often the dimensions are not independent, and a given dimension makes sense only as a subdivision of some other dimension. A table that shows the sales of products of various companies, for example, describes products that are specific to each individual company; company C_1 has products p, q, and r, but company C_2 only has product s. This structure can be expressed by a lexicographical sum of partial orders, where the expression order is the partial

---

[2] Strictly speaking, the table consists of the mapping $X \times Y \rightarrow V$, but since V is functionally determined by every element in the cross product, we can think of the table as being restricted to the elements in the cross product.

order of companies, and the factor orders are the orderings of each company's products. Lexicographical sum gives us the ability to handle nested tables.

The set of partial orders that constitutes a table can be inserted in the document's partial order structure just as if they were words or characters; a document can, without loss of generality, include elements that are complete tables. All the operators of the partial order model will be applicable to such a structure.

Discussion

Document modelling is complicated by the problem that definitions of 'document', like definitions of 'art', tend to invite counterexamples that overturn the definition. Standard Generalized Markup Language (SGML) for example, structures computerized documents in a static, hierarchical repository containing embedded markup. Yet computerization itself encourages rapid and frequent change to documents, as well as multiple (and possibly external) structures on documents. The conclusion we should draw from this experience is not that one model is better or worse; rather that any model is more likely to change the domain than capture it. The domain-specific approach to modelling is not helpful when the domain is too fluid. We should not try to found a document database system on an abstract definition of documents, any more than we attempted to found traditional database systems on abstract definitions of business.

The partial order model does not attempt to define documents, nor is it especially designed for documents. Instead, it follows the general philosophy of the relational model: find a well-chosen mathematical abstraction, and by its nature it will be applicable to many problems. We have seen that many structures in documents can be described as partial orders. The most important contribution of the partial order model is its extraction of order as an abstract concept, whose manipulation and update is fundamental to many problems in document management.

Markup-based approaches tend to encourage a hierarchical view of documents, not just because it is easier to handle hierarchical markup, but because it is easier if most structures in the document are derived from the underlying total order of the standard file representation. This assumption is useful for managing hierarchical and proximity-based relationships. It becomes a liability when trying to manage non-hierarchical relationships, such as tables or overlapping sections. It also leads to errors when the proximity that is in the representation is not part of the model; thus, the last word of one sentence is proximate to the first word of the next sentence, but the two words are not related, as they belong to different structures.

Partial orders are not limited to hierarchies, and so they can express tables and overlapping relationships in a natural manner. Containment is the most important relationship in documents, and hierarchies do express containment, but not all containment is hierarchical. The most general form of containment is the partial order.

SGML addresses the variety of structures in documents with a variety of mechanisms. The 'logical' structure can be represented by the element tags in the document, and the element declarations in the document type definition. The 'redundancy' structure can be represented by the use of entities and entity references. The cross-reference structure can be represented by the use of ID/IDREF attributes. Finally, the layout structure can be represented by CONCUR.

These mechanisms are not equally powerful or well-developed; CONCUR, for example, is not widely implemented or used (Barnard 88). Similarly, extension mechanisms for class structures are not part of SGML, and so they are typically expressed as guidelines (for example, the Text Encoding Initiative's *Guidelines* (TEI 94)) rather than enforceable constraints. SGML's mechanisms are also not mutually orthogonal; it is possible, for example, to represent a hierarchy with ID/IDREF values, or even with entities and entity references (indeed, it is possible to represent directed acyclic graphs with entity references). The lack of orthogonality in these mechanisms and their differing implementation-specific characteristics complicate the document modeller's problem.

The basic strength of the partial order model is that it describes the various structures of documents with the single abstraction of order, rather than through a variety of mechanisms. This unification of document structures makes it easier to combine and manipulate the components of the resulting structures, because closure is more easily obtained for a single abstraction and its few operators, than for a collection of distinct mechanisms. It can also be argued that it is easier to understand a document as a variety of instances of one class of structure, than as a single instance of a variety of classes of structures.

The contemporary approach to documents splits querying into two distinct parts: a specification of structural properties (such as 'paragraph' or 'section') and a value specification (typically specified by string searching). The problem with naive string searching is that it directly involves the user with the representation. The user must worry about such issues as case, embedded tags, accents, variant spellings, and punctuation (or rather, the typical user does not even think of these things, and so the search fails to be complete). The partial order model permits the data modeller to unify value-based searching with structure-based searching; instead of strings being a different kind of data value, they are partial orders of atomic values. Explicitly representing sharing exposes the difference between a data value (of which there is only one copy) and the position of that value in some order (of which there may be as many instances as there are orders). Including strings in the logical model also makes explicit important update issues, that are handled informally, if at all, in other systems.

The ability to have more than one ordering relation on a single base set is useful for capturing the many orders that can be imposed on a single text. Markup-based systems can represent multiple orderings, but simply representing them is insufficient; one also needs operators to manipulate, combine, and update these orders. The partial order model provides such operators.

Other applications of the partial order model

The partial order model is applicable to a wide variety of areas beyond documents. Any structure that is defined by dependency relationships is a candidate for management by partial orders. A few such structures are briefly outlined here:

Version control

Versions of documents (or software, or systems) are ordered according to their development, while variants are typically unordered or incomparable. The partial order model provides a natural framework in which to express these forms of (in)comparability.

Software construction

The program **make** is a tool for determining whether there are inconsistencies between two partial orders (the dependency graph and the temporal order) on a collection of software modules. **make**, however, has only this single query hardwired into its structure; a more general tool that would permit arbitrary queries and processing on the underlying partial orders could support many advanced operations on software modules.

Temporal data

Temporal information is ordered information. Current approaches to temporal data attempt to retrofit relational databases with intervals, leading to additional operators and complicated problems of closure. The partial order model provides a more general framework in which to address both problems.

Object-oriented structures

Inheritance is an ordering relationships between sets of objects. Multiple inheritance introduces the problem of ambiguity in subclass member access. Typical solutions to this problem are hardwired; choices are made in advance by the language or the system. If class hierarchies were treated as a partial order database, however, it would be possible to use dynamic queries to solve the problem of ambiguity in subclass member accessing.

Redundancy control

The theory of functional dependencies and normalization of relational databases is the most thoroughly worked-out approach we have yet devised to understand and control redundancy in data. Lee has shown that this theory reduces to certain types of partial orders among sets of attributes (Lee 83). Modelling our data with partial orders allows us to translate known properties of normal forms into our particular data domain.

Partial orders as an integration framework

It is unlikely that the partial order model as I have described it here is *the* model for enterprise integration. What I hope to have shown is that a unifying model has value, and that this particular model integrates a variety of document-related structures in a unique and useful way. If it is true that a wide range of activities in enterprises can be usefully modelled as dependency structures, then the partial order model may also serve as an integrating framework for them as well. The model has good qualities for this purpose:

- The model is a general-purpose one, neither a document model being extended to the enterprise, nor an enterprise model being restricted to documents. The model's generality means that it has more chance of wide applicability, and is more likely to be able to sustain changes in use.
- The model is based on an algebra. Algebraic specifications tend to be more declarative and less representation-dependent than traditional navigation-based approaches. Consequently, they tend to be more portable and to put fewer restrictions on the underlying implementation.
- The model is typeless: it needs no classes or data types to describe complicated structure. This is useful when the data domain is not clearly understood, and the only distinctions that can be made are to separate large collections of objects from one another. Later on, if these distinctions become important, they can be captured as classes or types, and type checking can be provided to control update.
- The model provides the ability to combine and manipulate multiple (even contradictory) orders on a given set of objects. Most models that attempt to deal with order assume there is one defining order, or else treat it as part of the implementation. The partial order model allows different parts of the enterprise to model data in different ways, and provides a means for contrasting and combining those models.
- The model is well suited to describing theoretical aspects of data management, such as redundancy control, consistency management, version control, distributed data, and transactions. These issues are important not just for software or document systems; at their most abstract, they underly much of the activity in an enterprise.
- The model spans the range from unordered sets (current relational systems) to totally ordered sets (current document systems).It thus provides a natural way to blend the two existing approaches, which is important for a gradual evolution of the enterprise from its current state.

References

Barnard, D. R. Hayter, M. Karababa, G. Logan, and J. McFadden (1988). 'SGML-Based Markup for Literary Texts: Two Problems and Some Solutions' *Computers and the Humanities* **22** p. 265-276.

Beach, R.J. (1985). 'Setting Tables and Illustrations with Style', CS-85-45, Department of Computer Science, University of Waterloo, Waterloo, Ontario.

Goodman, N. (1976). *Languages of Art*, Hackett Publishing Co.

Harris, R. (1986). *The Origin of Writing*, Gerald Duckworth & Co., London, England.

Lee, T.T. 'An Algebraic Theory of Relational *Databases' The Bell System Technical Journal* **62**(10) p. 3159-3204 (December 1983).

Lesk, M.E. (1979). 'Tbl—A Program to Format Tables' Bell Laboratories, Murray Hill, New Jersey.

Parker, D.S. (1987). 'Partial Order Programming', Technical Report, Computer Science Department, University of California, Los Angeles, California.

Parker, D.S. (1989). 'Partial Order Programming', *Proceedings of the 16th ACM Conference on Principles of Programming Languages*, p. 260-266, Austin, Texas.

Pratt, V. (1986). 'Modelling Concurrency with Partial Orders' STAN-CS-86-1113, Department of Computer Science, Stanford University, Stanford, California.

Raymond, D.R. and F. Wm. Tompa (1988). 'Hypertext and the Oxford English Dictionary' *Communications of the ACM* **31**(7) p. 871-879.

Raymond, D.R. (1992). 'Flexible Text Display with Lector', *IEEE Computer* **25**(8) p. 49-60.

Raymond D.R. and F. Wm. Tompa (1992). 'Applying Database Dependency Theory to Software Engineering', CS-92-56, Department of Computer Science, University of Waterloo, Waterloo, Ontario.

Raymond, D.R., F. Wm. Tompa, and D. Wood (1992). 'Markup Reconsidered', *First International Workshop on Principles of Document Processing*, Washington, D.C.

Raymond, D.R., F.W. Tompa, and D. Wood (1996). 'From Data Representation to Data Model: Meta-Semantic Issues in the Evolution of SGML', *Computer Standards and Interfaces* **18** p. 25-36.

Raymond, D.R. (1996) Partial Order Databases, Technical Report CS-96-02, Department of Computer Science, University of Waterloo, Waterloo, Ontario, Canada.

Shin, K.H., K. Kobayashi, and A. Suzuki (1994). 'Tafel Musik: Formatting Algorithm for Tables', *Principles of Document Processing '94*, Seeheim, Germany.

Tansel, A.U. and J. Clifford, S. Gadia, S. Jajodia, A. Segev, R. Snodgrass (1993).*Temporal Databases: Theory, Design, and Implementation*, Benjamin Cummings Publishing Company, Redwood City, California.

Vanoirbeek, C. (1992). 'Formatting Structured Tables', *Proceedings of EP '92* p. 291-309, Cambridge, England.

Wang, X., and D. Wood (1993). 'Tabular Abstraction for Tabular Editing and Formatting', *Proceedings of 3rd International Conference for Young Computer Scientists* Tsinghua University Press, Beijing, China.

Wang, X., and D. Wood (1993). 'An Abstract Model for Tables', *Proceedings of the 1993 TeX User's Group Meeting* **14**(3) p. 231-237, Birmingham, England.

14 INFORMATION INTEGRATION IN MAINTENANCE AND DESIGN PROCESSES: A MODELING EFFORT

Malcolm Bauer,
David Newcom,
and Danny Davis

Introduction

This paper describes an effort to generate and evaluate alternative potential improvements to a vehicle design process. Our approach focused on the analysis of the documents used in the vehicle design process. Understanding these documents and the rules and assumptions underlying them allowed us to find the outmoded parts of the process. Challenging the rules and assumption underlying the documents lead us to two solutions, each with a different kind of process and information integration, and enabled by different degrees of technology. We used simulation to compare the redesigned processes and the original process. The simulations predicted that the redesigned processes would result in considerable cost and time savings over the original process. The simulations also gave detailed predictions on the relative merit of each redesigned process which allowed us to evaluate the usefulness of the different degrees of technology. We first describe the overall process and the document flows. Then we describe our rationale for business redesign including a discussion of information and process integration. We outline the two redesigned processes and describe the modeling and analyses we performed to evaluate the designs. Finally, we consider all three designs with respect to information integration. Across the current process and the two redesigns we find there is a shift from information integration by document integration to information integration by process integration.

The business redesign effort was performed as part of an international summer program at Carnegie Mellon University (CMU). The business process redesign team consisted of five upper level managers from a variety of vehicle manufacturers (heavy work vehicles, cars, etc.) and one electronics company, and two faculty members from CMU. The process redesign effort is part of a larger research project to develop collaborative systems for blue collar mechanical workers and white collar design engineers in distributed companies.

The Problem

The process we redesigned was the design of new models of cars in a large international automobile company with special focus on how failure information gets fed back from garages to the design teams. When the first model of a car is released it usually has many design flaws that cause problems. These problems are handled by garages in the field and paid for by the car company during the warranty period. Information from the field is used by the engineering design teams to correct problems and is filtered back from the garages to the design teams through a series of documents. Repair costs for cars under warranty are significant and increasing as market pressure is causing the company to lengthen the warranty period.

Our Approach

There are two approaches to reducing the number of flaws. The first is to improve the initial design process so that the first release of a new model contains few or no flaws. The second is to very rapidly remove the flaws in subsequent redesigns using failure information from the garages. While the first approach may result in a more dramatic decrease in faults initially, the our group felt that there will always be a need for getting detailed feedback from the field about new releases of vehicles. Because it was of more general interest to the team members, we chose to increase and improve the information that design engineers have available when they make design decisions. We believe that more timely and accurate field data sent back to engineering design teams can have a major impact on performance (Carley and Lin, in press) and also on costs and customer satisfaction - the sooner the problems are redesigned out of subsequent models, the higher the customer satisfaction for newly bought cars and the lower the warranty costs for those cars.

Our group used the following methodology to develop alternative redesigned processes. First, we outlined the existing process at a relatively high level. This was necessary because not everyone in the group was familiar with the goals of the process and how those goals were currently accomplished. We needed to know the present status of the company to determine what changes were possible. We then determined the rules and assumptions underlying the major activities in the processes with particular emphasis on the information flows. This lead us to determine several problems with the current process. Next, we identified *technology enablers* to create a new way (with new assumptions) to accomplish the same task. This allowed us to sketch out two solutions to overcome the problems we identified.

Analyzing the Current Process

For each car that comes into a garage under warranty, a mechanic fills out a failure form describing the problem that has occurred. There are over 5000 participating warranty garages that send field failure forms back to the factory. Of these garages, only a small percentage are large, sophisticated company-owned garages. Company-owned garages send in field failure warranty information electronically. The remaining smaller garages mail in paper forms. In either case, forms are sent to a central location, and information about particular features are entered into a database. The electronic forms are automatically input and the paper forms are entered by hand by clerks. There is typically a 1 month delay for the paper forms. Design teams extract reports on the relevant aspects of the car they are redesigning and use the reports to decide what changes should be made in the next model. There are many design teams, each working on a particular subsystem of a particular car. Each team consists of 4 or 5 members from different departments (engineering, purchasing, service engineering, production, etc.) with some members serving on many teams. Each design team meets roughly every two weeks to discuss what new changes should be made. On average, it currently takes a design team three meetings or six weeks per design decision. The time from first recognition of a defect by a garage mechanic until a design modification request by the design team is about 6 months. This includes 3 months to accumulate a large enough statistical base of problems to make design recommendations with confidence. After 1 year of production, only about 10% of the problems are fixed.

Starting the Redesign

One of our first and key steps after laying out the current process was to identify *rules and assumptions* behind the major activities. Rules are the who, what, when, and where of getting an activity accomplished, and the assumptions are the rationale behind them (Hammer, 1995). Questioning the assumptions behind the process is an important step in identifying potential solutions. In our case, for example, the objective of having a mechanic complete a failure form is to get information. A rule is using a paper medium. The assumption behind this at the time was probably a paper form was the most practical way to capture and send information - other medium may not have been practical or developed.

In the course of performing this activity, we identified several factors that cause the engineering design process to be too slow for the current market. Some factors consisted of changing customer expectations, for example, customers are expecting greater reliability and better service including longer warranty periods. To capture these changing market needs, the automobile companies are insisting on shorter design cycles. The shortened design cycles increase the criticality for prompt failure reports from the field so that design changes take into account the field results of the previous year's model car. Others factors were tied to the cars themselves, for example, the number of car systems and the complexity of the cars has increased, causing more problems and making them harder to diagnose. To address these concerns the engineering design teams need to identify and solve problems in the existing cars quickly.

Identifying the Key Problems

We decided that the current method of getting information back to the design teams is too slow and the resulting extracted reports are not rich enough to allow for these quick decisions. In the current process, the only information coming to the design engineers from the field garages is through the failure forms. Understanding these documents and the rules and assumptions behind them was essential to the task of redesigning the work processes. The existing document stream connects geographically distributed parts of the company - maintenance (the garages) and engineering (the design teams). In the current process, information integration occurs when the individual forms are added to the database and the design teams generate the failure reports tailored to their needs. Now that design cycles are shortening the information arrives too slowly - the 1 month delay between when a mechanic writes a form and when it gets entered into the database is significant. More importantly, the information is inaccurate and incomplete - there is a mismatch in goals between the original document writers (the repair personnel) and document readers (the engineering design teams). The design teams need information to help them diagnose and fix design problems. However, the repair personnel are simply concerned with fixing existing problems in cars and not redesigning them. The failure documents contain information to the level that the mechanics need to fix the car (e.g. the distributor needed to be replaced) but the design teams need to know much more about the underlying causes of problems to redesign the car. As a result, the documents do not contain all the information that the designers need.

Proposing the Solutions

This analysis of the current process, driven by understanding the rules and assumptions behind existing documents drove us to a solution that involved bringing the design and maintenance processes closer together. In our case it was not just a question of making better use of existing documents but rather changing the nature of the processes that created the documents. For greater information integration we needed greater process integration. Before generating potential new processes that accomplished this integration, we identified technology enablers that would allow us to create a new ways (with new assumptions) to accomplish the same task. We then outlined two methods to accomplish the process integration, an easy to implement low tech solution (the "incremental solution") and a "radical solution" that takes advantage of innovative communication and collaboration technology. In the incremental solution, we integrate the processes by bringing the designers out to several of the company-owned garages for one week every two months. This supplements the bi-weekly failure reports by giving the designers direct hands-on experience with the car problems. It ameliorates the goal mismatch between the designers and the mechanics by moving the designers out to the field and allowing them to address in great detail the design problems with the current cars. The radical solution involves the creation of a central maintenance hotline team (CMHT) composed of expert mechanics and designers. The CMHT has access to a representative sampling of garages through remote audio, video, and computer links to the garages. The CMHT can "look over the shoulder" of mechanics in the field to advise them on difficult problems and at the same time confer with them about design issues. An interdisciplinary team at Carnegie Mellon University is currently developing systems with these characteristics. This technology forms the basis for our radical new process. The CMU team is developing and evaluating collaborative systems for use in contexts similar to the current one. The systems allow workers in the field to access on-line manuals, schematics, and other documents relevant to their work using high performance wearable computers with heads-up video display/camera system including audio input/output for hands free operation and wireless communication for mobile use (Smailagic & Siewiorek, 1996; Kraut, Miller, & Siegel, 1996). Use of such a system will allow the design team representatives in the CMHT to collaborate with mechanics in the field and bring a continual flow of relevant information to the design groups. It ameliorates the goal mismatch as in the incremental solution by allowing the designers to see and evaluate typical problems first hand and to develop a closer working relationship with the garages. In the radical solution, however, the designers will be able to share information with mechanics on a more frequent, continual basis.

Simulation of the Processes

In order to evaluate the redesigns, we ran a comparative simulation using the ithink simulation package (High-Performance Systems, 1994). Ithink is a commercially available visual process modeling tool built on top of a Dynamo-like programming language developed originally for simulating complex systems of differential equations. Ithink enables a systems thinking approach (Senge, 1990) to understanding complex systems. In Ithink, complex systems are represented as relations between different influences The approach differs from modeling frameworks such as Levitt's Virtual Design Team (VDT) (Levitt, Cohen, Kunz, Nass, Christiansen, and Jin, 1994) in that the focus is on modeling flows of information and the factors that influence these flows, rather than individual actions. Because the focus of our effort was on improving the flow of information into the design process, rather than in contructing a detailed model of the design process itself, this seemed to be a good approach to take.

Ithink allows for both high level and detailed representation and simulation of many kinds of work processes. There are three basic building blocks used in ithink models: flows, stocks, and converters. Flows represent transfers of "stuff" in a model, for example paper forms, cars, money, etc. In the model in Figure 1, flows are represented by the thick arrows with the round spigot attachments in the center, for example the connection labeled "faulty cars" between the customer and the garage below. Stocks are places where stuff going through the flows can accumulate. Stocks are represented by the rectangular boxes in the diagram below, for example the box labeled "cars fixed" in the customer box accumulates all the cars that are fixed. Converters allow particular stocks or flows to control the behavior of other parts of the system. They are represented by the circles with the thin arrows coming out.

In our simulations, we modeled the flow of cars into and out of the garages, the flow of documents, the design decision making process, and the effect of fixing design problems on newly produced cars. We "tuned" the model by matching it to known inputs and outputs of the current process. Once tuned, we used our underlying assumptions about the new processes to develop the simulations of the two alternative redesigned processes.

The Baseline process. Figure 1 is an ithink representation of the current or baseline process described previously. We describe the main components of the model and the additional assumptions we made in constructing the ithink representation. There are four main components in the model, each with an associated box in the diagram: customers, garages, Service Engineering, and the Product Design Team. Customers bring their cars to the garage, and the cars are fixed and returned to the customer in 1-3 days. This process is represented by the flow loop between the customer box and the garage box. Cars under warranty require a failure form to be sent to service engineering. The converters connected to the "Cars back to customer" flow start this new flow of failure forms on the right side of the garage box. The forms are first prepared by the mechanic and then go to the cashier. From there there are two ways the forms can go to Service Engineering, represented by the two flows going out of the "Cashier Processes form" stock. Forms go either by computer and are put directly in the fault database, or they are sent by mail and then must be processed by clerks before they are entered into the fault database.

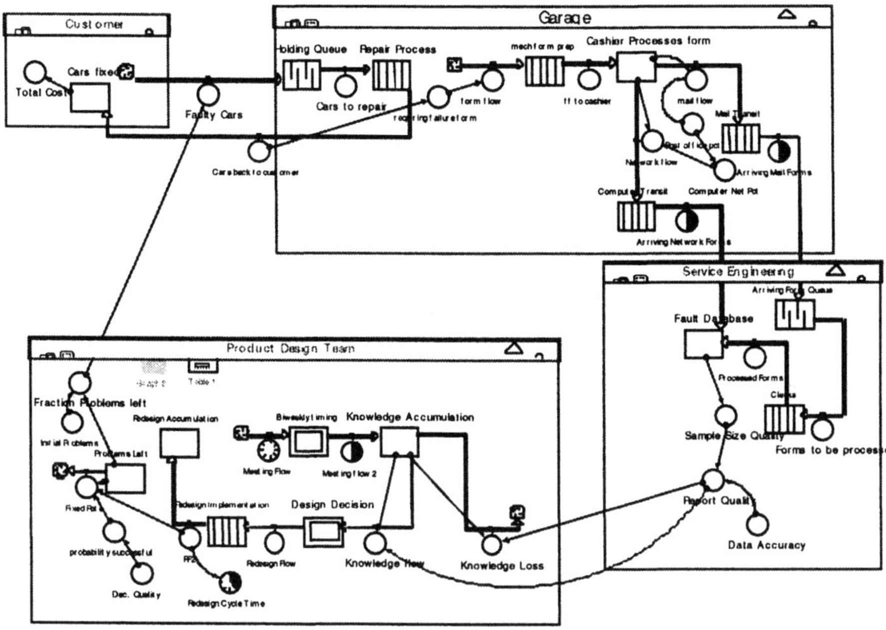

Figure 1 : Ithink Model of The Baseline Process

The Product Design Team uses the fault database to make design modification decisions to existing products. They use information from the field residing in the fault database to make this decision. The last part of the ithink model, the structure in the Product Design Team box, models this decision making process. We modeled the design decision process as an iterative gathering of information. When enough information is collected, usually after several meetings, the team makes a decision. Thus in the model, every two weeks a team meets and generates knowledge that will be important in making a design decision. If they generate enough knowledge they are able to reach a decision. In the model this means the knowledge accumulated is above a particular threshold. If they do not generate enough knowledge then the amount of knowledge they generate accumulates in the "Design Decision" stock. More knowledge gets added at the next meeting and if the amount is above threshold at that point then a decision will be made. (In figure 1, “Knowledge flow” transports the knowledge generated at the meeting to the Design Decision stock. The “Knowledge loss” flow removes knowledge that was lost due to incomplete or inaccurate information).

For the model, we decided that the quality of the report generated from the fault database determines the amount of useful knowledge a design team can generate in a meeting and thus the time it takes a team to make a decision. If the report is missing information or the accuracy of the data in the report is poor, then the design team will generate less knowledge at the meeting, making it less likely that they will make a decision during the current meeting. Report quality is affected by two factors, the size of the fault database and the accuracy of the data it contains. These two factors combine to determine the quality of the reports used to make design decisions. Based upon data from the company, we made the assumption that when there is little data in the fault database it causes the report quality to be low, and the factor associated with size of the fault database increases monotonically to a maximum when there are about a million forms in the database. We set the data accuracy of the fault database to 0.35. This assumption is based upon the fact that once the fault database contains a large number of forms, it still currently takes about three meetings (or six weeks) for a product teams to make a design decision. Setting the data accuracy to .35 causes the model of the design team to make a decision in this same amount of time.

In addition to affecting the time it takes a design team to reach a decision, we assumed that the data accuracy would affect the quality of the decision as well. In the model, the data accuracy also affects the probability that the modification the design team decides upon will successfully solve the fault in the car, as seen in the lower left portion of the Product Design Team box in figure 1. The probability of success increases monotonically with the decision quality, which in this case is equal to the data accuracy. When the data accuracy is at a maximum the probability successful is only 70%. This assumption is based on the idea that even with perfect data, the design team will still make mistakes. The rough percentages were supplied by the company representative in our group.

The last important connection in the model is between the Product Design Team and the "faulty cars" flow between customers and the garage. The basic idea is that as more design modifications are made, the rate at which cars breakdown decreases. The idea of diminishing returns is built into the model. So, for example, while in the first year the teams may solve 10% of the problems, in the next year, with the same amount of effort, they will only solve 10% of the remaining problems. Thus as time goes on it takes increasingly more effort to solve problems for a given product. This is an attempt to model the notion that the design team will solve the easier and more frequent problems first and the harder and less common problems later.

The output measures we settled upon for the model were the percentage of the design problem fixed, the total cost to the company due to repairs covered under warranty, and the cycle time for the design team to come to a decision. These measure were extremely relevant indicators of company's performance with respect to improving the flow of information from the field garages to the design engineers. We ran this simulation and compared the predicted measures to existing company data. All three measures were reasonably close to the measures for the actual current process. Although this is not a careful, scientific comparison, we consider it to be a simple "sanity check" on the model to determine if it is within ballpark range of the actual processes. We will discuss these results in more detail shortly.

New Process: Incremental Solution. Every two months, for one week, the team works in one of the selected company-owned garages to understand and diagnose for the most important faults. By meeting for a week at the garages, we assume the product design team will have access to detailed information about design problems. Rather than simply relying on the failure reports, the design team will be able to examine the failures themselves. Thus the quality of the data they use to make design decisions will increase dramatically. In the model this is reflected in an increase in the data accuracy from .35 to .8 for the week of the garage visits. We chose a value of .8 because it was slightly more that twice the data accuracy in the baseline model. The company representative in our group believed this was a reasonable increase to expect from visiting the garages. For the time it takes the team to reach a decision, we assumed the data accuracy would only be .8 for the week that the team was actually at the garage. For the meetings between garage visits, we assumed the data accuracy was the same as in the baseline case, .35. However, given this new source of data will affect all decisions, not just the design decisions made during the week out at the garages, we set the decision quality to a constant .8. These were the only changes made to the baseline model to create the incremental model.

New Process: Radical Solution.. In this solution, collaborative computer and telecommunication technology enables designers in the CMHT to advise and collaborate with the garages. The garages are equipped with a communication system for direct data /audio/video transmission to the CMHT and a direct data link into the central fault database. This will allow immediate and accurate fault data acquisition into central corporate fault database, removing the one month delay in the transmission of the failure reports. It will also afford the design teams deeper knowledge of the failures because the design teams will have the capability to see defective parts and discuss design and maintenance problems directly with mechanics in the field. Although this requires major changes to the real process, we predicted that its overall effect on the model would be to increase the data accuracy and the decision quality from 0.35 to 0.8 throughout the design period. We chose .8 because we did not think it would increase the data accuracy beyond that for actually visiting the garages (as in the incremental model) but given that the CMHT would have access everyday and could advise and ask questions about maintenance and design problems, we could not justify decreasing the data accuracy either. These parameter changes were the only changes made to the baseline model to create the radical model.

Analysis of the Simulations

The results of the 3 simulation runs (baseline, incremental, and radical) are summarized in the graphs in Figures 2 and 3. Figure 2 shows the impact of the redesigned processes on the company's ability to solve existing car design problems. The graph displays the fraction of remaining design problems over a 5 year period for each of the three alternative processes. One important indirect measure is customer satisfaction which is inversely proportional to the shape of this graph. For customer satisfaction, it is very important to remove design flaws quickly; every customer who buys a car with many design flaws is likely to be dissatisfied. As more problems are removed, new customer satisfaction increases. For the baseline case, 9 months go by before any problems are fixed. Then there is a slow, almost linear decrease in the remaining fraction of problems left. After 5 years, roughly half of the problems still remain. The incremental process has an 8 month delay before any problems are solved. However, problems decrease significantly starting in the second year. At the end of the second year about half of the problems are solved, and at the end of the fifth year there are only 7% of the problems left. The radical solution is most dramatic. Problems begin to be solved after 5 months. After 2 years, only 15% of the problems remain. Customer satisfaction for a client that buys the product after it has been on the market for 2 years is about three times higher for the radical solution than for the incremental and about 5 times higher than for the baseline.

Figure 3 displays the cumulative warranty costs over five years for the baseline, incremental, and radical process models. At the end of the first year there is not a dramatic difference between the processes. This is due to the fact that for all cases there is little data for the product design team to make design modification decisions. Towards the end of the year, as more cars enter the garages with faults, costs of the three processes begin to change. The warranty costs associated with the baseline process continues to grow roughly linearly throughout the 5 year period reaching a total of 952 million dollars by the end of the 5th year. Costs for the

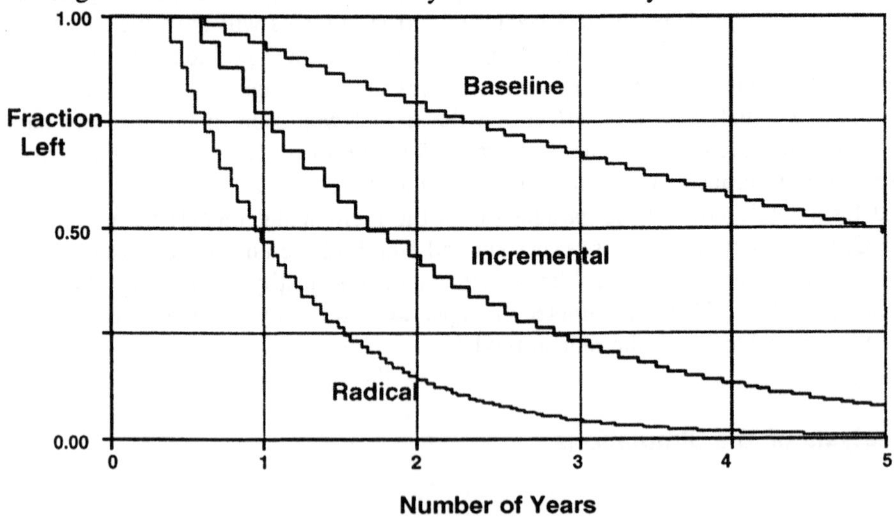

Figure 2: Fraction of Problems Left over Time

radical process begin to slow first, due to the fact that data reaches the product design team more quickly for this process. During the second year the effect of both redesigned processes on the warranty costs begins to appear. The costs for the incremental process begin to slow and level off after 5 years at 540 million dollars. The costs for the radical process slow even more quickly - after the first 2 years the costs barely increase. The total cost for the radical process converges to 302 million dollars. Thus over 5 years, the models predict that the incremental process will save 412 million dollars in warranty costs over 5 years and the radical solution will save 650 million dollars over 5 years.

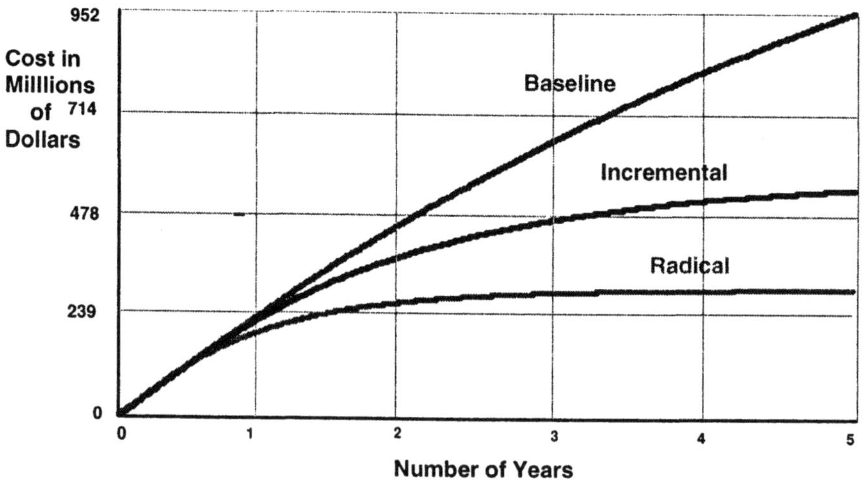

Figure 3: Cumulative Warranty Costs over Time

Cycle Time. One important measure for the processes is the time it takes the product design team to reach a design modification decision. In the current (baseline) case, the average time it takes for the team to reach a decision is 44.5 days. This matches the estimate of 6 weeks from the actual current process quite well. There is a slight decrease to 37 days for the incremental process. This is due to the increased data accuracy for the week that the teams visit the garages. There is a dramatic decrease in the cycle time for the radical solution. It takes an average of 19 days for the design team to reach each design modification decision. This is due to the increase in data accuracy to .8 for the entire design period afforded by the continuous flow of high quality data from the garages to the product team.

Overall, the incremental solution and the radical solution offer differing risks and benefits. Although we did not perform a formal cost estimates for the two solutions, the incremental solution involves no new technology and is easy to implement. We estimated no significant start up costs, and a yearly cost of 1.25

million dollars to allow the design engineers to visit the field sites. The cost of implementation and maintenance for the radical solution are harder to estimate. There are substantial implementation costs and maintenance costs for the new technology but cost of this technology is dropping dramatically. The simulations predict that the radical solution will save 238 million dollars more than the incremental solution in warranty costs alone over five years, perhaps justifying its initial investment and higher maintenance. More importantly, the simulation of the radical design predicts that it will solve all but 15% of the design flaws in the first two years of the release of a car, while the incremental solution does not reach that level until the fourth year. This could be a critical factor in the success of an automobile. Customers may be willing to wait a year or two for the manufacturer to work all the kinks out of a design, perhaps leasing an initial release, but they may not be willing to wait four years. This difference could prove critical to the success or failure of a model of car. While we do not claim this interpretation is the correct one, our point is that the simulations allow us to predict the performance of different redesigns with different types of process integration and answer questions about what impact these changed processes might have on a company's business strategy.

Across the current process and the two redesigned processes there is a shift in focus from information integration by document integration to information integration through process integration. In the existing process, the only connection between the product design team and the garages is through the automobile failure forms. Integration of the failure forms occurs when designers extract reports from the failure form repository based on specific queries. In the incremental solution the only time the maintenance and design processes are merged is when the engineering design teams are visiting the garages. In the radical solution, process integration occurs continuously through the combined activities of the maintenance and engineering design personnel in the CMHT and their active process connection to the garages. Overall there is a shift from a static one way connection with information being filtered to the product design personnel through extracted reports to an active two way exchange of information, with maintenance personnel engaged in the design process and product design personnel engaged in the maintenance process.

References

Carley, K.M., and Lin, Z. (in press). A theoretical study of organizational performance under information distortion. *Management Science*.

Hammer, M. (1995). *The reengineering revolution.* New York: Harper Business Review.

High Performance Systems. (1994). Ithink Technical Documentation. New Hampshire: High Performance Systems.

Kraut, R.E., Miller, M.M., Siegel, J. (1996). Collaboration in performance of physical tasks: Effects on outcomes and communication. To appear in *CSCW-96.*

Levitt, R.E., Cohen, G. P., Kunz, J.C., Nass, C.I., Christiansen, T., and Jin, Y. (1994). The "virtual design team": Simulating how organization structure and information processing tools affect team performance. In Carley, K.M., and Prietula, M.J. (Eds.) *Computational organization theory.* Lawrence Eelbaum Associates: Hillsdale, New Jersey.

Senge, P., *The fifth discipline: The art and practice of the learning organization,* Doubleday, New York, 1990.

Smailagic, A., and Siewiorek, D. P. (1996). Modalities of interaction with CMU wearable computers. *IEEE Personal Communications.*

Acknowledgments: We would like to thank our colleagues in the process redesign group, Hartmut Baumgart, Giancarlo Bertoldi, Bernd Breugge, and Hans Joachim Glas, whose hard work made this paper possible, and also the Carnegie-Bosch Institute for creating the summer program in which this work was done. We especially want to thank Jane Siegel for her feedback about this work.

15 THE LSS PROJECT: A CASE STUDY FOR INTEGRATING AN ELECTRONIC DOCUMENT REPOSITORY INTO THE LEGAL PROCESS

Thomas L. Sarro,
Gary A. Benson,
and Craig A.A. Samuel

Introduction

In June of 1993 a project initiative was begun at British Petroleum in Anchorage, Alaska. The goal was to build an electronic depository capable of supporting the document retrieval needs of the company's legal department there, and potentially for the entire corporation. Corporate litigation is information intensive, with storage requirements ranging in the hundreds of thousands of documents and millions of pages *for a single lawsuit.*

The primary motivation for this project was to eliminate the slow and cumbersome process of retrieving paper documents from storage. But in addition to fast retrieval, an electronic system could also fundamentally change the way in which the legal activities were conducted within the company [6, 7]. With this in mind, the following explicit goals were established:

- adequate *hardware/software infrastructure* for fast response (typically 1 to 4 minutes for a sophisticated search)

- extensive *document search capability*, using both 'fuzzy' and control field searching on the documents, using OCR text and a 'meta data' model appropriate to the legal information environment

- an intuitive *User Interface* providing data organization models which would allow users to share information generated by the system (such as document lists) easily with other users

- on-screen document image browsing

- high quality *multiple document printing* for all items in any generated list

- *geographic distribution* of users over all important corporate centers, including Anchorage, Houston and Cleveland

- a *distributed data model* to provide scalability of the system to an arbitrary number of concurrent litigation activities

A system has in fact been built using a client-server architecture which fulfills these intentions. It is referred to as LSS, the "Litigation Support System", and has been in production use since late 1993 supporting the large litigation efforts it was designed to handle. LSS has earned a high degree of acceptance by the user community within the legal department. The process of loading the system with the volumes of required data has been in progress since that date.

Since the first full roll-out of LSS in mid 1994, the system has grown considerably through the acquisition of additional document data. During this time LSS has aided the successful conclusion of three major litigation efforts, and is currently being configured to support two more. The overall design concept of LSS has also proven successful, particularly in the accommodation of document data distributed over multiple databases so that the document repository will never be overwhelmed by growth of the required information base.

The LSS Application Setting

The user community for this system consists of attorneys, paralegals, engineers and clerical workers. An important and time consuming activity for all of these people is the legal 'discovery' process whereby research is conducted to find information which is exchanged with other parties in a lawsuit. The primary purpose of LSS is to aid retrieval and access of documents produced in this 'discovery' process. The strongest collaborative activity is usually between the paralegal, attorney and engineering roles. When an attorney makes a request for information, an engineer and a paralegal work together to arrive at a 'discovery' set of documents that provide information relevant to the issue of concern. Although there is a high level of interaction between the legal workers, there are no easily discernible patterns from which a rigid workflow process model could be based. Rather, the interactions tend to be 'ad hoc', and are inspired by the creativity of the individuals involved in order to find solutions to the problems that arise. However, informal observation of the users revealed that the information they share often consists of either a document list, or the methodology for conducting a document search. Observing this dynamic, it was apparent that the legal workers needed:

- storable and sharable search criteria
- storable and sharable result sets

Prior to LSS, document searches were conducted based on less efficient manual indexing and to a surprising extent, individual's memories. Most onerous of all, the actual documents usually had to be delivered via messenger from off-site storage. In addition to being slow, this delivery mechanism had a potentially high error rate, and occasionally resulted in lost documents, probably due to misfiling of returned items.

With the advent of LSS, the off-site storage problems have been minimized. In addition, the legal workers now have search capabilities far exceeding anything previously possible, both in terms of speed and integrity. In addition, data abstractions have been provided to support the shared work functions in LSS. They are called 'Search Sets' and 'Document Lists'. These allow the LSS users to share the products of their work with colleagues in a totally unconstrained fashion which matches well with their natural 'ad hoc' work patterns.

An existing Wide Area Network provides geographical scope for the system to support legal activities in Anchorage, Alaska; Houston, Texas; and Cleveland, Ohio. A connection to Juneau, Alaska for use during trial has also been implemented.

Design Rationale & Scope of Implementation

As with nearly all commercial ventures, the LSS project was constrained by time and resources. The preponderance of available budget needed to be allocated to the extensive hardware infrastructure and data preparation requirements of the project. This meant that only those user features thought to have a high impact on the business process were considered for implementation. It also meant that commercially proven software tools would be used whenever possible to leverage the implementation effort. These included:

- document fileroom, fuzzy searching and image viewer (Excalibur)
- GUI construction tool kit (Odesta)
- relational database (Sybase with interactive SQL)

Also notable were the components of the system which had to be built:

- document searching and list displays (using the GUI toolkit)
- 'work set' sharing (using the GUI toolkit and Sybase)
- document search query construction (C language)
- database structure for driving User Interface and organizing a distributed data model for storing document index information (Sybase)
- multiple document printing (C language, PERL, GUI toolkit, and Sybase)

The possibility of imbedding a formal workflow structure into the system was also discussed and dismissed early in the conceptualization phase of LSS. Despite increasing use of this methodology [1, 3] it was not viewed as an important part of LSS for the following reasons:

- legal work processes did not fit into easily discernible patterns that could be used as the basis for a workflow model
- user acceptance was deemed more important than establishment of highly structured work methodologies
- work patterns would inevitably change in unpredictable ways due to the impact of the electronic repository and associated tools
- currently available tools were not powerful enough to implement user-configurable workflows

Rather than impose a structured workflow on the users, it was decided to facilitate their own 'ad hoc' work patterns by providing simple and elegant mechanisms for sharing their 'work sets' generated within LSS for refinement, approval, or commentary. This is reminiscent of a "common-sense" approach that has been discussed earlier [9]. Apart from certain very routine procedures, it is sensible to let trained professionals do their jobs as they see fit and not force them into pre-defined patterns. There is at least one example of a system that was found to be more effective after it had been made less restrictive [5]. The resulting implementation for this 'ad hoc' sharing is described in the sections below.

User acceptance was a major consideration for this project. Indeed, this is an important ingredient for success of any new system [8]. As mentioned earlier, a basic philosophy of the LSS development team was that reliability and fast response were the under-pinning for good system usability. The best User Interface design imaginable is of only marginal benefit if the features being controlled execute too slowly or unpredictably to be of any real benefit in accomplishing the tasks that the users need to do. This point was addressed by investing a large percentage of the project's resources into a first class hardware/software infrastructure that was not likely to be overwhelmed by typical use.

In addition, all system feature specification and User Interface design was be done in a participatory manner. This point was addressed by holding design meetings with user representatives during project conceptualization, and subsequently at frequent intervals throughout the implementation [4]. A very flexible GUI construction tool was used to fabricate all of the custom User Interface components, so that desired changes could be made quickly and with minimal impact on the overall system architecture.

During the first six months of LSS development (from mid 1993 to early 1994), implementation activities were prioritized to be able to deliver a basic electronic document repository to be used by an on-going litigation effort. This included establishment of the operating infrastructure, initiation of the document conversion process (indexing and scanning of relevant documents), establishment of the document fileroom environment, and establishment of search methodologies based on document index data. At this point, the available LSS features were made available to legal workers involved in a single (but important!) litigation effort. The second half year of development (thru mid 1994) focused on providing multiple litigation support, multiple document printing, optional fuzzy searching, 'work set' sharing, and additional legal environment specific features. This period of development also provided an opportunity to deploy a major new version of the GUI development toolkit, which provided an extensive procedural scripting environment to complement the existing visual GUI construction tools.

There were four primary individuals involved in the implementation of LSS (both hardware and software). These four people performed the following roles:

- Hardware Configuration Expert/Overall Project Coordinator
- Data Loading Expert/Local User Support Coordinator (4th Dimension)
- User Interface/Database Design & Implementation (ODMS, SQL, C)
- Document Fileroom Implementation and Support (Excalibur, PERL, UNIX)

During one year of intense LSS development, these four people were all fully engaged in the project (75 to 100 percent activity). Thus, it would be reasonable to say that the first 'completed' version of LSS took roughly four person years to finish, over a one year period. Through the end of 1995, these roles have dropped to about 25 percent each, with a somewhat higher rate of activity for the ongoing data loading and document fileroom support roles, and a somewhat lower rate for hardware support and software implementation. One could accurately conclude that it takes about one person year annually to maintain the system, however, the extended participation of all four roles for system maintenance has been critical to continued success and confidence that the users have in the system.

Apart from a rapidly growing document database, and support of several additional litigation efforts, LSS has been remarkably stable since its Phase II completion in mid 1994. It would be difficult to translate all of the hard costs associated with the aggregate of activities that continue to be part of the LSS investment into terms that would be useful or even comparable to other situations. However, the following additional cost factors should not be ignored when considering projects of this type:

- hardware acquisition
- software acquisition
- internal large scale hardware platform operations (e.g., servers)
- internal technical support for client platforms
- internal software support (e.g., advanced Sybase expertise)
- document conversion activities (e.g., indexing and imaging)

Finally, it should be noted that incremental improvements to LSS have been relatively painless and easy to deploy to the users. This is due to the use of a GUI construction toolkit which allows changes to be made in a localized manner with minimal disturbance to the basic structure of the system.

System Overview

The hardware configuration implemented for LSS is summarized in figure 1. The documents are stored on an 187 gigabyte capacity jukebox in scanned image format. A Sparc 10 workstation acts a controller for this device. This storage capacity can be increased via a hardware upgrade that would not structurally change the LSS configuration. The software which organizes the document repository resides on an RS 6000 based UNIX platform, as does a Sybase relational

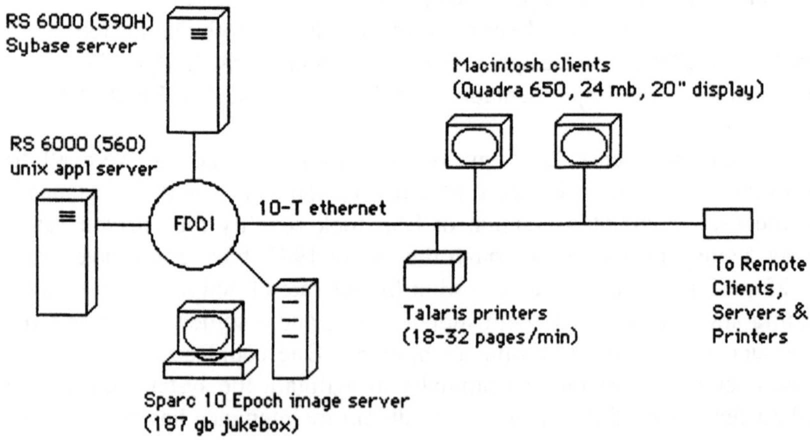

Figure 1: LSS hardware configuration

database engine used for accessing the document index information and other customized document structures (the document 'meta data'). These systems are located in Anchorage. Ethernet connects local Macintosh client workstations and Talaris printers to the server functions via TCP/IP protocols. In addition, ethernet connects a bridge to the WAN for remote clients, database servers, and printers. This is a fairly typical client-server architecture [2].

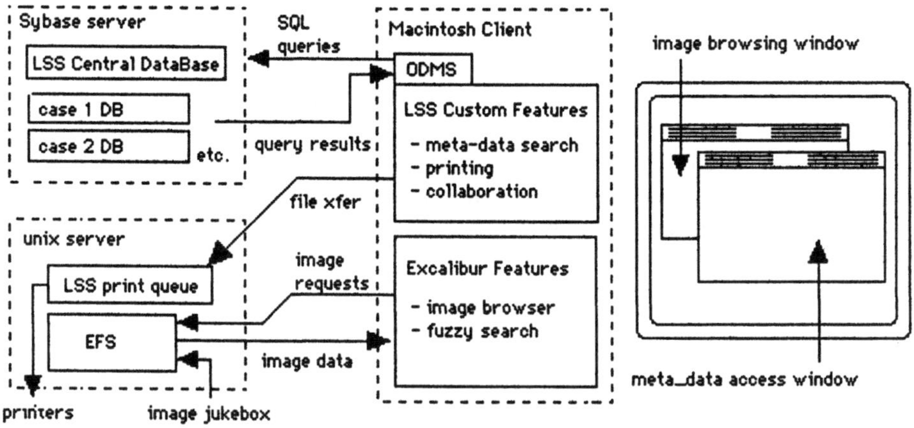

Figure 2: LSS Software Overview

A high level software description of LSS is provided in figure 2. As mentioned above, the client workstations run two applications simultaneously. One is the Excalibur client which interacts with the document repository software (Excalibur Fileroom System or EFS [11]) server on the UNIX platform. This server knows how to find requested images on the jukebox, and returns image data so the user can browse through documents on the display. The second application is a custom built portion of LSS, which provides a database structure and user access for the indexed 'meta data' which is essential for describing and categorizing the documents efficiently. The LSS custom application was built using a GUI construction tool kit provided by Odesta Systems Corporation which provides direct access capability to multiple Sybase databases. The Odesta product (Odesta Document Management System or ODMS [10]) is required in the run-time environment of LSS.

Figure 3 presents a simplified representation of the database schema used to store all of the system data not related to EFS. It is provided here primarily for reference, to give some idea of how the features to be described in the following sections relate to the storage structures in the Sybase server databases. Note that there is a single *LSS Central Database* and an arbitrary number of *Document Databases*, one to implement each litigation project being supported by LSS. The central database is required for ODMS, but is also used to drive pop-ups and other User Interface elements for each LSS user session. It also stores the 'work sets' data. The case specific document databases store the indexed document data for each litigation project. Also note that there are tables to support special litigation data such as depositions, exhibits, etc. This data is entered by LSS users as such events occur throughout the course of a litigation.

Hardware/Software Infrastructure

A more detailed description of the hardware and software components of LSS is not in the scope of this paper. In many respects this is appropriate, as the nature of present day client-server environments diminishes the importance of specific hardware component choices. For instance, the differences between Sybase running on an RS 6000 workstation and Oracle running on a Sun workstation would not be highly consequential to LSS. These choices were largely made based on the preferred vendor relationships with BP, and the availability of an existing operations and support organization for these systems.

Selection of suitable application/development software was similarly guided. It happened that both Odesta and Excalibur already had established relationships with BP, so it made sense to use these products. This is sound advice anytime a system is being developed within a large organization with such established relationships. In addition to lower software license costs (site licenses for these products already existed), existing relationships may smooth the way for specialized support or required enhancements to the off-the-shelf products. In the case of the ODMS product, required development environment features for the Phase II implementation of LSS were not available within ODMS until a major new version of that product was released at the beginning of 1994. Given the mission critical timing for the Phase I and Phase II deployments of LSS, this may be considered an example of 'just in time' scheduling, where release of an updated software tool was required to feed into an on-going development project.

Document Search Capability

The core capabilities of LSS are undoubtedly the ability to search previously prepared index data to identify a set of documents which fit within a desired category, and then the ability to access an image of each document in the set via the electronic repository. For the legal environment, such index searching has been
thought to be more important than any kind of open text or 'fuzzy searching' based on the actual text of the documents in the repository. This is true even though LSS does have the capability for 'fuzzy searching' (as a consequence of using the Excalibur product) and converted text for many of the documents is available in the

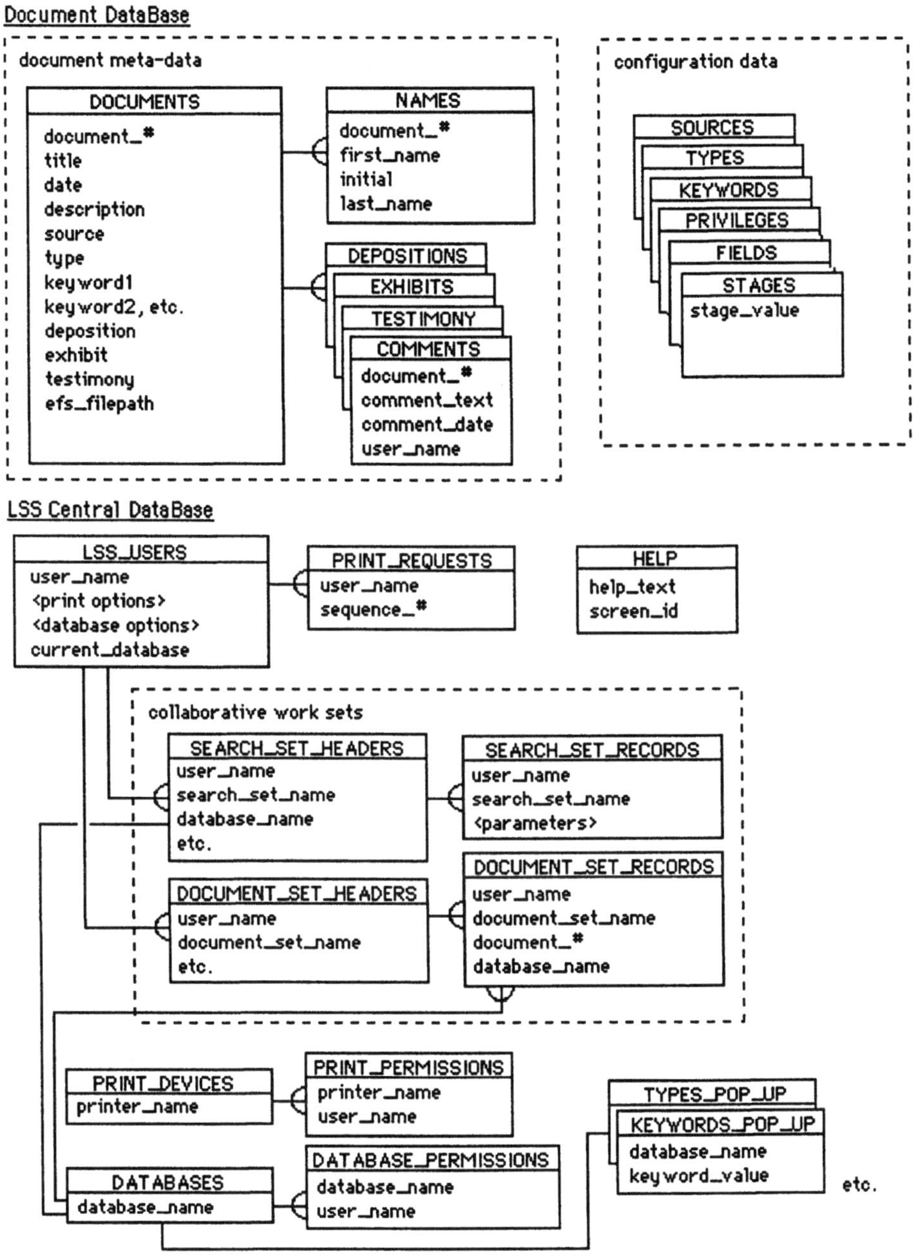

Figure 3: Simplified LSS database schemas

system. In the legal arena the *context* of a piece of information is frequently as important as the data itself. For example, it may be the case that finding all occurrences of the name *John Smith* as an author of any document may be important. A search of an index in which names are categorized by their context (author, recipient, mentioned name, etc.) will find this list easily and accurately, whereas the result of a fuzzy search would be a much larger set of documents with many instances of *John Smith* in contexts that are not of interest to the problem. Although there may be environments where non-contextual 'fuzzy searching' is preferred, LSS has been effective without depending upon it. The remainder of this section will focus on contextual searches based on index information for the documents stored in the relational database.

Looking back to the database schema presented in figure 3, it can be seen that the information used to perform document index searches is contained in each one of the document databases. There are five ways to search for documents:

- simple document/names search
- deposition exhibits search
- trial exhibits search
- expert testimony search
- complex document/names search

The first four search types are similar, in that simple forms are presented to the user with fields to fill in and pop-up selections to define the search categories of interest. They each operate on different domains, namely the *DOCUMENTS* table (with a join to *NAMES*), the *DEPOSITION EXHIBITS* table, the *TRIAL EXHIBITS* table and the *EXPERTS TESTIMONY* table. In the current implementation of LSS, searches across these domains are not possible, but this apparent deficiency does not seem to pose much of an inconvenience to the LSS users. The simple document/names search includes only a subset of the most common search parameters available from the join of the *DOCUMENTS* and *NAMES* tables, such as author's last name, a date range, several keyword selections, etc. These search types are only intended for simple and rapid access to the information in these domains.

The last search type provides a more comprehensive way to search for information in the *DOCUMENTS/NAMES* domain. This search mechanism provides the user with a User Interface tool which provides for the construction of a list of any available search parameter in this domain. In addition to being comprehensive, the complex search also allows the user to store the search criteria in a list. The mechanism for doing this is described in detail in the next section. The search is actually executed out of the information provided in this list. Each record in the list has the following format:

logical relationship parameter operator value

The logical relationship is either AND, OR, or NULL. The parameter is any item from the *DOCUMENTS/NAMES* domain such as last_name, title, or keyword. The operator is any operation which is relevant to the selected parameter, such as "equal", "not equal", "does not contain", "is null", etc.

The value is whatever data the document parameter should be compared to. In the source example given above, the parameter would be BP Exploration (Alaska), BP America, etc. An example search syntax built up using this mechanism might be:

NULL	keyword	=	"Legal Support"
AND	type	<>	"Memorandum"
OR	title	contains	"LSS"
AND	type	<>	"Memorandum"

This search would attempt to find documentation written about the LSS project, excluding memorandum which probably deal only with ephemeral issues surrounding the evolution and management of the project. If these were the issues of interest to the search, we would have explicitly asked for the memorandum only.

User Interface/Groupware Feature

The style of the User Interface implemented for LSS is fairly typical. Figures 4, 5, and 6 are presented here to provide a representative sample of the way data is displayed in LSS, how features are accessed, and to illustrate from the user's perspective some of the features of LSS that are unusual, if not unique.

Each user also has access to a list of current work sets, as illustrated in figure 6. Although simple, this information sharing model for collaboration provides considerable power to the users without binding them to the constraints of a pre-defined workflow. It also has the advantage of adding practically no additional cost to a project, since the user interface and data structures required to support the 'work sets' would need to be built anyway.

Image browsing within LSS is provided as an intrinsic feature of the Excalibur client application. The LSS document number (equivalent to *document_#* in the *DOCUMENTS* table) for each document has been loaded into an index table provided by the Excalibur client. A document number can be 'Cut' from the LSS client, then 'Pasted' into an appropriate field on the Excalibur client to display the image. This 'Loose Coupling' between the Excalibur client and the custom LSS User Interface has proven very workable for the LSS users

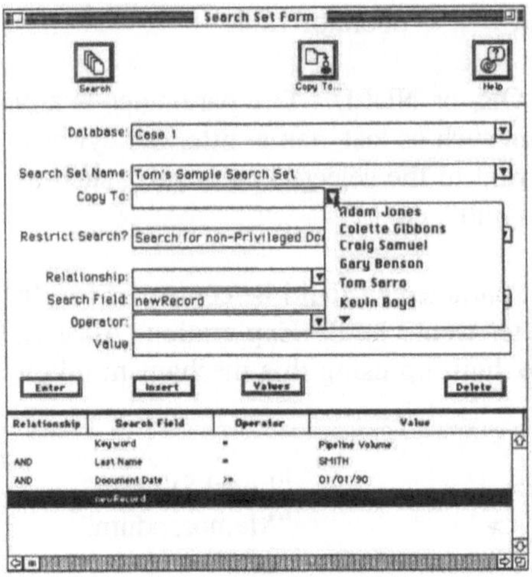

Figure 4: User Interface for sharing Search Sets

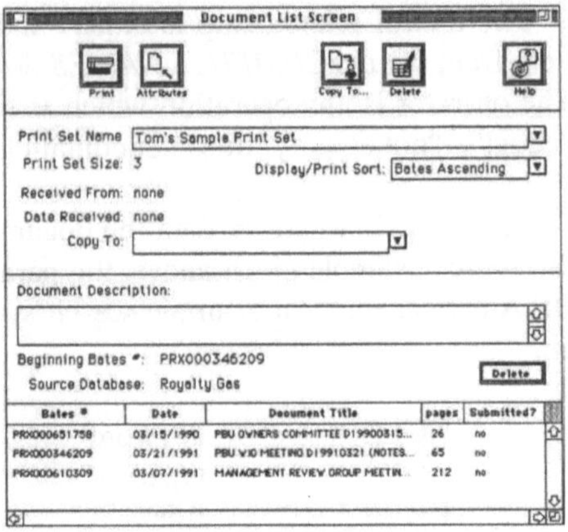

Figure 5: Interface for Document List Sharing

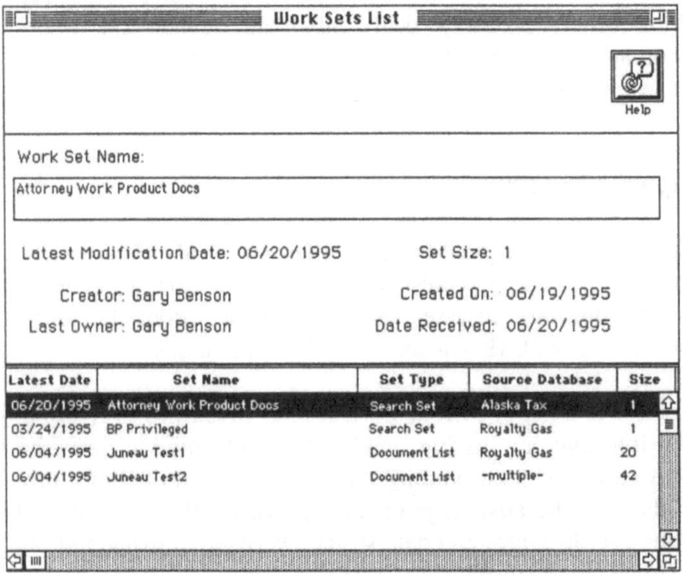

Figure 6: Interface for Work Sets Display List

Multiple Document Printing

One functional area in which none of the vendor tools provided much help was in printing the documents. The Excalibur client has a print feature, but can only handle print requests for one document at a time. This was far too onerous for LSS users, who sometimes needed to print batches of dozens of documents. A batch printing feature was implemented within the LSS client by creating an interface whereby the user could select the documents to be submitted for printing, as in figure 5 above. The user must select some document records from the list and then press the *Print* button to initiate the print request. Behind the scenes, a local disk file containing pointers to all the desired documents is created, and a File Transfer Protocol (FTP) request is made to copy this 'instructions' file to the UNIX environment. Once there, a shell script acts as a daemon to intercept this file and execute the print commands it contains, using appropriate UNIX commands for delivering each print instruction. One of the commands in this file is a printer device selection, as specified by the user via the LSS User Interface.

Geographic Distribution

The infrastructure supporting LSS is all located in Anchorage, Alaska. However, high speed links already connect the Anchorage based servers to LSS workstations located at BP facilities in Houston and Cleveland. LSS has provided a common means by which expertise in the Anchorage and Houston locations has been joined to work together on the same projects on a scale that was not common previous to the implementation of the system. The commonality of the data structures generated via LSS ('Search Sets' and 'Document Lists') is thought to be a strong contributing factor to this trend. The system has also been used in Cleveland to support an Alaska tax case. There has been at least one instance where a paralegal familiar with LSS was sent to Cleveland to support outside counsel located there. The ability to access LSS in close proximity to the outside counsel was a great advantage in this situation.

In preparation for a major trial an additional link between Anchorage and Juneau was implemented. This allowed LSS to directly support trial activities in the Alaskan state capital. However, an out-of-court settlement prevented the need for this particular trial, and the system was never used in the trial setting. With adequate Wide Area Network links, there is no technical obstacle to LSS taking on an international scope.

Distributed Data Model

An essential characteristic of the LSS implementation is that it is scaleable to accommodate an arbitrary number of lawsuits. The large amount of data being considered precludes the use of a single database for all of the litigations, as such an implementation would easily overwhelm any reasonable hardware configuration. Instead, it was decided to implement a separate database for each lawsuit. This presents some difficulty when a user wishes to search across multiple databases, but from a design perspective this is a reasonable compromise, since most searches occur only in the context of a single litigation.

While there is nothing new about de-centralizing data, the LSS model takes care that switching between database contexts has absolutely no impact on the user. This is done by arbitrating any database change from within a central database, which provides the information required to reconfigure the user's local parameters to be appropriate to the new database selection. For instance, different keyword sets are used for each litigation project, so any time the user moves from one litigation (or database) context to another, any User Interface element which displays keywords must be re-populated. The ease with which users can move from one database context to another can be seen by looking at figure 4. The field labeled *Database* displays the current database context. The pop-up button next to the field will provide all of the additional database contexts available to this user. By simply selecting a new option from the pop-up, the entire database context is changed automatically, and the user is ready to perform searches from within the new information source.

LSS in Operation/Future Goals

LSS has already successfully supported three major litigations in Alaska, and is currently being configured for two more. Each of the corresponding document databases is large, ranging from roughly 250,000 to 500,00 documents. After the initial three cases, the total number of imaged pages stored in the system was roughly 5 million, representing the equivalent of 58 tons of paper. As a replacement for the old hard copy filing system, LSS has been a success, reducing the time to access a specific document from up to two days to less than a minute. But the system has also added considerable value to the legal process at BP. Sophisticated index parameter searches can be accomplished in 1-2 minutes (instead of days), and the capability to immediately browse the document list makes iterative search procedures practical. Based on actual legal activity in the last year, it is estimated that three paralegals using LSS can accomplish the work of six paralegals and six clerical staff workers working in the pre-LSS environment.

It is possible that LSS may act as a stepping stone to the vision of a 'Paperless Trial', where discovery material can be shared among Plaintiffs and Defendants in electronic format, and material can be presented in the courtroom via interactive electronic display systems. For instance, BP has considered utilizing LSS compiled documents for mastering to CD-ROM format for subsequent use in trial.

The existence of LSS has also fostered collaboration between disparate organizations. In the most recent cases supported by LSS, all trial exhibits from all parties (several oil companies and the State of Alaska) were jointly prepared using a single imaging vendor and distributed using a compatible electronic format. While such cooperation is rare in the legal world under any circumstances, this could be the first instance in the United States where all parties in a lawsuit agreed to exchange data via electronic media.

Conclusions/Lessons Learned

The Litigation Support System has succeeded in minimizing the use of paper documents for BP's legal support requirements in Alaska. The system was built on the principles that strong user acceptance and adequate infrastructure were pre-requisite to meaningful user features. In light of this, user participation in the conceptualization and design process was intentionally high, and simple collaborative tools were selected which would not impede the user's ability to advantageously adapt their work patterns to exploit the new system. Over more than two years of production experience, we conclude that this was a good strategy, as the system has gained wide acceptance, and fostered greater collaboration among the legal support staff in the form of 'work set' sharing which has now become the norm among legal workers. The Herculean task of managing the many documents generated during major litigation has been made more time-efficient and cost-effective than was ever possible in the past.

Consistent with its design intentions, the most positive impact of LSS on the legal process at BP has been the rapid retrieval of specific documents. Once located, the document can be printed and reviewed in detail. This has been very helpful during deposition preparation. In particular, the ability to determine quickly (less than 15 minutes) whether or not a document has been produced has proven to be invaluable during court proceedings.

It has been found, however, that creating a document repository such as LSS is not entirely sufficient to replace paper documents. The major problem is the speed with which documents can be browsed on-screen. It takes roughly 5 to 10 seconds to display an electronic document page in LSS. This rate certainly impedes a trained professional, who can often flip through pages in a document and in a few seconds determine whether the content is of interest. In one case, documents that already existed within LSS were to be reviewed for possible production in a new litigation. It was deemed more efficient to review the original paper documents than to use LSS for this task, because of the different browsing rates. This factor should certainly be considered in any electronic document repository implementation.

Another lesson learned has been the relative value of keywords as a component of the document index data. In practice, document sets imaged for one litigation are frequently considered for production in subsequent litigations. This is convenient, since the documents are already easily available to LSS users. Unfortunately, the keywords selected for one litigation effort are rarely applicable to other cases. Rather than submit the documents for re-indexing, the keyword capability usually goes unused in these situations. This is not to undermine the overall value of document indexing. The title, mentioned name, date and status flag fields are used extensively to locate documents. However, the failure of the keyword concept in real-world practice may argue for a re-evaluation of the positive value of fuzzy searching, as a replacement for keywords.

Perhaps the most significant lesson learned is that an electronic document repository of this sort should not be viewed as an end in itself. The original managerial mandate for LSS was to replace paper documents with electronic images and to replace existing manual indexing schemes with a relational database. The truth is that once people (both users and management) begin to realize the latent potential in such a conversion, the expectation for the system increases dramatically. As just one example, the current support of the legal model in LSS, as represented by the depositions, exhibits, and testimony information storage was a last minute response to user feedback after the Phase II version of the system was deployed. The future trend for LSS, based on user needs and desires, is to implement a more sophisticated legal model, a more sophisticated document representation model and improved searching capabilities.

References

1. Abbott, K.R., and Sarin, S.K., Experiences with Workflow Management: Issues for the Next Generation. in Proc. Conference on Computer Supported Collaborative Work (CSCW '94) (October 1994), pp. 113-120.
2. Baker, Richard H.. Networking the Enterprise. McGraw Hill Publishers, 1994.
3. Black, D.B., Workflow Software: A Layman's Handbook. Inform, April 1994, Vol. 8, No. 4, pp. 52-59.
4. Floyd, C., Reisen, F-M, and Schmidt, G., STEPS to Software Development with Users. in Proc. 3rd European Software Engineering Conference (ESEC '89) (September 1989), pp. 48-64.
5. Gintell, et. al., Scrutiny: A Collaborative Inspection and Review System. in Proc. 4th European Software Engineering Conference (ESEC '93) (September 1993), pp. 344-360.
6. Hammer, M., and Champy, J. Reengineering the Corporation. HarperCollins Publishers, 1993.
7. Khoshafian, S, Baker, A.B., Abnous, R., and Shepherd, K., Intelligent Offices. John Wiley & Sons Publishers, 1992.
8. Markus, L., and Connolly, T., Why CSCW Applications Fail: Problems in the Adoption of Interdependent Work Tools. in Proc. Conference on Computer Supported Collaborative Work (CSCW '90) (October 1990), pp. 371-380.

9. Moran, T.P., and Anderson, R.J., The Workaday World as a Paradigm for CSCW Design. in Proc. Conference on Computer Supported Collaborative Work (CSCW '90) (October 1990), pp. 381-393.
10. Odesta Systems Corporation, ODMS Toolkit Reference Manual, Northbrook, IL, 1993 *(Note: Odesta is now part of OpenText Corporation).*
11. Excalibur Corporation, Excalibur Fileroom System User Manual, San Diego, CA, 1993.

16 DYNAMIC DOCUMENTS AND SITUATED PROCESSES: BUILDING ON LOCAL KNOWLEDGE IN FIELD SERVICE

David G. Bell, Daniel G. Bobrow, Olivier Raiman and Mark H. Shirley

ABSTRACT

Documents play a central role inside corporations as a resource for business processes, and paper has been the primary medium for distributing documents. These paper documents have not always been effective with respect to achieving the goals of the users of the documents, or of the corporations that have designed the processes. As documents are embedded into electronic media, it is possible to rethink their form, method of production and use. This paper is a case study of the redesign of a document-supported process for servicing Xerox equipment. Design and development of the new tools and process involved both the producers and users of the documents, so that they better fit the work practices of both groups.

The new electronic documentation more easily supports multiple styles of diagnosis, context-sensitive rendering of relevant information, and incorporation of current field learning into the support material. The co-development and commitment to ongoing evolution of the service process through field feedback reflects our desire to make the process accountable and responsive to the users, in contrast to the more common practice that uses new technology to hold people rigidly accountable to following reengineered processes.

This new process is currently in use by some of the Xerox field service force, and the population of users is growing. Measurements of impact showed convincing field service productivity improvement, using dynamic documents and processes that are adaptable to local knowledge and context, and support diverse reasoning styles.

Introduction: Looking at current documentation use

Within Xerox corporation, paper service manuals have been one of the main diagnostic support tools for field service personnel. These manuals have sections including parts lists with illustrative figures, block schematic diagrams, repairs and adjustments, and often the largest section contains diagnostic procedures called Repair Analysis Procedures (RAPs). Each procedure is distinguished by a primary symptom, often a status code that has been triggered from sensors in the machine. There typically aren't enough sensors in the machine to indicate a single corrective action, so the service engineer must make additional tests in order to determine which corrective actions are necessary to fix the machine. The RAPs are in the form of decision trees intended to direct the engineer through answering a series of questions based on tests, ending with a single corrective action that will fix the machine. The intention of the RAP is to make it possible for service engineers without extensive experience or training to follow the step-by-step process and find the problem.

But do customer service engineers (CSEs) really use these documents in the intended style? Are there other ways they make repairs? What else do they do on their job? To answer these questions, we spent time in the field observing service engineers. One of our group was certified on one product, and worked as a CSE for three months. He made trips with more than a dozen engineers servicing products with a wide range of complexity, speed and features. Another spent more than a month going on the job with dozens of CSEs with different profiles: central city and rural; specialists on a single product versus some who handle everything at a location; newly trained and local experts on a product.

The following vignette reflects early observations made during a time when the organization was in the process of competing for a national quality award (it won).

> During the first days when one of our team was going on calls with a CSE, the CSE initially thought our team member was a quality inspector. Although our member described his position and background, the CSE was very careful, showing only a pristine service manual, describing how

> he methodically followed the directive decision trees in the manual. It was his understanding that he was expected to follow these procedures precisely, since a company policy mandated that in order to provide quality customer service, all customers must receive the *same* service. Furthermore, he thought that CSEs were not allowed to make annotations in their manuals since that would mean all CSEs would not have the same procedures to follow. After the CSE got to know our team member better, he showed his "cheat sheet" with recent tips for difficult service problems that he used as an augmentation to the manual. In essence, he was keeping two sets of books: one to show quality inspectors, and one to use for a quality job!

This pointed to a clear gap between the documented processes provided in the service manuals and the actual work practices of field service engineers. We decided to look more closely at what was driving the discrepancy between the actual practice and the documented processes. Xerox was moving towards using technology to support service people in the hopes of gaining productivity, and we wanted to understand how the technology might be made to fit their practice rather than just more tightly implement the current process.

We started with our observations of service engineers using documentation on the job. We also held roundtables with different product and workgroups to gather their understandings of issues and practices in their work. There were problems reported traceable to the medium, the inflexibility of the document for different styles of use, and the lack of currency and completeness of the information. The manuals lose value because of their size and the inconvenience of inserting updates in the right place. Also, CSEs felt that some customers looked askance at a CSE using a book, asking "*Why don't you send someone who knows what they are doing.*" The form of the instructions cause problems as well. It is easy to follow a procedure in the manual exactly, but not always easy to understand why and where it is going – to extract the underlying rationale. For problems that hadn't been anticipated the documentation can lead the CSE astray.

The problems of documentation form are simply solvable by moving to computer-based documentation. With a laptop, an engineer no longer has to trade-off carrying tools and parts inventory versus the heavy manuals – and using a laptop gives even a novice the appearance of being "high-tech." But using a laptop doesn't make everything better. Circuit diagrams, block schematics, and some figures showing complex arrangements of parts are not very usable on small low resolution screens; paper versions of these graphics augment the laptop documentation. Also, simple translation of the decision tree documents to hypertext on a CD-ROM does not make the documentation easier to use in different styles.

Flexibility: Minding the styles

Observations of field service indicate that CSEs diagnose machines in different styles at different times. They use the documentation as a resource, rather than as a set of instructions – as Suchman [1987] describes in her seminal work use of plans for situated action. The following vignette represents an experience of the team member who was certified and worked in the field. It is indicative of how different reasoning styles are used, even within the varying context of a single diagnosis:

> As new service engineer, I started one call by methodically following the directive diagnosis procedures in the manual to identify the machine fault. When this failed, I called a specialist and described the visible symptoms (it kept jamming in the fuser area). The specialist gave me some tips relating recent similar failures in other machines, based on associations made to the symptoms observed on this call. When none of these helped, the specialist drove out to join me on site. At this point, the specialist first tried a couple of quick fixes that he guessed might solve the problem without explanation. Finally he resorted to a principled analysis using his knowledge of how the machine should be working. He finally deduced that the root cause must be in a gear on the far side of the machine, which proved to be cracked.

Four diagnosis styles are illustrated here, which are explicitly referred to by the Xerox documentation community [Smith, 1993]: deductive, directive, associative and part-swapping to fix a fault he intuitively thought might be the problem.

We refined our understanding of these styles through analogy with the Jungian type hierarchy for ways people perceive and interact with the world. Jung [1971] labeled styles *thinking, sensate, feeling* and *intuitive*. In the *thinking style*, a person uses abstract reasoning from principles; in the *sensate style,* a person is grounded in the details of the sensations and interactions in the world; in the *feeling style*, a person uses analogies with past experiences to guide present actions; in the *intuitive style*, a person leaps to (often correct) conclusions based on partial knowledge by recognizing a pattern and extrapolating. Let us consider how these styles are reflected in how a CSE might do his job.

In the *deductive style*, the resources that a CSE uses are knowledge of the structure of the machine, and the principles of operation of each of its parts. From an understanding of how parts fail in the field, they reason backwards from the symptom to a set of possible causes. Measurements and observations of the machine allow elimination of each hypothesized cause to narrow the diagnosis to a part that can be adjusted, repaired or replaced to eliminate the observed problem. Problems with this style include existence of an unknown failure mode for a part (e.g. a solenoid is slow moving in but not out), or an unusual pathway of interaction between subsystems (e.g. a signal traveling through a power supply) that makes an unusual or unexpected symptom appear. Then reasoning, no matter how carefully done, can be ineffective.

In the *directive style*, the resource that the CSE uses is the set of instructions, the Repair Analysis Procedures (RAP), provided with the machine. A RAP specifies a sequence of setups, tests and corrective actions. By answering the questions, the CSE is enabled to look at only local information. In this way, the CSE is led through the diagnostic decision tree. This works well when all possible faults have been anticipated by the author of the decision tree, but as machines age new problems appear. Another place where problems arise is in the interpretation of an observation or measurement: is that a smudge or a smear; is the voltage of 16.1 within what was intended by the author to be equal to a nominal 16 volts or not? And what about if the measurement was 17.2 volts?

In the *associative style*, the resource the CSE uses is a set of stories or cases about how machines fail, especially in unusual ways. The similarity between the described symptoms, state and context of use of the machine, and elimination of simple alternatives makes the case base invaluable as an aid to tracking down new, difficult or rare problems. But a case base is rarely complete; the unremarkable rarely gets included. And similarity may be difficult to determine.

In the *intuitive style*, the resources the CSE uses are tacit knowledge about possible faulty parts that can causes a specific symptom, which ones are most likely, and what has been replaced recently. Experienced CSEs can often look at the presenting symptom and a few copies coming through a machine, listen to it running, and make a very good guess as to what the root cause is. But in the extreme, doing this can be quite costly as a CSE could swap out any number of good parts before finding the one that cures the problem. This extreme is referred to as "shotgunning," implying a mindless replacement of parts.

Jung asserts that people have dominant ways of viewing the world, and are often most comfortable using a particular style. The parallel of the Jungian types and diagnostic methods of service engineers suggests that one could identify people's type and have interfaces suited to a person's dominant style. But we found that the use of styles was not only dependent on the person. It was also dependent on features of their situation such as the type of machine, the type of fault, etc. The mix of these varies by individual, work experience and the context of the particular diagnosis being done, yielding situated reasoning styles rather than individualistic reasoning styles. This work did not attempt to *manage* diversity by labeling individuals through standardized tests, but rather focused on *supporting* the inherent diversity of situated reasoning styles through the design of support systems.

Dynamic Documentation: A Minding the Styles Diagnostic Assistant

The dynamic documentation allows use of all four styles, shifting the emphasis from being a diagnostic director to being a diagnostic assistant. It attempts to capitalize on dominant styles, reinforce secondary styles, and mediate between effective utilization and ineffective extremes such as shotgunning for the intuitive reasoning style. For example, when using the dynamic documentation, if the CSE wants to jump ahead (intuitively) after making a few observations to specify a particular fault that seems most likely to them, the system will extract that part of the RAP which contains the minimum set of tests to confirm the guess given the current information. By providing confirmation test sets, assistance for the intuitive style is provided, and this moderates shotgunning.

Assistance in the deductive style is provided by allowing CSEs to enter test results in the order they find convenient. This is not always in the same order as the standard decision tree; but through additional information added to the documentation structure, what is displayed can be specialized to the current context, maintaining the logic of the decision tree while eliding questions already answered, and branches no longer relevant. To understand the operation of parts involved in the tests, the decision tree contains hypertext links to appropriate places in the documentation/principles of operation. Active block schematic diagrams could help show how different faults propagate in the system.

Assistance for the directive style is the context-sensitive rendering of the documentation that shows only that portion of the document that is relevant considering the tests and observations made. In addition, users can see a choice they make and the effect it has on the set of candidate root causes for the problem. For example, if an engineer initially decides that 17.2 volts is close enough to 16 volts, they immediately see which faults are eliminated. If one is eliminated that they think is very likely, they can go back and change their interpretation without needing to re-enter any other information. In addition, the laptop can be connected to the machine being repaired enabling reading of the machine's internal non-volatile memory. That data is used directly by the laptop diagnostic assistant to answer memory-specific tests in the decision trees.

Authoring Process: A Document-centric Knowledge Base

Context-sensitive assistance requires additional information that is not ordinarily part of existing documentation, so straightforward hypertext conversion of paper documentation is insufficient. The standard way of building flexible diagnostic aids is to build a rule-based expert system that deduces the next step to be taken in a diagnostic process based on the observations made. The authors have a long history of designing and building such systems [Bell et. al., 1991] but when we showed one to the document authoring group, they said that it didn't help with their work practice. They said that expert systems did not take into account many cognitive and training factors in generating decision trees, although they could appreciate the power of the flexible context sensitive rendering of information. They also were facing a challenge to their practice from another group that was developing full diagnostic aid in the expert system style.

We have since worked to develop a methodology that capitalizes on the knowledge and practice of the documentation group and the knowledge representation techniques used in building expert system knowledge bases. This merges into one activity two formerly independent authoring activities, standard documentation preparation and expert system authoring. To support this, we built a system we call SADIE, Service Analyst Design Interactive Environment that helps in authoring, annotating and previewing the new expert documentation. The authoring is done in SGML, a standard in the publishing industry for representing formatted documents. Annotations in the document source capture the extra knowledge required to support the context-sensitive re-rendering.

This document-centric methodology enables publishing of three outputs (paper, HyperText and expert documentation) from one document database. The expert documentation is viewed in PRIDE, a laptop-based expert diagnostic guidance assistant that supports interaction with the copiers in the field, extraction of internal machine data, and context sensitive rendering of the document based on that data and the history of the CSE interaction.

Another key benefit is that decision trees in legacy service documentation can be readily imported and reused. Old document sources are being converted to SGML, and portions can be annotated to support use in more flexible ways. Hence it is possible to incrementally move from simple translation of the medium from paper to hypertext to having more and more of the document using the flexible computational medium for expert guidance where most needed.

Currency: Learning from field experience

Making existing documentation more flexible helps improve its usefulness. But there is a problem of currency; often lessons learned in the field are shared as informal hints and tips since the formal documentation cannot keep pace with the learning that happens in the field. This is reflected in the need CSEs have felt to carry around "cheat sheets," and the observed use of war stories to share lessons.

> The practice of diagnosis is done through narrative, and the diagnostic process is preserved and circulated among the technicians through war stories, anecdotes of their experiences. [Orr, 1991]

Service manuals include diagnosis for known problems considered both complex enough and common enough to document. The initial set of known problems is envisioned in engineering and observed in limited lab testing. This knowledge base is augmented during alpha test of the product with a limited set of advanced customers. The initial documentation is then published.

But new problems keep coming up. After official launch a product is placed in many customer sites, some very different from the alpha test sites: from dry deserts to onboard ships; from the high altitudes of Denver to the low altitudes of New Orleans; and from the cleanliness of a doctor's office to the dust-filled rooms of a lumber mill. The contexts encountered also include machine operators and job types [Blomberg, 1986]. As the number of machines in use increases, the number of machine contexts increases, and the number of observed problems increases.

The same presenting symptom can have many different causes. The most frequent cause for a given symptom changes over time – because of new software releases, new hardware changes, and the effects of aging (e.g. wear). This affects both the ordering of causes for problems, and the set of top problems seen in the field. The six-year history of underlying causes for one presenting symptom, out of hundreds on the photocopier under study, was uncovered through interviews and historical data. Seven new causes appeared over time, and different causes dominated at different times.

As more problems are encountered by service engineers in the field, more solutions to those problems are found. Sometimes these solutions are found by the engineers themselves, other times by field service specialists (Tigers) and other times by product engineers. Attempts are made to incorporate new knowledge in the formal documentation, but distribution to the field takes time, since it can be significant work to incorporate the new knowledge in the existing decision tree, and it takes time to publish and disseminate a new version of the manual. Because of this constant discovery of new problems, some people say that service manuals are effectively out of date the day they are printed.

War stories and informal tips are useful for sharing lessons learned within a work group, but it is difficult to scale this up to work across a large geographically distributed work force. Face-to-face communication has limits of time and space, and understanding the value of a tip is harder if you don't know the person who is providing it. We have addressed this through a distributed tips-sharing and validation process.

Tip Sharing: The Eureka Process

Service engineers frequently invent new/better ways of doing things and sharing them locally. Unfortunately, current policies and infrastructure significantly limit the company's ability to capture any value from this learning beyond the local workgroup. The following story was told to one of us by a senior CSE.

> Decades ago when he started at Xerox, he submitted a suggestion on how to install a machine more efficiently. For six months he did not receive any feedback about the suggestion. Then he saw a published bulletin with his idea, attributed to the person who received the suggestion over the phone. After that, the service engineer did not submit any ideas until the launch of the Eureka process.

To provide an infrastructure and context that they could feel comfortable with in sharing their knowledge more widely, we worked with the field service community to create a process (named Eureka). Representatives of the field service force in France, including customer service engineers, hotline specialists, product specialists, Tigers and others, jointly designed a distributed tips validation process. In this form, a tip is a problem-cause-solution case. Tips are indexed at the same granularity as the documentation (presenting symptom), allowing easy cross-referencing between the tips case-base and the documentation. In this process, anyone in the field service community can author a tip and submit it for validation by a community of product leaders.

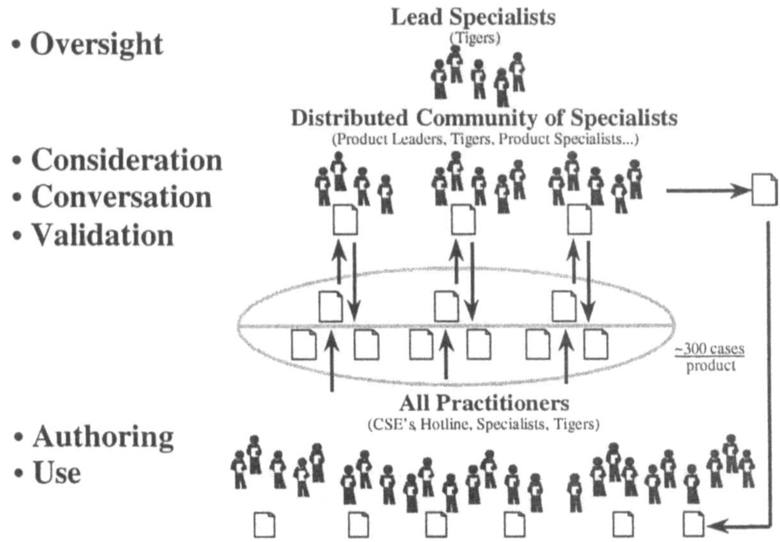

Eureka Distributed Tip Authoring and Validation Process

The French service community decided that the appropriate people to do validation should include those people who were already designated product specialists, and the Tigers who helped in the escalation process. They felt that these were the people who could check the validity, safety and efficacy of the suggestions. This validation community has several responsibilities: first, to talk with contributors about submitted tips, to make it better in both content and form, enabling submitters to learn from the conversation; second, to ensure the quality of tips before sent to the larger community; third, to combine redundant tips, and remove those that are no longer useful.

After a tip is submitted, tip authors can monitor the progression of their tips through the validation process. They get to see who claims their tip for validation, all the comments that person makes on their tip, and they get to have a conversation with the validator about their tip. Use of the system is completely voluntary, and extrinsic rewards are not used. When asked if a monetary incentive would be useful, a Tiger said "such incentives would corrupt the process." With the author's name on the tip, community recognition and improved reputation are rewards.

The process is changing the roles of community members. Customer service engineers are now spending more time thinking of new ways to diagnose broken machines and new ways to repair them to make them more reliable. They are sharing these tips with others in order to help both their local workgroup and the large field service community. One hotline specialist who we thought might have felt threatened by the system, welcomed it saying "This will allow us to spend more time figuring out how to handle hard problems, and less time on repeating solutions to problems we have already figured out." Most of the validation is done by people local to the district, rather than by the centralized group of Tigers who support the escalation process. Instead of being a bottleneck in a validation process, the limited number of Tigers are enjoying their role coaching a distributed set of validators.

Tip Authoring: Focused Reflection

Additional observations of field service workgroups have shown how members support each other to improve their overall performance. A useful practice we observed during a workgroup's meeting at the district office involved focusing the workgroup's reflection is reported in the following:

> The team noted that they were spending more on photoreceptors than the national average for 5090s, and were trying to determine possible causes. One CSE remarked on learning about a cause of stray light that makes photoreceptors age faster than usual. To prevent this, a flash guard needs to be installed rotated ninety degrees from what appears natural. Insertion of the guard the wrong way causes misaligned tabs to raise the guard slightly. Other CSEs realized they were indeed making this installation mistake. This shared insight allowed the group to improve its use of parts.

This type of focused reflection was not observed as a general practice, but was a local best practice. By focusing on one part in particular, the group shared information that might not otherwise have been shared. By selecting a part where performance significantly lagged national averages, they picked an area where there was likely something to learn. This focused reflection led to the generation of a local tip, for use within the workgroup. Tips generated in this manner can be shared more globally between workgroups using the distributed tips validation process. Validated tips are cross-referenced with the documentation, and may eventually be more tightly integrated into a future release of the formal documentation.

Results

Study of the practices of the people who prepared documentation for service, and the people who used them suggested a number of ways that related processes might be improved. The authors co-developed (with the users) systems that would take advantage of the new technological infrastructure that Xerox was planning to deploy (e.g. laptop computers and bulletin boards). The SADIE authoring environment and the knowledge-based PRIDE diagnostic system were ways of delivering expert guidance based on centrally prepared documentation. Tests were made of efficiency of authoring in the environment, and the diagnostic efficacy of the resulting knowledge-based system. To get acceptance of the idea of using field knowledge, two field tests were done. Columbus demonstrated the value of a tips database in use in the field. The Minitel based Eureka implementation demonstrated the scalability of the process for gathering and validating tips from the field, and their resulting use by the community.

SADIE/PRIDE: Comparisons with standard expert systems

Xerox has long been looking for alternatives to traditional documentation. As an experiment, they developed an expert system in a standard expert system shell. This system took roughly six work years to develop for one complex product. Measurements of a test when it was deployed indicated significant gains in reliability of diagnosis, and improvements in other metrics of productivity. The productivity gains in that experiment were used to justify the rollout of the laptops to the field. However, there were a number of problems in adapting that expert system to the field work practice. SADIE and PRIDE had to not only better fit the practice, but also needed to convince management that they would provide comparable productivity gains.

There are many contextual factors that make a direct comparison difficult. In order for service management to evaluate SADIE/PRIDE, they used two external companies and their products as benchmarks. The following criteria were used in the comparison: cost, modularity, maintainability, vendor, time, ease of use, and effectiveness. The first three were evaluated based on information about the companies. But time for development, ease of use of the systems, and effectiveness would have been hard to estimate without a common basis.

Xerox service management sponsored a "bake-off," a direct comparison of the three systems on a small problem set. This involved three separate authoring groups who built three systems to aid in the diagnosis of problems, and six students who had just completed their training on the product. Each student diagnosed eight inserted faults yielding sixteen data points per solution. SADIE/PRIDE did very well in this small test.

Service management concluded that although they considered it an advantage to be able to hold an outside vendor accountable, this was balanced by the risk of giving up control to a small vendor. For effectiveness, the small test was enough to believe that SADIE/PRIDE could be comparable to the commercial systems, but not conclusively proved since SADIE/PRIDE did not have an established track record. For the other five evaluation criteria SADIE/PRIDE was considered better. Since the bake-off, about a half dozen product programs have started development using the new system.

Columbus: A test of the effectiveness of tips

To test the usefulness of service tips, we worked with Rank Xerox France to sponsor Columbus, a field test of tips on one product, gathered from CSE roundtables. This test used forty service engineers using laptop computers and a mirror population of engineers with similar profiles as a control group. The CSE profiles were matched by dedication rate of the CSE, which refers to the percentage of time an engineer spends servicing a product. These rates were estimated by the number of calls each service engineer took per month on this product, and they were clustered by low, medium and high dedication rates for the test. The reference group had similar profiles, but was not given laptop computers. CSEs in test and control groups were also matched for experience and type of area they worked in (urban/rural). Results for the six month period were compared against the reference group, and against the national averages.

This field test did not include context sensitive rendering of documentation, but did include a simplified version of the *Minding the Styles* interface. It was designed, built and launched within three months, and the six month pilot showed overall measured improvement of 5% in service hours and parts usage. The low dedication rate engineers had the largest improvements, and they represent the majority of service engineers working on the product in France.

Eureka: Evaluating a new dynamic tips update process

Xerox has had a number of programs that have tried to capture field experience. Most have just used the Tigers to generate tips. Relatively few tips were generated for this case base, and its use was limited. The Columbus test only included a static database of tips, but no process for updating the database. Our field studies indicated that CSEs would help build a quality case base if given the chance. As a test, we sponsored the deployment of Eureka in France, a nationally accessible tips update and validation system.

In 1997, France has a field service force of about 1300 people, and about fifteen percent of that population is participating by submitting tips. Most tip authors are from the field, not from the central organization. Between one and two new tips are being submitted per day, averaging about one new tip per thousand calls, and there is an average of one access to the tips knowledge-base per day for each service person. Although only available for a few products at first, this participation convinced management that it was useful over the whole range of products.

Since the process is available to the entire country, there is no reference group; hence, comparative data on service effectiveness of these tips is difficult to obtain. However, France has improved its service productivity along a number of dimensions, becoming close to benchmark in Europe for some.

Discussion

Working with the field provided us an opportunity to understand the gaps between the documented processes for doing that work and the actual practices. Our work has helped to bridge the gaps, both by changing practice to be more effective, and obtaining management recognition of the value of some previously under-appreciated practices. To gain needed productivity, we did not engage in top-down reengineering. Rather, we engaged the field in reflecting on and improving their own practice, while we provided both technological support and help in development of new practices, processes and supporting technologies.

Redesigned documented processes use a novel document-centric authoring and publishing solution with several benefits:

- Production of three outputs from a single SGML document source.
- Incremental investment path for product programs yielding quick time to first benefits.
- Incremental learning curve for both documentation and field service communities.

The Eureka tips sharing process leverages the local knowledge of field service engineers. Its benefits include:

- Rapid turnaround on field invented solutions.
- A sense of recognition and empowerment for field service people.
- More fulfilling jobs for the Tigers and hot-line specialists.

When the solutions were introduced to the corporation, the accommodation for diversity through the minding-the-styles interface was in direct contrast to a prevailing desire to force service engineers to follow the directive procedures as prescribed. In the mid-eighties, the corporation created a new job title called product service representatives, and started hiring less skilled workers into the positions to perform routine work.

> The management of the corporation for which the technicians work has pursued a strategy of de-skilling through the use of directive documentation. . . . While de-skilling remains a management intention, one of the standard criticisms of de-skilling theory has been that it is much more accurate at describing management intentions than working realities. [Orr, 1991]

While the use of less skilled workers was considered a failure and was discontinued, the use of directive service documentation has remained, and in fact some parts of the corporation have tried to make the documentation more directive. With the introduction of electronic documentation, some other parts of the corporation advocated that documentation be used by progressively revealing one question at a time. Only when a CSE responds to a question is the next step revealed – in the hope that this would enforce compliance to the prescribed procedure. In that design, auditing capabilities could be used to see "what he [sic] did versus what he should have done," [from a specification documents of a technology group]. Our thrust has been to provide flexibility in how a CSE can use documentation, and auditing only to learn what will make the documentation more useful.

Conventional wisdom of service management has long held that performance improvements come by suppressing diversity by enforcing standardized processes. The thinking is that if diversity of practice is reduced, variance in output performance will also be reduced. Once this variance is reduced, then everyone improves together as processes are gradually changed (in "lock-step" as one service manager used to say). To change any part of the process, service engineers must submit process change requests, and only when a request is accepted are they officially allowed to vary from the process. Theoretically, customers with new and unique problems have to wait until a new procedure is published before receiving adequate service.

To avoid delays for customer problems not handled by the manual, CSEs have always used the freedom to work around systems. However, the introduction of technology that enforces compliance through audit trails can make it more difficult for service engineers to use work-arounds, and the goal of quality customer service can become lost in the very processes that were intended to improve it. CSEs need legitimate authority to deviate from standard procedure when necessary, and they need appropriate infrastructure for sharing successful new procedures.

The conventional wisdom relates to common interpretations of public policies of standards such as ISO 9000, and national quality awards, such as the Malcolm Baldrige Award. Some interpret the essential test of these policies to be "Do they do what they say they do?" [Patterson, 1995]. This results in a move to hold individuals strictly accountable to documented processes, and while this is clearly visible within Xerox, it is not really part of these national policies. In the Rank Xerox European Quality Award assessor's report, the following "Areas for Improvement" were listed [Palermo, 1993]:

- There is no evidence that the sharing of knowledge of internal best practices is carried out systematically.
- The approach is heavily "top-down" and the degree to which the "bottom-up" process can influence the policies is not clear.
- The extent of empowerment and how employees are empowered is unclear.
- The recognition system was very formal and management controlled. . . .

Corporations have a history of depending on explicit rules, especially to ensure safety [Yates, 1993]. Today, the push for strict adherence to explicit processes leads to an emphasis on holding individuals accountable to the processes the corporation has defined. Gardner [1995] claims that this trend means, "... new developments often originate outside the area of respectable practice." Our work has shown the benefit of holding processes accountable to individuals – that is taking into account and adjusting to their practices. The approach presented in this paper shows that significant performance improvements can result by recognizing and supporting inherent diversity rather than suppressing it. The balanced approach of holding processes and people mutually accountable not only yields benefits for individuals, but also benefits for corporate communities.

Acknowledgments

This work was made possible by the insightful ideas and hard work of many people including the following: Estella Verdouw, Chuck Vorndran, Al Turof, Mark Harmison, Bob Cheslow, Dan Marder, Tom Zapata, Kim Schwind, Judy Derring and Roger Vidal of Xerox Corporation; Eric Delanchy, John Sanderson, Serge Garniel, and Lawrence Armour of the Rank Xerox Organization. We would like to thank all those who spent time to talk with us in the field including Brian Van de Ahe and Bob Mayer among many, and all the other people who helped make these projects move forward. We would also like to acknowledge the support from the staff of our information center at PARC including Maia Pindar, Lisa Alfke and others. Various ideas in these documents have benefited from conversations with many at PARC including Jeannette Blomberg, Vicki O'Day, Markus Fromherz and other members of the Design Studies Group (Margot Brereton, Steve Harrison, Scott Minneman, Susan Newman and Randy Trigg).

References

Bell, D.G., Bobrow, D.G., Falkenhainer, B., Saraswat, V. and Shirley, M., "RAPPER: The Copier Modeling project," *International Logic Programming Symposium*, San Diego, CA, Oct. 28-31, 1991.

Blomberg, Jeanette L., "Social Interaction and Office Communication: Effects on User Evaluation of New Technologies," in Robert Kraut (ed.), *Technology and the Transformation of White Collar Work*, Erlbaum Press, Hillsdale, NJ, 1986.

Gardner, John W., Self-Renewal: The Individual and the Innovative Society, Norton & Company, New York, 1995.

Jung, C.G., *Psychological Types*, Princeton University Press, Princeton, N.J., 1971.

Orr, Julian E., Talking About Machines: An ethnography of a modern job, SSL-91-007, 1990.

Palermo, R.C. and Watson, G.H. (eds.), *A World of Quality: The Timeless Passport*, ASQC Quality Press, Milwaukee, WI, 1993.

Patterson, James G., *ISO 9000: Worldwide Quality Standard*, Crisp Publications, Menlo Park, CA, 1995.

Smith, Don, personal communication, 1993.

Suchman, Lucy, Plans and Situated Actions: The problem of human-machine communication, Cambridge University Press, UK, 1987.

Yates, JoAnne, *Control Through Communication: The Rise of System in American Management*, Johns Hopkins, Baltimore, 1993.

17 DOCUMENT AND PROCESS TRANSFORMATION DURING THE PRODUCT LIFE CYCLE

Abraham Bernstein and Christian Schucan

ABSTRACT
Based on our experiences[1] *in the corporate banking department of the Union Bank of Switzerland we are convinced that business, IT and organizational aspects have to be considered in an integrated way while developing IT-strategies. IT-strategies are crucial for an effective (business) development because they identify the constant and the changing parts of an IT infrastructure during product life cycle. In order to achieve this, we state three design invariants: the deep structure of the process, the dependencies within the process, and the information handled. We believe that identifying these invariants will lead to a deeper understanding of product-life-cycles.*

Introduction

Our field of experience is the information technology support for the corporate banking division of a bank. We believe that this area of studies offers some generizability to other service providing industries, due to the significance of information (as a facilitator and as a product in itself) in this business. Some insight from our observations should be applicable to the management of production-oriented business, since it is the nature of management as a task to be closely coupled to information flows and processes and therefore to information management. The statements made in this paper, are based on our experiences as project managers in several projects at Union Bank of Switzerland. They are observations made during our daily work and are not based on a specific empirical study or on a theoretical approach.

---

[1] Both authors worked as project managers for Union Bank of Switzerland

We differentiate between data and information. Information represented in a physical structure becomes data. With this view, data is information which is coupled to a physical structure. But data is not in every case information. Whether data represents information or not depends on the use of data. Only a meaningful context can turn data into information. As an example we offer the number 1996. This number is data when stored in a physical structure, but without context it is meaningless to the user. The number does not represent information. In addition to the context specification (e.g. the number represents the current year) the number has to add additional knowledge to the user, otherwise it does not represent information to him. For example, we observed systems that hold huge amounts of data. But since the users chose other information systems (especially paper-based document archives) or knew the facts in advance, the system had no value to them. Thus, it did not add any information to their work. A consequence of this view is that information can be represented in an unstructured document in the file system as well as in a strongly structured relational form in a database. The information does not change by this fact.

We also see a difference between process maps, which represent the surface structure of a particular process, and the 'deep structure'[2] of a process. A process map describes the elementary details of a particular process, and only describes one way to achieve the goal. It does not describe the action of achieving a goal without actually offering a special solution. We refer to the 'deep structure' of a process, an expression from linguistics, for the more abstract description.[3]

The Relation between Business, IT-Support and Organizations

When we are speaking about business support with information technology, we think about any piece of software, tool or method that is needed to provide, handle and manage information that is used to keep the business running or even more as a product of the business itself. This also includes aspects which only appear over time, i.e. within different levels of product development in the product life cycle. This is important for the design of document and process management systems. They have to be designed to support structural changes in documents and classes of documents. We observed this in our environment and recognized several problems:

- people work with different versions of software
- information of different structured documents is no longer comparable, because of the different data structure

---

[2] see Malone 1996

[3] 'John hit the ball' and 'The ball got hit by John' represent different surface structures for the same deep structure. (see Malone 1996)

- data can not be aggregated to provide the overall information about the state of the product and its selling because the data comes from different sources according to the level of development of the product and with that in different structures.

For example loan-granting in a bank: When a customer wants to build a house, he often gets mortgage from a bank. This business is handled via documents containing many pieces of information about the house and its value. The structures and contents of the documents change over time and differ from region to region. However the management needs the information of the total value of all mortgages over all regions and wants to compare this result with former results. Because the documents are stored in different places with different structures[4] (but with the same information represented) it is difficult to find and add the single values in order to calculate the total value.

We are convinced that only this global view on information management, that includes aspects of technology, economics and organizations, allows IT to become a strategic issue within the businesses. This overall view is necessary for IT projects to focus on the needs and to become an asset rather then an obstacle.

The use of IT support requires a major financial involvement. In order to justify the commitment of financial resources to IT projects, they have to be focused on areas where a major return on investment is to be expected. If this selection is accurately applied, IT appears no longer as a cost factor (as it does today in our domain) but as a business opportunity.

In the following, we explain this relationship and its consequence with the example of the corporate banking market in Europe. Over the last few years the corporate banking market in Europe; which has been mainly focusing on loans, has transformed into a highly saturated and competitive market. Loans have transformed into a commodity product, which differ mainly in pricing. In order to ensure survival in this market, financial institutions face a major transformation of their market appearance in terms of communication channels to their customers, products, product innovation, pricing and distribution. This transformation from a highly administrative loan-'granting' company to a cooperative customer-focused organization with a broad variety of products, can only be achieved by business process reengineering projects.

At the first glance the problem as we encountered it, showed two main problem areas. On one hand, existing loan-products had changed to a commodity product, which have to be produced cost efficient; in other words a major area for rationalization. On the other hand, new approaches to the business demanded

---

[4] location and structures for mortgage documents are defined bank-externally by law

support for customer focused product innovation and a new way to look at the relationship between financial institutions and their customers; in other words, a major area for invention.

A more profound examination of those two problem areas unveiled that they actually represent two different views on the same problem: the complexity of managing and coordinating a variety of parallel product life cycles. Since the managing process bases highly on information, i.e. gathering and distributing information, we have to manage the coordination of the processes and the respective information over time. The main information flow within an enterprise is document centered. Therefore, the coordination of processes and information over time largely incorporates the problem of managing the transformation from unstructured document centered information processing to highly structured database held information and its handling.

Product Life Cycles: Two Examples

Looking at money transfers, as an example, might help us to understand this transformation. The traditional way of money transfer was predominantly paper based. The customer produced a document to order and authentified the transfer. Following that, he handed over this transfer order to the bank. The bank checked the authenticity of the document, entered the transfer into their records, produced a charge notice for the originating account and a credit voucher for the beneficiary.

A more sophisticated approach was given by the introduction of forms for the documents mentioned. In this way, transfers could be processed faster because they could be handled by standard procedures with well-established processes. The next level of sophistication is the introduction of electronic forms processing. Money order forms are scanned upon arrival to the bank, important information as account numbers and amount of transfer are either entered manually or even extracted by OCR-methods. The introduction of an EDI-interface between the bank and its customers even allows an automated handling of the whole process.

If we focus on the documents throughout this 'evolution' of the money transfer process, we conclude that the representation of the data held in the documents involved gets more and more structured. Finally, it is even transformed into an electronic record. Parallel to this change, the processes get more structured and at last translated into computer programs.

Another example with a much shorter product life cycle are derivatives. Derivatives are usually constructed and calculated supported by spreadsheet calculations in order to estimate their value. This is a manual process handling highly unstructured documents. If they seem profitable, they are exposed to the market. Their handling is constantly improved (e.g. introduction of spreadsheet macros, short programs) and the documents involved are getting more structured with every refinement cycle.

At the beginning of this life cycle, production costs for this product are very high. This does not matter because customers are willing to pay the appropriate charges since there is no competition for this product. After a period of about three months, the derivatives start to become a commodity product. Therefore, their production has to be organized in a highly cost efficient way. Therefore, within the period of three months we have gone from product invention to cost efficient (rationalized) production.

It is important to notice that in both life cycles, the product remains the same, but the organization, the steps for the transactions, and the data structures changed. In addition to, this the second example shows a business opportunity that is only feasible by IT means, because the calculations for derivatives are rather complex.

Implications of the Close Link between Business and IT

The statements about the relationship between business, IT, and organizations as well as the two examples illustrate, that the use of IT has impacts on business **and** conversely. In consideration of this link between business and IT, we noticed two major consequences:

- IT has to fulfill the strategic business needs, and not only small isolated problem areas as it is today; i.e. it is not enough to support one version of a product and restart the development for the IT support for the next step in the product life cycle from scratch. Support for products has to be developed in a flexible way to assist the product life cycle and thus constantly improve. This is a long-term goal. In order to achieve this, IT has to be flexible enough to support the changes of the short-term business needs in the areas of organizations, processes and information and provide a coordinated information and process support.
- Business-strategies have to enclose IT strategies and to consider the business opportunities created by the availability of IT; e.g. availability of new products, speeding up product life cycles, or allow faster settlement of deals. IT is not just an add-on to the business strategy, but more likely part of the business strategy. With the use of IT, business and organizations are changed.

This has to be clarified in the business strategy by defining the role and the respective long-term goals for the IT support. If this is not done, IT can hardly fulfill the business needs.

Considering this, IT development within an enterprise is not a set of uncoordinated projects but a set of projects derived from an IT strategy which links IT with business and therefore helps to differentiate between long-term base-level development and short-term application development. When we are thinking of a better integration of documents and processes, this last point becomes crucial because otherwise uncoordinated projects create structural clashes. Therefore document and process technology are part of the long-term development. In our banking environment it is a declared goal that document and process management have to be part of the base-level architecture of IT. We think that the following problems are the major problems when trying to establish this base-level architecture:

- existing information bases (databases and document usually just handled by the file system)
- existing monolithic applications
- heterogeneous structures - changing technology
- changing business and thus, continuous development of products (product life-cycle)

Considering these impacts and the findings explained in the examples, we need a way to design a document and process support that makes a distinction between constant and variable structures. We therefore have to find the invariants of this change.

The Three Design Invariants

We observed that most product life cycles have invariants which are partly defined by the product. The first invariant is the deep-structure of the production process. A loan application consists of an application (or some kind of contact, in which information is exchanged, be it directly or indirectly), an approval process, and a third process in which the funds are made available to the customer. These processes are invariant to the changes of the loan product. This structure does not define when the customer and the bank actually meet the first time (if ever), or whether a formal loan application has to be filled.

We found dependencies (see Malone & Crowston 1991) to be an other invariant. Coming back to the loan granting process as an example, no corporate loan is being paid without some kind of approval. So the approval process is a prerequisite on the third sub-process of loan granting[5].

[5] For a more detailed explanation on processes and dependencies please refer to (Malone & Crowston 1991)

Reconsidering the money-transfer example, helps us to identify the third invariant. The actual information (as opposed to data) never changed. A money transfer always contained information about the originator, the receiver and the amount to transfer. The physical representation changed from-free form text to EDI-records, but its information stayed the same. So information is the third invariant. It is important to know which information is relevant for the business, which information is created by the business, how the management of information has to be implemented from the business point of view and what influence time has on information.

We by no means claim that this list of invariants is exhaustive, but our experience in several projects showed, that it helped us to think about the product life cycle in this manner.

Conclusion

Reviewing a number of examples within our institution, we discovered that the structure of the data (the data model[6] spoken in IT terms) changed, but not the information passed throughout the process. In addition, we could see that the detailed process map changed, but not the deep structure and the dependencies within the overall process. Furthermore, we discovered a very strong dependency between the data model and the processes.

These discoveries lead us to the conclusion that the following points are central for managing the change:

- We have to find the invariants of this change, i.e. the deep structure of the process and the dependencies within the process, as well as the information handled.
- We have to build a data model and a process map according to the invariants which supports a design for change.
- These two models can not be constructed independently from each other. They are strongly coupled.

In order to ensure these points, we need a tool which not only helps us to create data models and process maps but also supports the identification of the invariants. In addition it has to actively support change. This means it has to be capable of handling different versions of models and the transition process between them.

---

[6] We do not speak here about a physical data model, where the storing strategy (e.g. file system, relational database, text documents, etc.) has to be taken into account.

We also need a technology which allows a smooth transition from unstructured documents to structured data and processes. In the case of documents, this could be achieved by active documents and the use of technology similar to the Web and Java. In the case of processes we have to integrate unstructured processes, supported by groupware products, workflow management, and database-like nested-transaction management.

References

Malone, T. W. and Crowston, K. (1991). *Toward an interdisciplinary theory of coordination* (Technical report #120). Cambridge, MA: Massachusetts Institute of Technology, Center for Coordination Science.

Malone, T. W. *How Will You Manage in the 21st Century? From Command and Control to Cultivate and Coordinate.* MIT Center for Coordination Science, Unpublished discussion paper, May 1996

18 FORMING THE RESEARCH AND DEVELOPMENT WORKPLACE: DOCUMENTS AS THE GLUE IN THE PROCESS DESIGN

Turid H. Horgen,
Charles D. Kukla,
William L. Porter,
and Gregory W. Zack

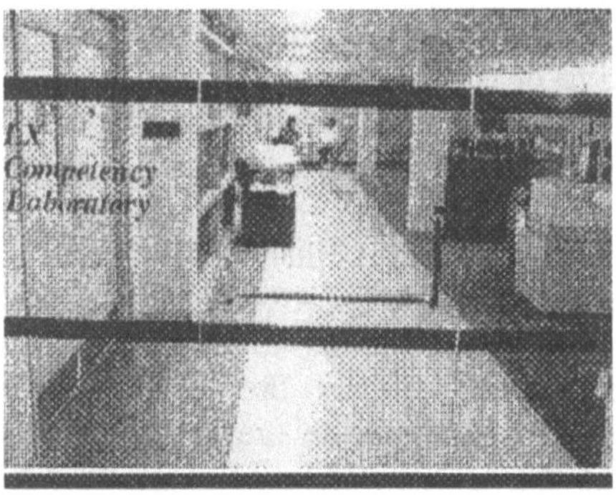

Documents are a powerful resource for constructing and negotiating social space. John Seely Brown suggests that the social life of the document is not widely recognized, and that seeing documents as a means of *making and maintaining social groups,* not just as a means of delivering information, makes it easier to understand the utility and success of new forms of documents.[1] The paper investigates how establishing documentation of a situation can help understand issues of importance in a work group and can be instrumental in constructing a new work place and work processes which focus on integration of effort. Our focus will be on how joint use of documents can support collaborative processes in a way which sparks innovation. Through an example from a case study, the paper addresses how the study of best work practices and the documentation of different viewpoints about communicative spaces gradually shaped the vocabulary for design requirements for a new work

---

[1] John Seely Brown and Paul Duguid "The Social Life of Documents," Esher Dyson's Monthly Report Oct. 1995.

place.[2] The result was a work place which fostered innovation, creativity, and learning, and which simultaneously was itself the most effective marketplace for new technology.

The R&D laboratory whose story is presented here, named LX, is among the leading laboratories in its field, and has become a benchmark for the research center it is a part of, the Joseph C. Wilson Center for Research and Technology in Webster, New York. The laboratory has undergone a dramatic change in its work process, which can be attributed in part to its participation, through a living experiment, in a re-invention of its work setting and work place technology. Both the communications and spatial innovations of this experiment had profound impacts on work process and team behavior. The changes ranged from achieving a new team identity and a shared mission for the lab to undertaking a commitment to generate the knowledge base for the company's twenty-first century marking technology. This laboratory's new place for team work was built, worked in, and evaluated over a period of 16 months.

Laboratory for Remote Collaboration

The vision of the Wilson Center is to be the industry benchmark in the capture of new technology opportunities contributing to color marking systems, and to position Xerox as the leading supplier of color document systems. The Center is faced with the need to develop processes which allow rapid, cost-effective deployment of the results of its research and technology development. Xerox is committed to making its research and technology development process continuously more efficient and effective as product design cycles become shorter. Part of this commitment is willingness to experiment with the work setting of core research and development teams in order to find ways to improve work outputs and processes within the organization.

One such effort to speed the process of technology and product development is the LARC (LAboratory for Remote Collaboration) concept.[3] LARC's mission was to develop computer technologies, systems, and applications to enable highly effective remote cross-functional teamwork. To validate the collaborative technologies developed by LARC, a pilot project was created in the newly formed LX lab at the Wilson Center. The intention of the LARC Workplace Pilot was to focus on creating a work environment that would allow the LX lab best to accomplish its mission, and contribute new work tools such as new space and new technology to enhance the work processes and outputs of the lab. The LX members became at a certain point the real drivers of the experiment, and the collaborative

[2] Toward Process Architecture "New Work Practice Discovered through Making a New Place — The Xerox LX Common." SP/ORG Report 1996

[3] The Laboratory for Remote Collaboration (LARC) project was created as a collaborative research and development project between Digital Equipment Corporation, Xerox Corporation, and Design Research Institute at Cornell University; and later the SP/ORG group at MIT School of Architecture became a partner in the project.

way of working became natural both within the group and in meetings with vendors or possible business partners. The LX lab became a real working model and test bed for introduction, assessment, and diffusion of new technologies, work spaces, and work processes for group communication and collaboration.

Supporting a collaborative process

The MIT SP/ORG contribution to the project was to analyze the work in the laboratories participating in LARC, in order understand in what kinds of work the participants could be remote from one another, and in what kinds they needed to be face to face. In the course of doing that, SP/ORG were asked to give input to the spatial arrangement for co-location of part of the LX lab, and run a four-day workshop to detect and document work processes which would be essential to the spatial and technology solutions for the lab. The lab members were asked to participate in a work place design experiment which would benefit the group, providing new space for part of the laboratory and new computer technology to support their work. The workshops were facilitated by Chuck Kukla, a research consultant from Engineering Services at Digital Equipment Corporation, and Turid Horgen, an architect and research associate at the MIT School of Architecture and Planning. William L. Porter, Professor of Architecture and Planning at MIT, helped analyze the workshop material and was part of developing the strategy for the design of the workspaces. Greg Zack, manager of the Xerox section of Design Research Institute (DRI) at Cornell University, was the initiator and overall leader of the LARC project, and was directing the technology component.

In this paper we will examine that the role the documentation of the first week of intervention, including the documents created throughout these four days, played in the design, implementation, and consolidation of the new lab. Some of the material from these workshops also formed a basis for the technology plan for the lab, most notably use of Xerox LiveBoards, Digital's Workgroup Web Forum document repository, and other PC- and web-based collaboration tools, but this technology plan is outside the scope of this paper.

Graphic process tools and documents for developing space/technology concepts

Monday morning August 1, 1994, the LX lab members met for the first time as a laboratory, though most of the people had worked together before, on either xerography or another Xerox-related research project. The opening of the first session, the introduction to the workshop, was interesting in a certain way: all the workshops were held in the very room the LX group would later inhabit. It was a large empty room, about 4000 square feet, newly renovated as research space from part of the old model shop. One portion of the area was built as laboratory space, and another portion was planned as an open office environment with work stations made of Steelcase furniture, in the so-called "Harbors and Commons" concept. The

Harbors and Commons furniture had already been purchased, and occupied one corner of the open office area, still crated in cardboard. In another corner were a rectangular table and chairs, where a few lab members were already waiting when the LARC consultants arrived. The lab manager took the consultants aside, and told them to be cautious in their conducting of the workshop over the coming week, as he knew that several members of the lab were apprehensive that the new space plan would be a ploy to create office cubicles at the expense of private offices. The presence of the Steelcase furniture actually later helped the lab members to be more articulate about space requirements for their research environment.

With this at first puzzling opening the workshop started. The LARC consultants explained the agenda for the week, saying that it was important for the consultants to understand the work processes and what people actually were doing in the labs. A list of labs to visit was handed out, and a timetable of a series of structural events designed to help discover the group's work practices. The consultants explained that they would record all events, and develop a set of documents which would be used in a collective design process. Immediately people began to make suggestions and additions to the list, what they thought the consultants needed to see in order to get a grasp of the work.

The lab members met for 1 1/2 hours every morning over a period of four days, received homework each day, and discussed the results of homework the next day. Through documenting each event carefully, and looking at the resulting documents and discussing the meaning of them, collaboratively the LARC team and the members of the lab gradually built a set of potential images of the new lab. The table of events lists some of the documents produced, day by day, from the various different workshop events. After four days the concept for the new workplace was conceived. There were still controversies to be resolved, though, such as whether valuable lab space should be given over to a conference room, and how many Steelcase harbors should be used, etc., and the idea would go through several iterations over the next couple of months, before the LX lab agreed to build what they had invented: the LX Common.

The spatio-technology strategy developed through the workshop combined two leading ideas for improving the work process: "co-location of project groups," and "the laboratory for remote collaboration." From various discoveries throughout the workshop the idea of the LX Common was conceived. Pieces of what later became the Common were "found" in the existing work environment, or invented in collaborative drawing sessions and cardboard games. The documents from these sessions were crucial in establishing the language for this design to happen.

The resulting space design is based on a central meeting and gathering place, surrounded on one side by four experimental laboratories and on the other by about 10 offices. A kitchen with whiteboard wall, another discussion area, and an enclosed conference room are on the periphery of the space. The Common, about 20' x 35', contains a large modular meeting table in the center, a pair of LiveBoards at one end,

TABLE OF EVENTS

This table illustrates the structural events and examples of documents produced which took place during the four day workshop.

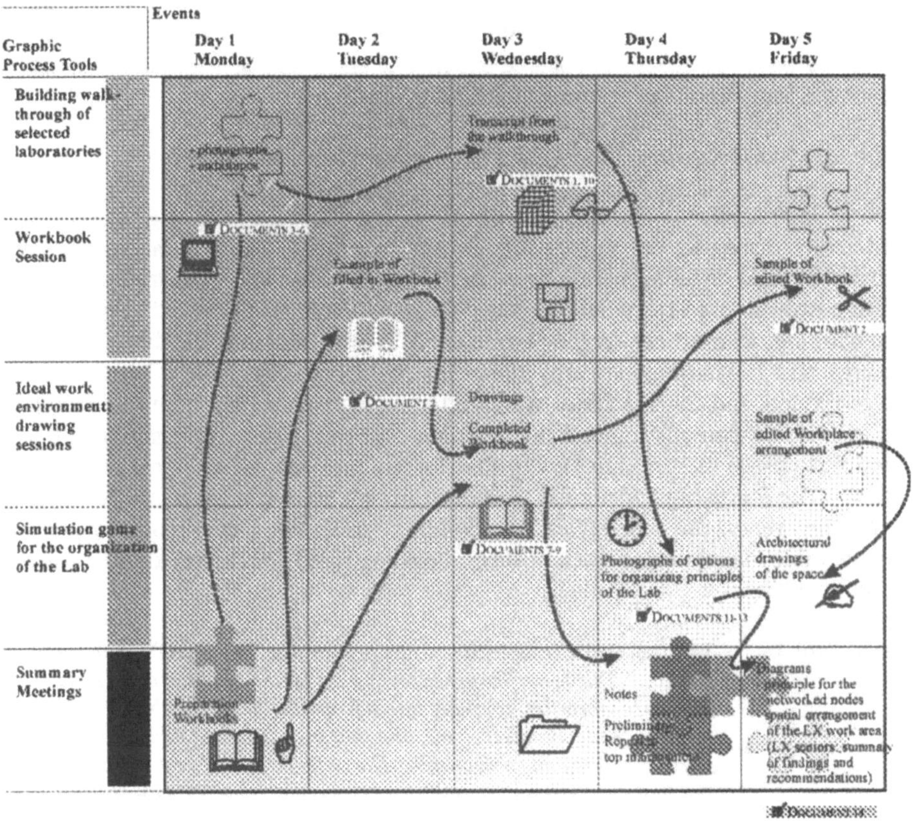

four workstations, a telephone, and within a few feet a scanner, a copier, a printer, a fax machine, and a video-preparation workstation. Traffic flow through the Common is continuous, by design. The LiveBoards serve as a presentation medium for PowerPoint slides, as an electronic whiteboard during meetings and for 2- or 3-person working sessions, as the means of accessing private or group or public information through a Web browser, and for display of group announcements. These last two capabilities combine to provide the group's Active Project Information Center, or APIC.

Documentation of the laboratories

The first structured event, the "*lab walk-through*" is a place-specific inquiry into lab members' experience, and served as the initial meeting between the LARC team and the LX members. The LARC consultants visited 10 selected individual laboratories spread out in three buildings in the Wilson Center, and met with a host in each lab, who introduced the consultants to other lab members, and who provided a short description of how the work was performed. The LARC consultants took a set of pictures and slides of the overall work area, and of specific points of interest, and audio taped the conversation. Its function was to establish a common reference to the work environment in which the LARC team would build their experiment, the "laboratory for remote work," so that the ideas they exchanged about space and work practices would be based on a shared experience and a shared vocabulary, in order to shape the same points of reference for later evaluation and design.

Changing work teams and work processes – stable work setting

The Wilson Center is challenged with providing space for working teams that are physically dispersed but must work closely together. The LX laboratories were located in three different buildings on the Xerox Webster site. The traditional layout for the two- to three-story buildings was to have laboratories located in the center of the building, with offices on the perimeter. While in principle this design allows for change and flexibility, in reality the research laboratories have now accumulated large fixtures and test machines which often have taken a long time to develop and build, with delicate instruments that are time-consuming to set up again, and it is not feasible to move these fixtures every time one might want to redesign a research program. The following "document" (a walk-through transcript excerpt) illustrates that over the years the open flexible building structure has become rigid with "immovable" laboratories, each of them developed and fine-tuned to one or another specialty of work.

Document 1

Illustrating the complexity of this proposition, one researcher describes his fixture: *"This lower fixture is an optical table. And it is damped to minimize vibration, coupling into it from the floor. It is being used in another mode, however, here, and that is as a precision underlay to all the various subsystem components. The optical table is pretty precise, but it's not that precise—and it weighs several hundred pounds. If you were to move it, you will torque the thing in several dimensions, and it will not relax completely. ...It was three months for us to do it the first time. ... I would strongly recommend against moving this particular fixture, just of the mechanical alignment problems that would certainly entail if it were moved. We have requirements for about 50 amps of power to run all the various componentry around it. We require compressed air to run some of the fixtures. Some of the materials that we use in the process of, we know, have their characteristics change with temperature. So we do need to at least monitor what the temperature is around here and keep the directive of that. Ah, some process characteristics are also affected by the amount of humidity that's in the air. There are a number of subcomponents that we operate at high voltage. So we have to manage some effluents from there. There's some ozone generation that takes place. The volume of the laboratory here pretty much sops that up, but it would be a concern if it were moved to a smaller physical space. We are sensitive to the amount of workspace that we have around here. If one of these things comes out to make adjustments inside, we have to obviously have a place to put it."* (Transcript of workshop. August 94)

The people in the lab tell a story about their workplace, and that story gets taped and transcribed, and becomes a piece to design with. The transcript from the walkthrough represents a documentation of the conversation that took place, is a document in the project, and becomes the beginning of a language to understand the work process. The stories in the transcript help to shape the understanding of the key problems to solve, and gradually to build the leading ideas that shape the work environment. The specific conversation above became crucial in the later design of the place.

The work is not routine

The walkthrough process helped elicit stories. The LARC consultants asked: "What's stable here in this environment?" because they could not find anyone's work staying the same—"no day was the same." The process of work and a workday would be described like: "you come in, and you figure out a problem, and you design something to test it, and you run the test." There was nothing really stable except the setting: the resources and tools available. The question then became what were the commonalities among the different types of work that go on at the Wilson Center and in the LX group, that the LARC workplace pilot could support in some particular way?

Descriptions of work would start with a particular kind of event—usually an event that had upset the routine, something not going the way it was supposed to. The description was conveyed as a narrative, as opposed to a procedure or a linked set of goal-oriented activities. The work was composed of both routine and non-routine activities. Documentation and a thorough analysis of these documents from the walkthrough helped to identify the key sets of activities central to achieving the mission of the lab.

In addition to the recording and transcription of people's discussion of their places during the walkthrough, photographs documented the artifacts and technologies used by the different actors in the story, and the edges or boundaries of the places named in the story. Presenting the transcripts of the initial story and the pictures from the labs to the lab members the following day helped to evoke other stories about activities taking place in the same space. The overlapping stories, and the events that triggered them, revealed critical patterns and dependencies of artifacts, tools, and technologies in the workplace. Often the stories would reveal contradictions about what was important. Work was done in the dark and the light, the lab needed to be both clean and dirty, or private and public, the focus was in the front or in the back, the lab was for an individual and a team.

The stories revealed overlapping activities occurring in the same place. The shifting emphasis of what was important between problem solving and planning indicated a workplace with limited and committed resources with alternating uses, unforeseen events disrupting ongoing routine work and having to be solved within a particular time-frame. The focus of work would shift from place to place, during the day and in the course of the project time. Questions of inquiry in a walkthrough are typically aimed at "what is happening here, in this place." With the LX lab, when the LARC consultants asked, "What happens here?" the response was to ask, when?—"Do you mean today, yesterday, or what is planned for tomorrow?"

A collective inquiry of individual workplace

The focus of the next event, *the workbook* was a tool to step outside one's intimate knowledge of one's own environment, and review it individually, or collectively with one's co-workers. On Day 2 of the workshop the lab members were asked to circle and color photographs of each lab taken during the walkthrough. Working in groups of two and three people, people were asked to mark aspects of these images that they found important, either positively or negatively, with respect to four fundamental issues about the work place: *appreciation (like/dislike), change (wish to keep/abolish), safety, and efficiency.* The challenge for LX group, as it turned out, was to be the subject of their own research, taking their enclosed environment apart, deconstructing it, and rebuilding it to be a more useful support for their research.

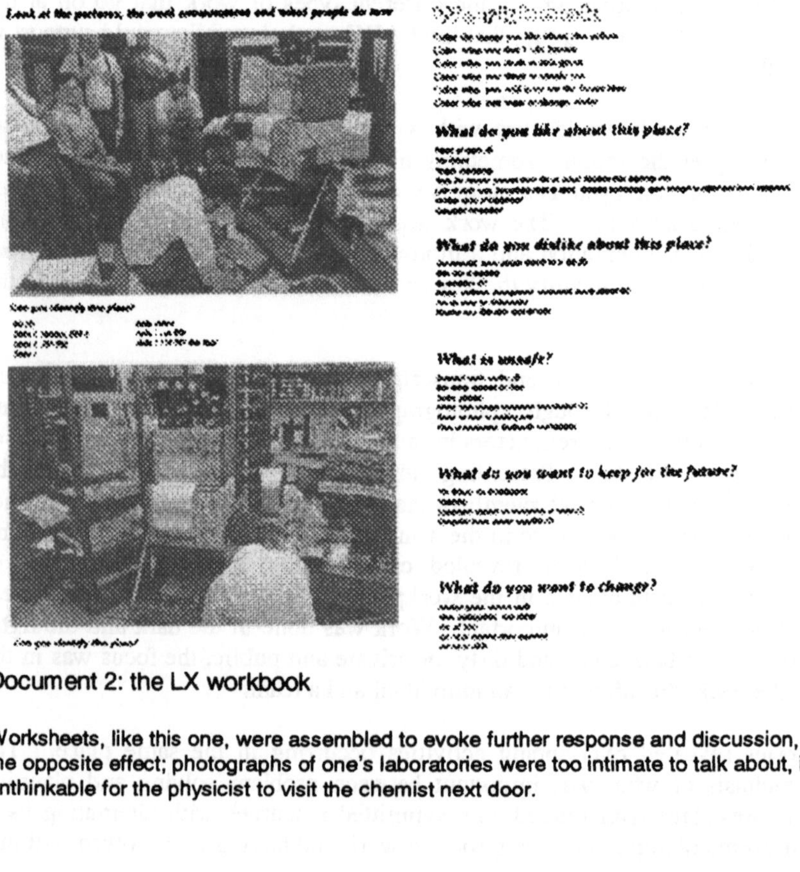

Document 2: the LX workbook

Worksheets, like this one, were assembled to evoke further response and discussion, but had the opposite effect; photographs of one's laboratories were too intimate to talk about, it was unthinkable for the physicist to visit the chemist next door.

The workbook is intended to be a graphic document to prompt discussions about issues of importance in the existing workplace, in order to diagnose dysfunctional pieces, and suggest improvements. It was puzzling to discover that with the LX group this tool did not function the way it was supposed to.

The laboratory as a secret place

After 10-15 minutes of almost complete silence and no activity in the group when it had been handed the workbooks, the LARC consultants quickly changed the agenda, said people would get the workbooks as homework, asked them to fill them out individually rather than as a group, and introduced another exercise instead: the drawing of the ideal work place. When the consultants met with the group the next day, they looked briefly through the workbooks the lab members brought with them, and discovered that people basically had commented on their own lab, and not touched other places which also were presented in the book. It was still puzzling why a picture of one's workplace could have such an effect that everybody immediately clammed up. For more than 20 years that Horgen has been using this method, this had never happened. Quite the opposite: the discussions always get very lively, people are very appreciative that somebody actually has taken a picture of their own environment, and it is not unusual that they ask to keep one of the books as their private picture book. Xerox had the opposite reaction, and why was this?

Our initial interpretation was that the labs were an intimate part of the work; some people had worked in the company for more than 30 years (we would often hear the phrase "when we grew up here"); and that it was hard to step "outside" something one had built with one's own hands, and pull it apart. One of the consultants actually took a photograph of the integrated fixture lab, made an overhead slide, pulled out the different objects in the photograph, circled them, and said here is a workbench, here is a computer rack, one could think of piecing it up and building it again. This did not help—photographs of one's laboratories were too intimate to talk about.

The full significance of silence among the LX members the LARC consultants did not fully understand until almost a year later, when the group for the first time organized a walkthrough within its various labs, and we discovered this was the first time most of the lab members had visited the other labs in the group—the reason no one had had anything to say about each other's laboratories was that no one had ever really *seen* each other's laboratories, or known the work which went on there. Most people would work in isolation in their labs, and only ask co-workers to come in if they needed help with a test result which did not quite work the way it should, or invite close collaborators or people within the same discipline to look more closely at a specific experiment, etc. To open up one's lab to the whole group, the way we did when we presented the workbook, was quite unusual.

Working face-to-face across disciplines

The common assumption is that information technology can facilitate communication to any degree desired; therefore there is often no attention paid to the need for face-to-face or face-to-machine communication. The idea of "the Laboratory for Remote Collaboration" originated in the need for technology to support collaboration over a distance. The workbook exercise, though not successful, made it evident that the creative exchange and progress of ideas that come about because two people or more are present in the same place, and have easy access to the data they are working on, is critical to speeding up the innovation process. The purpose of the information technology then becomes to "make differences smaller" across disciplines in a team, in addition to providing information to the individual.

The fundamental work the LX team conducts is xerographic research. This entails integrating many work processes such as simulating behavior of new designs, conducting experiments on test fixtures, assembling components and complete marking systems, testing materials, and analyzing image quality. To do research in this field requires the competency to solve problems between fields, instead of within a field; the learning of xerography is a parallel activity to the development of the work process of the research itself. Unlike the other competency laboratories in the Wilson center, the LX lab contained all the competencies needed to develop a future technology in one group, yet most of the members who joined LX came from labs that had been more specialized in some particular aspect of xerography, such as paper handling or photoreceptor design. Hence they were faced with the challenge of working as a team with people from different backgrounds who were skilled in areas different from their own and whose vocabulary for describing their work was sometimes unfamiliar. The challenge for designing a new work environment is to get the requirements for each of the working components discussed and understood within the group, as well as within the discipline.

Places where work happens

The documentation of the walk-through revealed work practices of critical importance to the group, such as spontaneous meetings in the corridors or around the test fixture, or in a meeting room in the midst of four other labs. The work requires continuous dialogue, which takes place any place work happens. The nature of the work implies closeness of collaborative researchers to each other, putting any kind of data available in front of a whole group as three or four researchers engage in a dialogue while looking at it. These kinds of meetings happen on the spur of the moment, as an immediate outcome of what is happening in the workplace, and the knowledge developed is part of the corporate memory which often is difficult to find in more formal settings. Collaboration in the form of problem-solving meetings, or meetings to discuss interpretations of findings or new ideas, does happen in offices, mainly by invitation. More often, though, it happens in front of a machine when a

Document 3-6

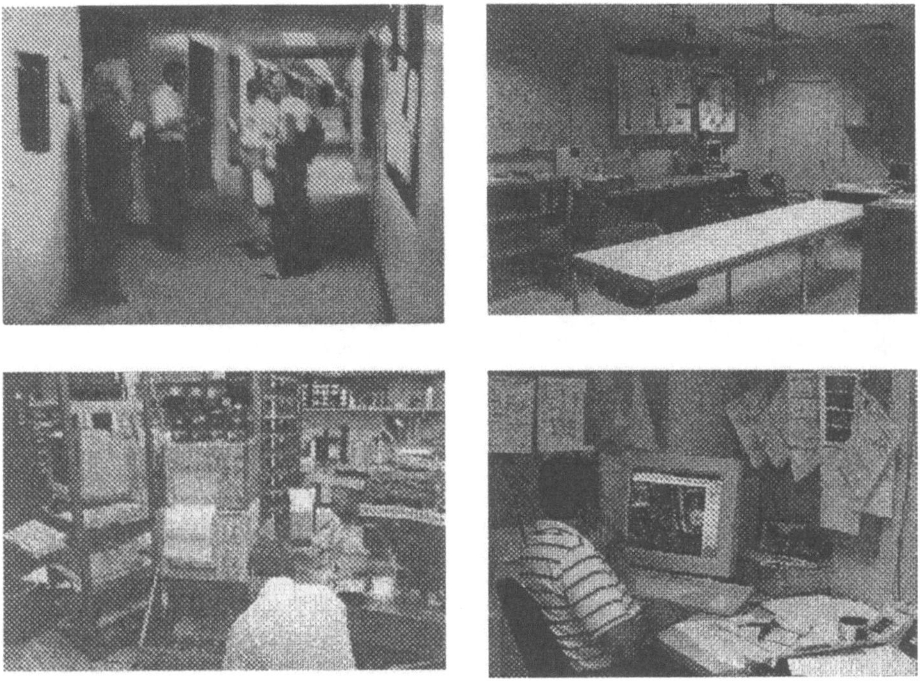

problem occurs, or in the doorways (where small whiteboards are hung on the inside of every door, or any other place where one could possibly fit).

Documenting and understanding the elements of workplace structure

A third event, "*the ideal work environment*" session produced a set of user-generated drawings, *based* on what the lab members find important in their own work environment, with notes of suggestions and explanations. In one session each of the lab members was asked to make a drawing of the ideal laboratory, and choose the level of aggregation—whether the drawing would be of the work station, the office, the laboratory, or the whole campus—and the members were asked to explain the drawings to each other. From this information the facilitators could analyze the different concepts, taking them apart and rebuilding them into different types of office space, lab space, and meeting areas. Drawings from such an exercise usually are of three types; the slight improvements of existing places, the partial changes, and the breakthrough designs.

Document 7-9 The ideal lab environment

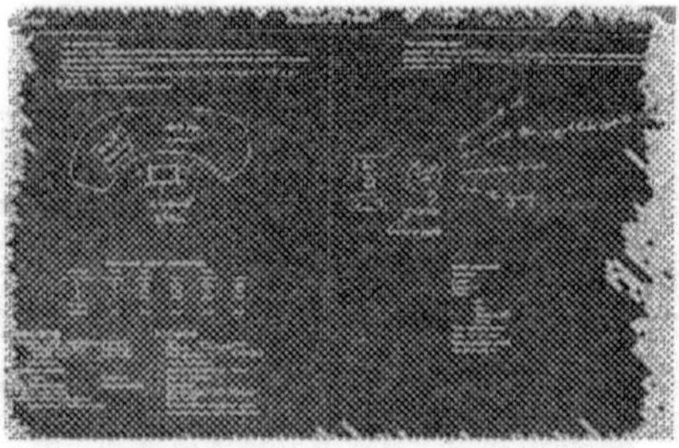

Same as before: The drawing sessions always produce documents which trigger discussion and invention, and challenge the traditional concept of lab space. Most people draw what they already have, with minor practical improvements.

"The workplace at the beach": The LARC consultants asked "If you have all the money in the world, if you have the decision power of the President of Xerox, how would you organize the LX lab or your individual work place?" Many will make drawings of ideas and expressions which represent partial change of the arrangement of work.

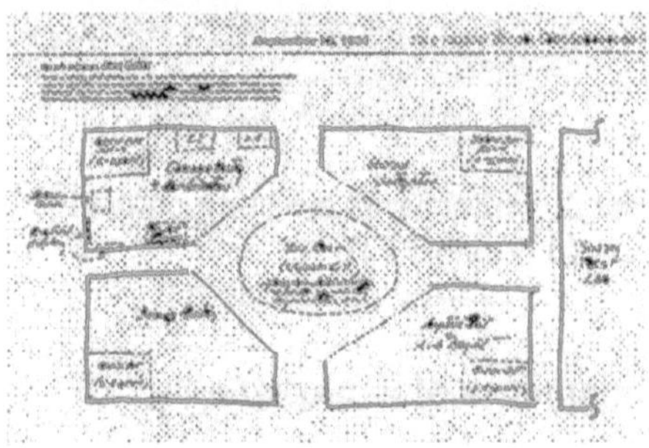

New typology of space: In the drawing exercise there always will be one or two people who will make drawings which represent a breakthrough concept, a different typology of spatial arrangement. The idea of channeling information generated in the labs into a general discussion and presentation area was more clearly expressed in a drawing in a workshop a month later, in one of the platform teams.

In order to develop work areas and meeting places which could support innovation, the LARC team needed to better understand what kind of work was going on when "we do serious work"—as one scientist put it, "when we need to think hard about a problem we have." The LARC consultants needed to ask themselves "what is happening in the situation where one tries to frame the problem one shall work on?" A researcher has a theory about something and a visitor comes into his office and they look at the screen. Or one researcher would say, "I need the whiteboard to scribble on, because I think with my hand as well as my brain." And the researchers would have this white board, writing on it, and might also need to have a computer screen, or two screens, to look at at the same time. And all of them emphasized the "spread-out place," "to get around the data." The data need to be present in the place of work. The following document illustrates the ideas expressed in the drawing session.

Document 10

M: As long as I have a space for someone to come in and look at my results on a screen in real time, rather than I print it out and take it outside to show. ...The screen is as important as paper. ...The left side [of the screen] is space for the visitor to sit and look at it. The visitor has to be able to look at the screen.

M2: Is there any value... of informal conversation and interaction and—you know, there's all kinds of ideas what that might mean in terms of common space and lounge space, whatever. Is that something that's relevant to your work, to your idea of casual encounter and exchange of ideas?

M: Yes. I think I may be wrong, but—experimentalists do experiments, which is very easily described verbally. But the theoreticians, sometimes you have to show them the equations, the numbers, the curves. It's more important for the theoreticians to have their space, either desk top, or blackboard, or white-board.

M2: That I understand. But I'm more interested in the value to this organization of casual encounter and exchange of information.

M: When we get together, sometimes -- we haven't gotten together just the two of us, but, X and I get together just casually, but we need a blackboard. We need a blackboard to think on because we think with our hands as well as our brains. I mean, when you write down equations, you think as you're writing and you cross out as you erase.

M2: ... you're walking down a hall and you meet X. Do you have a casual meeting in the hallway?

M: No. Not necessarily.

T: So ... you have to see the conversation.

M: Yes. It's not easy to just talk. You have to see something.

M2: What I'm getting at is if you're standing in line to get a coffee and the guy in front in you is waiting in line: "What are you working on these days?"—and the conversation starts up.

M: That's not a serious conversation. I mean, that can be a serious conversation, but that's more casual.

M2: Well, I understand that, but certain companies have found actually tremendous merit in those conversations... And to the extent that they have actually starting supporting them and reinforcing as a behavior.

M: Well, when we get into serious, what I call serious conversation. And we obviously have the coffee pot, where we stop and we start talking about the status of experiments, we start talking about status of models, and we talk about all kinds of different things. The weather and our latest vacations and so on. That might lead, that casual conversation might lead to a serious one that otherwise might not have taken place. ....But the real serious, what I call the serious conversations, take place in the office, with a blackboard, with pencil and paper, right? ....And when you have these conversations you go to a place of business where you can use your aids, like the computer screen or paper or white-board.

M2: I also wanted a work area which to me is a desk, privacy, what I call a spread area, because even though you may have a graph on the computer, you may

> want to have six or seven graphs at the same time and it's not convenient to look on a screen so you want to see what the trend is or something like that. So you need, what I call, a spread area. ....And I've participated in intellectual properties activities which I don't get into but that's another team, committee, whatever. I would also like to have—an ideal situation would be a LiveBoard that's near this meeting area so that you work with that. I don't care if it's in a circle or square or rectangle. (Excerpts from transcript from the Drawing session.)

The drawings can be seen as a wish list for a better workplace, but more importantly they represent diagrams which contain elements of the future workplace. By looking at the transcripts of the conversation from the drawing session together with the actual diagrams, the consultants could identify eight different types of offices, and five different types of meeting rooms, all serving different purposes. A drawing of an ideal workplace becomes a diagram which illustrates an idea. The diagram presents a picture of an idea; however, the diagram is not the idea. Working across media, such as on paper with a pencil; on the computer; or by extracting principles from composite drawings onto a flipover chart as a summary in a drawing meeting, or as an afterthought onto a set of new diagrams of types of workplaces, as was done in the LX workshops—changes our understanding of the potential of the design.

The diagram allows one to explore an idea before one builds anything. The drawings of the ideal work environment in the LARC pilot development are such diagrams; they represent ideas of how better the lab members might work together. In the conversation between the scientists, they could see each other's diagrams, and react to them, and each person could react, as well, to what he or she had drawn on the paper him/herself. Within the act of drawing the diagram, the researchers in the laboratory at Xerox were actually discovering options they never discussed or thought about. The idea of the common, with the curled or broken corridor as a "divider" with fuzzy edges, and with the meeting area in the middle, can be explained and communicated in such a diagram. Also the drawing from the one of the platform groups, later used by the DRI designers to develop the idea of the APIC, is a diagram of spatial and technological interrelationships.

Communication less frequent in the LX lab than the platform teams

The lab members were spread out in three buildings. Two were adjacent, one of these including what was intended to be the LX central work area. The third was 15-20 minutes' walking distance away. In the morning of day 4 the participants in the *cardboard game workshop* were asked to circle the main workplaces, and the communication between their main workplaces and other members of the group they would need to talk to, draw lines to show either on a daily or weekly basis. The maps below show the communication pattern of LX and, for contrast, that of a platform development group that was being studied at the same time. While the platform group's map was filled with lines, one could hardly detect any lines between the LX members. It is not obvious what this means, but the LX lab was a newly established research and development team, while the platform team was more mature and was working with a tight schedule and a clear understanding of their technology tasks and deliverables.

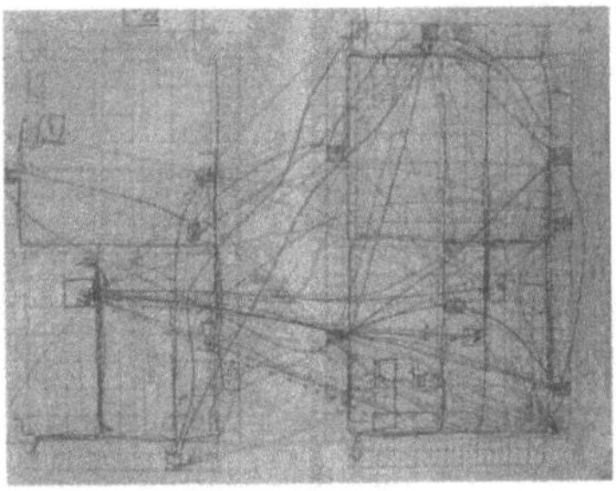

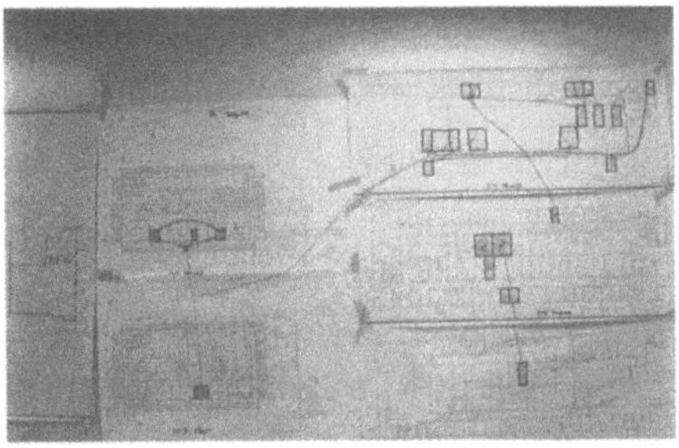

Document 11-12

Maps of laboratories and communication patterns, the LX lab (Day 4, August workshop) and the platform lab (September workshop)

Structuring the work and the communication processes

The games serve well to clarify roles people play in actual change processes, to illustrate the kinds of issues that arise and to force reflection on them, and to highlight the kinds of skills required, producing interesting alternatives. They have also been useful in illustrating new relationships among the actors of the work environment, relationships that can serve as concrete examples of how behavior in everyday work practice might be changed for the better.

Document 13

Interactive design game lays out a possible organizational structure of the lab. The game is a collection of cardboard pieces in different colors and sizes, with what they should be represent left up to the participants, to be organized in different relationship towards each other, in order to understand the proximity of functions and the communication links between them.

The problem people worked on was: given the LX work area, which contained enough office space for only about one-third of the LX lab, and with the LX common as "a center in the center," using the New England Town as a metaphor; who should be close to the "common" and who should live in the periphery of the town? In the course of developing these, each stage of the process was photographed. The lab members were grouped two by two, then gradually in larger groups, in order to explore the principles for the lab organization, and the relationship between face-to-face collaboration and work at a distance. Existing and ideal communication lines were drawn. In the second round the game was redefined to represent devices for communication.

Different types of meeting places needed

People need access to the same information in order to collaborate on the same technology. It was the original idea of the LARC project that information technology could help provide such access. However, the workshops concluded that to collaborate effectively people need to meet face-to-face. In order to speed up the innovation process people need to interact: they need to talk, they need to look at the same data at the same time, they need to make decisions together. The common area illustrates one of several spatio-technological strategies. In this area the engineers could post any information charts they thought were important to conducting the design process. The meeting area would afford direct visual or electronic access to information in people's laboratories or offices, but it would also provide space where one could display charts, photographs, and maps—electronic or otherwise—whatever represented the current problem.

The need for multiple representations

The need for a central place to display the overall research picture was best developed in the drawing session with the LX group, and later in the "situation room" sketch drawn by a member of a platform group. An individual workplace large enough to allow for two or three people grappling with data and ideas, and the shared spaces next to the integrated fixture, are important to the culture of experimentalists and engineers, and are also conducive to the sharing of multiple representations of research phenomena, which enhance problem-solving capability. The face-to-face meeting places provide a useful informational redundancy, so that the workers can check to see whether they and their co-workers are reading off the same analog devices, for example, or so that they can combine their experience to understand the test-sheets produced. Interpretations of production phenomena cannot be confirmed by reference to multiple data sets, but another person, whose experiences are different from yours, may hear something differently from the way you do, so he also acts as a check on your interpretation; or when the researcher sees that his colleagues' head is cocked, indicating that he is puzzled by something, he may figure out what is wrong more quickly than the other can. In these ways, a face-to-face team situation enables each person to make use of the other's sensory capacity in order to direct and adjust the line of thinking.

The need to meet in the middle of the work

The conference room used for two of the platform teams had the traditional "situation room" setup, with an oval table; there was a centrality in the orientation of the room, with a wall for projector displays at one end, and chairs along the wall at the opposite end. The more senior people would sit at the upper front part of the oval, the less important would sit at the lower part of the oval. The technicians—the people who actually knew about the problem which had occurred—would sit on the chairs along the wall, out of the main flow of the meeting. And they had no way to display anything about the problem visually or through seeing the actual fixture. The displays in the room might be formal presentations of some known technology; whereas the apparatus and the artifacts actually connected to the problem the technicians would be trying to understand, or the parts which were the cause of the breakdown, would not be present.

A problem that people in the platform teams brought up was the lack of immediacy in these latter meetings—how it might take two or three days to assemble the people with the authority or knowledge to solve an important problem, and when the people were assembled, it was hard to bring back the situation in which the problem had occurred. The more efficient problem solving—if only one could have the necessary people there—happened in front of the machine, or when people were congregating outside a lab door. The design question became how to bring the work into the conference room, or the conference room into the middle of the work.

Document 14

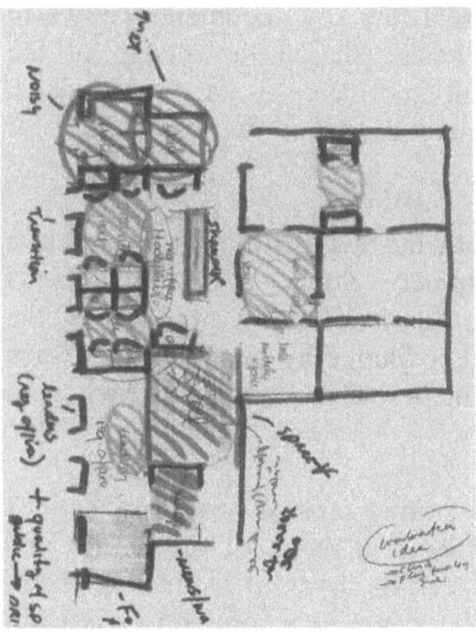

Drawing summarizing the key concept for the LX work area: The workshops revealed two principal types of meeting places, with variations of meeting areas within these two types: informal and formal. Informal meeting places were those where meetings are not scheduled, and are open to anybody who wants to sit down and participate in what's going on. Formal meeting places were those where people are invited into meetings that are common to the whole group, or common to the people working adjacent to the meeting area. One knows immediately when one is an intruder in a meeting like this.

Documents as glue in building a research community: what to be learned

The documents from these seminal workshops described above became crucial vehicles for mobilizing the group to assess its work processes as well as its work environments and for forming a new work place. These documents were created as an integral part of the evaluation and design process. They included photographs, audio-taped conversations, communication maps, cardboard games, yellow trace, letter paper, flip charts, computer-based displays, slides, and films. Thus, 'documents' refer to almost anything that contains a record of some kind and that can be referred to independent of their authors, though it is conceivable that, under some circumstances, ephemeral oral or visual representations, for example, improvised and un-recorded theater, might qualify.

The documents were created in a collective work process, where everybody could see and hear what another person suggested and could comment on it and discuss it. The documents showed also how a not-yet-understood problem can be worked on in an open and collegial manner, in which expertise on the work itself is combined with expertise on work place design. The participants gradually discovered bits and pieces of knowledge about the work which bore critical importance to the new place to be built. Throughout the process, documents were an indispensable agent in recording work practices, triggering new ideas, arguing positions, and recording decisions. For the participants to have imagined and invented the workplace without documents is unthinkable.

How, then, do documents function as 'glue' in building any community of research? Shared knowledge, perhaps signaled by a few key documents known to most of the participants, constitutes a strong basis. Shared knowledge of the particular set of documents strengthens membership and increases its value. Indeed, most disciplinary groups are formed in part around a commonly shared body of knowledge, of literature, and of artifacts.

In this paper, we speak in particular of the documents that are the by-products of a process of working together to reshape the workplace. Some of these documents may serve to re-represent the shared knowledge base. Thus, by-products of the current process can reinforce the already shared knowledge by restating it in ways that are germane to the problem at hand. But the main role of such by-products is to record and articulate the work of the group.

The documents that are the by-products of a working process have implications for the formation of a research community, partly as a result of the nature and content of the documents and partly through the efforts invested in making them. Participation in making the documents engages the group in a common enterprise.

This activity in itself helps to form the basis for further working together, regardless of the topic. The very activity of document making by the group means that, like a garden to the gardeners, it is a collective product, and there can be pride and sense of accomplishment in its making, reinforced simply by viewing the results. The production of documents may provide a diversion that permits better communication, as talking while walking affords a focus other than the other person, under which conditions it may be easier to raise and to discuss certain issues.

Working together calls forth distinctive modalities of relating to one another. These modalities may be quite different from approaches to problem solving or finding that are professionally defined, which might, for example, be characterized as 'logical,' 'systematic,' and 'scientific.' For example, people have "roles;" which in turn suggest actors, directors, producers, stagehands, and the other participants in dramatic production. Roles also suggest players, as in games. Gaming permits playful use of artifacts, hence encourages thought about unconventional uses, opens up 'lateral' thinking process, and encourages reinterpretation and re-understanding as a function of context rather than meaning inherited. Because people can assume different roles, it opens up the possibility of empathetic understanding of other roles in a group, particularly because in a game or a play, one may have to assume any of several roles over time or, as in some theater productions, more than one role at the same time! People tell stories to one another. Narrative construction implies a linking of causality and time, though in the hands of an expert author, these are treated knowingly. Memory is enabled by recording of the trace of the narrative development of the group; the group has its own story that has evidence to document it; this evidence can be used to cue memory of the participants and can be used as well by historians to attempt reconstruction of the group's process. Moreover, each modality has characteristic ways in which it becomes documented. And each carries implications for how cause and effect are to be described.

Architects use diagrams to bridge between ideas and form. Ideas in diagrams are often more compact and communicative in a short time than through spoken language. The representation and the idea often become inseparable. The diagram's power is its capacity not only to suggest an idea, but to be manipulated in various ways that diagrams permit. Another aspect of its power is its lack of precise reference to anything in particular. This enables many to participate in a discussion where the understanding of the diagram by each individual may not be precisely the same, but where there is enough overlap to continue the conversation until stronger agreement is achieved. As with any representation, its weakness is that it does not have all the characteristics of the finished product. Nevertheless, because of the advantages of diagrammatic representations, participants in a group process often turn to them and, as a result, produce diagram-filled documents.

The language of the document, whether it be symbolic, diagrammatic, pictorial, or verbal, serves to develop a kind of patois for the group that belongs to no one else and that helps to reinforce the uniqueness and the identity of this particular group. The idiosyncratic marks and diagrams, not to mention the special contextually defined words and phrases, expand and define the shared domain of the working group. They expand the special language by means of which the group can communicate. And they preserve the individuality of many of the participants by means of the contributions each has made to the construction of the language. The documents serve as guardians of the language and model its use.

The circumstances within which a group operates may be exciting and challenging, but they also may be burdensome. Shared difficulties, expressed in documents of protest, clarify shared interests and act as binding agents. The documentation of protest may be cryptic and not understandable by outsiders to the process, but can also bind in the same ways that other specialized knowledge defines and binds various communities. And clarification of other aspects of the circumstances of work can only build a shared sense of being-in-it-together, subject to the same forces acting upon them. Documents that express these circumstances, and especially that express the unique bearing of the circumstances on the group, reinforce the group's identity and mutual inter-dependence.

In projects for modifying the workplace, it is the range and variety of documents, their relationship to the various individuals and disciplines contributing to the team, their identity that is independent of these prior relationships, that signal the likelihood that a group process has worked well and that it will be carried over into other settings. A more profound result was that this style of collaboration in problem-solving across disciplines became the new working style of the group in their own research and development work. The lab members discovered that the new workplace was much more conducive to working in teams, and to looking at representation of data in public, using electronic documents as well as handwritten notes and whiteboard drawings in their creative process. This way of working became natural both within the group and in meetings with vendors or possible business partners. Thus the workplace change process led to important changes in their own work practice.

19 UNDERSTANDING OF BUSINESS AND ORGANIZATIONAL ISSUES SURROUNDING INTEGRATION: REDESIGNING MIT'S PUBLISHING SERVICES

Barrie Gleason

At MIT, a reengineering team charged with developing a new business model for providing publishing services has a unique opportunity for promoting innovative information management[1] at the Institute. There are two stories which unfold in this presentation. The first is a chronicle of the team's work, including a brief history of events and a sketch of the new business model. The second is a description of opportunities for innovative information management which the new business concept affords. In conclusion are the lessons learned in this work.

Brief History

The status of publishing at MIT is well documented in a 1994 report prepared by the Publication Services Review Group (PSRG) for the Senior Vice President. A cross-functional group of staff members, PSRG began their work late in 1992. They met for over a year, using traditional and TQM methods to collect and review data, assess problems, test assumptions, and develop recommendations.

Their report suggests new ways of producing publications at MIT, all of which were expected to generate cost savings and combine separate tasks into better integrated processes. Two recommendations called for changes in how the Institute's central publication services were structured and delivered. The other recommendations dealt with policy and how individual departments and centers maintained accountability regarding the production of their publications. The

PSRG also recommended incorporating existing services into a new organization.

The report identified several key institutional priorities: the need for (a) a communications strategy based on the Institute's mission; the need to develop and communicate (b) editorial and design standards, to achieve greater (c) financial accountability among those who produce publications, to provide (d) better information about publication processes and available services, and to provide (e) higher quality, more cost-effective service.[2]

MIT initiates reengineering

At the same time, MIT was initiating its reengineering effort. Along with many other research universities, MIT faced fundamental shifts in its relationship with the federal government, starkly exemplified by the decline of funding for research and changes in MIT's contribution to the indirect cost of research. No longer were incremental measures such as budget cutting and downsizing (which the Institute had already tried) enough to address relentless increases year-to-year in the budget deficit.

In a town meeting held in November 1993, President Vest discussed MIT's need to reduce the gap between income and expenses by \$40M and reduce the number of jobs by 400 over a three- or four-year time period. (In May 1995, President Vest amended that figure to 600 jobs.)

In March 1994, the Senior Vice President introduced MIT's reengineering effort. This effort was geared toward simplifying the business processes that support the Institute's academic and research enterprises, while improving quality, enhancing customer service and reducing costs. Initial reengineering efforts focused on broad areas such as student support, management reporting, and the buy/pay process.

What was the problem? One example was the buy/pay process, which included the functions involved in acquiring a product or service for use at the Institute, from determination of need (by an individual or project) to paying the bill (by accounting). In fiscal year 1994, MIT maintained a vendor database of over 45,000 suppliers, conducting business with over 14,000 of them and spending over \$240M in the process. Eighty-seven percent of MIT's total purchasing transactions were for under \$500, and accounted for less than 3 percent of the total.

Early reengineering teams who reviewed the buy/pay process believed that MIT could take advantage of its buying power much more effectively; realize significant economies of scale by managing the vendor database; and improve the Institute's ability to measure performance and service quality of suppliers. They developed a set of supplier consolidation principles, which were to: (1) reduce the cost of acquiring goods and services; (2) improve the quality of service to the MIT community; (3) improve the buying process; (4) channel buying behavior through incentives rather than mandates; and (5) build strong partnerships with MIT suppliers. Their belief was that the Institute could save millions of dollars by applying these principles to the purchase of a wide range of products and services, from temporary help to travel to publishing.

Reengineering team created

Under the auspices of supplier consolidation, several reengineering teams were formed to simplify the buying processes at the Institute. In March 1995, a team was created to review how MIT purchased its publishing services. The key administrative areas represented by this five-person team (called 'P-squares') included the MIT Libraries, Public Relations Services, Sloan School of Management, the Industrial Liaison Program, and Graphic Arts, Operations. (Three of these individuals had served on the original PSRG team.)

The team's charge was to analyze the process as it currently existed (what is the work? how is the work performed?); interview customers and suppliers; search for industry's best practices; and create a vision of a new process. The team began their work by reviewing the recommendations in the 1994 PSRG report.

Since costs related to the purchase of publishing services at MIT had never been tracked consistently, the $8M estimate for fiscal year 1994 was conservative. Although there were in-house suppliers of these services (Design Services in Public Relations Services, and Graphic Arts in Operations), three-quarters of MIT's work was handled by outside vendors. The vendor database, managed by the Purchasing Office, included more than 500 print suppliers alone.

In July 1995, the reengineering team presented its initial findings to the Institute's Steering Committee, a group of senior administrators led by the Senior Vice President, who provided oversight to the Institute's reengineering effort. The team described the flow of work to produce print products and publications at the Institute. These processes were characterized by decentralized coordination and specification of projects; uneven efforts directed at channeling design and print to in-house operations; and little coordination of outside suppliers.

The reengineered workflow proposed by the team would improve the buying process and reduce costs (see below). The Steering Committee's reaction to the proposal was positive, but they wanted more information. In response, the Senior Vice President asked the team leader to identify the individuals who could work together to refine the business case. The reconstituted team (PubServ) retained two members of the original team, representing MIT Libraries and Public Relations Services, and added two new members, who represented the Institute's Purchasing Office and Information Systems.

Bold New Business Model

PubServ refined the concept of a central publishing services bureau for coordinating the purchase of publishing services at MIT. Their solution took the shape of a publishing services bureau that was a single, coordinated channel for publishing activities. By providing different levels of service and points of entry, the bureau would be flexible enough to accommodate customers who differed in terms of their requirements for service (requiring many options, or few options, from a broad array); their background and experiences in publishing; and in the nature of the publication with which they were concerned. For example, the bureau could manage an entire production cycle on request, by identifying appropriate writers, editors, proofreaders, 'html' coders, or photographers, to support production, and recommending printers with expertise and equipment to match specific job requirements. On the other hand, the bureau might simply recommend a short list of preferred vendors.

The bureau would be staffed by teams of brokers, who operate in a learning environment, and would promote a strategic view of publishing by helping Institute publishers to determine which publications were necessary to produce; to develop and manage budgets; and to exploit electronic publishing. As specialized purchasing agents, the brokers work with customers to match their unique publishing needs with the appropriate levels of service. The brokers do not provide design and print services themselves; instead they identify those suppliers who provide unique, expert publishing services, and are interested in developing business partnerships with MIT.

Brokers negotiate favorable contracts and partnership agreements with these suppliers. On an ongoing basis, to assure quality control, they monitor the performance of vendors and evaluate the extent to which customers are satisfied with services provided by vendors and brokers alike. In addition, brokers are prepared to clarify to customers their responsibilities in the publishing process.

The bureau is staffed by a team of eight individuals, six administrative staff and two support staff. The six include a director; four professional brokers with combined expertise in design, print, electronic publishing, and purchasing; and a graphic designer. The purchasing broker is responsible for all of MIT's publishing purchases, whether channeled through the bureau or not. The two support staff who work in the bureau support the director and the purchasing broker respectively, but may assist other brokers as required. The director has a joint reporting relationship to the Director of Public Relations Services and the Senior Vice President.

In PubServ's view, the bureau's director is a skilled manager whose enthusiasm for implementing a strategic vision for publishing in infectious; whose creativity in managing collaboration is exemplary; and whose strong commitment to customer service is a model for the Institute. While the brokers bring unique talents to the bureau, they also share certain core competencies in publishing technologies, customer service, and problem solving. In their work, they function as a high performance team.

The underlying rationale for providing a range of publishing services is simple: Better informed customers make better publishing decisions and better use of Institute resources. The bureau's services are designed to facilitate 'doing the right thing.' PubServ was certain that a more formal publishing strategy could save MIT several millions of dollars per year.

Getting There

How did the reengineering teams develop their vision of the new process? Three examples of their work are worth mentioning.

Interview customers

To learn more about the customer's point of view, PubServ conducted three meetings, resembling focus group sessions, with a total of 26 participants from various academic and administrative offices at the Institute. These individuals were involved with different aspects of the publishing process, from budgeting to desktop publishing. Some were self-selected volunteers; others were identified as key 'stakeholders' in publications at MIT. In the sessions, the reengineering team described the new concept for publishing services, then posed the following questions: what do you like or dislike about the new concept? what is missing from the design? what is your experience with internal and external suppliers? would you use this approach to purchase publishing services?

The participants clearly wanted higher levels of customer service in meeting their needs, however those publishing requirements were met. They evaluated customer service not only in terms of how well the supplier listens to the customer, but also in the supplier's ability to rethink, or redesign, a project based on the customer's unique requirements. Institute publishers wanted to see higher levels of quality control in both processes and products.

Later, PubServ conducted in-depth individual interviews with 28 members of the MIT community who represented different customer constituencies. They included satisfied and dissatisfied customers of the internal organization providing design services, and those who purchased services from external vendors. In general, these customers were acutely aware of the enormity of MIT's publishing problems and were eager for change. They identified improved service as support with visual identity programs, with articulating their requirements, and managing their publishing work systematically. They wanted design choices, or options, which helped them to lower costs. They also believed that unless change at MIT was supported 'from the top,' it would not succeed.

Run pilot project

In order to test their assumptions about workflow in the bureau, PubServ worked with the Director of Communications[3] at the Sloan School of Management to design a pilot project. The director, an experienced and sophisticated communications professional, was already planning the redesign of the Sloan's alumni/-ae publication *MIT Management*. He was eager to work with the PubServ team as if he were a customer of MIT's future publishing services bureau. Together, the PubServ team would act as a broker in the bureau.

In a typical bureau scenario as envisioned by the team, the prospective customer schedules a meeting with one of the bureau's brokers. Together, they develop a publication plan by addressing questions regarding the purpose of the publication, its primary audience, budget allocation, and the means to evaluate the publication's impact on the intended audience. The broker and customer discuss alternatives regarding print and electronic versions of the publication. The broker recommends several designers, and possibly printers, from the bureau's database of preferred suppliers. The customer may decide to work directly with these vendors, or ask the broker to manage the entire job.

Acting as the broker, PubServ provided the names of four design firms to the Director of Communications. The team contacted the design firm principals to ask if they were willing to participate in the reengineering pilot project. Although the interview between each designer and the customer would be 'the real thing,' PubServ requested that team members sit as silent observers during these interviews in order to learn more about the process. Four unique design firms, including the internal service, agreed to participate, and the interviews were scheduled.

Later, the communications director met with the team members to evaluate the four design proposals submitted. Together, they articulated criteria for evaluation, which included the designer's awareness of process and opportunities for cost savings; attention to information design; and his or her listening skills. The director selected the designer, and began work on the redesign with his staff and the design firm. He continued to meet with PubServ at intervals to describe the evolution of the project, the end result of which was a dramatic and energetic new publication called *R.O.I.* (Return on Investment), published by Sloan three times annually as a print newsletter and on the World Wide Web.

From a broad array of potential services, the broker offered this unique customer assistance with a publication plan, electronic publishing, design options, clarification of Institute purchasing policies, and production assistance. In a written testimonial submitted to the Steering Committee, he commented, 'Although we have considerable experience in this field, working with the broker team has proven extraordinarily useful in several specific (and sometimes unexpected) ways.'

Interview designers

To order to test its business assumptions, PubServ planned a series of interviews with designers who work as freelancers and heads of well-known design firms in the Boston area. Before each meeting, designers were provided with a set of statements outlining 'givens and assumptions,' which reflected the themes and ideas in the team's vision of the bureau. Billing these sessions as conversations, the team encouraged designers to react candidly to reengineering assumptions, and to tell the team whether or not they would consider doing business with MIT in the future.

Statements which represented 'givens' of the new business included the following. Given: That the publishing bureau represents a new way of doing business, which ensures dollar savings, more efficient workflow, and improved levels of service quality to the Institute. Given: That design is not MIT's core business. And, Given: That electronic publishing has created a dynamic, fluid, and ambiguous context in which to rethink information design and access. Designers agreed with these statements.

Discussions of business 'assumptions' with these designers were informative. For example, the team had made the assumption that the design broker need not be a designer. However, designers disagreed; they believed that the design broker *should* be a designer in order to more readily gain the respect of colleagues (customers and vendors) and bring a working knowledge of appropriate software technologies to the bureau. The team also assumed that together with outside vendors, brokers could work to achieve design coherence and Institute visual identity. Interestingly, the different designers interviewed were of one mind in their feedback. They were convinced that creating and implementing a visual identity for print and digital media should be the first order of business for the bureau, and that brokers and outside vendors could undertake this effort *together*.

Approval

In November 1995, PubServ made the second presentation regarding the redesign of MIT's publishing services to the Institute's Steering Committee. In this meeting, they described the results of the pilot project conducted to clarify business processes and define the work of the bureau. They described the bureau's organizational structure and staffing and presented a financial model which reflected savings opportunities for the Institute. Finally, they specified the factors critical to the success of such an endeavor. In December, PubServ presented to the Senior Vice President the working draft of a business plan for the publishing services bureau, which included job descriptions and the first year's budget.

In February 1996, the Senior Vice President asked the team to proceed with the final phase of its work, transition to the new way of doing business. In July, he formally announced the establishment of the Publishing Services Bureau to the MIT community and senior management's decision to close the internal services (Design Services, Public Relations Services; and Graphic Arts, Operations). In October 1996, the newly hired Director of the bureau began to interview applicants to fill the bureau's broker positions.

Innovative Information Management

The reengineering teams' vision of a bold new way of doing business offers opportunities for promoting innovative information management, that is, *how information is used and structured in MIT's print and electronic publications*. Four of these opportunities, described in detail below, include promoting the use of the publication plan, creating an MIT identity, developing the electronic catalog, and agile publishing.

Using the framework of the publication plan to clarify the publishing process for *a specific publication*, the broker promotes understanding of the business value of documents and the information they contain on the part of the individual publisher. At the Institute level, the bureau's director and brokers work through the identity design process, development of the electronic catalogue, and application of the agile publishing framework to accomplish the same purpose.

This work encourages publishers to examine, and make explicit, the interrelationships that exist among documents; existing and emerging technologies which support their publication; and the business processes, or work practices, of the organization. Central to this dynamic is information. Progress in managing information occurs with increasing awareness of its Ôimpact, value, and cost' to the organization.[4]

Publication plan

The vision

Brokers in the new Publishing Services Bureau will assist customers with developing comprehensive plans for publishing projects. They assist with forecasting new jobs by helping customers prepare realistic production schedules and accurate cost estimates, and provide expertise in needs assessment of an organization's publications. By promoting an audit strategy to review effectiveness of publications, or communications programs, brokers encourage customers to link planning and evaluation with the organization's budget process. Brokers also assist customers in developing evaluation strategies for their own publications, in order to assess the extent to which a publication addresses the purpose(s) for which it was created.

The reality

Working with the reengineering team to develop a publication plan (in the pilot project), the communications director at Sloan was encouraged to 'rethink the document.' By stepping back in order to engage in more rigorous and thoughtful planning, he was able to articulate the purpose and context for a redesigned publication and how he wanted it to perform (document and business process). By understanding the advantages of publishing on the World Wide Web, he was able to anticipate and accommodate this new technology in the design of the publication (technology and document). And by producing Sloan's alumni/-ae publication as a newsletter in print and on the World Wide Web, he hoped to influence behavior on the part of the publication's key audiences—alums, corporate sponsors, and the business press (technology and business process). He anticipated that a larger percentage of the audience would come to rely on the publication as a source of information and engage more actively in the Sloan community.

In summary, by 'managing' the interactions among document, technology, and work processes, the communications director enhanced the value of information in the publication.[5]

These shifting, evolving dynamics influenced information design in the publication *R.O.I.* in important ways. In print, its size and format were attention grabbers. Most articles began and ended on a single page for ease of reading. Content was written to be newsworthy and fresh, to avoid a self-congratulatory attitude. The newsletter engaged readers in ongoing conversations by posing questions, asking advice, and in subsequent issues (both print and digital), publishing the replies submitted by readers. Their responses helped shape the content of future issues.

Sloan's communications director has set the stage for further organizational change. By extending this framework and strategy to other publishing work at Sloan, he and his creative team will begin, slowly but surely, to influence the way people think and make decisions. (This signals future change in the document and business processes as the requirements of *internal* customers are defined more clearly over time.)

The future

PubServ believed that Sloan's story heralds a different future for publishing work at the Institute as publishers of information and documents begin to appreciate more fully the business value of what they do, from the low budget brochure published by a small administrative office trying to claim a publishing budget, to the myriad documents and publications produced by the School trying to corral its budget.

Table 1. Enhancing the value of information

Document
Articulated purpose and context for information
Created design templates for print and digital versions
Specified performance measures for publication
Planned reuse of text and images

Technology
Published in print and electronic formats
Provided access to newsletter articles via the World Wide Web

Business process
Planned *R.O.I.* as centerpiece of communications strategy
Linked changes in publication to customer response
Reduced annual publication costs by 25 percent
Developed shared language for rethinking the document

By spelling out different levels of effort—(1) decisions to print, or not; (2) evaluation of performance-oriented content; and (3) design of information to convey meaning—the opportunity exists for achieving greater coherence within the School's publications, and, no less significant, cost savings that benefit both the School and the Institute.

Identity

Since MIT has no clear, consistent identity system in place for the use of its logo or logotype, another opportunity for innovative information management concerns the identity design process for the Institute. In interviews with the reengineering team, without exception, customers and vendors expressed their interest in design coherence and visual identity in print and digital media. MIT publishers believe that an identity is very important for their unique organization, and would respect the Institute's visual identity *if there were one*. Designers were consistent in their recommendation that a visual identity should be in place before brokers and vendors could work together efficiently.

In the view of designers, the effort to create a visual identity serves as the springboard for developing a comprehensive communications strategy for the Institute. Approached thoughtfully, this opportunity is especially compelling because it addresses the joint business goals of reengineering: reducing costs and improving the quality of service to the Institute.

How might this happen? In the immediate future, mapping a communications plan for the Institute would be a two-track effort: one track to deal with establishing a visual identity; the other to deal with training brokers, customers, and vendors within the publishing bureau on guidelines for its application. Only when they begin to speak the same language, that is, articulate the context for problem solving, would these constituencies begin to think operationally as well as strategically, to manage costs as well as affect revenues.

ECAT

In the future, the Publishing Services Bureau will promote its publishing services via the electronic catalog, or ECAT. Currently under development by another supplier consolidation reengineering team, ECAT is an on-line sourcing, pricing, ordering, and payment system for purchasing from MIT's supplier partners. From their desktops, Institute customers would use the Internet and the World Wide Web to view current and complete product descriptions and illustrations, as well as information regarding pricing and availability. Catalog 'pages' display products and the reduced prices negotiated between MIT and supplier partners.

From its World Wide Web homepage, the bureau will describe the services it provides, such as lists of MIT's preferred vendors, and offer printing products, or commodity-type items, such as business cards, or letterhead stationery. In a typical scenario, the customer reviews design options for business cards from the electronic catalog. After selecting a design, he or she completes an information template on the screen. The customer may view paper stock samples and ink colors by visiting the bureau, or select directly from the on-line catalog. The printer, with whom the bureau has negotiated a partnership, receives electronic notification of the new print job, completes the job, and delivers business cards to the customer's desk the following day. Over time, the bureau tracks volume orders for each design in the catalog and interviews customers who place special orders. Brokers review both process and product to verify that business card orders meet quality, cost, and delivery time standards.

It's not hard to imagine the bureau providing flexible on-line templates for other basic document formats, such as brochures and newsletters, to assist publishers with small budget projects. By observing patterns in customer requirements over time, the bureau can begin to anticipate needs and tailor service options to address them. These are opportunities to influence the quality of publications (consistency in look) and manage additional cost savings (in time and dollars) for the Institute.

Content-driven publishing

The fourth opportunity for promoting innovative information management described in this paper, is content-driven, or agile, publishing. In 1994, when the Center for Coordination Science, Sloan School, sponsored their first workshop at MIT on 'Rethinking the Document,' Rob Haimes introduced the concept of content-driven publishing. In this conceptual redesign of business processes around publications, content resources were stored in a central repository, with form separated from content. Content providers focused on creation of content that met the needs of the target audience, while design and production people provided 'containers' into which that content could be poured. Contents of the repository, or database, were available in electronic and print formats to support a wide range of customer requirements for information.

> Structuring content for repurposing and using more sophisticated templates (or rule-based design models) ultimately leads to an increasingly dynamic and automated publishing process—one that can become central to supporting a company's business objectives.[6]

Haimes' presentation sparked the curiosity of a handful of MIT colleagues who applied the model to one of the Institute's official reference publications, the 'faculty picture book.' They wanted to understand what it would take to create an information infrastructure (with information and images) that supported a wide range of business activities from production of faculty directories to standard faculty reporting and research grant applications.

What came to be known as the 'agile publishing working group' designed a template of information to describe the individual faculty member and listed business applications for this information. They researched total costs for print picture books already published across campus in order to compare current and future solutions. And they identified key implementation issues to address, which included privacy of information, copyright, and information ownership.

Reviewing this work-in-progress, the reengineering team found many strengths in the content-driven publishing model: the application of market and design/production models (which specify context); the reuse of information elements; distribution of publishing decisions; and the potential for standardization *and* customization in documents. While the team believed that the publishing strategy supported the work of the bureau, they were not convinced that pursuing this particular project was the *bureau's* work.

Two years ago, when the agile publishing working group was considering a central repository for information on faculty, the World Wide Web (WWW) had not yet overwhelmed the campus. Since then, individuals, departments, and SchoolsÑin increasing numbers, with uneven resultsÑhave become their own publishers. Today the content-driven publishing model may be more useful as a framework for understanding how publishing work is organized, and how it could be organized, in other words, how a broad base of resources is linked in ways that allow people to design and deliver organizational messages across a wide range of media. For this or any other publishing project to rely on a *content* repository requires collaborative effort among administrative offices to integrate information and the work processes of information collection and distribution.

Lessons Learned

There were important lessons learned in redesigning MIT's publishing services that lead to better understanding of the business and organizational issues surrounding integration. They include the following:

- The original PSRG report identified institutional priorities, which the publishing services reengineering teams were later to support. However, in hindsight, the incremental approach reflected in their recommendations for change did not adequately address the serious problems in the Institute's buy/pay process for publishing services.

Reengineering provided the opportunity and appropriate methodology to introduce wide-ranging changes, new ideas as well as ideas floated by other working groups and task forces, which had been in the works for years, but never implemented. Reengineering changed the rules of the game, enabling cross-functional teams to think about the 'best practice' scenarios, rather than what appeared to be more practical solutions tailored to accommodate political realities. Redesign of the process by the reengineering teams was fundamental, radical, and dramatic.

- One problem that dogged the work of the publishing services reengineering teams began as a semantic confusion, that is, lack of a precise definition of the process under study. This often led the (parent) supplier consolidation and publishing services teams in different directions. In their pursuit of 'best practice,' for example, the supplier consolidation team focused their research on different printing companies, comparing how outside vendors organized their work with internal operations (at Graphic Arts). However, what the publishing services reengineering teams had in mind was a broader view of the process, to include design, and other creative services, along with print.

  This confusion played itself out in several ways, for example, in differing agendas of the two key process owners (the Senior Vice President responsible for Graphic Arts and the Director of Public Relations Services), and in development of a financial model that did not adequately consider how supplier consolidation principles applied to the creative, collaborative nature of design work.

  Consequently, short circuits in communication and decision-making often delayed PubServ's progress and distracted the team with reengineering's implementation problems rather than the task at hand. Critical work that remains for the Publishing Services Bureau is to develop a clearer understanding of how supplier consolidation principles apply to the Institute's purchase of design and creative services.

- Writing the business plan for the new publishing services bureau was a daunting process for the reengineering team. However, PubServ was strongly committed to the long-term planning that this effort required. The team anticipated that revising the plan on an annual basis would be an essential part of the bureau's work. They conceived of no stronger statement regarding a *bold new way of doing business at MIT* than spelling out the bureau's vision and the terms of its accountability to the Institute in a business plan.

Conclusion

In 1990, an independent research report on information access at MIT painted a grim picture of how MIT's administrative culture actually inhibited the flow of information.

> The inappropriate extension of MIT's original cultural attitudes [entrepreneurial philosophy] to its growing administrative sector has fed the development of a complex, fragmented, politicized and sometimes redundant organizational environment in which information is power, and thus something to be closely held rather than shared.[7]

The report suggested that the most important element in the effort to integrate information, its collection and distribution, was cultural. Cultural organization and commitment to implementing integration were more important than the technology used.

Six years later, in 1996, MIT's culture *is changing*. Reengineering has been the necessary catalyst. Evident in the redesign of MIT's publishing services described here are important cultural changes in how work is done: through teamwork, collaboration, focus on the customer, accountability, and a different understanding of the business value, for *all* the Institute's constituencies, of integrating information and processes.

Table 2. Key dates

1990	Independent research report describes problems with information flow at MIT.
1992	Senior Vice President appoints PSRG task force to review MIT's publishing services.
1993	President hosts town meeting to discuss MIT's financial picture.
1994	PSRG submits report to the Senior Vice President (January). Senior Vice President introduces reengineering of MIT's administrative services (March).
1995	P-squares reengineering team formed under supplier consolidation to review Institute's publishing services (March). P-squares makes initial presentation to the Institute's Steering Committee (July). PubServ formed to proceed with redesign (August). PubServ makes second presentation to the Steering Committee (November). PubServ presents business plan to the Senior Vice President (December).
1996	Senior Vice President asks PubServ to proceed with transition to the Publishing Services Bureau (February). Bureau's Director begins work (October).

This presentation is a snapshot in time of important work in progress. The reengineering team responsible for the business plan considered the bureau's work to be a dynamic, learning process, in which brokers, vendors, and customers learn from one another, and evaluate their own and one another's work. Redesigning publishing services at MIT opens opportunities to improve quality and levels of service, while reaping business rewards. An especially intriguing aspect of this work is the application of theory to practice, reflected in the Center for Coordination Science's influence on rethinking both document and process in this practical application in its own backyard. Let's continue the dialogue!

Footnotes

[1]*Processs Innovation*, Thomas H. Davenport, Harvard Business School Press, Boston, MA, 1993, p. 66.
[2]Report of the Publications Services Review Group, MIT, February 1994
[3]For clarity, the text refers to the director. However, these important changes at Sloan were designed and implemented by a talented team of three communications professionals.
[4]Davenport, p. 72.
[5]Adapted from presentation by David Levy, Xerox PARC, 'Document Stability and New Media,' at the Center for Coordination Science workshop Rethinking the Document: New Ways of Creating and Sharing Information, January 1994.
[6]Rob Haimes, Managing Workflow and Content for Agile Publishing, *Color Publishing*, 1994, p. 29.
[7]The MIT Information Access Project (INFACS), Information Flow and Needs Analysis Study and Recommendations, Discworks Consulting Associates, Cambridge, December 1989, p.3.

20 PROCESS REDESIGN IN EDUCATION: THE CASE OF DOCUMENTS

Munir Mandviwalla and Anat Hovav

ABSTRACT
This paper investigates the use of process integration tools and techniques in education. We argue that process thinking is an important strategy for improving education. An adaptation of business process redesign to learning is presented. The paper focuses on the documents process by analyzing the use and role of documents in education. The potential benefits of applying electronic document management technologies to the documents process are highlighted. "Proof-of-principle" is shown in a case study classroom application of document process redesign. The results of the case study are reconciled with a follow-up case study that focuses on the views of administrators and faculty. The paper concludes by examining the implications of redesigning documents processes with information technology.

Introduction

To many the University is an institution of "higher learning," the "academy," a participant in the "global village." However, at the most basic level the university is a service organization. Society is demanding better results from this service organization. This paper presents an adaptation of Business Process Redesign (BPR) to higher education. BPR is the "analysis and design of work flows and processes within and between organizations" (Davenport and Short, 1990; p 11). BPR focuses on processes and uses of information technology (IT) -- the key enablers of change in information intensive service organizations. BPR thus represents an integrated and structured approach for analyzing and improving educational processes through IT.

The "process" approach is different from traditional efforts in education that focus on improving content. Moreover, there are fundamental differences in the assumptions and terminology of BPR and higher education. This paper adapts BPR to education. The adaptation is termed "learning process redesign" (LPR), (Mandviwalla and Hovav, 1996).

We first present a brief description of LPR as a general framework to study learning processes in higher education. There are three potential levels for applying LPR; interorganizational, interfunctional and interpersonal. The focus of the paper is the interpersonal level. Next, we emphasize one critical process in education -- document handling. The section describes both, document handling in general and in the classroom. Next, we outline the attributes of Electronic Document Management (EDM) and the role and impact of redesigning the documents process in education with technology. An in-depth classroom case study application of LPR to documents is presented. A second case study involving instructors and administrators focuses on the feasibility of redesigning educational document processes. The paper concludes with a summary of the potential effects of redesigning educational document processes with IT and future research possibilities.

Learning Process Redesign

Based on Davenport and Short (1990), a learning process is defined as "a set of logically related activities (informational and physical) performed to achieve a defined learning objective." Learning processes include an objective and learners. A set of learning processes form a learning environment. (Note: the term "learning" in this paper is analogous to "education" and should not be confused with the cognitive process of learning). Table 1 outlines generic learning processes and shows their relationship to business processes. Table 2 links the capabilities of information technology (IT) with potential learning benefits.

Tables 1 and 2 are applied in the remainder of this section to identify areas for redesign and brainstorm potential technology options. The individual ideas presented below are hardly new -- what is useful is the ability to consider and compare a large portfolio of ideas as part of an overall structured approach.

Interorganizational. Universities are typically self contained entities. They require very limited external partnerships in order to survive. Their main partnership is with their customers (students), alumni, governmental agencies, and funding agencies. However, the volume of these transactions may not be high enough to justify implementation of EDI and similar technologies. There are few linkages among universities. There are very few cross-university courses, programs, or research projects. Universities may need to form linkages in the future to survive funding constraints. They may also need to collaborate to meet demands for more flexibility. For example, Hamalainen et al. (1996) describe the educational brokerages of the future that will integrate educational organizations, publishers, training companies, accreditation institutions and students using the geographical, sequential/temporal, and informational capabilities of the Internet.

Business Process Dimension and Type	*Learning Process Dimension and Type*	*Examples*
Entities		
Interorganizational	Inter-university	joint courses across universities
Interfunctional	Inter-course	learning communities across courses
Interpersonal	Interpersonal	student-student, faculty-student interaction
Objects		
Physical	Learning equipment	loan out test tubes and notebook computers
Informational	Learning materials	distribute class notes
Activities		
Operational	Teaching	lecture, class discussion
Managerial	Administration	course scheduling, curriculum development

Table 1: Types of Learning Processes (adapted from Davenport and Short, 1990)

Interfunctional. Administrative and academic departments are typically independent entities in most universities. The pressure to streamline administrative work and contain cost is increasing the need for cooperation among administrative departments. Industry pressure for multidisciplinary training and research is increasing collaboration among academic departments. Administrative departments are trying to rationalize their existence and form links with others. Academic departments are exploring all types of linkages at the program, faculty, and course level. Administrative departments could apply the tracking and workflow capabilities of IT to streamline interfunctional processes and the disintermediary capability of IT to directly link faculty among departments.

Interpersonal. The focus of this paper is on the interpersonal level. Specifically, student and faculty interaction involving informational objects (course material) in operational activities (teaching) -- these processes are typically termed "classroom" activities. In higher education, an important determinant of success is the productivity of the customer (student) and the line employee (faculty) in creating the product (education). Consequently, a redesign of the faculty/student interaction should reap a high payoff. Focusing on high impact processes is consistent with the BPR approach (Davenport and Short, 1990). Moreover, it is the

IT Capability	*Learning Impact/Benefit*
Transactional	transform unstructured logistically difficult processes into routine transactions - automatic assignment of students into teams - workflow forms for selecting and assigning project topics
Geographical	transform information with rapidity and ease across large distances - distance learning
Automational	replace or reduce human labor in a process - programmed learning
Analytical	bring complex analytical methods to bear on a process - use of modeling and simulation tools for learning
Informational	bring vast amounts of detailed information into the process - digital libraries and databases - supplemental information
Sequential/Temporal	change the sequence of tasks in a process, introduce simultaneity - anytime anyplace learning
Knowledge Management	capture and dissemination of knowledge and expertise - intelligent tutors - sharing assignments for peer evaluation
Tracking	detailed tracking of task status, inputs, and outputs - keep track of readings, student assignments, teams - organize information
Disintermediation	connect two parties within a process that would otherwise communicate through an intermediary - direct electronic contact can reduce reliance on teaching assistants
Socio-Emotional	improve motivation - on-line learning communities

Table 2: IT Capability and Learning (adapted from Davenport and Short, 1990)

unique interaction among faculty and student that differentiate universities from other service organizations.

Figure 1 presents a general Learning Process Redesign (LPR) framework that meshes together the learning theory of Hills (1979), the computer mediated communication framework of McCarthy and Monk (1994), and BPR as outlined by Davenport and Short (1990) (see Mandviwalla and Hovav, 1996 for further details). The organization of the framework is a simple adaptation of other frameworks that follow a factor, process, and outcome structure. The key element that ties the framework together is the view of learning as a process. A learning process in this paper is defined as a set of logically related (informational and physical) activities performed to achieve a defined learning objective. The definition is based on Davenport and Short's (1990) definition of a business process. Learning processes include an objective and learners. Process thinking also leads naturally to a functional decomposition of educational processes where one can imagine decomposing a classroom into a set of interrelated processes such as:

A. Questioning. Starts when a student or instructor asks a question. The overall process usually involves a question, response, and then confirmation.

B. Discussion. A series of exchanges among at least two participants.

C. Documents. Prepare, copy, distribute (and collect) materials.

This paper focuses on redesigning document processes. Documents are an important learning tool in education. Documents also generate revenue when they are books, case studies, and articles.

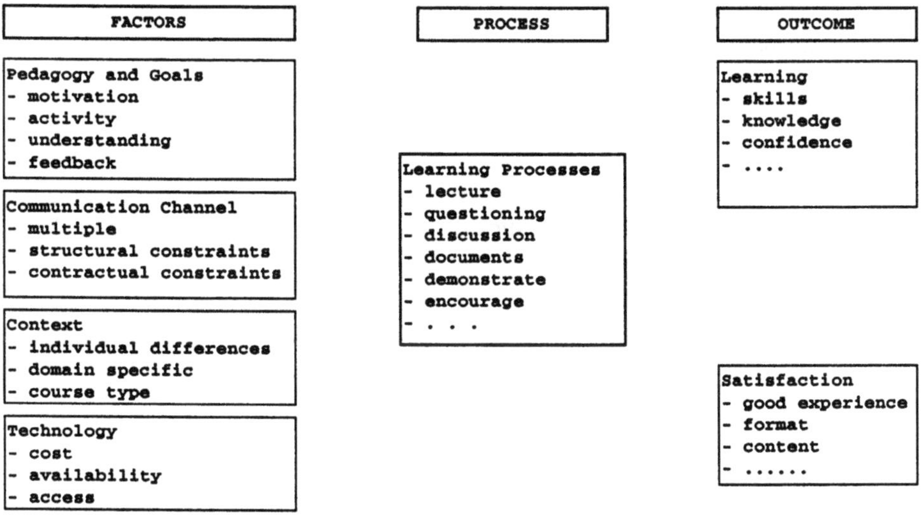

Figure 1: Learning Process Framework (from Mandviwalla and Hovav, 1996)

Document Processes In Education

Documents (Overall)

A document is "recorded information structured for human consumption" (Levien,

1989). US companies spend between $94 to $120 billion dollars a year to distribute, store, and process paper based documents (Skapinker, 1991). Document processing is a well-established topic in organizations and research. For example, document process redesign is routinely included in many re-engineering efforts. Researchers in workflow, office automation, and computer supported cooperative work and the emerging "electronic document management" area address document processing. However, document processing in educational organizations is rarely researched. A literature search on the topic revealed no usable references. This is surprising given that it is through documents that a major part of learning takes place. Document processing can be decomposed into the following activities:

- Creation
- Storage
- Organization and structure
- Transmission, retrieval and sharing
- Updates and manipulation
- Disposing

Documents used in learning are different from standard business documents. Table 3 outlines the key characteristics of educational documents based on Kind and Epperndahl's (1992) framework for analyzing business documents.

Attribute	*Documents in Education*
Growth	The total number of documents does not grow as rapidly as in other service organizations; there is a cycle of growth and then disposition in a session; most documents are distributed to external sources (students).
Updating	As new sessions start there is a high frequency of updating followed by a stable period until another session starts.
Origin	Most documents are generated internally (e.g., lecture notes); exceptions include supplemental material and books.
Layout Structure	Educational documents are less structured than most business documents. There is no pre-established key or a pre-defined format.
Legal	There are no legal requirements for maintaining documents or the length of time they should be kept or accessible to others; one exception is student's exams.

Table 3: Analysis of Educational Documents

Documents (classroom)

In the classroom faculty/student context, important documents include assignments, syllabi, reading supplements, lecture notes, and so on. A simple documents process involves the instructor creating the material, getting it copied, and handing it out to students. More complicated document processes such as assignments also involve the management of incoming documents from students. For example:

A) the instructor composes the assignment on their word processor,

B) prints it out and sends it for copying,

C) brings the copies to class and hands them out to students,

D) the student reads the requirements and works on the assignment outside or in-class,

E) the student prepares the assignment for submission,

F) brings it to class on the specified due date,

G) hands it in for grading,

H) the instructor evaluates the assignment,

I) assigns and records a grade,

J) brings the graded assignments to class, and

K) hands them back to the students.

Table 4 lists problems with traditional document processing in classrooms and potential redesign objectives. Several of the problems are discussed further below:

- **time** -- there is a significant amount of lead time required to setup a document such as getting it copied, waiting for the next class to hand it out, and so on,
- **no update** -- once the document is copied and handed out to the student it is difficult to update or clarify the content,
- **manage delivery-receipt** -- the instructor needs to manage the delivery of some documents, some students miss class and want to get the handout from the instructors office or the next week, some want it faxed to them, in other situations the student says they already submitted the assignment and the instructor has no record of it,
- **duplication cost** -- there is a cost involved in duplicating documents. This places a limit to the amount of supplemental materials that can be provided to the student, and
- **limited by medium** -- the process is automatically limited to material that the student can understand via written text on paper and tasks that can be submitted on paper.

Problems	*Objectives*
Lead time needed to prepare & distribute	Reduce the lead time needed to prepare, distribute and receive
Impractical to update documents that have been distributed	Provide up-to-date material Reduce document errors
Manage delivery and receipt	Track the delivery and receipt Reduce class time spent on delivery and receipt
File and retrieval time Duplication and storage cost	Reduce labor and cost involved in document's preparation
Medium of paper is limiting	Increase the richness of class material
Type and amount of feedback	Improve feedback providing to students
Difficult to share	Increase accessibility Increase sharing

Table 4: Documents Process Problems and Objectives

Electronic Document Processing

Electronic document management (EDM) technologies can be used to redesign and address the above process and information integration problems. Examples of EDM include FileNet, Canofile, Image Gen and MARS (Cooper 1992). According to Sprague (1995) the potential benefits of electronic document management include:

- Lower real estate cost for storage
- Improve communication
- Any time any place retrieval capabilities
- Distant collaborative work
- Improve productivity
- Improved customer service
- Improved quality of the information
- Preserving historical records

The following list presents generic advantages of redesigning the classroom documents process in higher education with EDM technology. The list is based on the basic geographical and sequential/temporal bridging, automational, analytical, informational knowledge management, tracking, and disintermediation capabilities of IT and EDM (see Table 2):

Storage
- No physical limits to the length of each document
- Reduce real estate and administrative costs such as filing

Organization and structure
- Electronic documents are programmable and can become interactive learning tools
- The richness of the medium may improve the quality of documents and feedback on student assignments
- Electronic documents can improve comprehension and readability by including multimedia such graphics, voice, video, and hyperlinks to other documents
- Living documents can be created such as a book that is continuously being updated

Transmission and retrieval and sharing
- Electronic documents provide an instant low cost typographic quality publishing medium
- Distribution channels outside the classroom
- Available any-time any-place
- Students are provided with a large number of documents without prohibitive copying expenses
- Increase the ability to conduct collaborative learning since electronic documents are easily shared
- Long lived discussions about documents can be recorded and shared on related technologies such as bulletin boards

Manipulation and updates
- Assignments are editable, allowing instructors to provide detailed and reusable feedback. For example, it is easier to broadcast a comment to all students. Electronic response is often more readable than a handwritten response
- Easy to track, search, and update electronic documents
- Compress the time needed to prepare and update material, resolve issues, and correct errors

Case Study 1 -- Classroom Implementation

Redesign and Technology

The documents process was redesigned using world wide web (WWW), electronic mail (Email) and bulletin board technologies. The World Wide Web provides a multimedia channel for distributing assignments and other documents. Electronic mail with file attachments provides an efficient channel for collecting and returning assignments. Bulletin boards provide a simple mechanism for discussing issues related to a particular document. These technologies are widely available for little or zero cost in educational environments. Traditional EDM technologies are costly and typically require significant infrastructure and human resources.

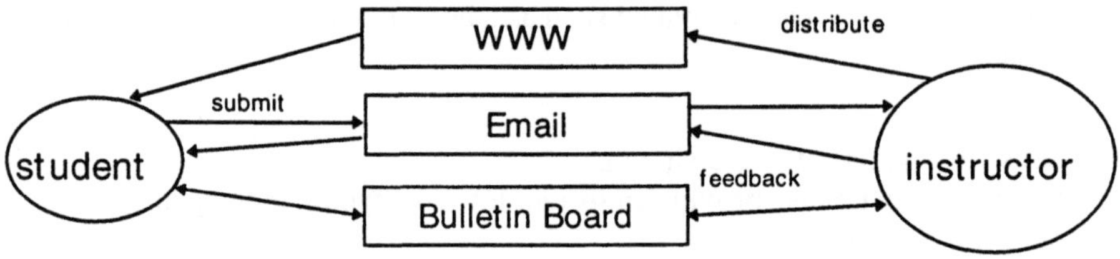

Figure 2: The Redesigned Documents Process

Activities	*Traditional Process*	*Redesigned Process*
Creation	Instructor creates a paper document	Instructor creates a document on the WWW
Storage	Documents are stored at the instructor's office	Documents are stored electronically
Organization	sequential	Hyperlinks
Transmission	Manual delivery in class	Available on the WWW any time any place
Retrieval	In class	Any time any place
Manipulation	Limited	Multimedia
Updates	Limited and costly	As needed at little cost
Disposition	Ad-hoc	Simple archiving and removal

Table 5: Redesigned Documents Process

Figure 2 shows the redesigned processes. Table 5 compares the activities of document management in traditional setting and in the re-designed environment. The instructor distributes static material on the WWW. Students submit assignments as Email file attachments. The instructor distributes grades and comments back on Email. Discussion about assignments and other class documents is conducted on a special Internet newsgroup termed the "bulletin board." Dynamic information such as changes in due dates, clarifications, and so on are broadcast by the instructor on Email and the bulletin board.

A consistent and easy to use interface was constructed to provide access to course materials (see Figure 3).

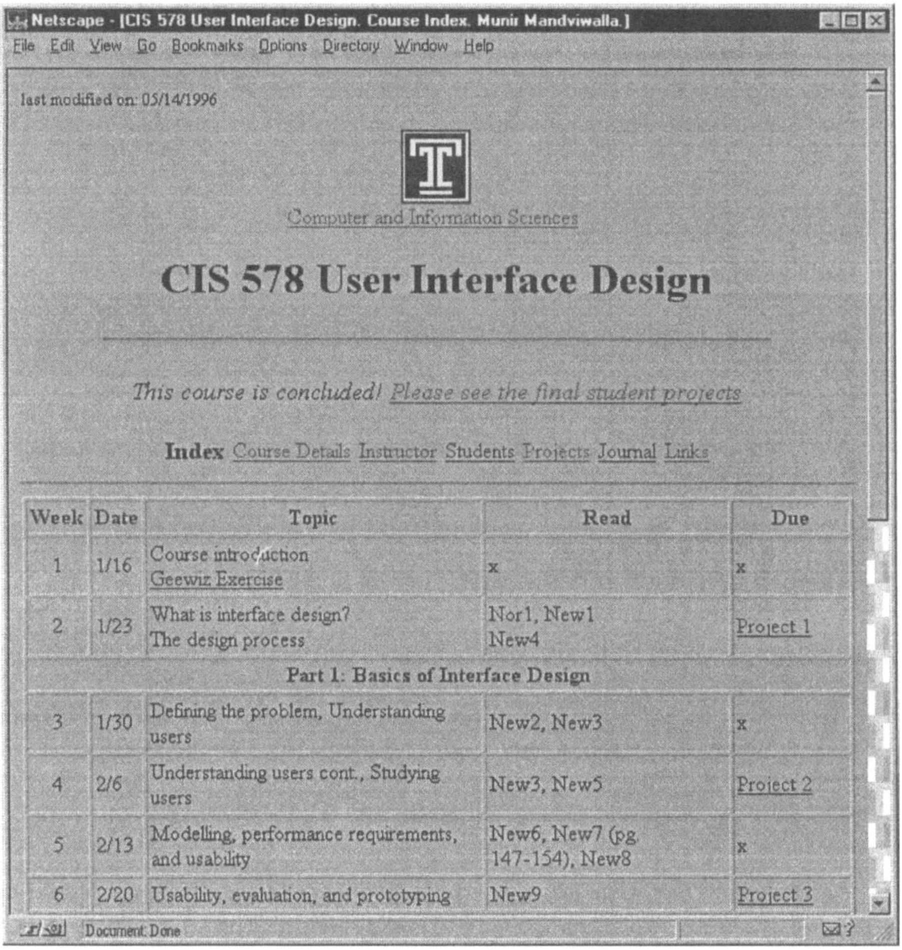

Figure 3: Sample Course Document

The course material was structured as follows:

- Index page (see Figure 3). A one stop entry point for all commonly used course material. Assignments are available directly by clicking on links on the course schedule.
- Custom menu. A pseudo menu structure that provides consistent and quick access to course information (see the line starting with the large type boldface word "Index" on the middle of Figure 3). This menu was repeated on every course page. The use of large type and boldfacing indicates the currently selected page.
- Update information. Every course includes a line at the top showing when it was last updated. This allows students to quickly check the update status of a page.

Other course documents include:

- Course details. "Syllabi" type of information (except for schedule, assignments and reading list). The goal was to place all relatively stable information on a document that students could print out and keep for reference.
- Instructor/Students. Information on the instructor such as contact hours. The student page includes names, Email addresses, pictures, and links to student home pages.
- Project/Journal. Information on projects and journal requirements.
- Links. A rated set of WWW links applicable to the class topic.

Procedure

The document process redesign was implemented between Fall 1993 and Spring 1996 and involved approximately eighty students in five undergraduate and graduate courses. The study captured multiple sources of data such as questionnaires, evaluations, protocol analysis, and log files.

The document redesign process was implemented in the courses using the following procedure. At the beginning of each semester, students were provided printed copies of the syllabus, introductory training on the WWW, and documentation on uploading and downloading files. Students were told that all further documents would be distributed on the WWW, all assignments were to be submitted through Email, and all feedback would be sent out on Email. Students were also encouraged to use electronic technologies to exchange documents amongst each other. The courses included several team projects.

Results and discussion

In this paper, we present an in-depth analysis of one advanced graduate course with eleven students (the results are consistent with the results of other courses). Overall, the students agree that the redesign of the documents process is useful because it helps in class preparation, the lead time is reduced, delivery/receipt is simplified, and documents are updated frequently.

Table 6 summarizes the data captured through questionnaire's, review of usage, and class materials. The remainder of the section highlights the more interesting aspects of the study.

Access. There was positive response to electronic access despite the fact that most students printed all the electronic documents and that only some of the documents made innovative use of the medium. It was the ability to retrieve documents from any place at any time without being limited to one physical location (the class room) at a given time (class meeting) that seems to have contributed to student's satisfaction with electronic documents.

Managing electronic documents. Managing electronic documents seems to be easier for both students and the instructor. However, they also seem to "slip through the cracks." Students had to be reminded repeatedly about assignment due dates. The concept of "contractual constraints" (McCarthy and Monk, 1994) may partially explain this phenomenon. When a physical paper document is handed to the student, it establishes an implicit understanding between the instructor and student that the document has been received and will be acted upon. Further automation of the process could solve some of these problems. For example, automatically sending reminder messages to students before a deadline and creating a formal on-line submission process for assignments so that receipt of a document is immediately acknowledged.

Update notification. Another problem occurs because on the WWW it is hard to keep track of changing information. About half the class (45%) felt that frequent updates made it difficult to keep track of material. Even though every course document included a label at the top, identifying when it had been changed. However, this still requires that students have to manually check course pages or that the instructor announces changes. Both solutions are problematic -- manually checking pages is a large burden while there is no guarantee that instructors will always remember to announce changes.

One solution is to use an automatic update notification system. A key problem is granularity -- students will need to be able to control when they are notified of changes and to prioritize the notification. For example, set the notification trigger based on changes to due dates, requirements, or other criteria. The document designer will need to use an advanced tagging system such as SGML to enable this level of sophistication.

Students. Students seem to like using electronic documents including electronic submission of assignments. The key issue for students is the ability to reliably access all the technology. There were frequent network problems during the study causing high levels of anxiety among some students.

Process Objective	*Result*
Electronic access is useful	95% agreed
Access helps prepare for class	73% agreed
Reduces lead time	All documents were available on-time
Delivery and receipt of documents	All documents were on-line
Provide additional documents	Links to 28 supplementary documents
Improve the quality of documents	- New type of assignments were created - 73% thought quality improved
Useful to update documents	91% agreed
Improve feedback	Students were provided on-line feedback
Assignments more challenging than other classes	73% agreed
Shift the responsibility of retrieval to the students	91% agreed
Useful to have course handout on WWW	91% agreed
Useful to have supplemental material on the WWW	100% agreed

Table 6: Documents Results[1]

Instructor. From the instructor's perspective, it is very useful to electronically distribute documents and supplementary information while collecting assignments through electronic mail. Any time any place access reduces the lead time needed

[1] All percentages are based on a five point scale where 1 = "strongly agree" and 5 = "strongly disagree." In the tables, agreed includes those who responded either 1 or 2, disagreed includes those who responded 4 or 5. Markus (1994) follows the same presentation strategy.

to prepare documents, the course can be fine-tuned on a weekly basis, and it is easier to track who has submitted what and when.

Technology. The technology used to implement the redesign in this case study is relatively primitive compared with integrated systems such as Lotus Notes. Several students had trouble with the cumbersome nature of the technology. However, the cost and accessibility of Notes and other sophisticated process integration tools is high. Most educational organizations already have access to WWW, Email, and bulletin board technologies. The tradeoff between integration and accessibility will hopefully disappear in the future.

Case Study 2 -- Administrator And Faculty Survey

The first case study is limited because the instructor was the same in each course, all the courses were on computing, and the subjects were computer literate commuters. To achieve truly generalizable results we would have to conduct a very large scale experiment and try to control for a large number of variables. Such a study will have to be done across universities, using the same technology and training in all the institutions involved and controlling for subject area effect and teacher effect. It will require the participation of many institutions, departments and classes. We do not believe it is viable to do this experiment and it may not be relevant in the first place. Any change in educational processes is highly dependent on the instructor. The results will vary on the instructor. A more pressing concern is applicability, i.e., is it feasible for other instructors and universities to apply the ideas generated as part of the research.

To check the applicability and feasibility of our results, the redesigned processes and related technologies were demonstrated to a group of administrators and faculty (8 administrators; 9 faculty). At the end of the demonstration, the group was asked to fill in a survey questionnaire. Table 7 summarizes the results.

Overall, administrators favored electronic document processing while faculty seem more cautious. Several faculty members were also concerned that using electronic documents will hinder disadvantaged students. Students that do not have access to the WWW at home or work will not benefit from the re-designed process.

Informal chatting with the group suggests that administrators are more familiar and accepting of process integration techniques and tools. This may have to do with more traditional office environment of administrators. In contrast, faculty are less familiar with "process thinking" and more aware of the difficulties of improving education. This is not surprising given that most efforts to improve education focus on improving content. To fully take advantage of process integration efforts universities may need to formally train faculty on "process thinking."

Process Objective	*Administrators*	*Faculty*
Reduces lead time	100% thought that preparation time will increase	66% thought that preparation time will increase
Delivery and receipt of documents	63% agreed on potential	50% agreed on potential
Improve the quality of documents	100% agreed on potential	78% agreed on potential
Useful to update documents	88% agreed that updates will increase	75% agreed that updates will increase
Improve feedback	87% agreed that feedback will improve	38% agreed that feedback will improve

Table 7: Administrator and Faculty Survey

Future Research

Our case study presents more questions than answers. There is a need to study the advantages and disadvantages of electronic feedback. This paper concentrated on one type of relationships, interpersonal. There is a need to study the use of electronic documents in interdepartmental and interorganizational settings. Is it viable to develop standard electronic communication among universities (similar to standard purchasing/invoicing developed by the retail industry)? Is there a need to develop electronic communication with granting institutions? If so, what technologies should be used? Further research is needed on the richness of electronic documents, the ability to create new types of documents involving assignments and reading supplements by integrating audio and video and text, and the ability and feasibility to produced customized class material.

Conclusion

Our experience with redesigning the documents process using IT leads us to suggest the following propositions:

1. Electronic distribution, collection, and discussion is more convenient than a paper channel because there are no geographical or temporal limitations

2. Electronic distribution and collection of documents will results in more frequent incremental improvements to class materials
3. Students will be able to access class materials much further in advance
4. There will be increased use of sharing of information
5. The length and depth of feedback will increase

The main contribution of the paper includes adapting BPR to learning, analyzing the documents process, and in demonstrating through "proof-of-principle" case studies that process integration techniques and tools can improve education.

References

Cooper, P (1992). New ways to DIP into information. *Accountancy,* 110 (1191), 62-63.

Davenport, T. and Short, J. (1990). The New Industrial Engineering: Information Technology and Business Process Redesign. *Sloan Management Review*, (31) 4, 11-27.

Hamalainen, M., Whinston, A. and Vishik, S. (1996). *Communications of ACM,* (39) 6, 51-58.

Hills, P. J. (1979). *Teaching and Learning as a Communication Process.* New York: Wiley.

Kind, J. and Eppendahl, F. (1992). The Need for Office Analysis in he introduction of Electronic Document Management Systems. *Document Image Automation,* 12(2): 31-35.

Levien, R. E. (1989) The Civilizing Currency: Documents and Their Revolutionary Technologies, *Xerox Corporation*, Rochester NY 1989.

Mandviwalla, M., and Hovav, Anat. (1996). Redesigning the Questioning, Discussion, and Document Processes. *Proceedings of ACM Special Interest Group on Computer Personnel Research Conference (SIGCPR),* Denver, April 11 - 13, 1996, 326-337.

Markus, M. L. (1994). Finding a Happy Medium: Explaining the Negative Effects of Electronic Communication on Social Life at Work. *ACM Transactions on Information Systems*, (12) 2, 119-149.

McCarthy, J. and Monk, A. (1994). Channels, conversation, cooperation and relevance. *Collaborative Computing*, 1, 35-60.

Skapinker, M. (1991). Warm for Form. *BYTE,* April 1991 p. 166.

Sprague, R. (1995). Electronic Document Management: Challenges and Opportunities for Information System Managers. *MIS Quarterly*, March, 29-49.

21 KNOWLEDGE WORKER SYSTEM FOR PROCESS INTEGRATION

Wayne J. Schmidt

The Situation

Complex and highly distributed organizations, as which the Department of Defense surely qualifies, depend upon their ability to integrate and execute the business processes. The vast majority of the Department of Defense's 700,000 civilian employees are involved in the day to day processes required to manage such a large organization. These processes are similar to commercial business processes. In both the Government and commercial sector, efficient and repeatable processes are key to quality decisions. In the commercial sector, business processes are starting to be considered a strategic business asset. In the government sector, Business Process Reengineering is an effective way to cope with fewer resources and deliver a product more efficiently.

The Federal Government is often criticized for not becoming more efficient. The General Accounting Office reported to the Governmental Affairs Committee that federal managers do not have the essential information required to perform their jobs, despite investing more than $200 billion on computers over the last 12 years. Senator Roth, committee chairman observed that:

> 'There is a more subtle issue here that needs to be highlighted--it is not enough to buy computing capacity. Modern organizational structures and management practices are required before computers can yield meaningful cost savings and capability improvements.'

Complicating the problem is that the business process is seldom static and even less so in this era of downsizing and rightsizing. In addition, new regulations and laws continue to force changes in key processes. In the case of the Army, the impact is significant.

> "The Army is undergoing its largest restructuring in terms of dollars, personnel, facilities, equipment and operations since 1945 ... perhaps in its history." (MG John Little, Chief, Assistant Chief of Staff for Installation Management).

The decline (25-30%, FY 92 -FY 99) in Base Operations resource levels and a commensurate reduction in manpower necessitates rapid implementation of new technologies as a mechanism for change. Thus, the Army is pursuing a goal of

> 'Complete installation-level process and functional redesign to off-set the impact of downsizing and continuing resource constraints.' (Installations: A Strategy for the 21st Century, page 16)

Success in this climate requires an ability to rapidly implement the results of Process Re-engineering and Improvement across Federal Government. Urged on by the National Performance Review and the Government Performance and Results Act (GPRA) of 1993 (PL 103-62), many agencies including the Army are embarking on Business Process Reengineering. Defining the business process including relevant guidance, documents and the information they contain and workflow is a critical part of Business Process Reengineering. Often, implementation of a new process structure or change in the organizational structure causes a loss of institutional knowledge. Chaos ensues until new processes are structured and inculcated into the organization. Resolving this chaos into a new shared articulation of the business process is essential to avoid loss of productivity and customers.

The ability to execute a business process depends upon a sound infrastructure. "Infrastructure" refers to those embedded services that allow the organization to perform its central mission and function. The primary effectors in the infrastructure are the managers and staff. They define requirements, allocate resources, review programs, analyze data, provide guidance, gather and disseminate information. Managers and staff normally do not perform the agencies primary function but rather provide essential support services. They do not deal in hardware or product but rather in *information*. They keep the information flowing and thus, the infrastructure effective. Managers and staff are therefore "knowledge workers," i.e., professionals who add value to a process or physical product through analysis and distillation of information in concert with the leveraging power of automated support systems.

A prime problem facing knowledge workers in execution of processes is 'What is the Process' and 'Where are the documents and referential material I need?' Traditionally, organizations deal with process problems via printed documents: policies, procedures, standard operation processes, regulations and guidelines. These documents attempt to specify WHO is to do WHAT, WHEN and HOW. In large organizations, like government, regulations attempt to insure consistent performance across widely dispersed organizational units. Regulations purport to print institutional memory; however, printed documents are, by their nature, limited in their distribution, currency and specificity. Filing systems were developed to handle documents. These systems were focused on 'operational' documents and did little to help knowledge workers.

The challenges

The current infrastructure presents the knowledge worker with a variety of challenges:

- Increasing number and complexity of tasks
- Exploding information volume
- Distributed decision environments
- Loss of institutional knowledge

The number and complexity of repetitive tasks is increasing. In today's automated environment, the information needed to make a decision is available, but only if the knowledge worker knows WHERE and HOW to access the information. It is typically located on a variety of computers, each with its unique operating system, applications packages, query structures and file formats. Remembering the steps to access information across these environments is difficult and error prone. In the past, clerical staff performed repetitive tasks such as updating letters and documents. Now, knowledge workers do this with computers and word processing systems.

Information is exploding in volume. Yet effective decision making demands the ability to correlate and evaluate information quickly and rapidly. The quantity of information is rising at an exponential rate (doubling every 10 years), but the ability to cope with this growing mass of information is rising linearly, at best. In addition, the complexity of organizations is increasing, especially in terms of interrelationship of functions. No longer can we classify decisions as "comptroller" or "personnel office." Knowledge workers must make decisions across traditional functional areas. This requirement necessitates access to information outside the traditional stovepipe information systems.

Organizational and decision environments are increasingly complex. The decision making process now requires more players, more information and more communication. Knowledge workers face both a cyclic set of tasks but also an increasing number of ad hoc tasks. These tasks, because of their high visibility and short term nature, tend to receive top priority. The longer range and once-a-year tasks fade into the background until their due dates are imminent. Shifting events and dates produce complex and dynamic schedules. The resultant changes are often "lost in the mail" and do not reach the knowledge worker until it is too late for an effective response.

Turnover of personnel is always an issue and a complex decision environment exacerbates the problem. A new knowledge worker may understand neither the process nor the product. A motivated knowledge worker will seek guidance from others, which causes a loss in productivity for the knowledge worker's tutor. Attempts to retain institutional knowledge through regulations and procedures are effective only when tasks are very specific and well defined. Higher order decisions are a value added function and not amenable to written procedures. In addition, keeping procedures current is difficult and expensive.

The objective

The objective of the Knowledge Worker System (KWS) is to provide a synergistic performance support environment that assists knowledge workers in fulfilling their responsibilities. KWS is not an application designed to perform a specific function but rather an integrated environment that interrelates existing applications and multiplies knowledge worker productivity within a complex task environment.

KWS is an automated tool that enables a work group to share an online model of the business process for both process execution and improvement. Using this on-line model, KWS reminds knowledge workers which tasks are due and when, details steps for task execution, provides easy automated access to the required documents, and links to existing automation systems. KWS will remind personnel WHAT tasks to perform and WHEN; the system will retain procedural information (HOW to accomplish) and automate many repetitive tasks. By enhancing productivity, KWS will free up personnel to do the creative and complex tasks in which humans excel.

The Knowledge Worker System will provide the following capabilities:

- Retain an on-line model of the business process and provide dynamic scheduling for organizational tasks.
- Capture and store institutional knowledge.

- Provide procedural information about what and when a task must be done and how it was historically performed.
- Provide a framework for attaching expert systems and other productivity tools.

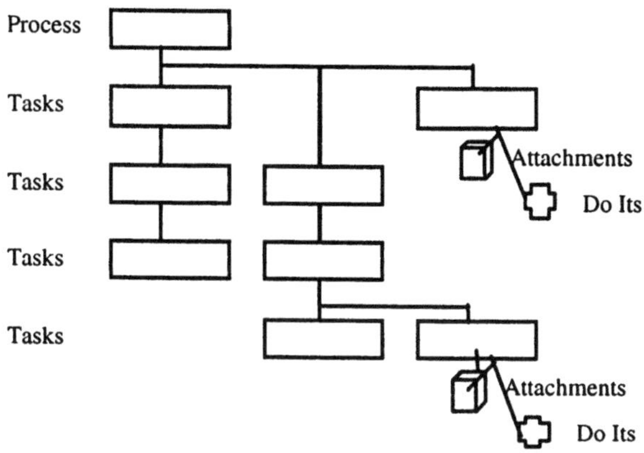

Figure 1. Hierarchical Process Structure

Model of Business Process

Knowledge workers' daily activities are dictated by pre-determined tasks that are part of a prescribed sequence of events, which lead to a completed product. Generally, higher headquarters determines the overall *process* and *calendar*; thus, the knowledge worker has little control of timing and due dates. The knowledge worker initiates actions, analyzes information and produces products according to the preset schedule. However, the process is not situated, but changes as regulations and business goals evolve.

This schedule, albeit preset, is subject to change. Changing the schedule is easy; determining the effect and notifying the *critical* knowledge workers is much more difficult. Task completion requires careful work planning, scheduling and coordination with related activities and a myriad of ad hoc tasks and meetings. Further, as the task progresses, it must be periodically re-planned, re-scheduled and re-coordinated. KWS will accommodate changes in the work schedule by reflecting their effects on related activities, adjusting due dates and providing information about the impact of the change.

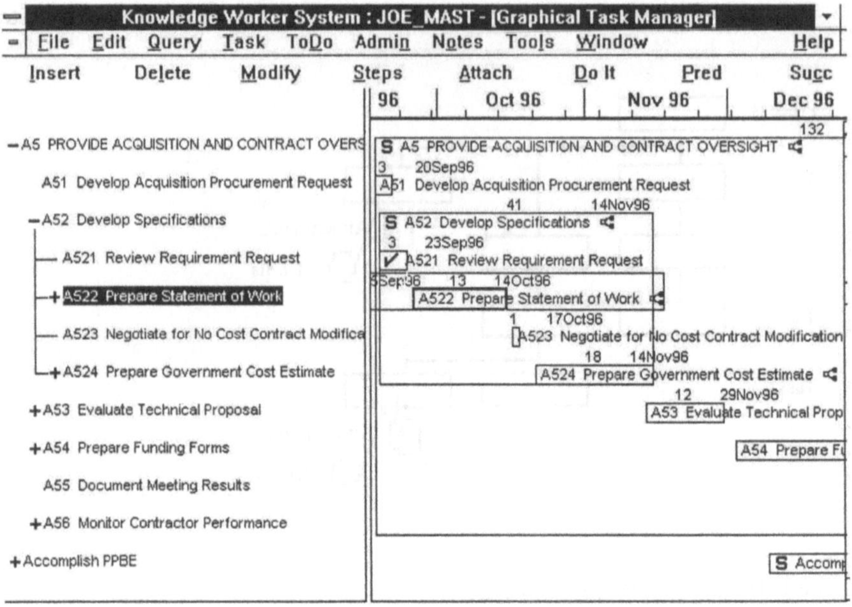

Figure 2. Process Representation

Process information within KWS is structured as a hierarchical model (figure 1). Each process has both an assigned organizational entity and a due date. As processes are displayed by organization, each organization has an immediate reference to their critical missions. In addition, each knowledge worker can see where their task fits into the overall process. Processes decompose into tasks which are assigned scheduling information and performers. Tasks can be further decomposed into addition levels of tasks. This decomposition continues until a task is a single unit of work completed by a single or group of knowledge workers in a given period of time. These are the tasks that appear on the *To Do* list. The process structure is more completely described in a USACERL Technical report 96/32, January 1996, Dynamic Task Scheduling for the Knowledge Worker System, by Brown, Sucur and Schmidt.

Each task can have steps. Steps are detailed context specific procedural guidance on the performance of a task. Steps are the mechanism to capture the organizational specific knowledge required for effective execution.

Processes and tasks are displayed by KWS in either a graphical or textual window. The graphical representation (figure 2) shows the task hierarchy on the left with a time scaled representation on the right.

Tasks are rescheduled by KWS and thus provide both a multi-user calendar and the ability to move tasks within boundaries and determine the effects of proposed changes. The scheduled tasks are presented to the knowledge worker in the form of a *To Do* list with a date due, a priority and other scheduling details. A calendar highlights the days when tasks are due.

Processes can be represented in three different formats depending on the type of process being modeled. 'One time' processes can be positioned at a particular point in time and when completed do not reappear. 'Cyclical' processes repeat in a periodic manner. For example, developing the budget for next year usually occurs at a particular time. A cyclic task is created by using a template and then cycles of the process are created. Changes to the template will be reflected in any new created instances. 'Ad hoc' processes are stored in *Task Palettes. Task Palettes* are defined for a variety of topic areas and process that relate to the area are placed on the *Task Palette* (figure 3). These tasks can then be dragged from the *Task Palette* to the *To Do* list or the hierarchical task structure to create new tasks.

Capture and Store Institutional Knowledge

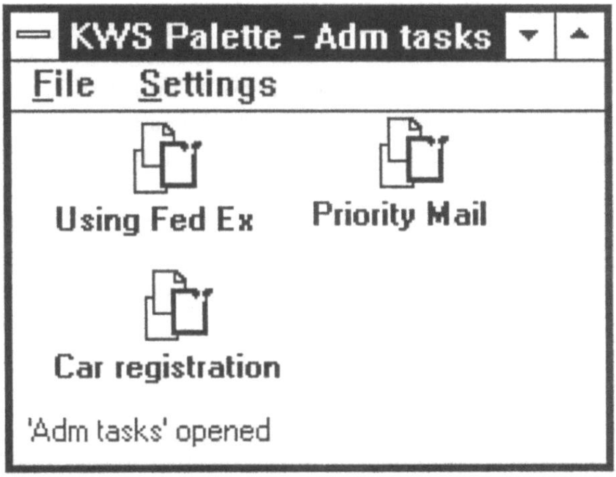

The capture and storage of institutional knowledge is critical to the success of KWS. Process description and task related documents are of particular importance in capturing institutional knowledge. KWS captures both of these aspects and integrated them into a task orientated methodology. The initial information regarding tasks, processes, steps and calendar information can be gathered and entered a variety of ways. A person who is familiar with the overall function or mission can observe job practices and capture those tasks and procedures. Each task is then assigned to a particular knowledge worker. There are a variety of Business Process Reengineering tools available in the commercial market. The difficult part is to capture task steps and products. This decomposition should be done as a natural by-product of the task performance, not as an added function.

'Document management' is a term used to refer to the storage, retrieval, tracking and administration of documents. The term originated with the use of manual file cabinets and has successfully move into the computer era. However, the concept relates to the management of documents outside of the business process that created the documents. Documents are classified into subjects, years, types, key words etc, but lack a connection to the process. In addition, many electronic documents, spreadsheets, animated presentations, databases, and embedded audio and video clips resist the conventional file cabinet approach. Often only the end artifact is stored. Later when questions arise, the back up documents are not available and must be recreated. Often at considerable expenditure of resources and energy. The present system of "paper storage" is not adequate to support a knowledge worker. Too often the paper record cannot be located. In addition, the document provides only the result, with no hint about the decision process, the base data, or the location of automated records. Simply saving data in machine readable form is not adequate. Finding the correct document among the hundreds or thousands on a hard drive is tough, finding the "right data" among the 200 diskettes left by a departing employee is a futile task.

The Knowledge Worker System integrates the processes with the information required to perform the process and the results of execution. This information is linked to the task that created it. Now, information retrieval is based on searching for the task ex *Develop Budget for 1997* rather than searching the c: drive. All the draft documents, spreadsheets and other information are readily available.

Documents are grouped into Attachments and are linked to the related task. If a task has documents, (figure 4) the attachment symbol appears to the right of the task. Attachments can be linked to any task or steps. Attachments can be any digital information created by some tool, ex referential, guidance, notes, spreadsheets, documents, presentations. The attachments are shown in the *Attachment* window (figure 5).

Documents may also be linked together to avoid duplicate storage of referential material and to provide for workflow between tasks. Each document creation creates both the document and a link form the task to the document. Subsequently, the document can be linked to additional tasks. Any modifications performed on the attachment becomes visible to all of the tasks to which the document is linked. The **copy** function allows users to create a new copy of the attachment and link it to the desired task. Any relationship to the previous link is removed and the use is the creator of the new document. Copying and linking are both subject to security permissions.

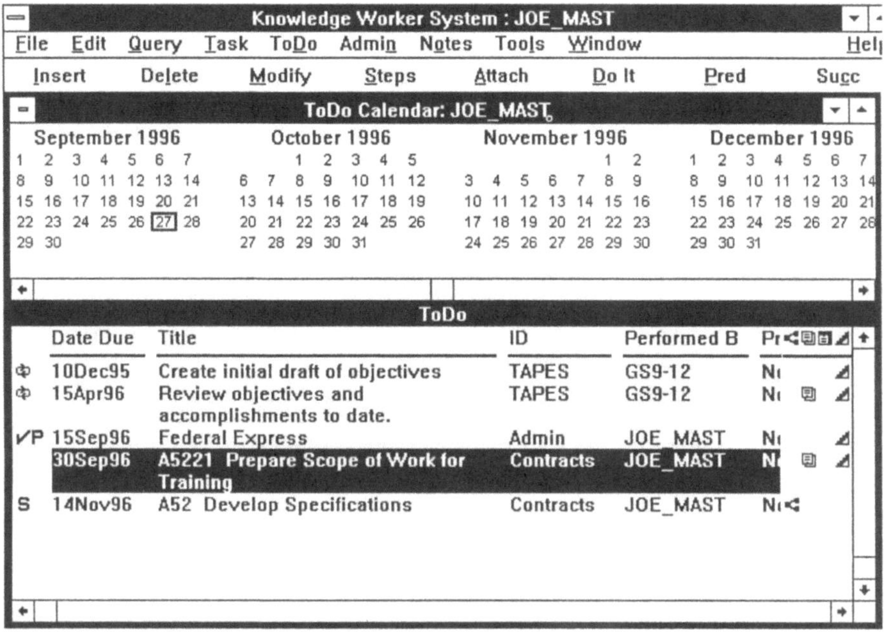

Figure 4. Task List with attachment icon.

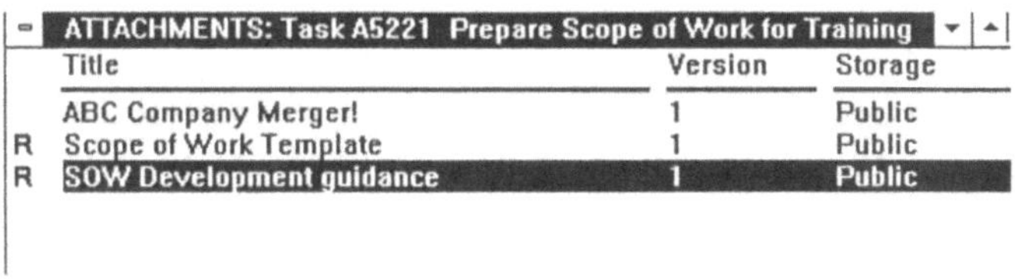

Figure 5. List of Attachments.

KWS provides the basic document access and management requirements. The requirements include support for document creation, storage, retrieval, tracking, security, media selection, versions and viewing. Document creation is accomplished by importing an existing document or creating from within KWS. As a document is created an Attachment Profile is created and stored. This attachmnet profile is shown in figure 6. This profile contains:

- Title
- Version
- Description
- Application
- Storage Type

- Attachment Type
- Context
- History
- Access Rights
- Links

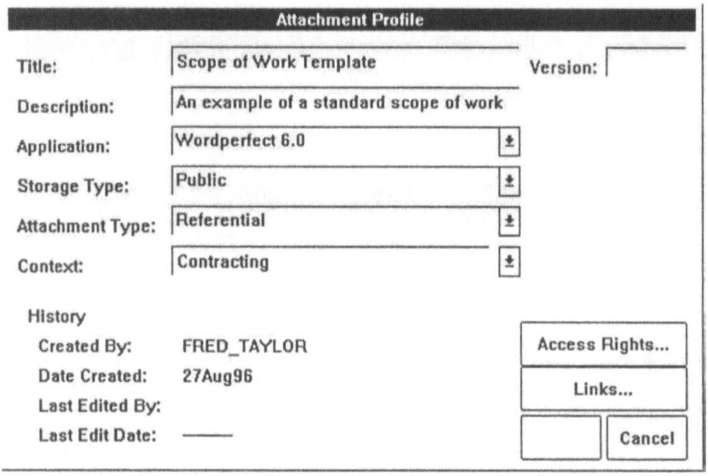

Figure 6. Attachment Profile

Title is a descriptive name given to the document. For an individual task the Title should be unique with Version numbers used to track copies. However, multiple attachments list may have the documents with the same title.

Version contains the version number of the attachment file. KWS provides the capability for users to quickly create new versions of a document through the Version option. When a new version is created, a copy of the attachment is made, the highest version number of the selected attachment is incremented by 1 and assigned to the new version of the attachment. The version creator will then be the owner of the new version which will be reflected in the **Attached By** field value. All other profile information remains the same and the user is no longer allowed to edit the **Attachment Title**. This restriction is imposed to maintain the relationship between the original document and its revisions. Allowing a name change would essentially change the attachment to a copy of the original not a revision.

Application identifies the tool used to create and edit the attachment. The users selects the Application value form a list of available applications.

Application share across a work group are identified with a common name and selected from a master applications list. This list contains information about the application and the command line to launch the application. Thus the knowledge worker can simply select edit from the button bar and the correct application is launched with the attachment as the target.

Storage Type identifies the storage location type of the attachment. The available values for Storage Type are public, private, or removable. Attachments with Storage Type **Public** are stored on the KWS shared file server on the local area network, storage type **Private** are stored on the user's KWS workstation, and **Removable** are stored on user designated removable media such as floppy or Bernoulli disks. The directories for Public and Private attachments are defined by the KWS system administrator during the KWS installation process. When an attachment file is designated as "Removable", the user is prompted to specify the drive and directory of the removable media for storing the file and 2) enter a description used to physically identify the media. KWS will then store this information and use it to assist the user in subsequent retrievals of the attachment For example, if the attachment file '*Training Plan for 1997"* is stored to the user's Bernoulli disk labeled *Training* in drive d:, KWS will display a message to the user requesting that they *"Insert Bernoulli disk titled Training in drive d:\" to retrieve the attachment file "Training Plan for 1997".*

Attachment Type identifies if the attachment is referential. Many attachments are used as guidance and are not changed by the user. Attachments with this property are labeled with an **R** preceding the attachment.

Context is used to assign a 'subject' property to an attachment. It can also be used to support existing standards for document management.

History provides information on the attachment usage. It includes the name of the knowledge user who created the link. This value is used by KWS to determine who has subsequent modify rights to the attachment's profile. If a user other than the one who created the link establishes another link to the attachment file from another task, the original creator will still maintain ownership of the link and will be the only one able to modify the attachment's profile. If another user makes a copy of the attachment file and links it to another task, a new attachment profile is created and the user copying the attachment becomes the creator. The date created and who last edited the file are also saved.

Access Rights indicates who has authorization to access the attachment. Current options are View Profile, Read/Copy, and Read/Copy/Edit. View Profile allows users to view the attachment profile, but not to access the attachment. Read/Copy allows users to view the attachment profile and read or to make copies of the original attachment. Read/Copy/Edit allows users full rights to view, copy, or edit the attachment as well as view the profile.

Links show the links that this attachment has to other tasks and steps. Additional information can be found in USACERL Report 95/38, September 1995, Document Management for the Knowledge Worker System by Kappes, Schmidt and Sears.

Provide Procedural Information

The procedural information about what, when and how a task was historically performed is a key element in KWS. The *To Do* list and calendar provide the initial information.

The scheduler furnishes the information central to the organization's goals and process. It provides a description of the task along with the steps required for performance. Each step can contain examples of documents and forms, references to regulations, historical notes and links to related steps in other tasks. The knowledge worker can easily modify the steps to incorporate new information. This process not only helps the current knowledge worker keep track of current progress but retains institutional knowledge. Humans tend to forget the details of tasks and when called on to repeat, must spend considerable time answering the question "what did I do last time?"

In many cases, the movement of a document is an integral part of a process and must be integrated into a performance support environment. KWS provides the ability to automatically move a document from a task to a successor task. It should be noted that the intent is not to provide a highly structured environment to push invoices through a billing process. Rather the focus is on knowledge workers who may spend days authoring a document and several days reviewing other's work. In addition, the number of documents may vary from one execution of the process to another, or the flow may change because of a change in guidance or process.

Additionally, many complex organizations have field units, each of which has the same basic set of operating procedures. Once a Knowledge Worker environment is established and the tasks/steps information captured, it can be mapped to a new location with only minor changes. Minor variations in the steps may require some customization but the basic step information, regulations, help information and products will be similar.

Provide a Framework for Attaching Productivity Tools

The Knowledge Worker System seeks to organize the efforts of knowledge workers. However, they still need access to the 'tools of the trade'. In many cases, this included access to email, the Internet, remote computers, databases and other applications not associated with documents. These types of applications can be linked to the applicable task. Again, this integrates the process and put the focus on process/task rather than tools/ applications. The linking of application to task is accomplished via *Do Its*.

Both tasks and steps can have *Do Its*. Pointers to other applications can be created and then linked to a task or step. The knowledge worker can then execute the application. *Do Its* can be Windows batch files, Visual Basic programs or simply links to existing applications. A complete set of dlls and vbxs are available for developers to communicate with the Knowledge Worker System. Thus a Visual Basic program can create new attachments and add them to the appropriate task or step.

Status

Knowledge Worker System (KWS) addresses the need for a highly intelligent, innovative system that will enhance productivity, capture institutional memory and reduce the stress on personnel that is prevalent in an event-driven, high-demand environment. Knowledge Worker System Ver 2.5 is complete and available for implementation within the Federal Government. An evaluation version is available by contacting the author.

KWS is implemented in the client server environment and is thus intended run over a local area network. Work is currently underway to expand this environment to include multiple servers over a wide area network. The process knowledge server is an SQL or ODBC relational data base with a client running under Windows 3.1. Documents are stored on a network file server or optionally a commercial file management system can be used. Microsoft Access is used for the evaluation version and can be used for small workgroups.

Several pilot projects are underway to test KWS and provide feedback into future versions. Initial estimates point to a 25% increase in productivity. We estimate that implementation within just the US Army, Corps of Engineers will result in an annual savings of $120 million.

22 WEB PUBLISHING AND CHANGES IN DOCUMENT PRODUCTION

Pål Sørgaard

ABSTRACT

With the current rapid diffusion of Internet and the World Wide Web, many organisations establish Web services and hence become providers of digital documents. Based on eight smaller case studies and theoretical work with dialectics, this paper discusses the organisational implementation of the World Wide Web among information providers.

A Web service typically takes its starting point in the current production of documents using conventional word processors. Creating a Web service results in a major extension of the chain of tasks related to document production. Current practices in document production are not necessarily well suited for this extension of the task chain.

Concepts from dialectics can be used to characterise systems development as construction, evolution and intervention. In an analogy to this interpretation, three approaches to the implementation of Web services are derived: technology oriented, tradition oriented and change oriented approaches.

Two of the cases, both from the Norwegian public administration, are clear examples of a tradition oriented approach, although both started in a more technology oriented manner. While this appears to be a typical course of evolution, those two cases also reveal important unrealised possibilities, indicating that the organisation behind the Web services probably have not found its final shape. Realising these possibilities involves a more change oriented approach. This observation confirms the relevance of applying ideas from dialectics to the use of World Wide Web.

Introduction

The use of the World Wide Web (Berners-Lee *et al.* 1994) has grown rapidly from 1994 to 1996 (American Internet User Survey 1996; Chon 1996; Pitkow and

Kehoe 1996a, 1996b). As a technology, The World Wide Web (or the Web for short) makes a distinction between information "consumers" (i.e., those using a browser) and information "providers" (i.e., those making information available on a server). For many organisations, this development represents a major change in document production. While word processing used to address the production of printed documents, word processing now becomes part of a longer task chain. The outcome of these changes is far from obvious, and is in itself an interesting phenomenon to study.

As observed by Blomberg (1988), different groups and different organisations may implement the very same technology in different ways. Analyses of the differences in the implementation of the Web may give us a better insight in the interplay between technology and the context where it is applied. The Internet and the Web represent a *common* infrastructure, and hence the electronic audience, other (possibly competing) organisations and political and social conditions may play a role (Star and Ruhleder 1994).

One language to talk about the use of technology, and its link to the context of the work, is the language of dialectics. Dahlbom and Mathiassen (1993) use dialectics to characterise systems development as construction, evolution, and intervention. This gives us a way to talk about different approaches to Web implementation. The contradiction between construction and evolution is important, and ways to handle that contradiction characterise different implementations. This paper applies these concepts to the organisational implementation (or just implementation) of Web services. Levy and Marshall (1995) discuss assumptions behind digital libraries, and come up with related criticisms of simplistic assumptions, while also criticising unreflected conservation of some features of current libraries.

Providing a Web service involves many people, directly and indirectly. Gasser (1986) uses the terms task chain and production lattice to describe integration of work and computing. Schmidt and Bannon (1992) work on similar ideas, addressing interdependent work and computing support for the extra work — articulation work — needed to make the collective efforts function smoothly. Both of these approaches are relevant when discussing the implementation of Web services.

The Internet and the Web have important limitations. The address scheme of Internet needs revision (Eidsnes 1994; Hinden 1996), a far from trivial problem. The functionality of the Web is limited compared to the potential of hypertext technology (Trigg 1996). In addition, important standards like HTML have not settled (Paoli 1996). This does not imply, however, that current use fully utilises the potential of the Web technology as it is today. Therefore, current use will be compared with some ideas for possible future development.

In summary, there are good reasons to study current use of the Web. This paper uses eight Scandinavian cases, a potential bias of the paper. The paper deals with two cases in more detail, both from public administration in Norway. Moreover, the Web services studied are all externally oriented services. There are no examples of so-called "intranet" applications studied here.

The next section gives a brief introduction to the Web and to digital documents. The following sections describe the research approach taken, including an introduction to the cases and to applied theory, and describe three approaches to the implementation of Web services. The last two sections discuss some issues in more detail and present some conclusions.

The Web and Digital Documents

While technology for producing and disseminating digital documents has been available for quite a while, it was through the rapid diffusion of the World Wide Web that this kind of technology became practically applicable to a large number of persons and organisations. The rapid emergence and acceptance of new job titles like "Web-master" and "HTML-programmer" are interesting pieces of evidence of this development. For an introduction to the Web, see Berners-Lee *et al.* (1994) or one of the many textbooks, e.g. Flynn (1995).

The Hypertext Markup Language (HTML) was initially designed as a language for *communication* on the net, deliberately designed so simple that computers as well as humans could generate it (Berners-Lee *et al.* 1994). As with other components of the Web, it was built using well-recognised standards: HTML is defined as an SGML (ISO-8879, Standard Generalized Markup Language, (see, e.g., van Herwijnen 1990; Travis and Waldt 1995)) Document Type Definition.

The Web supports a broad range of other kinds of documents than HTML. In this way, the digital document concept of the Web includes audio, video, graphics, etc. The core document representation is, however, HTML. HTML is understood by all browsers, and it is through the HTML syntax for "links" that the Web gets its hypertext capabilities.

HTML is an evolving standard. The first version was simple and left most of the presentation issues to the browsers. Later there has been a massive introduction of extensions for defining colour, size, background and formatting. These extensions are not supported by all browsers. Given the dominance of some vendors, some of the openness of the Web may get lost. This development is criticised, see, for example, Paoli (1996) and several articles available on the net[2].

Digital document technology increases the practical feasibility of "virtual" documents, documents generated "on demand" (observe, in line with Levy (1994), that this is a relative, not an absolute difference). The content of virtual documents may depend on when, where, and for whom they are generated. Virtual documents may look like static digital documents, but in fact be generated from underlying

[2] See http://www.yahoo.com/ Computers_and_Internet/ Software/ Data_Formats/ HTML/ Extensions/

information sources (Gruber *et al.* 1995). Digital documents can even contain executable code themselves, the documents becoming dynamic entities (Reinhardt 1994). These differences complicate document management. Authors are no longer in complete control of what readers view, making it harder to figure out what to write in the first place (Hendry 1995).

Currently there is a tendency to actually encode and *store* documents in HTML. In this way, the Web becomes a large collection of relatively static and preformatted documents. The potential of virtual documents remains unexploited in this way. In this paper we look into the implementation of the Web in some information providers, finding good reasons for this rather "conservative" approach. We also identify a potential for virtual, digital documents and for other technically and organisationally radical solutions.

Research Approach

The research presented in this paper rests on theoretical work and on a series of smaller case studies performed during 1995 and 1996 by the author, his students, and colleagues in the "Internet" project.

Eight Web services were analysed, through inspection of the services and interviews with people responsible for the services. Three cases are from public administration in Norway, two of these will serve as the main cases of the paper. We have followed the cases from public administration since they started (we still follow them), giving us a chance to look into the changes taking place over time. Three other cases were selected to get a picture of Web use in Scandinavian newspapers. Finally, a library and a public transport organisation were selected as they were so clearly different from the other cases.

In the "Internet" project we have developed a Web service. We did this primarily, of course, to disseminate our results, but also to get experience about possibilities and difficulties.

The main point in this paper, however, is the development of theory. The theory presented is inspired by the cases as well as by studies of dialectics. We observed quite early that many services started as initiatives in the DP departments, while control later passed over to units responsible for information or public relations. It also became very clear that several organisations deliberately took a careful, even conservative, approach, with heavy focus on reliability and responsibility, and with less emphasis on technical ambitions. These observations called for a dynamic theory, a theory that could help us explain the changes and better understand the forces behind the process.

Overview of cases

For ease of reference each case is here given a short presentation and an acronym.

PB is a major public bureaucracy, consisting of several large independent units. Most employees have PCs, using AmiPro, Microsoft Word and WordPerfect for word processing (for more details about this case see Braa and Sandahl (1997)). In 1993 PB introduced e-mail for most employees, and in 1995 PB launched a common, externally oriented Web service. This service is considered politically important. The Web service is operated by a newly established unit within the section for documentation in the department for common services. The Web unit receives documents for publishing via electronic mail, on floppy disks, and sometimes on paper. Documents (i.e. files) are normally received from the authors, but large publications are often obtained from a print shop.

SR is a major public institution for statistics and research. SR produces a broad range of reports, ranging from widely circulated yearbooks, via quarterly magazines and weekly newsletters to a large number of reports and research papers on various specific topics. SR has its main office in the capital and a secondary office in "Skogby" 100 kilometres away. Johansen and Myklebust (1996) have made a detailed study of the early history of the Web service in SR.

GI is a government information office, providing information to the public and advising other government offices on their information policies. GI runs an experiment whereby so-called mail journals (i.e., indexes of incoming and outgoing mail) are made available on the Web to a selection of newspapers. This service can be used to glance through the journals, just as looking through the physical copies of the same journals in the press centre of GI. One aim with this service is to provide rural newspapers with the same information as newspapers based in the capital.

JP, **GP**, and **DB** are newspapers in Denmark, Sweden and Norway, all running Web services. JP runs an extensive news-service for paying subscribers, GP runs some of its news and a lot of classified advertisements, and DB runs a "network tabloid" with some new services. These cases are described in more detail by Eriksen and Sørgaard (1996) and by Eriksen (1997).

TI is a prototype of a transport information service run by a regional public transport company. The service finds optimal connections between any two stops at a given time. Development of this service stopped for financial reasons in the autumn of 1995 and the service ran unchanged one year later.

CL is a computing science library using the Web to provide traditional library information with technically advanced solutions: a separate server has been programmed to interface the library database to the Web. All customers of the library have access to the Web service, and customers and library staff all use e-mail (Hegna 1995).

Concepts from dialectics

In their discussion of the nature of systems development, Dahlbom and Mathiassen (1993, 1997) apply the dialectical scheme of thesis, antithesis and synthesis. As an example of this kind of analysis, they propose three characterisations of systems development, namely as construction, evolution and intervention.

Systems development seen as construction expresses the view that the problem of the development project is given, and that the main challenge is to handle the *complexity* of the problem. The role of the users, if recognised at all, is to provide information and approve decisions (Dahlbom and Mathiassen 1993, ch. 4).

In the evolution approach to systems development the problem is still seen as given, but the main challenge is *uncertainty* about needs, rather than the complexity of the solution. Hence trying out solutions and listening to users become important. "The decisive move from construction to evolution is when you give up deductive rationalism for an empiricist, inductive, experimental approach" (Dahlbom and Mathiassen 1993, p. 108). The challenge is to develop and adapt the technology to fit with *current* work practices.

Seeing systems development as intervention recognises that systems development is not separate from the life of the organisation. Systems development is part of organisational change, and is subject to organisational games, co-operative as well as opportunistic behaviour, and is also subject to the *contradictions* and *conflicts* of the context of the development process. The role of the systems developer easily becomes that of a change agent (Dahlbom and Mathiassen 1993, ch. 6). Changes may come early or late, but denying the interventionist nature of systems development is naive. Dahlbom and Mathiassen exercise some care, however, to warn systems developers against always working as dialectical thinkers, analysing conflicts and bringing contradictions into the open. Development work will in this way be in constant turmoil and it will be hard to know when a computer system can be delivered (Dahlbom and Mathiassen 1993, p. 69).

Production lattices and interdependent work

In his analysis of the integration of computing in everyday work, Gasser (1986) uses the concepts of task chain and production lattice. Gasser's work is based on the use of grounded theory (see, e.g., Strauss (1987)) and the application of the concept of articulation work (see, e.g., Strauss *et al.* (1985)). In a complex set of tasks we can choose to pick out sequential task chains. In work these chains intersect, and a complex, co-ordinated structure of intersecting task chains is referred to as a *production lattice* (Gasser 1986). Schmidt and Bannon (1992) discuss many of the same concepts, addressing *interdependent work* and the role of articulation work therein.

While the work with this paper has not applied grounded theory, the concepts of production lattice and interdependent work are extremely useful to talk about the organisation of work behind a Web service. In all cases but CL, the Web service is run by a separate unit, and the server is a separate machine outside the network of the user organisation. Thus, authors are dependent on the Web units to get their material on the Web. The Web units depend on the authors to deliver texts, and their work is highly dependent on the quality of the delivered text with respect to ease of conversion to HTML. Possible developments like providing documents with links and producing virtual documents from databases provided by the authors, will lead to further interdependencies between Web units and authors.

The complex set of tasks behind a Web service can naturally be described as a production lattice. We can use the shape of this lattice as a way to express ourselves about the organisation of work behind the service. Innovative uses of Web may require changes in the lattice far away from the Web units, typically affecting those producing text in the first place.

Approaches to Web implementation

In this section the concepts of construction, evolution and intervention are used to characterise how organisations implement Web services. The concept of production lattice is used to describe and *symbolically* illustrate the differences. The common legend to these illustrations is in Figure 1.

Figure 1: Kinds of tasks

Technology orientation

When the idea of systems development as construction is applied to Web implementation, focus is on issues like setting up connections, getting the server running, and how to compute the information to be provided. Less emphasis is put on the organisation or on the needs of the supposed consumers of the information. The case of TI is a good example of this kind of Web service. While the service does a good job in searching for optimal connections, it falls short in ordinary usability. As an example, it is of little help when the traveller misspells the name of a stop. Moreover, it will only give the times for one connection, quite inadequate for travellers who do not know exactly when they will leave or who risk to get delayed. The underlying technology is quite advanced, and the "deficiencies" of the service can be explained by the origin of parts of the design: some of the routines were originally designed for use from cellular phones. Another example is the popular name service of SR, where it is possible to check how many people in Norway carry a specific name. The answers are provided by searching a static file extracted from the national register, not on searches in the register itself. The connection to the underlying work of keeping the national register up-to-date is very weak.

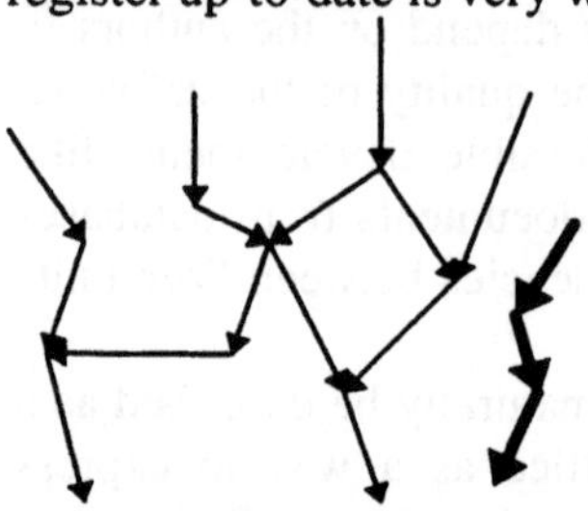

Figure 2: Production lattice of technology orientation

In this paper, this is referred to as a *technology oriented* approach, characterised by innovative services which only to a little degree are adjusted to meet the needs of the consumers of the information. A typical weakness of this approach is its lacking connection to the work in the organisation. The document production lattice is not only unaffected, there is practically no connection between the Web service and the production lattice (see figure 2). We all know the result: lots of outdated Web pages. The main strength of this approach is its ability to focus on the potential of the available technology: offering services which do not have counterparts on traditional, paper based services.

Tradition orientation

Seeing systems development as evolution directs the focus towards aligning the Web service with the current document production lattice, making current material available electronically, and making sure that there are proper editorial routines to ensure that what is made available on the Web is indeed material which is supposed to be released.

The three newspapers, JP, GP, and DB, provide services similar to their paper editions, with little impact on the document production lattice. The journalists write as they are used to, and the Web units pick their material from the ready to print electronic copy of the paper (Eriksen and Sørgaard 1996). This is referred to as a *tradition oriented* approach to the implementation of Web services.

The Web unit in PB has little control over the shape of the documents it receives, making them available on the Web on an "as is" basis, taking whatever steps which may be needed. As often as possible, automatic conversions to HTML are performed. This does not always work (this depends on the use of document templates and their paragraph styles; styles are often overseen (Sørgaard and Sandahl 1997)). In extreme cases, documents have been retyped by personnel at the Web unit. Nearly the minimum of what is needed to get documents on the air is done. Little is done to equip documents with an appropriate hypertext structure, with internal links as well as appropriate links to other documents. In practice, authors have no simple way of including links in the documents they write. Moreover, PB has an explicit policy of being careful with links to other sources, mainly to avoid references to incorrect or "unsuitable" information.

The story at SR is quite similar. There is a wide variety of material available from SR's Web service, most of it identical to printed reports. Since early 1995 the weekly newsletter is available on the Web at the same time and with the same contents as the printed newsletter, the text for the Web copy being captured from the material which goes to the printer. SR is consciously striving for a more and more "mature" service.

At a few occasions the Web service of PB has been able to provide reports before printing. This has stimulated debate on important political issues, and also drawn attention to the new medium. SR has released a statistical report where most of the tables are only available on the Web.

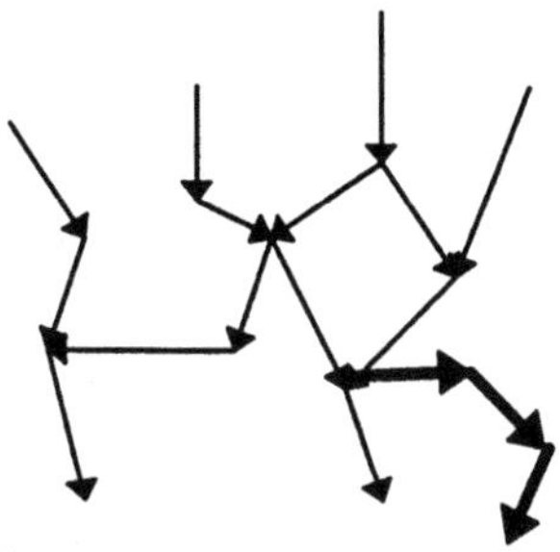

Figure 3: Production lattice of tradition orientation

In terms of production lattices, this approach can be described as the Web units hooking into the existing production lattice, with no other changes to the work organisation (see figure 3). The units responsible for the Web services in PB and SR appear as appendices to the existing organisation (Braa and Sandahl 1997). We made a similar observation in the study of the three Scandinavian newspapers (Eriksen and Sørgaard 1996).

The main weakness of this approach is its conventional services, resulting in an under-utilisation of the potential of the technology. In its extreme, the Web services offer nothing which is not also available on paper, reducing the Web to an alternative (and often secondary) distribution channel. With this approach there is often a lot of extra work being performed to provide the contents of the service. Still, the positive aspects are important: the services have a basis in the policy of the organisation, making it clear that the services are official and trustworthy. Moreover, in this approach maintenance and future availability of the services are considered important.

In total, SR, PB, and most of the other cases are strongly tradition oriented, in the services they provide and in the way work is organised.

In a dialectical discussion it is important to emphasise the contradiction between the technology oriented and tradition oriented approaches. There is no simple way of combining the technical creativity of "Web-hacking" with the serious information policy of newspapers or of public administration. Uncontrolled mix of the two could easily result in a wide variety of designs, pages not being maintained, dead links, and other problems often encountered in private home pages. From the point of view of an information policy, this would not be acceptable. There is also a considerable risk that a lot of time would be spent by individuals learning HTML and developing their own pages. Moreover, such a mix would only be feasible if everybody had access to the server, which in some cases could result in intolerable breaches of security and data integrity. Therefore, if we accept that the case organisations in question implement the Web in order to provide serious services and not to do exploratory tests, there appears to be a lot of sense in aligning the services with the ordinary information activity, thus ending up as tradition oriented services.

Change orientation

As said above, there is a contradiction between the technology oriented and tradition oriented approaches, with no simple compromise in between. The synthesis, parallel to intervention, is a *change oriented* approach to the implementation of the Web. A synthesis in dialectical terms supersedes or overthrows the contradiction between thesis and antithesis, in this case through a change process where work organisation and technology are mutually aligned in a way which allows new services and more benefit of the technology. A change oriented approach represents a third alternative which provides something qualitatively new compared to the two other approaches. Such an approach is clearly more radical, implying changes in technology and in work and responsibilities of many people. The document production lattice is changed. Tasks related to authoring and tasks related to Web publishing will be intermixed, perhaps end up being seen as different aspects of the same tasks. Some tasks may become obsolete, and some new may be needed. These different changes are illustrated in figure 4. Such changes may create conflict and resistance. There will be costs and increased interdependencies between tasks. There is no claim in this paper that a change oriented approach always is to be recommended, but it is stated that it is only through this approach that the possibilities of the technology can be fully realised.

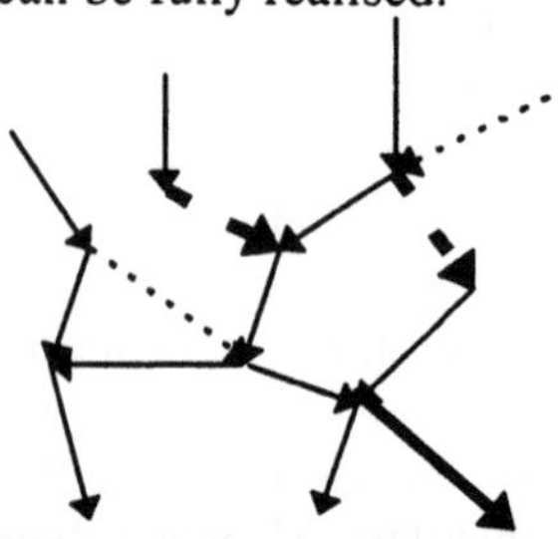

Figure 4: Production lattice of change orientation

It is hard to find clear cut examples of this approach, but CL may serve as a moderate example. Due to the way the university organises its libraries, CL has a computing scientist with training in librarianship in its staff, thus overcoming the traditional divide between technology oriented and content oriented personnel. The Web is used to provide traditional library information with technically advanced solutions: a separate HTTP-server has been programmed to interface the library database to the Web, resulting in up-to-date information about books, whether they are available for loan, etc. Several traditional functions of a card-index are implemented: having found a book it is easy to find all other titles by the same author. Ordering literature is integrated with search, so that all relevant information from the search is brought over to the order, resulting in higher quality orders, and library staff spending less time fixing incomplete orders. Reminders are automatically generated and sent via e-mail: If nobody has reserved the book, the borrower can renew the loan by simply replying to the reminder message (no need to enter any text). The library staff reports that the volume of work in the library has not declined. The customers have become more aware of the library's services, and consult the library staff for more advanced queries than before. These changes are not only due to the Web, it is the other way around: it is the smooth integration with existing infrastructure (notably e-mail) which makes the new solutions possible.

Discussion

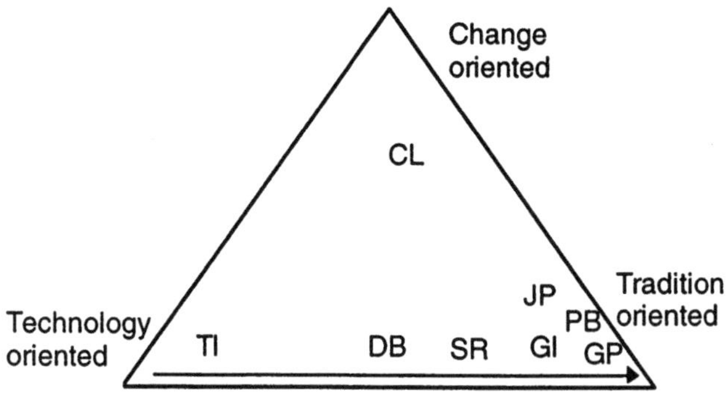

Figure 5: Classification of cases

The three approaches to the implementation of Web services span a wide variety of alternatives. Clearly, most of the case organisations have taken a tradition oriented approach, as has been illustrated in figure 5. There are good reasons for this choice of approach, but still there are some issues that need to be discussed. In this section two issues will be brought forward: the history of the services and the challenges they are facing today. Doing so we can better appreciate the dominance of the tradition based approach as the *current,* but not necessarily permanent, approach to the implementation of the Web.

History of early adoption

In all cases but two (CL and GI) the initiative to start the service came from the DP department or from some external event. In SR the founding event was an initiative from an access provider suggesting that SR's information would be suitable for the Web. The access provider helped in establishing the service. In TI a major upcoming sports event created a certain euphoria with respect to implementing modern technology. In the newspaper JP the people behind the paper's "computer club" had set up a Web service to provide software to its members; this service has later grown into the paper's official electronic edition.

The exceptions are interesting too. In CL work had been going on to develop an electronic customer interface to the library for 2–3 years. When the Web became available it was soon decided to switch to that technology, as the Web supported the concept of a common electronic information service at the department and since most concerns over different platforms were handled. In GI the Web was selected as user interface for the second test of the service. A previous test of a similar system had been conducted, revealing several problems related to the establishment of an inter-organisational system for low volume use running on solution specific technology (Kluge 1994).

Given the way many of the services started, it makes sense that the responsibility for the services in an early period rested with the DP departments. In both PB and SR there was an explicit, somewhat conflict-laden, shift in responsibility away from the DP departments to departments with responsibility for information or documentation. Later things settled, and there is now a smooth co-operation between DP and Web units. For both SR and PB the role of the service as an official information channel is emphasised.

The cases reported are all from organisations where the Web was first implemented in a time when the technology still was relatively unknown. This may have impacted the way the Web was adopted. Today, everybody has heard about the Web, there is an abundance of popular writing, and there are many tools. Therefore, we should be careful when generalising from the cases mentioned. Future implementations of the Web may follow a different pattern.

Emerging changes

While an analysis of the current implementation of the Web in PB, SR, and several of the other cases results in an understanding of the reasons behind mainly tradition oriented approaches, we should also be aware of some emerging signs of change.

One important disadvantage of a tradition oriented approach is the cost of converting word processing files *as they are made today* to HTML. In SR and PB there are attempts to impact the use of word processing. The use of relevant document templates is encouraged and it is called for awareness of possible Web publishing of the documents. Within PB, authors of large documents that will be published on the Web are encouraged to contact the Web unit beforehand.

Within PB and SR, some documents are printed by external print shops. The manuscripts of these documents are normally passed on floppy disk to the printer, where they are marked up (typically in SGML). There are often important, last minute corrections to these documents. Such corrections are made to the copy in the print shop and not to the various source files of the document, be they word processing, spread sheet or other kinds of files. As a result, a correct electronic source of the document is not available. In the beginning the Web unit in PB duplicated the corrections in their copies of such files. Now they receive documents from the print shops to better handle late corrections in documents (Braa and Sandahl 1997). This has expanded the interaction between the Web unit and other units involved in the document production lattice, calling for increased integration of technical solutions. Similar developments take place in SR, where the production of high-quality (in terms of layout and accuracy) numerical tables is close to the *raison d'être.*

SR has started development of a facility for interactive access to statistical material, a sort of "statistics on demand" derived from databases authorised for this kind of use. This represents a move towards use of virtual documents (Gruber 1995).

Unaddressed challenges

In spite of emerging changes, there are several issues that are not addressed by the current services.

Today, the possibilities of the medium do not get realised, not in terms of providing access to background material (through links to relevant sources or to otherwise unpublished material), nor in terms of providing public insight into the administrative processes of public administration. Interestingly, one public committee in Norway (working on personal integrity issues) used the Web to interact with the public. The Web pages of this committee were not, however, located on the service of PB, but on a server operated by the University of Oslo.

The practical limits of the Web are different from those of paper. The limits set by a printed weekly newsletter do not have to apply to articles on the Web. Why should such articles have to stick to the length constraints, possibilities for colours and graphics of a newsletter? Why should there be a weekly production schedule? Would it not make sense to include links to relevant data files as well as other articles on the same topic? Such topics can only be addressed when authors are aware that they write also for a new medium.

Today, a journalist searching in the electronic mail operated by GI can request a copy of interesting documents. The responsible organisation checks whether the document can be released, and then sends the document to the journalist. Most documents can be released, but the principle is that release of a document should be decided at the time of request, not when the document is produced. When most documents exist in electronic versions, an attractive solution would be to make the documents themselves, and not only the mail journal, available on the Web. This would require, however, a change in principles for public insight in public administration.

Taken together, these issues entail major challenges to the organisations. They demonstrate the unrealised potential of the technology, that there are difficulties in using the Web precisely as previous media. In the long run one may question the relevance of services that give little or no extra information compared to what is available on paper. The issues also demonstrate, however, that realising the potential entails major, and expensive changes to the organisations and to current information and publishing policy. This is the core of the problem, and the main thrust of a dialectical analysis of the cases.

Although the Web has become widely used, it has not found its final shape. We have, for example, seen rapid changes in the capabilities of the more widespread Web browsers, and we have also seen major changes to HTML, some standard, and some as proprietary extensions (see, e.g., Paoli (1996)). Implementing the Web will therefore not be a single shot process, instead it will be like chasing a moving target.

Conclusions and Further Research

Most of the cases studied have implemented their Web services in a tradition oriented approach, aligning the technology to fit with the current work organisation while not fully utilising the potential of the technology.

Concepts borrowed from dialectics are useful in this context. They help us appreciate the contradiction between technology oriented and tradition oriented approaches. The theory helps explaining the current implementations as sensible, conservative compromises dealing with existing forces and with uncertainties in the technology. The theory also addresses the shortcomings of these compromises, making the potential and possible consequences of change oriented approaches clearer to us.

Dialectics is a dynamic theory. Current compromises are "current." There is every reason to expect changes. The exact nature of these changes cannot be predicted from a discussion of this kind, but it seems clear that there is an immense potential in integrating Web publishing with ordinary document production, and hence radically change the scope of ordinary word processing. Emerging signs of changes in this direction have been observed. How this work will be organised is, however, an open question.

The discussion in the paper calls for further studies. Cases of change in document production should be studied in order to reveal patterns of change as well as deficiencies of the technology. Change-orientation may require new practices in development of the services. Systems development techniques should be evaluated in this context. Well-designed prototypes could help exploring new possibilities and also help communicating ideas for changed work organisation.

As stated, the development of HTML and other parts of the Internet may impose decisive uncertainty, stimulating the selection of tradition oriented approaches. At the same time, HTML is inadequate as a format for document representation in some of the cases studied (e.g., in the case of statistical tables). Other formats for document representation need to be evaluated and tried out. Moreover, the possible impact of changes to HTML should be studied to give information about the impact of different kinds of standardisation processes.

Finally, most of the cases presented here started with a rather technology oriented approach. Future adopters of the Web could be followed up to see if this pattern remains or disappears as the technology has become more well known.

Acknowledgements

While nobody but the author should be held responsible for any deficiencies of this paper, I deeply acknowledge the contributions of my students and colleagues. My students Bjørn Magnar Myklebust and Bent Østebø Johansen did a great job with SR, so did Anders Vindvad with GI. My colleagues Kristin Braa and Tone Irene Sandahl have worked with PB. The studies of the newspapers were done together with Lars Bo Eriksen. Tor J. Larsen and Kristin Braa helped me shape the paper. Bo Dahlbom stimulated and participated in several discussions about the use of dialectics to describe approaches to the organisational implementation of the World Wide Web.

This work was supported by the Swedish Transport & Communications Research Board (Kommunikationsforskningsberedningen) through its grant to the "Internet project," http://internet.adb.gu.se/.

References

The American Internet User Survey: New survey highlights. Technical report, Emerging Technology Research, 1996. http://etrg.findsvp.com/ features/ newinet.html.

Tim Berners-Lee, Robert Cailliau, Ari Luotonen, Henrik Frystyk Nielsen, and Arthur Secret. The World Wide Web. *Communications of the ACM,* **37**(8):76–82, August 1994.

Jeanette L. Blomberg. The variable impact of computer technologies in the organization of work activities. In Irene Greif, editor, *Computer-Supported Cooperative Work: A Book of Readings,* pages 771–781. Morgan Kaufmann, San Mateo, California, 1988.

Braa and Sandahl. Standardization and flexibility in the distibution and exchange of documents, 1997. In this volume.

Kilnam Chon. Internet inroads. *Communications of the ACM,* **39**(6):59–60, 1996. Introduction to special section.

Bo Dahlbom and Lars Mathiassen. *Computers in Context: The Philosophy and Practice of Systems Design.* Blackwell, Oxford, 1993.

Bo Dahlbom and Lars Mathiassen. The future of our profession. *Communications of the ACM,* **40**(6):80–89, June 1997.

Håvard Eidsnes. Practical considerations for network addressing using CIDR. *Communications of the ACM,* **37**(8):46–53, August 1994.

Lars Bo Eriksen. On the limited impact of network publishing — three cases of Internet news publishing. In *Proceedings the 30'th HICSS,* Hawai'i, January 1997.

Lars Bo Eriksen and Pål Sørgaard. Organisational implementation of WWW in Scandinavian newspapers: Tradition based approaches dominate. In Bo Dahlbom et al., editors, *Proceedings of the 19th Information systems Research seminar In Scandinavia,* pages 333–349, Lökeberg (Göteborg), 10–13 August 1996.

Peter Flynn. *The World Wide Web handbook.* Thomson Computer Press, London, 1995.

Les Gasser. The integration of computing and routine work. *ACM Transactions on Office Information Systems,* **4**(3):205–225, July 1986.

Thomas R. Gruber, Sunil Vemuri, and James Rice. Virtual documents that explain how things work: Dynamically generated question-answering documents. http://WWW-

KSL.Stanford.EDU/ people/ gruber/ virtual-documents-htw/, 1995.

Knut Hegna. The University of Oslo's informatics library and the World-Wide Web. *VINE*, (99):24–31, June 1995. Theme issue on the World-Wide Web in Libraries.

D. G. Hendry. Breakdowns in writing intentions when simultaneously deploying SGML-marked texts in hard copy and electronic copy. *Behaviour and Information Technology*, **14**(2):80–92, March–April 1995.

Eric van Herwijnen. *Practical SGML*. Kluwer, Dordrecht, 1990.

Robert M. Hinden. IP next generation overview. *Communications of the ACM*, **39**(6):61–71, 1996.

Bent Østebø Johansen and Bjørn Magnar Myklebust. World Wide Web i offentlig tjenesteyting: Dokumentasjon av en tidlig innføringsprosess (WWW in public service: documentation of an early introduction process). Master's thesis, Department of Informatics, University of Oslo, August 1996.

Anders Kluge. Offentlige elektroniske postjournaler i pressen (Public administration mail journals used in the press). Report 886, Norwegian Computing Center, Oslo, December 1994.

David M. Levy. Fixed or fluid? Document stability and the new media. In *Proceedings of the European Conference on Hypertext Technology'94*, pages 24–31, Edinburg, 1994.

David M. Levy and Cathrine C. Marshall. Going digital: A look at assumptions underlying digital libraries. *Communications of the ACM*, **38**(4):77–84, April 1995.

Jean Paoli. Extending the Web's tag set using SGML: The Grif Symposia authoring tool. In *Fifth International World Wide Web Conference*, Paris, May 6–10 1996. http://www5conf.inria.fr/ fich_html/ papers/ P18/ Overview.html.

James E. Pitkow and Colleen M. Kehoe. Emerging trends in the WWW user population. *Communications of the ACM*, **39**(6):106–108, 1996.

James E. Pitkow and Colleen M. Kehoe. WWW user surveys. Preliminary results, Graphics, Visualization & Usability Center, Georgia Institute of Technology, 1996. http://www.cc.gatech.edu/ gvu/ user_surveys/.

Andy Reinhardt. Managing the new document. *BYTE*, **19**(8):91–104, August 1994.

Kjeld Schmidt and Liam Bannon. Taking CSCW seriously: Supporting articulation work. *Computer Supported Cooperative Work (CSCW): An International Journal*, **1**(1–2):7–40, 1992.

Pål Sørgaard and Tone Sandahl. Problems with styles in word processing: a weak foundation for electronic publishing with SGML. In *Proceedings the 30'th HICSS*, Hawai'i, January 1997.

Susan Leigh Star and Karen Ruhleder. Steps towards an ecology of infrastraucture: Complex problems in design and access for large-scale collaborative systems. In Richard Furuta and Christine Neuwirth, editors, *ACM 1994 Conference on Computer Supported Cooperative Work — CSCW'94*, pages 253–264, Chapel Hill, October 22–26, 1994. ACM Order Number 612940.

Anselm Strauss, Shizuko Fagerhaugh, Barbara Suczek, and Carolyn Wiener. *Articulation Work*, chapter 7, pages 151–190. The University of Chicago Press, Chicago/London, 1985.

Anselm L. Strauss. *Qualitative Analysis for Social Scientists*. Cambridge University Press, Cambridge, 1987.

Brian E. Travis and Dale C. Waldt. The SGML Implementation Guide: A Blueprint for SGML Migration. Springer, 1995.

Randall H. Trigg. Hypermedia as integration: Recollections, reflections, and exhortations. Closing keynote, Hypertext'96. To be published.

23 PAPER DOCUMENTS: IMPLICATIONS OF CHANGING MEDIA FOR BUSINESS PROCESS REDESIGN

George L. Roth

'I loved the tactile nature of work in the 20th Century,' said Jean, a senior document technician, in an anthropological study of insurance workers in 2016. A smile was on her face, and her eyes cringed with the bittersweet memory of the times as she fondly reminisced. She told of how she was connected to her work in ways that are different than today. Jean, now nearing 50, started as a customer service representative in 1990. She remembered, 'I miss the paper. We used to have a sense of our customers. We did what was important to them.'

Introduction

Office settings in the 21st Century will undoubtedly take on a different character from what we see today. The development of computer and telecommunications equipment over the past four decades allows almost unlimited options for organizations in creating new working arrangements. The predominant use of paper as *the* media for recording, storing and transmitting information is now giving way to new electronic forms. Not only is information technology providing faster access to, and easier routing of documents, it is enabling new approaches, such as workflow mapping, task sequence optimization and flexible worker scheduling. These innovations are likely to dramatically change the nature of work. Yet, current trends are paradoxical — the paper industry reports record use of its parchment as managers and workers wonder they improve work in a new electronic world.

Foretelling the future of work through an understanding of the conditions preceding a paperless offices was my interest as I undertook this ethnographic study. ·In 1990 I began a study of two insurance companies replacing their paper documents with electronic images while reengineering the associated business process (Roth, 1993). Understanding a paperless office involved observing transitions from a paper-based environment and capturing the thinking and actions of people as they created a new office landscape.

This paper describes the transition from paper documents to electronic images at Dover Service Company and Harwick Insurance Company.[1] Both companies reengineered business processes as they moved paper document information onto networked computer systems. To provide a context for what happened, I briefly review imaging systems technology, reengineering change strategies and the research approach used in this study. For each company I review their background and describe strategy formulation, technology selection, preparation, implementation and outcomes for the use of imaging systems in one business process. I conclude this paper with considerations for how organizational conditions determined, and were reified by, a change process combining new technology with physical work requirements to influence what business improvements were achieved.

Document Image Management Systems & Reengineering

Computer-based document image management systems are a combination of imaging, data entry, computing, display, communications, mass storage, printing, and software technologies. Input, in addition to keyboard data entry, is done by scanning papers to create digital bit-mapped images. Specialized programs scan, store, display and route imaged documents. Local area networks transmit these images so that they can be displayed on people's desktop workstations. Optical disk jukeboxes store and provide access to millions of imaged documents. Today's imaging systems makes the "paperless office" envisioned decades ago by futurists (Toffler, 1980) a current reality.

Devices for producing, reproducing and storing documents have long influenced communication and control in work places (Yates, 1989). Many office activities, such as sequential hand-offs and routing of documents, are based on the physical and material characteristics of paper. These historical approaches and activities have created linear, time and labor intensive processes. Existing organizational processes can be reconsidered once paper-based information is available in digital form:

[1] All names of people and companies are pseudonyms.

> *Only a minute amount -- perhaps as little as 2% -- of all "information" handled by companies today exists in digital, computer-manageable forms. The vast untouched remainder -- letters, documents, drawings, contracts, shipping information, photos, and more -- continues to accumulate on desks only to be carted away by truckloads to rows of filing cabinets and micrographic departments (Booker, 1990: 67).*

Office workers are expected to more easily perform routine functions using document image management systems. For example, they can simultaneously work from the same document, access files without searching records rooms, automatically track work, and monitor document access.

Organizational changes are needed to achieve maximum benefits from this new technologies. Former professor Mike Hammer (1990) calls for "obliterating, not automating," the way work is done. "Business reengineering," a term popularized by Hammer and Champy (1993:32) is the "concept of fundamentally changing the way work is performed in order to achieve radical performance improvements in speed, cost and quality." Consultants use phrases like "radical redesign," "quantum leaps," and "fundamental rethinking" to characterize the ideals of business process redesign. These ideals are part of the change strategy at both Dover Service Company and Harwick Insurance Company.

Research Methods and Sites

Dover Service Company and Harwick Insurance Company both make extensive use of paper documents. Image management systems were expected to reduce the tedium of handling paper documents. In initial interviews I found executives, managers, technologists, and workers at each company unanimous in their expectations for business improvement and better working conditions.

My research spanned more than one year of intensive on site, participant observation. Figure 1 presents the time line for the technological change process and research activities at both companies studied.[1] Field work started in March of 1991, shortly after each company had selected TopImage systems, and several months before these systems were installed. I immediately began observing work practices so that I could compare them to what unfolded. Although I studied numerous uses of imaging systems at each company, I focus on the description of two business process changes in this paper — new accounts forms in Dover's Processing Department and title and ownership assignment forms in Harwick's Customer Service Department.

The work in the companies and business processes is similar. Work involves processing paper-based information, responding to customers' telephone inquiries, and performing activities on mainframe computer systems. The two departments are paper-intensive areas where service capability, speed, and efficiency are considered important. Table 1 provides a general overview and comparison of

Dover and Harwick. The two firms are similar in terms of work and new technology and differ in terms of management style, training practices and implementation methods. Given the similarities in these two firms, the influences of management style and technology implementation practices on outcomes can be discerned. Understanding the influences of management style and implementation practices requires examining company backgrounds before proceeding to business process changes. Dover Service Company and its change processes are described first, followed by changes process at Harwick Insurance.

Dover Service Company

Dover Service Company, a subsidiary of Dover Insurance, manages mutual fund investments. Dover Insurance established the mutual funds subsidiary in the 1960's to provide clients with additional investment options. The company had been profitable until the "black Monday" stock market crash in October of 1987. At the end of 1988 a new CEO was appointed. He is a twenty-year veteran of Dover Insurance, having held top financial management positions. For the two prior years he was Dover's Chief Information Officer. His recent success in achieving business improvements with technology influenced him positively towards "those young tigers that ... use PC's, and are willing to try new things."

As he took the helm of the mutual funds operations, the new CEO consolidated investment and retail operations from separate locations into a new building. He also expanded operations by starting new divisions to attract investment brokers and to service new, non-Dover Insurance customers. The business plan was to double assets in three years by expanding to outside the existing customer base, improving service, and acquiring other mutual fund companies. Investment in information technology was a central part of a strategy for integrating and improving administrative operations. To improve service, work performed by outside companies was moved in-house. Customer service and administration work was to be handled by a newly created subsidiary, Dover Service Company. In May 1990, shortly after it was formed, an experienced executive from a competitor was hired as Dover Service's president. A start-up staff of fifty included internal transfers, new hires and people from the previously contracted outside companies. By the end of the calendar year Dover Service employed one hundred people, and a year later it grew to one hundred and fifty employees.

In my initial interviews managers described Dover Services as a new organization unencumbered by entrenched operating modes. They emphasized a service quality approach, making special efforts to motivate and reward staff for service initiatives and frowning upon adherence to bureaucracy and rigid rules. Managers described the company as unique because there were only four levels between president and workers, half the number which other companies had. Technologists and executives conceived the organization as having a clean slate for providing the best possible customer service. Managers and workers discussed participative decision-making, and valued a team approach. Workers did, however, express some skepticism. They were hired with promises of a new customer-oriented approach, but at least initially, they found themselves performing the same tasks in the same ways that they had in previous jobs. Workers eagerly awaited advanced technologies, including document imaging systems, that would improve working conditions. The Processing Department is representative of the work and changes Dover Services undertook.

The Processing Department

The Processing Department handles customer, insurance agent and investment broker documents. There are two managers, each of whom is responsible for three teams of four or five account specialists. Each of these teams has an appointed team leader who distributes and checks on work. Team leaders are knowledgeable on all transactions, while account specialists may only be familiar with two or three transactions types.

Approximately one thousand documents arrive daily. The mail room brings them to a mail desk throughout the day. Account specialists are assigned, on a rotating basis, to sort, time stamp, and log incoming documents. Documents are sorted into batches of similar types, counted and placed in holding baskets. Team leaders get and distribute the batches to the account specialists.

Account specialists are assigned to teams, and team members sit in adjoining office cubicles. The corner partitions where adjoining cubicles meet are at a lower height making it easy to converse and exchange documents. Account specialists often help one another with various transactions, in part because it is cumbersome to switch functions on the MFA system. For example, when setting up a new account on the MFA system it is not easy to perform a "look-up" function on another account. Account specialists would call out, "is anyone in look-up?" and another worker would respond and do what is requested.[2]

New Account Forms

New account forms is what was later chosen as the first business process to improve using imaging systems. The flow of work and use of computers in this process (see Figure 2) is typical of paper-based processing work.[3] Many work procedures used at Dover Service are based on what was done at the contract companies that had previously done the work. People hired those companies, both managers and workers, instituted procedures they were familiar with. The reasoning for why things were done the way they were could not always be explained by the workers who performed them.[4]

Imaging Systems for New Account Forms

After a TopImage system was selected, a phased approach[5] was planned that called for seventy percent of all paper documents be imaged and electronically routed with one year. The phased approach provided a framework for the business process change and system development plans.[6] Technologists asked that managers consider scenarios for "rolling out" the imaging system and propose improved work flows. As managers raised questions (about project scope, clarity on long term direction, understanding the effect on workers, and accessing MFA systems) technologists dismissed these concerns, telling managers that these issues would be worked out. Technologists wanted systems were to be "brought in and used without changing the normal course of business."

Technologists' activities included analysis of existing paper documents processing methods, specification of TopImage features to be utilized, business process change recommendations, and software programming to govern system functioning. They expected imaging systems to provide benefits as work flow software were combined with work changes, however, they believed *any* use of the imaging system would provide improvements over existing paper-based methods.

Managers were interested in how work would be done using the imaging system. They expected benefits to come from the process changes that became possible with the new technology. As technologists studied paper document processing, managers also wanted them to propose immediate improvements. Technologists, however, focused their data collection and analysis efforts on specifications for work flow software.

As technologists worked with the imaging system, they wanted to select a single function as a focus for their efforts. Managers did not want an imaging system for only one function. One manager said, "the real issue will be separating out the types of work that are handled on the imaging system and the types of work that continue to be done with paper." Managers wanted the imaging system to manage all documents, not automate single functions. Technologists responded, "it doesn't matter as much which one we do, but [that we] start with just one function first." In the plan under which the TopImage funding was approved, technologists committed to delivering a work flow program by a particular date (August 1). The only way to meet their deadlines was by focusing on a single function.

Although technologists conducted preliminary analysis to determine which function they should start with, the one function approach influenced subsequent activities. In the analysis, technologists promoted their own interests by carefully managing the information they provided managers. Managers were responsible for operational business results; imaging documents was just one of many initiatives they were involved in. As technologists took charge of the imaging project, managers complied as it was one less thing for them to worry about.

Technologist's analysis started by documenting existing work flow. They expected that "there would be efficiencies gained by [using the imaging system to] just moving the information faster."[7] Spurred on by project schedules, technologists sought to quickly obtain the information they needed to begin programming. Managers appointed a worker team. This team was to provide information, map out the overall work flows, propose changes, and help determine the needed imaging system features. Working with a team, however, took more time than technologists had anticipated. Technologists were concerned that the worker team's goals of process improvement by mapping and analyzing work flow hindered their implementation plans. They did not want to take the time, or see the need, to educate a team on imaging system capabilities. It was their role to determine business improvements through imaging technology:

> *I have been brought in to implement a system, and that is the goal I need to work toward. If we are not implementing, I am not doing my work. We can't spend the time to be creative and just think about how work might be done in the future, we need to have something implemented according to schedule.*

One technologist expressed concern that "things not get out of hand with being creative." He actively limited creativity in order to move the mapping team along.[8] As the mapping team's efforts proceeded, technologists directed team members to think about automating, rather than altering, work:

> *We want them to think about this in terms of an automated solution. It may be that they don't want to change anything... Automation itself makes it better. There are two opportunities for change -- automation and change in work... The objective and process are two different things.*

The technologists' manager wanted to implement the imaging application quickly to learn from the experience. He responded to managers' improvement desires by saying that they preferred analysis to decision-making. He would not allow project schedules delays because the workers had regular work to do and could only meet a few times a week. With an unmoveable deadline, managers allowed the workers to meet daily.

When work flow maps were completed, alternative imaging system uses were discussed.[9] In a meeting of technologists with executives and managers, the decision was made to focus imaging efforts on new account forms. A consulting firm had completed a work flow study for regulatory purposes six month's earlier. The consultants' proposed changes were to be used. Technologists were to stop querying workers and develop program specifications using the consultants' recommendations. Managers and the mapping team were to review the consultants' report, and if they wanted changes, they could make them only by getting the consultants to alter their report.

As technologists followed this mandate, one commented that, "it seemed like a three ring circus."[10] Although the introducing change was cumbersome, these directions moved implementation forward, as indicated in the following technologist's comment:

> *It is clear what I have to do, and there are deadlines for me to meet. If I have a problem, I go to [the project manager] and the way in which it is resolved is clear. We didn't have that before... I hate to say this, but if I waited for the business people to decide what they should be doing, it would have taken a long time.*

During the two weeks that followed, technologists worked twelve hour days, locking themselves in a conference room. Only basic imaging functions for new account processing could be programmed to meet deadlines. The work flow application would use only new account forms for non-retirement accounts received with a single check. These specifications limited the imaging system to being used on only ten to twenty percent of the one hundred and fifty new account forms received daily.

The technologists' manager reviewed the work flow program specifications before they were shown to managers. The new design basically mirrored existing the paper-document procedures (see Figure 3).[11] Managers wanted more features, and proposed delaying the implementation. Technologists refused to delay implementation. As software was finalized, technologists, wanting to interact minimally with workers, asked that only one team be trained on the new system and that mail room people separate out new account forms with single checks. Managers chose the team of four account specialists and team leader they considered best able to adapt to new working methods. Account specialists were enthusiastic, they said being chosen to work on the imaging system was prestigious. Also, the relief from repetitive processing of paper document was appealing.

Technologists created a fanfare when the system was first used. There was a ribbon cutting ceremony with the Dover Service President, and a presentation and demonstration as the first documents were scanned and processed on the imaging system. On the first day of operation, fifteen forms were processed. A number of errors were encountered. While account specialists were at lunch, technologists fixed several errors and installed updated programs. More complicated problems were also discovered.[12] These problems disappointed managers, as did the fact that the system handled only a small percentage of documents.

The work flow system impact on Processing Department work was not beneficial. The ability to inquire into new accounts was not useful because so few forms were processed on the system. A department manager raised concerns that technologists needed to immediately add more capabilities, otherwise, "the system will get the reputation of being a joke." The system was slow and account specialists had to wait for forms to appear on the screen.

When managers or workers raised their concerns, technologists described their issues as resistance to change and new technology. When the new account program was first installed the team leader told me that workers were slow to start but that they would soon learn and become faster. After several days of processing imaged new account forms, the team leader's attitude changed, saying, "this will kill us!"

The team leader told managers that twenty more people would be needed if all work was to be processed using the imaging system. Account specialists' enthusiasm for the imaging system waned from having to wait for it to display documents. One account specialist commented, "it is so slow, I could fall asleep waiting for it;" another made the following comment while the system verified index information:

> *Between the times I enter things, I have to sit and wait. It is horrible! I get sleepy, I can't concentrate, just look how long this takes!*

Waiting for images and data entry forms frustrated workers. They were accustomed to working swiftly, rapidly keying in information, and moving on to the next screen. When using the imaging system they sometimes had to wait as much as thirty seconds for new screens. After several weeks of using the system, following installation of revised software, the slow system performance became "totally unacceptable" to the Processing Department manager. Processing imaged forms took longer than processing paper forms. Account specialists using the system were frequently asked to work overtime to complete their tasks. The manager requested that only a few forms be processed until the system performed better. As the Christmas and New Years holidays approached,[13] the team leader further curtailed imaging system use. The team leader told me they used the imaging system, even if it took longer, because it was the "politically correct thing to do." Eventually, because of people taking vacations over the holidays, the team leader stopped using the imaging system altogether.

Using the imaging system took 40% longer than comparable paper-based procedures (see Figure 4 for timing and work flow comparisons between paper- and image-based processing). Detailed comparisons between the improved work flow software and paper document processes are shown for the time required to complete the review, set-up, and quality control functions in Table 2. The data for these functions are representative of other functions; the use of the imaging system required account specialists to perform additional tasks, and the tasks themselves took longer.

People at Dover's accepted the imaging system failings, although problems were downplayed. The people involved expressed their desire to learn to improve other imaging system efforts. Open discussion of issues was, and continued to be, difficult. The other company studied, Harwick Insurance Company, followed a similar change process. Harwick's changes were also initiated by executives promoting imaging systems, and technologists dominated preparation and implementation activities. Harwick's project was greater in scope and complexity and took place in a more authoritarian culture.

Harwick Insurance Company

Harwick Insurance Company is one of the oldest US life insurance companies. The company's principle business is life insurance; other business units included disability insurance, pension, and mutual fund investments. Harwick had operated with an annual profit for over one hundred years. Like other insurance companies, Harwick's financial performance diminished because of real estate investments made in the mid-1980's. When rating companies downgraded Harwick's investment, business declined as policyholders cashed in and transferred policies. Harwick reduced its costs fifteen percent in 1988 by offering an early retirement option, but additional cost cutting measures were still needed.

Imaging Systems at Harwick

Harwick's management wanted to use new technology to help it operate more efficiently. In searching for possible alternatives, technologists had taken one of their top executives to visit Mutual Assurance, another insurance company in the area. The executive was reluctant to make this visit, thinking Harwick couldn't afford or benefit from imaging systems. She described her surprise as follows:

> *I have never had such a revelation as I did when I saw what they did at Mutual Assurance... Well, I was very frightened. Frankly, when I saw what was going on I thought "Oh my God, I'm seeing the future and they've got it." Mutual Assurance is one of our big competitors... and I thought this is really scary because they will take this, where they clearly know how to do it, they will take the team that did it and they will put them right down in their insurance administration area, they will be able to lower their cost structure by 30% and they will kill us.*

Shortly thereafter, by coincidence, Harwick executives heard that the executive who had sponsored Mutual Assurance's imaging system was looking for a new job. In the process of interviewing her, Harwick's executives learned her strategy for imaging systems and business change. A Harwick executive described his expectations in hiring her as their Chief Operating Officer (COO):

> *[The COO] comes on board, we don't have to do a pilot project. She's got it all straight, exactly what she wants to do... The whole idea of hiring [the COO] was that she had already done a pilot project. So there was never any discussion of doing a pilot project.*

When the COO started, she knew her proposals were supported by other executives. Both business and technology operations reported to her, giving her responsibility for business results and control over technologist resources. The

COO's vision was to develop a "business process platform for the next decade."[14] Technologists, excited about their prospects under new management, presented the COO with a proposal for an imaging system feasibility study two weeks after she had started. The COO told them not to do a feasibility study but rather instead immediately send out requests for proposals. "Let them find the labor savings," was what the COO wanted.

The request for proposal was sent to two vendors -- TopImage and Great Big Computer (GBC). Technologist held a meeting with vendor study teams at the end of August to explain the study processes and project goals. The objective of their study was "to create the best business case for image processing, minimizing disruption in the business areas as much as possible." Managers from each department were assigned as contacts for vendor study team. The managers were to provide organizational charts and work flow overviews, arrange meetings, and designate workers to be interviewed. TopImage and GBC study teams spent two months studying different departments, submitting their proposal as requested in November 1995. The choice of the TopImage system was strongly influenced by the COO; she knew she could depend upon the company who had supplied the imaging system at Mutual Assurance.

Following the selection of the best vendor, an internal proposal was needed for other executive's approval. Needed expenditures were justified through staff elimination savings. When the COO reviewed the proposal, she stated that initial savings estimates were too low. Meeting on what they described as a "cold and rainy" Saturday in late November, technologists worked with division managers to find the eliminations needed to satisfy financial targets:

> *It was a combination of [the COO's] numbers and what we got, as we got closer ... in terms of the costs of what it would take to achieve the benefits. We went up and down, and it finally settled down, where we finally said it is going to cost us this many workstations, it is going to cost us this much per workstation, we need to achieve these kinds of benefits over two years. Balancing the scale, we need to go after one hundred and sixty-nine people, and then we went out looking to see where those ... people would come from.*

Technologists and managers argued about how many jobs the technology would allow them to eliminate. A technologist described the situation as follows:

> *The discomfort was very high in the business area about those numbers. The technology side was more comfortable because technology people were more confident in terms of envisioning what image, queue management, work in process management were... I think they were struggling with trying to imagine how this technology could improve business process to the point where it would save a tremendous amount of staff, tremendous amount of labor, and collapse transaction costs down significantly.*

To achieve expected savings, technologist positions would also have to be eliminated once the system was implemented. The new proposal projected greater savings than what either vendor proposed. It did, however, meet the COO's approval. The COO championed the proposal through company approval processes. By the time Harwick's board of directors approved the expenditures in January, preparation activities were already underway. The plan called for the multiple teams "rolling" through departments to redesign business processes, deploy PCs, as they prepared and implemented imaging systems. There was a SWAT team for business redesign and three technical project implementation teams for application specification and programming. Customer Service was one of the departments where imaging systems were implemented.

Customer Service Department

The Customer Service department handles life insurance policy inquiries. It consisted of eighty-three people in five units. Four units were geographically organized, containing service consultants and service representatives (reps) assigned to agencies. A fifth unit, the Support unit, contained other staff that handled technical insurance issues and non-standard policies. Consultants respond directly to customers and agents, handling phone calls, incoming mail and writing letters. Reps handled routine work, consisting mostly of processing forms. "Form" work, which included surrender, loan, and title documents, was done by entering information for documents into different mainframe computer systems. In addition to forms, reps supported consultants' requests. They frequently wrote interoffice correspondences, letters, agency memos, and electronic messages. The company mail room sorted letters by region and delivered them to the Support Unit. Support specialists logged the incoming mail into the Harwick Track system, sorted it by agency, and distributed it to consultants and reps. One type of work, which became a focus of imaging systems, was processing title documents.

Title Processing

Title documents are the forms that clients and agents submit to designate changes to insurance policy ownership, beneficiary, cautions, and assignments. Title documents are processed in batches.[15] Each title document requires entering information into mainframe systems, making and sending copies to other departments, holding processed documents in thirty-day temporary files, and then sending them to archives (see Figure 5). Reps did title work by first reviewing batches, sorting documents into piles with similar issues, [16] and then processing each pile.

Title documents are processed by keying information from customers' forms into the TAA (Title Administration Application) system. TAA is a fifteen year old mainframe application that is somewhat cumbersome. As legal clauses are keyed in, special symbol codes are entered around important words. Reps frequently reference their Title Manual to determine codes and confirm that the phrases used meet company legal requirements. Minor alterations to wording are made, if needed. Then, if a client does not reject the new wording by returning the confirmation letter they are sent, title changes are considered approved. Title documents requiring significant changes are returned to clients with an explanatory cover letter. Reps estimated titles to be half to three-quarters of their work load.

Imaging Systems for Title Processing

The COO's technology initiatives provided several new systems for Customer Service. These included Harwick Track, a program to log, track and report on service requests; UltraFind, a system that retrieved and displayed on one screen customer information from multiple mainframe databases; Correspondence Creation, a system that automatically generated customer letters using mainframe database information; and TIP (Title Image Processing), an imaging system that scanned paper documents in the mail room and electronically sent them to reps for processing.

The TIP system combined imaging systems with mainframe database access capabilities. TIP was part of an overall effort to improve customer service work. As the project began, technologists spent the first two weeks meeting each morning with reps to understand what they did. Technologists determined that beneficiary form information would no longer need to be keyed into the mainframe database, but could instead be stored as imaged documents. Beneficiary information was only needed when paying claims. Ownership, assignment, and caution type of title information still needed to be keyed into the mainframe database as field offices needed this information. Imaging capabilities would not be available to field offices for some time. Eight different databases are used in processing title documents. All these databases would be automatically updated by TIP.

Technical complications and the ambitious scope of TIP prevented it from being ready by the original implementation date. The three programmers and two business analysts worked under constant pressure, averaging sixty hours per week, for five months on TIP. When completed, TIP consisted of 20,000 lines of code, representing over two man-years of software development efforts. Two reps were asked to test TIP as the new implementation date neared. Schedule pressures, and being late already, limited technologists' abilities and desires to consider their input at this stage. Service reps, not privileged to information about financial plans, were also fearful that TIP would result in layoffs. Reps were fatalistic, saying they would just keep on working as they always had, hoping to retain their jobs.

The Customer Service department was reorganized as TIP was installed. A new department, called the Processing Unit, consisting of all service reps was formed.

Three of eighteen rep positions were eliminated. Staff reductions were based on technologists' calculations, which the Processing Unit's manager described as follows:

> *The assumption with image was that the work would be quicker and easier than with paper, but I don't know where they came up with that. If you look at the work from A to Z with paper, and then with image, they said it would be faster. But, I don't think that they tested that! They had a chart where they said on single policies it would go from seven minutes for an existing change on paper to five minutes in the system... With multiple policies it would go from something like ten to six minutes... Based on their analysis I had to cut three people.*

With TIP, the TAA computer system now simply indicated that an imaged beneficiary designation was on file, and no longer directly provided that information. Field offices that required beneficiary information were to request that it be faxed to them, which could be automatically done using the imaging system. Title documents were still received logged documents into Harwick Track by the Support Unit, who then sent the documents to the Paper Management Unit. The Paper Management Unit scanned, indexed and then automatically routed documents (see Figure 6).

TIP altered the way reps worked by presenting documents as images on PC screens and leading them through a set sequence of image and mainframe screens. Reps still needed to key the same information into mainframe systems. Less keying was needed for beneficiary documents, but more was now required for other title documents as their indexes had to be verified. After verifying, or if necessary correcting index values, a new title inquiry screen presented client policy information from multiple systems. After the initial inquiry screen, screen sequences varied according to document type. Ownership, assignment, and cautions were processed in much the same way as paper documents had been. The difference was that TIP now automatically sequenced reps through mainframe and image screens, waiting for their input at each point.

Reps commented that they did not like the extra index verification work, having to follow a predetermined screen sequence, nor have to wait for screens. The ability to determine the order in which items were processed was no longer an option. For beneficiary changes imaged documents were displayed and reps simply approved new designations. While imaging beneficiary documents reduced keying, it created another problem when wording did not match acceptable legal standards. A rep explained:

> *...the interesting thing with image is how it is used in title. If people leave a word out, or add a word or two, we can't fix it. In the manual process we used to add those words to make it comply to our legal requirements and send them out the confirmation. Now, we have to reject more cases.*

Reps had long been trained not to accept title clauses which didn't comply with legal standards. Many more beneficiary documents were now returned. Returning title documents was cumbersome because originals were difficult to retrieve from Paper Management Unit. Reps therefore sent printed images back.[17] Reps were told by managers not to say anything negative about TIP. If they talked negatively, they were complaining, which was not what management wanted to hear.

Imaged title work was not all reps did. They continued to process paper documents for other financial and administrative work. As they concentrated on image work, other work continued to arrive in paper form. Processing imaged documents took three to four times longer than paper documents. After one month of TIP use, title backlogs had increased dramatically. Most reps had over two hundred title packets in their electronic work queues. The reps' manager struggled to cope,[18] wanting to return to paper processing but couldn't because, as she said, "that would be telling people it was okay to go back." She feared being perceived as having lied to the reps about the imaging system's ability to help them with their work. When the department manager talked to technologists he was told that their difficulties related to the reps' learning curve — they needed to use the system more efficiently.[19] With difficulty, the manager obtained approval for reps to work overtime. By then, however, backlogs were enormous.[20] Even with overtime, reps were unable to substantially reduce backlogs. One rep said that she had never before experienced such pressure and stress, saying, "we can't help it, the work is still more than we can do." Finally, seeing no other choice, the manager stopped sending title documents to the Paper Management Unit. Reps worked down the image backlogs and went back to processing paper title documents.

The decision to halt TIP's use was not widely publicized. Executives were uninformed about reps' difficulties with TIP. After a month-long moratorium on sending title documents to the Paper Management Unit, the planned resumption of TIP was delayed. During the month reps had processed most imaged title documents, but paper documents were still stacked on their desks. It was not until a month later, following repeated threats from technologists, that scanning was resumed for title documents. Reps used TIP only on a limited basis to process "clean" single policy beneficiary, ownership, and assignment changes. Four reps were initially "volunteered" to process imaged title documents. Each week more reps received title work through TIP.

My structured observation data (see Table 3) found that it took 3.3 times longer to process documents using TIP than what it had taken using paper documents TAA.[21] Even beneficiary changes, where the title system saved keying operations, took 3.2 times longer. Ownership changes, representative of other types of title work, took 3.5 times longer.[22]

The hierarchical Harwick culture, and fears for their jobs, made it difficult for people to speak openly about imaging system difficulties. When imaging systems did not produce expected improvements it was not possible for different groups to collectively examine problems. Instead, managers and workers covered up their actions and did what they thought they needed to do to survive. Technologists used their power to force imaging system use, require managers to reduce staff, and determine how information was presented about imaging system progress and accomplishments.

Discussion

Changes at Dover and Harwick are epic tales filled with irony. Despite the best efforts of everyone involved, no one wanted to settle for what was accomplished. Yet, the imaging projects were all written up in company and industry organs as successful and having achieved exalted outcomes. Executives were recognized within their company and industry for their leadership in these improvements. However, I was unable to substantiate these benefits. Workers endured increasing pressure on production, were limited in their abilities to learn new system capabilities, forced to reduce quality, and generally left demoralized from the paper-to-image transition. Technologists charged to deploy the imaging systems struggled to implement needed features. Technologists could, however, positively represent their achievements by carefully selecting what information they presented. Managers were continuously challenged to keep workers motivated, constantly vying to get technologists' attention in providing real productivity-enhancing capabilities while trying to smooth the work disruptions in the transition.

In a more detailed discussion of these changes (Roth, 1993), I utilized a metaphor of physical waves to explain the character of organizational social and technological change process. An organizational social-technological change process is made up of waves of activities involving different stakeholder groups — executives, managers, technologists and workers.[23] Each wave of activity is a temporal phase the builds upon what preceded it in contributing to eventual outcomes — formulating a strategy based on historical context, selecting a technology and change process within that strategy, preparing the technology and planning the change, implementing the technology and making organizational changes, and, finally, using the technology and new work arrangements in achieving outcomes. Social-technological change is shaped in those wave of activities by the roles, perspectives, thinking and actions of the various stakeholder groups. Across all of the six projects in the two companies I studied, benefits in service, speed, and productivity fell far short of what was anticipated. Multiple measures (ongoing interviews and participant observations, pre- and post-change survey of worker attitudes, motivation and satisfaction, and structured observations and timing of tasks) confirmed the decline in working conditions.

The various participants and their multiple, and often divergent, perspectives on accomplishments creates a complex situation upon which to base analytical comments. The question of what happened in these companies depends upon what data is used and how it is interpreted. What I offer is my own interpretation which, because I was not a participant is different from what executives, managers, technologists or workers said. My analysis does, however, benefit from having insight into these multiple understandings.

Outcomes

Clarifying salient outcomes provides a basis from which to consider what influenced the change process and imaging system results. The obvious outcome in both companies is that the transition from paper documents to electronic images did not resulted in expected benefits. One consideration for this outcome is that the study of change in organizations is constrained by the timeframe in which it is considered. My detailed descriptions came from a year-and-a-half residency at each company. However, a follow-up a year later showed little change.[24] The follow-up, as well as what is observed during the time, indicated a second consideration beyond not achieving expected outcomes — the difficulty of these organizations to learn and improve over time. The year later follow-up found only minimal limited effort still applied to improving technology use and making changes, consistent with what other researchers findings about the nature of social-technological improvement projects (Tyre and Orlikowski, 1994).

The inability to improve business processes was not based on technological inadequacies. The imaging systems passed technical tests (system performance, access speed to documents, time to retrieve and display images, and so on) in each company. Ongoing difficulties in achieving benefits relate to a fit between how people work and how technology was implemented. Tasks were carried out using electronic images much as they had been using paper. Neither company achieved expected benefits nor showed an increase in its capabilities to do so over time.[25]

Planned changes are motivated by what people with control over necessary resources consider to be possible. The range of change possibilities relate to people's conceptions for how work is done and could be improved using imaging system capabilities. That range of what is possible is progressively narrowed over time as decisions are made on the design of business process and selection of technology features (Thomas, 1994). The extent to which those people charged to carry out work, and those people responsible for using technology features, are involved in specify changes influences the range of work/technology options considered.

As new technology, like imaging systems, creates new possibilities for organizing work it requires social innovations to determine and realize what is technologically possibly. These social changes are difficult to achieve, particularly for technically oriented people because they can not effectively be imposed on others nor directly discerned through set analytical procedures (perhaps this is much like technological opportunities that are difficult for socially-oriented people to understand). And, whatever changes are made, after they are completed the knowledge that has been created in that process generally provides important new insight into what could be better. The only certainty in business process redesign is that once implemented there new knowledge about additional improvement opportunities. To apply that new knowledge, collective learning capabilities are needed. From this perspective *the extent to which the change process facilitates or inhibits collective learning determines the benefits organizations can achieve in transitioning from paper to new electronic media.* Examining paper document characteristics and issues in their transition to electronic images, and then the human aspects of business process integration, illustrates complexity of the undertaking and the consequent need for collective learning to achieve expected benefits.

Paper documents to electronic documents

Business processes in insurance companies are based on many decades of refinements in using and managing paper. The techniques to process paper documents relates to the physical characteristics of paper documents, mainframe transaction processing and database computer systems, and their broader organization into tasks and work. Although a new technology, like imaging systems, can be effective in some aspects of working with documents, it may not prove as efficient as paper when employed in identical ways. Examining how existing business processes are optimized around paper documents, information systems, people and work organization reveals these challenges.

Paper is a technology for information capture, display, transmission and storage. Forms are used to gather data. Paper displays information, reading a paper document simply requires adequate light to see it (i.e., a "solar powered" display). Documents record the products, services and obligations a company provides its customers. Paper is also a media for transmitting information. The material nature of paper limits its information transmission speed. Courier, postage and overnight deliver services have enhanced paper usefulness as a transmission medium. Converting document information into electrons and sending it at near light speed across telephone wires anywhere in the world, as facsimile machines have done, illustrates how electronic technologies enhances paper's capabilities.

Like with fax machines, once scanned into the document imaging systems, computer networks rapidly transmit information to workers. Once a document is imaged, however, information display becomes more time consuming. A computer screen is required to view information. The time to display a document on a screen is relatively short (or print it), in the area of several seconds. While seconds are short time periods, they are long for common tasks such as flipping through documents. A simple task like spreading documents out to look at them suddenly becomes time consuming.

Much of people's "work" in paper-intensive environments consists of reading information from documents and entering (typing) it into specific screens and fields on their desktop terminals. The terminals send the information to the mainframe computer, which processes transactions and stores them in databases.

What is done today embodies remnants of a time when computing was costly and labor was relatively inexpensive. Work procedures are based on considerations that people can more easily be taught simple, repetitive tasks than mainframe system can be programmed to meet people's requirements.

Existing mainframe systems exerted a continuing influence on work procedures as documents are imaged. As documents can be displayed on computer screens, the mainframe input windows were essentially the same as those of the earlier terminals. The new process was similar to what was previously done, with workers having to more, rather than fewer steps.

A batch style of work organization takes a relatively long time for any one document to pass completely through processing. Papers move in batches as information from each document is keyed in one screen at a time. After each procedure, paper sits in batches for the next processing step. The time that the paper just sits and is not processed was never considered critical when all work was completed within one or two days of receipt. Imaging system capabilities allowed a document to be processed through all functions, different from the batch organization where multiple documents where processed at each function. The new task organization required workers to look at the different pages of the document on their computer screen as they searched for the information to entered into the fields required by the mainframe. Paging through documents required several seconds for each new images to be displayed. In addition, the sequence by which workers performed tasks was controlled by the imaging system. Work flow software only allowed people to do tasks in the sequence that had been programmed.

Considering the characteristics of paper, and the improvements that are possible when information on paper is converted to electronic images, vast improvements in efficiency and effectiveness should have been gained. It was the promise of these gains which informed the *technical* thinking that led to strategy, influenced selection and guided imaging system implementation. What the technical thinking *failed* to consider was how to realize improvements in the context of people being required to performed tasks within the emerging constraints of new imaging and old mainframe systems.

Change and business process integration

The abilities of people to work with one another and with technology determines what benefits organizations gain when implementing new technologies. Although imaging systems created opportunities for improving the speed with which work is done, difficulties in changing business processes limited what gains were realized. For the most part, the paper-based processes were replicated. These processes were optimized for paper's characteristics used in combination with existing information systems. The change from paper to an electronic medium for recording, transmitting and storing information was *not* superior in all aspects. Both organizations had difficulty in organizing people, systems and work so as to leverage imaging systems' strengths and avoid its weaknesses.

The common outcomes —that both organizations' business processes were largely unchanged — is an indication of a persistent difficulty beyond any single organization. Although the goal was to enable radical improvements, the various people and groups involved, and the way they interacted, made it difficult for either organizations to change effectively. Each major stakeholder group — executives, managers, technologists and workers — held different expectations. Neither organization had the capability to examine how these expectations compared with one another. It was presumptions of conflict, beyond actual verbalized conflict, that constrained people's interactions and communication, and heightened defensive, surreptitious and political behaviors, thereby continually limiting the information that was available for improving imaging system use or redesigning business processes.

When initial problems arose in implementing imaging systems, technologists used their technical expertise, leadership positions and control over project resources to respond. They managed the information that was generally available on project progress and coerced managers and workers into compliance with the technical and financial imperatives. Technologists acted this way, in part, because they perceived managers and workers concerns as resistance to change and new technology. The more that technologists controlled and coerced, the greater the resistance of managers and workers. These behaviors escalated in both companies. When managers and workers collected and presented evidence that new business process and imaging systems were not providing benefits, it was discounted and dismissed. It was only through the use of carefully planned, politically correct, opportunistic excuses that managers and workers were able to avoid using imaging systems and return, although only temporarily, to paper documents.

The way in which the change process unfolded and people resorted to control and coercion to further their particular interests limited the long-term improvement abilities of both organizations. These collective behavior patterns are consistent with defensive routines and conditions that limit learning in organizations (Argyris and Schön, 1996). The ways in which activities were carried out undermined trust, restricted communication, and left little common ground to work together to create business processes that effectively integrated electronic document systems, existing information systems and workers.

Conclusions

When I have presented this material, I have often been asked, "So, what's new?" The question troubles me for two reasons. First, the question is generally followed by a statement that twenty years of history in implementing information technology are consistent these descriptions. I am left wondering why people have a knowledge of these issues and yet there is so little improvement. Both Dover and

Harwick hired well known consultants and had their people trained in the most renowned methods. Despite the genuine efforts of everyone involved, actual improvements fell far short of expectations. Imaging systems made it more, rather than less, difficult for the companies to improve.

Second, the question implies that there are obvious solutions. General solutions aren't obvious, in part, because audience members react by suggesting what one group or another should have done. For example, engineers tend to frame the solutions as related to technical issues — better analysis, more user involvement, improved design or faster technology. Manager talk about political issues — equitable distribution of resources, change of governance, more control for managers, or representation of less influential groups. People generally want to act on solutions from their perspective. They respond with their well-known problem solving strategies. These tried-and-true strategies have served them well in the past, at least as far as they have been able to recognize. My experience is that the responses from these audiences actually replicates what took place in the organizations studied.

There is a complexity to social-technological change in organizations which requires considering different perspectives and extends beyond the domain of traditional problem solving approaches. What is needed is a reconsidering the nature of the problem. The problems which surface are not behavioral *or* technical; they are a combination of behavioral *and* technical issues. Problems need to be examined in relation to one another, as a inter-related set. The socio-technical systems approach (Mumford and Ward, 1968; Trist, 1981; Pava, 1983) has long advocated this approach, proposing joint consideration of technology and social issues. However, the organizational understanding of the coupling of social systems and technology continues to be underdeveloped, in part because participants consider issues from their own perspective. In looking at issues as an interrelated system, there is a need to encompass and embrace multiple perspectives — that of executives, managers, technologists and workers. The different ways in which various groups perceive activities, and inability of organizations undergoing dramatic change to examine their perceptions and assumptions, leads to many difficulties found in examining change. The nature of social-technological change in organizations is that it relies on the participation and involvement of a broad and diverse group of people, many of whom have different backgrounds, beliefs, and basic ways of seeing and thinking about the world.

Many of these groups can be conceived of as organizational subcultures (Schein, 1992). As subcultures these groups my have unique ways of operating, hold different beliefs and values, and think and act based on different assumptions for how the world does and should work. These subcultures have different roots — workers and mangers perhaps in their local organization, technologists in their profession, and executives in a larger financial community. In studying managerial subcultures across organizations, Schein (forthcoming) found three distinct cultures. Each of these managerial cultures focuses on different issues, and has particular goals and orientations which makes them more aware of particular problems. An operator culture is organizationally based, and conscious of the need to function as teams and build capabilities for longer term improvement. The executive culture focuses on organizational performance, particularly money and cost control. Engineering culture sees organizations as having problems to solve, and seeks to employ technical solutions which don't require human intervention as a way of improving the organization. These different cultures of management use the same words, but they have different meanings and expectations for what is to be done based on what they say.

In viewing organizations as cultures, it becomes clear that problems will arise as organizations seek to improve themselves because members from each subculture will have different goals. They will fail to recognize that while they use the same words, they may often misunderstand one another at very basic levels. In creating and maintaining their own distinct identity, various subcultures hold different perspectives on what is held to be common, accepted as normal or generally understood. These varying perspectives create boundaries that are largely conceptual and thus "generally less visible and less easy to define" than physical boundaries (Schein, forthcoming). The invisible nature of cultural boundaries make it harder for people to understand when they have violated them, and such errors are often covered up and not discussed. They bound the systems of meaning which make subgroups unique and effective in their collective action, and at the same time different from the larger organization.

In order to address problems which span organizations and are without unique solutions, organizations must learn to create a common meaning for concepts used by different members, a shared understanding of individual and organizational goals, and an acceptance of different groups' varying motivations and perspectives. To be able to do so requires creating social conditions which foster individual and collective learning. Particular social conditions — valid information, free choice, respect and integrity — are necessary for organizations to improve over time (Argyris and Schön, 1996). Not only are these conditions necessary for ongoing improvement, they are also what is needed initially. An absence of conducive social conditions allows for only minor, and as was the case here, often ineffective changes to be made. With only minor changes in business processes possible, the use of a new technology which is not universally superior to its predecessor brings out its weaknesses. At Dover and Harwick, imaging system implementations without fundamental business process changes resulted in work processes which were not as efficient and effective as those using paper.

What is lacking in organizations undergoing technological change is a capability for creating shared understanding about issues associated with implementing computer systems, guiding social changes, and improving business processes. This capability comes from creating the slack in project schedules to take time for open discussion, the safety for individuals to surface issues, and an acceptance and consideration of various people's different perspectives. Unless executives and technologists join with managers and workers to create better conditions and capabilities for learning, organizations undergoing technological and social change will gain only limited benefits from their efforts.

Acknowledgements. The author wishes to acknowledge the support for this research that was provided by the MIT Center for Information Systems Research and The Marketing Science Institute.

References

Argyris, C. and Schön, D. (1996) **Organizational Learning II: Theory, Method and Practice**, Reading, Ma.: Addison-Wesley.

Booker, E. (1990), "Not as new and strange as it seems," **Computerworld** November 5, 67-75.

Dubashi, J. (1990), "Image ... is everything," **Financial Week**, October 16, pg. 55-56.

Hammer, M. (1990), "Reengineering Work: Don't Automate, Obliterate," **Harvard Business Review**, 68, 4, 104-112.

Hammer, M. and Champy, J. (1993) **Reengineering the Corporation, a manifesto for business revolution**, New York: Harper Collins Business.

Mumford, E. and Ward, T. (1968) **Computers: Planning for People**, London: Batsford.

Pava, C. (1983) **Managing new office technology: an organizational strategy**, New York: Free Press.

Roth, G. (1993) "In Search of the Paperless Office: The Structuring Wave of Technological Change," unpublished doctoral dissertation, Sloan School of Management, Massachusetts Institute of Technology, Cambridge, Ma.

Roth, G. and Senge, P. M. (1996) "From Theory to Practice: research territory, processes and structure at an organizational learning center" **Journal of Change Management**, Vol. 9, Issue. 1.

Schein, E. (1992) **Organizational Culture and Leadership, Second Edition**, San Francisco: Jossey-Bass.

Schein, E. (forthcoming) "Three Cultures of Management: The Problem of Managing Across Conceptual Boundaries" **Sloan Management Review**.

Stone, P. S. (1990), "Winning the war against paper," **Institutional Investor**, September, 253-254.

Thomas, R. (1994) **What Machines Can't Do**, Berkeley: University of California Press.

Toffler, A. (1980) , **The Third Wave**, London: William Collins.

Trist, E. (1981) "The SocioTechnical Perspective" in A. Van de Ven and W. Joyce (eds.) **Perspectives on Organizational Design and Performance**, New York: Wiley, 19-75.

Tyre, M. and Orlikowski, W. (1994) "Windows of Opportunity: Temporal Patterns of Technological Adaptation in Organizations" **Organization Science**, Vol. 5, No. 1.

Yates, J. (1989), **Control through Communication, The Rise of System in American Management**, Baltimore: John Hopkins University Press.

Figures and Tables

Figure 1 Time Line of Organizational Change and Research Activities

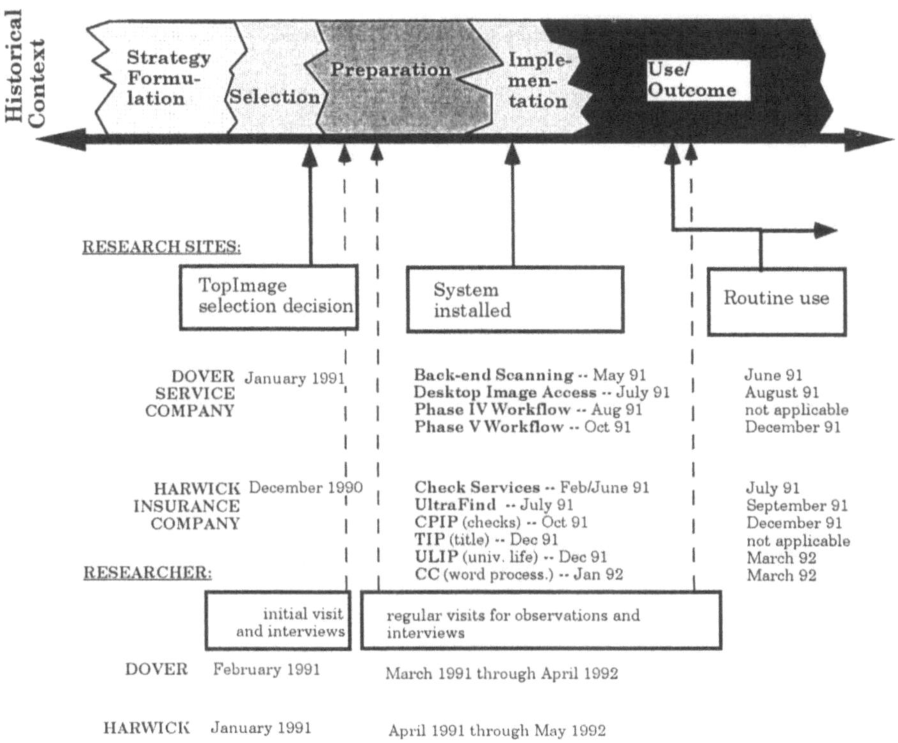

Table 1 Overview Of Research Sites

Company/ Description	Dover Service Company	Harwick Insurance Company
Business	Mutual Funds/Life Insurance	Life & Disability Insurance
Age	1 year	100+ years
Major Issue	Managing Growth	Cost Control
Management Style	Team/participatory empower people workers provide service	Directive/hierarchical functionally specific workers are expense
Executives	Positively Focused Vision to Transform	Positively Focused Vision to Transform
Imaging Goal	Service Capability	35% productivity gain
Implementation method	Involvement/participative consensus driven	Top down/expertise based, power driven
Department -work:	Processing process applications, paper work	Customer Services mail, correspondence, forms, phones
-staff:	30	83
-titles:	account specialist	consultant, analyst, service representative
-volume	mail: 25 K/mo.	phone: 17K/mo. mail: 25K/mo.
-imaging applications	Phase IV work flow Phase V work flow	TIP (title)

Figure 2 Tasks sequence for processing paper new account forms

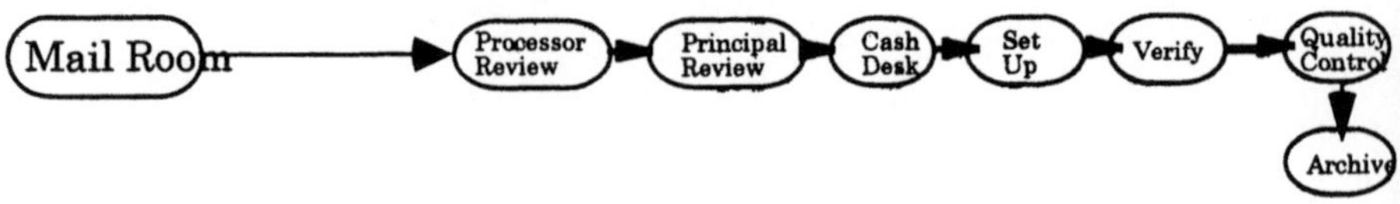

Figure 3 Tasks sequence for processing imaged new account forms

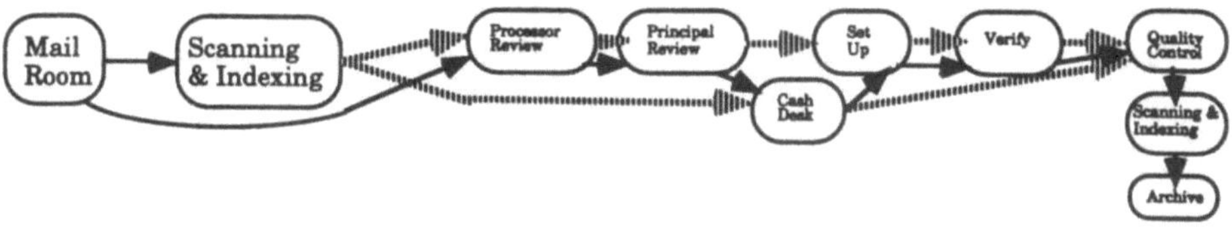

Figure 4 New Account Work Flow & Timing Of Tasks
(timing information from structured observation data)

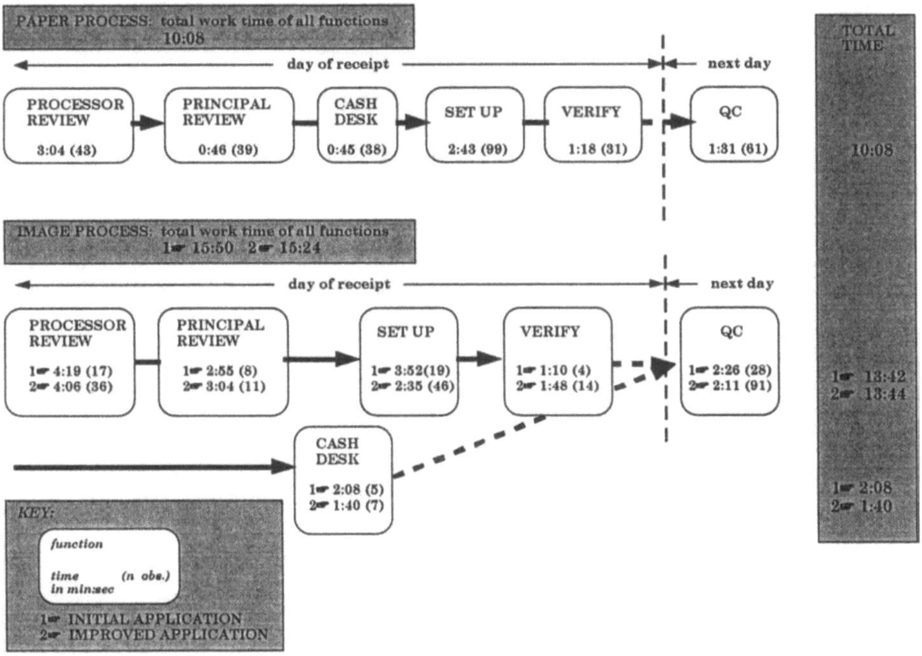

Table 2 Structured Observation of New Account Forms Processing
(time to accomplish functions/tasks in minutes and seconds)

PAPER NEW ACCT. DOCUMENTS			IMAGED NEW ACCT. DOCUMENTS		
FUNCTION/TASK	**TIME**	**n**	**FUNCTION/TASK**	**TIME**	**n**
OVERALL TASK AVE.	**1:54**	**315**	**OVERALL TASK AVE.**	**2:41**	**193**
PROCESSOR REVIEW	**3:05**	**43**	**PROCESSOR REVIEW**	**4:06**	**36**
			Select Proc. Rev. Funct	0:30	2
			Next Document	0:29	29
Review Document	1:01	17	Review document	1:26	45
			Enter Index	1:25	12
			Enter Check	0:22	6
Check Rep No.	0:49	16	Check Rep No.	1:00	3
Check Soc. Sec. No.	0:43	24	Check Soc. Sec. No.	1:19	13
Get Discount No.	0:51	8	Get Discount No.	0:35	3
Get Letter of Intent No.	0:41	1			
Update Acct. Info.	0:57	7	Update Acct. Info.	0:30	1
Stamp and Write	0:49	38	Print	0:19	3
Write Note	0:48	14	Write Annotation	0:10	6
Sort Documents	0:36	21	Approve/Complete	0:19	28
Track	0:34	12	Pend Document	0:12	6
Get or Return Items	0:46	9	Get Printed Image	3:34	2
ACCOUNT SET UP	**2:43**	**99**	**ACCOUNT SET UP**	**2:35**	**46**
			Select Acct. Setup Funct	0:17	10
			Next Document	0:14	35
			Wait	0:18	9
			Move Windows	0:18	5
Review Doc. & Enter Info	1:30	74	Review Doc. & Enter Info	1:30	50
Stamp and Write	0:47	57	Edit Index	0:30	6
Write Note	0:36	30	Display Document	0:14	15
Sort Documents	0:31	56	Complete	0:16	39
Get or Return Items	1:21	18			
Copy Documents	1:41	6			
Calculate	0:41	6			
QUALITY CONTROL	**1:31**	**63**	**QUALITY CONTROL**	**2:11**	**91**
			Log on MFA	0:52	11
			Select QC Funct	0:18	12
			Read Queue	0:33	8
			Next Document	0:25	46
			Wait	0:15	5
			Move Windows	1:40	4
Check Acct -- no errors	1:11	39	Check Acct -- no errors	1:11	62
Check Acct -- errors	2:05	15	Check Acct -- errors	1:21	9
			Update Acct. Info.	1:12	8
Sort Documents	0:39	11	Display Document	0:25	24
			Complete	0:31	61
			System Errors	1:20	7

Figure 5 Paper document flow for title processing

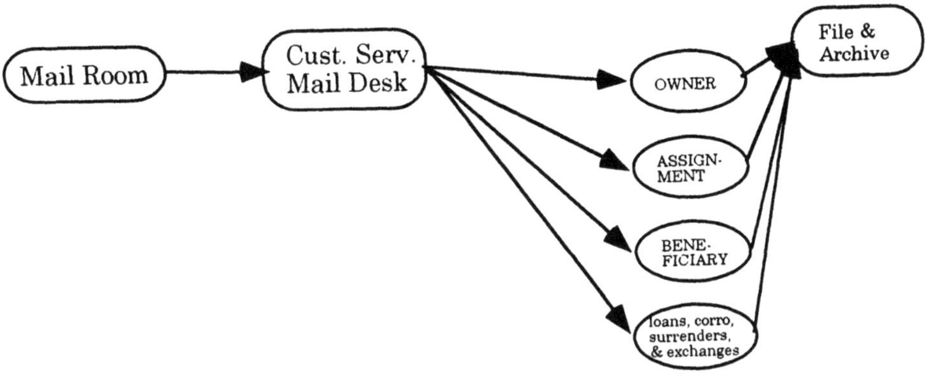

Figure 6 Flow of paper and electronic documents for title processing

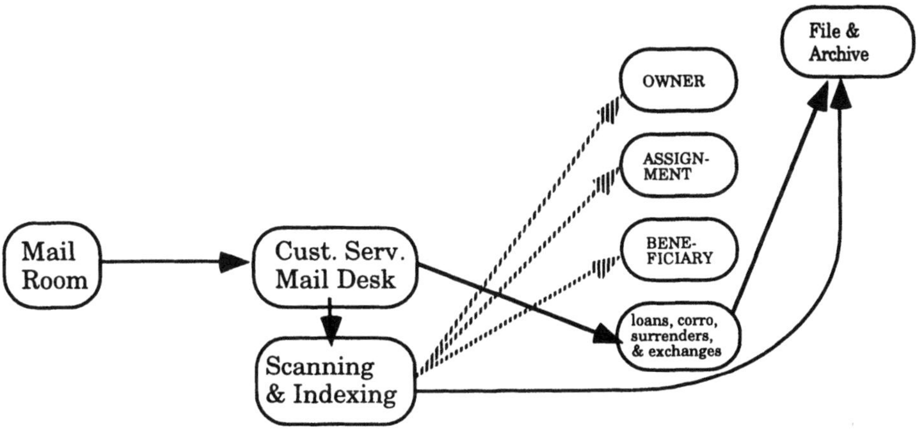

Table 3 Structured Observations for Title Forms Processing

PAPER NEW ACCT. DOCUMENTS			IMAGED NEW ACCT. DOCUMENTS		
FUNCTION/TASK	**TIME**	**n**	**FUNCTION/TASK**	**TIME**	**n**
AVERAGE OF ALL FUNCTIONS	**1:56**	**47**	**AVERAGE OF ALL FUNCTIONS**	**6:20**	**30**
OWNERSHIP CHNG.	**3:29**	**11**	**OWNERSHIP CHNG.**	**12:18**	**4**
			Select Work	0:22	5
Review document	0:22	6	Review document	0:36	9
			Verify Index	1:07	3
			Select Function	0:28	5
Inquire in System	0:23	17	Inquire in System	0:16	3
Enter Info.	0:39	20	Enter Info.	1:38	8
			Print	1:01	2
Write Note	0:17	3	Write Note	0:32	5
Track	0:18	2	Track	0:35	3
Write & Send E Mail	1:00	2	Approve/Complete	0:26	10
Sort	0:20	9	Cancel	0:33	2
BENEFICIARY CHNG.	**1:46**	**22**	**BENEFICIARY CHNG.**	**5:06**	**6**
			Select Work	0:16	4
			Next document	0:15	7
			Wait	0:21	3
Review document	0:10	1	Review document	0:26	7
			Verify Index	0:24	8
			Select Function	0:46	6
Inquire in System	0:19	15	Inquire in System	0:13	8
Enter Info.	0:58	27	Enter Info.	0:46	2
			Request Title Letter	0:20	5
			Write & Send E Mail	2:23	2
			Track	0:19	5
Write & Send E Mail	0:55	1	Approve/Complete	0:13	11
Sort	0:15	12	Cancel	1:38	1

Endnotes

[1] Field work was conducted during seventy-nine days at Dover and one hundred and seventeen days at Harwick. My routine was to be at one company the first two days of the week and at the other company the last two days of the week. Field notes detailed what I observed, noted specific conversations and captured observations and my thoughts about them as they occurred. Structured observation and questionnaires supplemented the qualitative data.

[2] Account specialists' work involves entering information from documents into the MFA system. They describe their work as more than data entry because of the business and system knowledge required to perform their duties. Many, however, commented that their tasks are repetitive and boring. One told me that he hasn't yet found an interesting task, "all of them are tedious."

[3] Account specialists receive new account forms and attached checks in batches of about twenty. Each application form is assigned an account number by removing self-sticking labels from a computer-generated sheet of numbers. The account number sticker is also placed on the application forms and deposit slips. Check amounts and customers' last names are written on paper deposit slips. The account specialist then reviews the form. Customers' personal information — age, income and total assets — are often left blank. This information is required for an investment suitability review that must be performed before the application is accepted. If the information is missing, the account specialist has to call the agent (insurance agent or investment broker) or customer to complete it. For forms that are completed, account specialists search the MFA data base for other accounts the customer may have, and to confirm proper agent registration (the agent receives a commission based on the investment amount).

Once the MFA database check is completed, that batch of new account forms are taken to team leaders for principal review (to confirm investment suitability). Account specialists either wait while team leaders signed forms or simply dropped them off and collect them later. Once applications are approved, account specialists enter account information into the MFA system. New accounts forms are then also logged into a tracking system. Deposit slips and checks are taken to the cash desk, batch cover sheets are stamped and initialed (with account specialists' designated number) and the complete batch is placed in a basket where it awaits the next step - verification.

Verification is performed by a different account specialist than the person who entered the original information. Using the MFA verification function, account specialists re-key account information. The MFA system automatically compares the original and verification entries. Discrepancies are displayed on the screen and the account specialist selects one of the options or makes corrections. When verification is finished, account specialists again stamped the batch cover sheet and placed verified applications into a bin to await quality control. Quality control takes place the next day, after the overnight batch processing on the MFA system has entered the new account information into the MFA system database. In quality control, the information on the data base is checked against the form to confirm that it has been properly recorded. The final step is stamping the batch cover sheet and placing the completed forms in a basket for microfilming.

[4] Pre-authorized checking is an example of a procedure that was performed in a particular way. Account specialists first wrote information from account application forms onto pre-authorized checking worksheets and then keyed the worksheet information into the MFA system. When I asked an account specialist why he didn't just directly key the information in the MFA system, he told me that he did not know — he was told to do it that way. When he had asked a team leader about alternative approaches, he was told to just do the task work the way he was shown.

[5] These phases were the conceptual basis for developing detailed plans for imaging system implementation. Phase I, "Electronic Documents," involved scanning documents that had previously been microfilmed. Imaged documents would be accessed using an imaging workstation in the research department. Phase II, "PC/Windows Roll Out," involved installation of PC workstations in Processing and Customer Service Departments. Phase III, "Image at the Desktop," added image retrieval capability to PCs; TopImage, MFA, and MiniComputer sessions would be simultaneously accessed and displayed in multiple windows. Phase IV, "Basic Workflow," was also called "front-end processing" because paper documents would be initially scanned as workers processed imaged documents. The technologist wrote, "Front-end processing will be used to scan incoming mail, and ElecFlow will be used to route document images to the appropriate groups/individuals." The final planned phase, Phase V, "Advance Workflow," consisted of work flow enhancements for more "effective management of documents and more effective indexing and retrieval."

[6] A phased approach also simplified technologists' task by allowing them to scan particular types of documents and develop software for the functions they were associated with sequentially.

[7] Several technologists suggested workers merely continue what they were doing and, "then they [technologists] could look at that [work flow] and reengineer efficiencies with a new process." They interviewed individual workers, asking them what they did, the source of their work, and what happened once their work was completed. Their efforts included describing, flow charting, analyzing, and proposing work flow alternatives.

[8] Technologists were confident that imaging systems would themselves provide business process improvements, concluding that business changes were not mandatory. Their assumption was that processing documents using the imaging system provided improvements.

[9] Workers on the mapping team wanted transfers, a function where money is transferred from one mutual fund account to another. Technologists advocated new account forms, a function where new account application forms information is entered into the computer database to establish new mutual fund accounts. Workers preferred Transfers because they required passing documents back and forth between Processing and Customer Service. Transfers were also a higher volume of work. Processing new account forms required no Customer Service involvement. Technologists considered new account forms as more visible to executives, and they were what was in their preliminary plans.

[10] When technologists encountered problems with Financial Service Consulting's recommendations, they discussed them with managers. Managers then talked with Financial Service Consulting staff and negotiated changes. The consultants, not familiar with detailed work flow activities, generally made whatever changes managers requested.

[11] The process was sequential, requiring application forms to go through the principal approval process before checks were deposited. The technologists' manager wanted some improvements in the process — he suggested the imaging system be used to conduct tasks in parallel. Specifically, he required checks to be deposited immediately after scanning. If applications were rejected, they were to be noted on error reports, and the customer would be issued a reimbursement check instead of returning their original check (which would by then have already been deposited).

Technologists proposed the new accounts process where checks were deposited immediately. Managers, however, required safeguards depositing checks. Technologists and managers agreed to a work flow where checks were held until forms were approved, with the understanding that safeguards to allow immediate check depositing would be programmed later.

[12] For example, completed forms could be accessed for quality control on the same day that they were processed. Quality control involved checking the MFA data base after the nightly batch run to confirm the proper establishment of the new account record. Quality control on the TopImage system was not supposed to be possible until the day following the new account data entry. One account form disappeared, never arriving in the principal review queue and no records of it could be found in any of the electronic queues. That new account was processed using the original paper form.

[13] Higher year-end paper work volumes and special projects made the holidays a particularly busy period.

[14] She invented terms and creative images to communicate her ideas. "Single View" is the strategy for computer systems that provide one easy way to access information on the nine different systems the company used to service customers. PC workstations are the "Master Hubs" that present workers with "View Fields" for their functions. "View Fields" are customized screens for sales, telephone servicing, forms processing, and other specific functions. The basis for the Single View strategy is a series of Integrated Personal Computer (IPC) projects. IPC projects utilize centralized imaging system servers, sophisticated PC workstations that display document images at workers' desks and business process reengineering techniques to streamline tasks. Imaging systems were the "sizzle" to sell the company, the COO said. What was really behind it was a way to improve business processes.

[15] The alternative method would be to complete all steps on a single form, reps first completed step one on all forms, then step two, and so on.

[16] Sorting was a common practice in processing title forms; documents were separated according to whether the work was "clean" or "dirty." "Clean" title work was the title transactions which could be processed in a straight forward manner. "Dirty" title work was more complex, requiring references to title manuals, asking questions, or returning the form to the client for corrections or additional information. Up to half the incoming title work was said to be "dirty."

[17] The printed image of a title document was what the customer or agent then made changes on, initialed and sent back. These were then again imaged, and routed by the imaging system. The ability to read text on documents that were imaged repeated times diminished, making it hard to work with them.

[18] At the end of December, while coping with increased document volumes from Customer Service and Universal Life, the Paper Management Unit scanned some title document batches more than once and others

in the wrong date order. Title documents logged into Harwick Track were not found in the TopImage system.

[19] The manager had two reps time the processing of title work on TIP versus paper documents. Five assignments, nine beneficiary changes, and two ownership changes were processed in two hours forty-nine minutes on TIP. During the test, TIP had stopped running for twenty minutes. Not including the down time, average time per title change was 9.3 minutes. Five assignments, ten beneficiary changes and two ownership changes were processed using paper documents in twenty-four minutes; average time per title change was only 1.4 minutes. Technologists did not accept this test because it was not performed by "objective people."

[20] The more documents there were in workers' queues, the slower the performance of the TopImage index accessing and image retrieval functions.

[21] These timings, made after reps had been using TIP for at least three weeks, examined only the processing time for reps and did not include extra time involved in sorting, separating, scanning, and indexing title documents.

[22] It was difficult to record large numbers of title document observations. When the title system was first introduced, I wanted to wait until workers had adjusted to the new system. However, given the scenario I have described regarding the use of the title system, it was difficult to determine when a "steady state" of use was achieved. Also, because of the stress workers were under, and uncertainty they felt in processing title documents using TIP, they were somewhat reluctant to have me observe them. I only recorded structured observations when workers approved of my sitting with them.

[23] I examine different occupational and stakeholder groups — executives, managers, technologists and workers — and their expectations, influence, roles and activities in the change process. While designation of stakeholder groups as executives, managers, technologists, and workers appears broad-brushed, in conducting interviews and observing people I found that individuals within these groups had similar outlooks, interests, responsibilities, and organizational experiences. The executive stakeholder group consisted of CEOs, Presidents, COOs, and Senior Vice Presidents who had some role in strategy formulation and decision-making related to imaging systems. Individuals in this group were the top management in each company, those ultimately responsible for business success or failure. Business, line, or department managers, referred to simply as managers, were responsible for daily business operations. Managers themselves did not perform customer service and processing work, but supervised workers who did. Technologists were responsible for imaging system specification, development, installation, and operation. Individuals in this stakeholder group included managers and individual contributors with the management information systems (MIS) organization. Technologists included business analysts, consultants, programmers, and project managers. Their backgrounds and expertise were in business, systems analysis, and computer system programming. The fourth stakeholder group studied was workers, or "users," in technologists' terminology. Workers processed documents, responded to phone calls, serviced customer requests, and performed all other activities associated with these functions. These people had titles including service representative, customer service consultant, analyst, communications specialist, operations specialist, and support specialist.

[24] At Dover, a year later, in the summer of 1993, there were changes, but little affect on outcomes. Use of the imaging system for new account forms processing never resumed. Managers were still uncertain of where imaging system benefits would occur and how they would have a greater role in specifying changes. The Processing Department hired only one person and assigned one manager part-time to work on imaging system developments. A new project to "front-end" scan all incoming documents in the mail room was undertaken and completed. This imaging application provided statistics and management reports, but it did not produce productivity benefits as documents continued to be processed in paper form. The head of the technologist group had left the company for a promotion to Vice President at another insurance firm.

At Harwick, also a year later, the Customer Services department had been part of a divisional reorganization into functional, task-focused departments. Managers were in different positions, none had any involvement in imaging projects. No technologists remained assigned to developing imaging systems. TIP is still used for only single policy changes, and although a task force of managers and workers investigated improvements, nothing came of their suggestions. Managers and workers were told to figure out how to do their jobs better using the imaging system. A combination of additional training and strict adherence to procedures for using the imaging system is how it was explained to me that improvements were made in the speed of processing documents. Technologists advocated another new information technology. As imaging system efforts slowed, new initiatives to replace administrative mainframe systems had begun. Workers were still pressured to accomplish more work and morale continued to decline. Few workers dared speak up. When three workers together wrote and complained about working conditions to the CEO, the COO reprimanded them.

[25] From that longer term perspective, Dover seems to have had, and maintained, more of that capability than Harwick. At Dover, people were more openly able to acknowledge that imaging systems as they were implemented did not provide expected improvements as they where able to cease using it where it was ineffective. At Harwick, the imaging system neither provided expected improvements nor enhanced the companies abilities to improve over time. Suggestions were ignored, complaints were suppressed and workers were coerced to work in ways which complied with using the system.

24 GUIDING ENTERPRISE CHANGE: A GROUP EXERCISE IN INFORMATION AND PROCESS INTEGRATION

Srikanth Kannapan and George Roth

Introduction

The *1996 Working Conference on Information and Process Integration in Enterprises* (IPIC'96) brought together researchers and practitioners representing diverse perspectives (information technology, business, social/organizational) with common interests in "rethinking" the role of documents in information and process integration. We took this opportunity to conduct an innovative group exercise involving the conference participants during a breakout session at the end of the conference.

Using a case study of enterprise change as a context, we simulated two types of organizations composed of functional and cross-functional teams respectively, assigned people to teams, and gave those teams specific, realistic, and focused problems to work on. This context enabled participants to operate in ways that were similar to the settings they worked in: as core or peripheral participants of teams which must integrate information and technology with business process designs. The process of problem solving allowed conference participants to communicate their perspectives on how to guide enterprises through changes in the role of documents, and enabled them to apply their expertise while learning from each other.

This chapter archives the rationale behind the group exercise, the materials used for the exercise and some of the presentation materials prepared by the groups.

Breakout Session Requirements and Metrics

Our overall requirements for the breakout session evolved from an exploration of different ways of bringing to bear the diverse perspectives that the participants represented on a focused problem within an enterprise in the field of information and process integration. We viewed the breakout session as an opportunity to engage participants in a/an:

- Group activity: to create professional interactions and a sense of community among participants through "doing" something. Use the informal setting of the exercise for sharing of knowledge that is tacit.
- Game: to do something in a lighter spirit at the end of the conference. Allow for the informal conversations that are of high value to participants, but often difficult to accomplish in busy conference settings where much of what is communicated comes from presentations.
- Exercise: to gain awareness of new perspectives and insights in a specific context, e.g., (a) integration of diverse pieces is hard, needs special attention, (b) integration involves changes in work process and social structures, (c) answers are context dependent. Create new knowledge for "rethinking the role of documents" including both know-how and know-why — being able to apply the theoretical insights gained from research into behaviors that produce expected outcomes.
- Experiment: to observe results of different organizations of people working on the same problem (e.g., by alternative designs for assigning people to teams.) Provide organizational insights that guide effective enterprise change and proper integration of new information technology with business practices and document-based information.
- Conference differentiator: create an event that is interesting and memorable - evolving in content and style over a series of conferences. Use feedback from this session to plan future sessions.

We developed some fairly simple evaluation metrics for this pilot version of the breakout session:

- People who participate find the exercise engaging.
- People who participate feel they gained some new perspectives and insights.
- A significant proportion of conference participants take part in the breakout session.

We developed a simple feedback form to make the above assessment.

Breakout Session Development Process and Rationale

The success of an experiential learning exercise depends, in part, on careful planning of the session. Creating an environment where the exercises are organized so that participants know what to do, and can focus on the issues posed to them, helps facilitate their learning. We took the following main steps in designing the breakout session:

I. ***Scheduling***: We scheduled the breakout session on the second day of the conference program so that participants would already have had to chance to hear the presentations, meet each other, and become aware of specific research issues and experiences in practice:

Session 6: Strategies for Success: Lessons from a Failure Case
1:40-2:05 Case Presentation: "Paper Documents: Implications of changing media for business process redesign"
2:05-2:20 Group Exercise Set-up
2:20-2:30 Break
2:30-3:30 Group Exercise (Team and inter-team work)
3:30-4:00 Presentation preparation
4:00-4:45 Collective Wisdom: Presentations and Discussion
Breakout Session closing remarks and feedback

II. ***Identifying detailed breakout session requirements***: These requirements relate to the kind of interactions we wanted among the participants, and what we thought was feasible to achieve within constraints of time and size of groups:

- Focus on a single problem situation to keep things as simple as possible.
- Have many small teams, with the problem solving requiring both interaction within the teams, and among teams to a lesser extent. The basic idea was to simulate 2 "organizations", each with about 4 teams of people.
- Don't make exercise very open-ended. Focus on getting operational details in place for further development in the future.
- Incorporate the characteristics we want: group activity, exercise, game, experiment and conference differentiator. Experimental aspects would however be minimal for this pilot version.
- Leave sufficient time for reflection, debriefing and discussion after the exercise is completed. This depends on setting realistic time frames for problem-solving activities, especially for a large group, and managing time carefully within those activities.
- Nothing is so practical as an actual experiment - be sure to block out time before the actual session to do a dry-run.

III. ***Selecting a case study***: We chose George Roth's case study of the efforts of an insurance company ("Dover") to improve its paper-based new-accounts work process with a major deployment of new electronic document imaging technology (see Chapter 23 of this book). The case brings out the pitfalls of not taking an integrated approach to co-evolving technological, business and social aspects of information and process.

IV. ***Estimating participation:***

- Maximum expected participation: 60.
- Total estimated number available for participation in breakout session:40-50 (because it is on a Friday afternoon and people tend to leave early.)
- Total expected actual participation in breakout session: 35-45.

We needed a way to gauge breakout session attendance in advance as well as the background and characteristics of participants. So we used a questionnaire as part of on-site registration. The questionnaire helped us assess the number of participants and assign participants to appropriate roles on teams. (The exercise design described below is scaleable between 32 to 56 people.)

V. ***Assessing resources and logistics***:

- We had access to only one room, but we sectioned it into 2 demarcated areas - one for each simulated "organization". Each "organization" was to have 4 groups of 4-7 people each sitting around a table. The room would become noisy, but we were asking the MIT faculty club to rent screens to separate the room into 2 areas with partitions between tables.
- The tables would be arranged by support staff during the break after the breakout groups are announced.

VI. ***Refining and documenting the group exercise design:***
- see Materials for Session Organizers and Materials for Participants appended to the end of this chapter.

VII. ***Testing the group exercise:***

- We conducted a dry-run breakout session with steering committee.

Simulating Organizations

Participants were grouped into 2 "Organizations" - RED-Dover and BLUE-Dover. There were 4 teams and one leader in each organization as shown below. Each team was to have 4-7 people. Participants were assigned to teams based on their answers to the Questionnaire (appended to the end of this chapter). The Materials for Participants contains details on the exercise (appended to the end of this chapter). Participants were also given a copy of the Dover case study (excerpted from Chapter 23 of this book) along with the Materials for Participants.

The layout of the tables and chairs for the teams to use during the exercise is shown below:

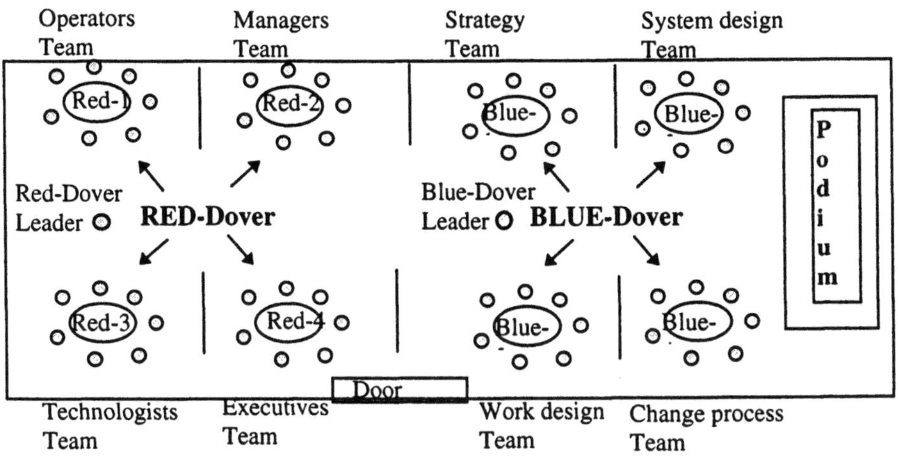

Both organizations solved the same exercise, i.e., addressed the same questions posed in Materials for Participants. But the teams in each organization were formed with different organizing principles:

- Teams in RED-Dover were specialized by functional roles (that we called *perspectives*) and addressed different *aspects* of the problem, viz., Strategy, System design, Work Design and Change-process management:
    - Team Red-1: Operators
    - Team Red-2: Managers
    - Team Red-3: Technologists
    - Team Red-4: Executives

- Teams in BLUE-Dover were cross-functional (incorporating different *perspectives*) but focused on specific *aspects* of the problem as follows:
    - Team Blue-1: Strategy
    - Team Blue-2: System design
    - Team Blue-3: Work design
    - Team Blue-4: Change process

The two organizing principles embody different bases for division of labor and management of problem complexity. Each functional team in RED-Dover allows for greater uniformity (and potentially less discordance) in the perspectives within the team during problem solving, but must address all aspects of the problem at hand. In contrast, each cross-functional team in BLUE-Dover can focus on a single aspect of the problem, but must potentially deal with widely varying perspectives within the team (representative of different organizational functions) during problem solving.

Each team's members were expected to interact among themselves, and occasionally at their discretion, a designated coordinator of the team was to walk over to another team in the same organization to exchange some information and coordinate the problem solving process. The organization leader was to walk around to all 4 teams (within the same organization) to help coordinate their activities, and take responsibility for achieving the overall task of the organization within the scheduled time. The materials for the participants included guidelines for managing the problem solving process (provided at the end of this chapter.)

Results of Group Exercise

The group exercise was successful in that it could be observed that most of the participants were engaged in animated discussions and applied themselves with enthusiasm to the focused problem-solving situation described earlier. The number of participants (32) was close to the estimated number. We obtained completed feedback forms from 26 participants. The feedback results were substantially positive from data obtained from the feedback form (a blank form is appended to the end of this chapter.) Over 60% of the participants who returned feedback forms said the group exercise was engaging and provided them with new perspectives and insights. About 20% said they had mixed feelings about the exercise and yet more than half of this category still thought they gained new perspectives and insights. None of the participants who returned feedback forms thought the group exercise was uninteresting.

There were numerous suggestions for improvement ranging from rescheduling the group exercise to the first day of the conference to the choice of a more challenging problem to solve. The proportion of participation from the full IPIC conference participation was approximately 50%. The main reason for non-participation by the other 50% (as obtained from results of the initial questionnaire) was that some people planned to leave before the last session of the conference. (As we expected, the fact that this session was on a Friday afternoon did seem to affect participation.)

We attempted no formal study of the simulated organizations during the problem solving process. However, it could be informally observed that despite the overall tone of the exercise being a combination of light-hearted game-playing and serious exercise, participants were being fairly true to their assigned roles (e.g., as managers or technologists) possibly because the participants were self-selected into roles that matched their background based on responses to the questionnaire.

There appeared to be a distinction between the styles of functioning between the two simulated organizations as well as in the results they produced. For example, some of the members of the functional teams in RED-Dover observed that while there was some challenge in working within their team to address all the different aspects of the problems, there was a greater challenge in working with the other teams to integrate solutions (possibly because several teams tended to revisit similar aspects of problems from different perspectives.) In contrast, some members of the cross-functional teams of BLUE-Dover commented that even though each team focused on a specific aspect of the overall problem (e.g., systems design), the discussions within their teams were quite insightful (requiring even explanation of vocabulary) and bordered on being contentious. But integrating the solutions of different aspects of the problem was apparently less of a challenge.

Some of the presentation material used by the groups are appended to the end of this chapter. The presentations of the two simulated organizations themselves were very engaging for the participants and stimulated a lot of reflection, questions and discussion. (A detailed analysis of the results of the presentations and discussion is beyond the scope of this chapter.)

In summary, based on the metrics we developed and the feedback we received, we believe we achieved the goals of the group exercise that we set, and plan to develop such exercises further by learning from this experience.

Acknowledgments

The most critical success factor for such a group exercise is participation; we thank the participants for taking part in the group exercise with sincerity and enthusiasm. We would like to thank the rest of the steering committee members of IPIC'96, especially JoAnne Yates, for participating intensely in the design and organization of the group exercise. We also thank Chris Foglia and Roanne Neuwirth of MIT for timely help while conducting the group exercise.

Materials for Session Organizers

Guidelines for Managing Breakout Session (Nov. 15, 2:00pm-5:00pm)

⇒ Give out questionnaire during IPIC'96 registration

⇒ Get filled questionnaire

⇒ Make organizations and groups. Select/request candidates for organization leader and assign leadership roles for each organization. Make assigned locations at tables. Create orgn./team/location assignment sheet and make copies. At dinner, make announcement of organization and groups.

⇒ For late-comers and second-day arrivals - remind participants about breakout session on second day afternoon and ask for filled questionnaires ASAP.

⇒ Make minor adjustments to breakout organizations and groups as appropriate and print out lists with assigned locations on layout drawing of room. Update orgn./team/location assignment sheet. Make copies.

⇒ Make **updated** announcement of organization and groups. Handout copies of orgn./team/location assignment sheet.
2:05pm-2:20pm;

⇒ Oversee layout of room and gathering of groups and organizations
2:20pm-2:30pm; break time

⇒ Ask groups to take assigned tables as indicated on orgn./team/location assignment sheet.
2:30pm; after break

⇒ Guide/manage group process and time
- Guide expected roles for organization leader, team coordinator, team member
- Guide expected interaction among teams members and between teams in same organization
- make sure organization leader gets team coordinators to meet at 3:30pm

2:30pm-3:30pm

⇒ Guide preparation of presentation of material (1 presentation per organization)
3:30pm-4:00pm

⇒ Manage results presentation of each organization
- manage layout of room and presentation location and equipment
- position steering committee and G. Roth as "focus audience"
- request all IPIC participants to gather for presentations
- manage presentation timing and Q&A
- make closing remarks and summarize
- ask for filled out feedback forms

4:00pm-4:45pm

⇒ Remind people to fill out breakout session feedback forms available in packet of material, and collect filled feedback forms.
4:45pm

Materials for Participants

- **Please <u>fill out the brief questionnaire</u> below.**
- **Pull out this page and return it during site registration.**

Questionnaire

A game-like group exercise is scheduled during the breakout session Nov. 15, 2:00pm - 5:00pm derived from a real-life study of the experiences of an insurance company (fictitiously named "Dover") which recently undertook a major effort in deploying state-of-the-art document imaging systems to replace its paper-based systems.

- Will you be **participating** in the breakout session exercise (2pm-5pm, Nov. 15)?

  Yes No

  If "Yes" please read attached material before breakout session.

- If "No" to above question, please help us understand why you are not participating:

  ____

If you plan to participate in the breakout session exercise, which of the following types of teams can you best contribute your expertise to:

Information/Process-support Technologies ____
Business, Operations Management ____
Work design, Work-practice, Social Issues ____
Enterprise Strategy and Planning ____

Materials for Participants

IPIC'96 is about bringing together somewhat diverse perspectives (information technology, business, social/organizational) with common interests in "Rethinking" the role of documents in information and process integration. The purpose of the breakout session is to explore topics in this area through a game-like group exercise in a realistic and focused problem context derived from a real-life study of an insurance company (fictitiously named "Dover").

Your Exercise Context

Dover was previously an enterprise with a paper-based new-accounts business process. An electronic document based process was sought as a replacement. A "solution" provider was contracted. The change process was initiated - a variety of technological, work-process, social, and management issues came into play. The result of the change fell well below expectations.

The Dover situation has been studied by an academic researcher (George Roth). His report (please **read Appendix A** of this packet of material) was given to Dover's board of directors, who were not initially aware of the issues and problems at Dover. The board is now aware of the issues and are questioning how they should proceed to solve the problems.

You are part of one team out of 4 problem-solving teams formed within "Dover". During this breakout session your expertise is sought as part of a team to solve the following problem playing the roles of technologists, managers, executives and operations specialists examining aspects of enterprise strategy, work design, systems design, and change-process management.

Your Exercise Problem

This is a "Diagnose and Propose-Better-Way" Exercise. Based on your understanding of the context of your organization (see Appendix A) you are called upon to help your organization answer the following questions:

1) **What went wrong at Dover?**
- For example: use some form of root cause analysis.

2) **What should Dover have done?**
- For example: develop some policy and change process guidelines.

3) **What should Dover do now?**
- For example: identify some action items.

Results Expected

Your team is expected to answer the above questions while addressing specific issues assigned to your team (posted on your assigned table during the breakout session). Your team's results are to be integrated with the results of other teams in your organization for a **10 minute overhead-transparency presentation (at 4:00pm)** to the "board of directors" of Dover - the board is interested in both practical suggestions and more abstract models of solution. The IPIC'96 steering committee will pose as the "board of directors" representing people with backgrounds and interests in enterprise integration technologies, business process engineering, document modeling and management, and work-practice studies.

⇒ **Roles** to play and **Guidelines** to manage your problem solving process are provided.

Roles to Play

Note that your team is one of **four** collaborative teams (assigned to adjacent tables during the breakout session) addressing different issues. To solve the overall problem, your team may need to occasionally interact with the other teams. To facilitate such interaction, at the discretion of your team, the coordinator of your team may walk over to another team to exchange ideas and information. Conversely, coordinators from other teams may visit your team.

Specifically, the roles to be played in solving the problem are as follows.

Team participants will:

- first designate a team coordinator and a scribe.
- work with other team members and organization leader (designated by session organizers) to answer the questions posed.

Team coordinators will:

- facilitate discussion within team, walk over occasionally to interact with other teams.
- work with other team coordinators, the organization leader, and possibly other participants, to integrate results of each team and make presentation material.

Organization leader (designated by session organizers) will:

- coordinate the teams and help manage problem solving process and schedule.
- provide additional guidance to team coordinators and participants as necessary to develop unified presentation of results.

A Guideline to Manage Your Process

1:40-2:05 **Case Presentation**: "Paper Documents: Implications of changing media for business process redesign",
George Roth, Center for Organizational Learning, MIT

⇒ Participants have previously read Dover case and hear case presentation.

2:05-2:20 **Group Exercise Set-up**

⇒ Participants listen to session organizers for breakout session instructions.

2:20-2:30 **Break**

⇒ After break, tables are ready for participants to take their seats.

2:30-3:30 **Group Exercise**
(Team work with some inter-team communication)

⇒ Each team decides on a coordinator and scribe for their own team.
⇒ Organization leader goes around each team and gets to know each team coordinator.
⇒ Each team discusses the case among themselves and the coordinator facilitates, and the scribe uses the flip-chart to capture discussions and results.
⇒ The team coordinator walks over to other teams occasionally to get inputs.
⇒ The organization leader keeps teams aware of timing.

3:30-4:00 **Presentation preparation time**
(Team coordinators work with organization leader, and possibly other team participants.)

⇒ Organization leader asks coordinators to bring flip-charts together

⇒ Organization leader facilitates creation of a coherent set of answers to the questions posed, designates the presenter and helps create **10min** presentation material.

4:00-4:45 **Collective Wisdom: Presentations and Discussion**

⇒ Designated presenter presents results (**10 minutes**)
⇒ Q&A
⇒ Breakout Session closing remarks and participant feedback

IPIC'96 Breakout Session: Feedback Form

- Was the group exercise an engaging experience for you?

  Engaging   Mixed   Uninteresting

- Did you think you gained any new perspectives and insights through this group exercise?

  Yes   Marginally   No

- Do you have any suggestions for improvement of the group exercise for the next IPIC (particularly if your found it uninteresting)?

  ____

- Do you have any suggestions for a different kind of activity for a breakout session in the next IPIC?

  ____

- Please tell us anything else you think would be useful for us to hear.

  ____

  ____

Red Dover

What went wrong?

- technology driven solution ignored social aspects of process
- ignored business strategy and process focus
- overly aggressive schedule

What should Dover have done?

- focus on interface between groups
- include operator rep on design team
- develop schedule that allows time to understand work

What should Dover do now?

- determine customer needs
- redesign business processes with cross-functional teams
- define pilot (implementation)

Presentation Materials from Groups

What went wrong? **Blue Dover**

- 800lb gorilla syndrome
- No pilot
- No matrix
- Goal was 'PR' not change in process, schedule pressure based on 'PR'
- No strategy to facilitate change
- Change in work process not recognized
- Human factors ignored

What should Dover have done?

- Communicate with Strategic Team
- JAD: Joint application design (confront knowledges, collaborative design, surface values)
- Identify change in direction of work working with strategy, work design, systems teams
- Players learn, communicate
- Introduce technological elements
- New roles for players - adjust
- Prototype, establish metrics, pilot
- Evaluate, monitor people's satisfaction, cost schedule, train users

What should Dover do now?

- Rebuild trust
- Fine tune, analyze change process - plan, keep what works and useful
- Implement change process
- Monitor

Note - Not all team members agree - a utopian solution?

Presentation Materials from Groups

MIX
Papier aus verantwortungsvollen Quellen
Paper from responsible sources
FSC® C105338

If you have any concerns about our products,
you can contact us on
ProductSafety@springernature.com

In case Publisher is established outside the EU,
the EU authorized representative is:
Springer Nature Customer Service Center GmbH
Europaplatz 3, 69115 Heidelberg, Germany

Printed by Libri Plureos GmbH
in Hamburg, Germany